i

Richard Crist

—————

BLENDER STEPS

CREATE PHOTOREAL STILL IMAGES AND ANIMATIONS USING BLENDER 2.63, THE AMAZING FREE 3D ART TOOL

A TRUTH ENGINE BOOK

Published by Truth Engine Books.

ISBN-13: 978-0-615-70966-6
ISBN-10: 0-615-70966-4

Warning and Disclaimer: Every effort has been made to make this book as complete and as accurate as possible, but no warranty or fitness is implied. The information provided is on an "as is" basis. The author and the publisher shall have neither liability nor responsibility to any person or entity with respect to any loss or damages arising from the information contained in this book.

CONTENTS

PART ONE: WORKING WITH THE BLENDER INTERFACE

PART TWO: GEOMETRICAL PROPERTIES

BMesh system, faces can have any number of sides). 79

PART THREE: MATERIAL PROPERTIES

PART FOUR: LIGHTING AND ENVIRONMENT

PART FIVE: TOOLS THAT ARE OF GENERAL USE—THAT IS, TOOLS THAT CAN BE USED IN CREATING BOTH STILL IMAGES AND ANIMATION—BUT THAT ARE PRIMARILY FOR USE IN ANIMATION

PART SIX: ANIMATION

PART SEVEN: CREATION AND ANIMATION OF PARTICLES, HAIR, FLUIDS, CLOTH, SOFT BODIES

PART EIGHT: CREATING AND RETRIEVING SCENES

PART NINE: POST-PROCESSING

PREFACE

This book is not a series of lessons, but a reference book to use as you work. It is a reference book both for beginners and for those who have struggled for some time to learn Blender.

If you are completely new to Blender, at some point you will sit down to begin your first Blender session; you will begin to build your first model.

Now imagine that, to help you any time you need assistance, there is a Blender pro standing next to you. Imagine that you tell him what you want to do, and he tells you exactly how to do it, step by step.

That is how this book teaches. There are only a few very short lessons that you ought to commit to memory—the rest is on-the-job training. You will not need to do exercises; rather, you will be able to work on your own project from the very start.

This book is not about studying; it is about doing.

WORK FLOW

After you have downloaded Blender (from www.blender.org):

Read the Introduction of this book. The part about datablocks might be a little difficult, but don't worry about it—knowing about datablocks will make things easier, but it's not crucial for you to have this knowledge, especially at the beginning.

You should know that you can find the following topics in Part One : Cancel an operation, Undo, Re-do, Perspective, Change point of view, Open a Blender file, Save your scene, Save a render, and Render.

When Blender opens for the first time, you are looking at the default "primitive" cube. You can view this cube more fully by changing your point of view (T13, p.10). Here is a suggestion for your work flow: **begin building your scene** by starting to work on the initial cube, or add another mesh object (T27, p.62) and work on that. Cut/subdivide the faces to create a finer mesh (T52, p. 81 ["loopcuts" can be especially useful—see T52, B, p.81], T54, p. 83). You might want to smooth the edges by following the steps given in T55, p. 87. You should familiarize yourself with the Blender coordinate systems (T24, p. 32). Select (T22, p. 20 [to select an "edge loop", see T22, step 101, p. 27]), transform (move from place to place, rotate, or scale—T25, p. 33), and extrude (T26, p. 58), vertices, edges and faces to add features and to shape the object. To merge vertices, see T48, p. 79. You can also sculpt the object (T56, p. 87).

Then, if your object does not yet have a base material applied to it, give it one (T61 and T62, p. 107). Then, you might wish to apply different materials to different parts of the object (T66, p. 109). You can change the substance color of any material (T68, p. 111). Read the overview on the material properties (T71, p. 116). Make a material transparent (T72, p. 117), or mirror reflective (T73, p. 118). Add a texture (T74, p. 120 to T76, p.128). Change the texture's properties (T77, p. 128). Do Texture Painting (T77, step 117, p. 145). Do Projection Painting (T78, p. 158). Apply a ramp (T79, p. 165). Use Vertex Paint (T80, p. 167).

Set up lighting (T81, p. 170, to T83, p. 171). Create a sky (T84, p. 179) or put a background image into your scene (T87, p. 182).

If you are modeling an animal or human character, to prepare for animating your model, build an armature inside it (T88, p. 185, to T92, p. 204). You might want to apply "Inverse Kinematics" to the "rigged" model so that it will appear to move naturally when animated (T93, p. 205). Apply "Constraints" to limit the way the character and other objects can be posed or positioned (T94, p. 207 through T103, p. 214). Create "Shapekeys," which are instrumental in animating changes of object shape (T105, p. 215). Animate your scene (T106, p. 218, through T118, p. 239). Create and animate hair, fire, water, jiggling objects, cloth or particle streams (T119, p. 240, through T124, p. 250). Do post-processing to add effects (use the Compositor (T129, p. 253)), or to splice scenes and other footage together and to create transitional clips, etc. (use the Video Sequence Editor (T130, p. 264)).

At any time, you can **create a new scene** (T125, p. 252) or **retrieve a stored scene** (T126, p. 252).

INTRODUCTION

―――――

Expressions:

"LClick" means "left click and release"

"MClick" means "click middle mouse button (push scrolling wheel down) and release"

"RClick" means "right-click and release"

"Scroll" means "turn scrolling wheel"

"LClick & hold" means "left click and hold"

"MClick & hold" means "middle click and hold"

"RClick & hold" means "right click and hold"

"press" means "press and release (a key on the keyboard)"

"press and hold" means "press and hold"

"CTRL+Z" (for example) means "press & hold CTRL while pressing Z"

"CTRL+LClick" (for example) means "press & hold CTRL while LClicking"

"CTRL+ALT+Z" (for example) means "press & hold CTRL while pressing & holding ALT while pressing Z"

Some Blender buttons are hard to refer to because they are not labeled, and their appearance changes according to how they are being used at any given moment. They are best identified by their position. In the picture below, the presence of the 3D View window icon at far left shows that you're looking at the 3D View window header. (A window's "header" is the strip that runs along the edge of the window.) This picture shows where the **Mode** button is, where the **Viewport Shading** button is, and where the **Pivot** button is. You need to know how to find these three buttons in order to follow the directions in this book.

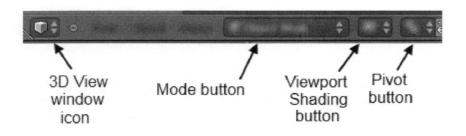

3D View window icon   Mode button   Viewport Shading button   Pivot button

---

Directions in this book will often look something like this:

Go to the "Properties" window: ▣ > LClick the "Material" button: ◉ > Go to the "Options" panel > Put a check mark into the little box next to "Vertex Color Paint"

The meaning of the sequence in this example is this:

1. Go to the **Properties** window, which is the window with this icon ▣ at the left end of its header; If you don't see such a window anywhere on your screen, you'll have to open one, either (a) by simply changing an existing window into a Properties window (go to topic **T1, p. 7,** to see how to do this), or (b) by first splitting an existing window (see **T2, p. 7**) and then changing one of the two resulting windows into a Properties window (see **T1, p. 7**).

2. Then, if the "Material" button ◉ is not already "enabled"—that is, if it's not already brightened, LClick the button.
3. Then go to the "Options" panel (You may have to LClick the black triangle to the left of the panel name to see the contents of this panel.).
4. In the "Options" panel, put a check into the box to the left of "Vertex Color Paint".

You will see buttons of this type: ◀ Energy: 1.720 ▶ . For a button like this, you can change the number in three ways: LClick on the little arrows to left and right; OR: LClick on the number and type in a new number, then LClick anywhere or press ENTER; OR: LClick & hold in the body of the button and drag right or left (you can keep dragging even beyond the button's borders).

In order to create models in Blender, you have to use the raw materials that Blender supplies to you. These raw materials are things that they call "objects". Blender classifies its objects into these general and special types:

General Types	Special Types
Mesh	Plane
	Cube
	Circle
	UV Sphere
	Icosphere
	Cylinder
	Cone
	Grid
	Monkey
	Torus
Curve	Bezier
	Circle
	Nurbs Curve
	Nurbs Circle
	Path
Surface	NURBS Curve
	NURBS Circle
	NURBS Surface
	NURBS Cylinder
	NURBS Sphere
	NURBS Torus
Metaball	Ball
	Capsule
	Plane
	Ellipsoid
	Cube
Text	
Empty	
Group	
Camera	
Lamp	Point
	Sun
	Spot
	Hemi
	Area
Armature	Single Bone

Unless you've changed the opening scene using CTRL-U, when Blender opens, it presents you with an object of the *general* type "Mesh" and of the *special* type "Cube."

Using the directions below, you could build a complex model from this cube without adding any other objects (you could start, for instance, by creating new faces by extruding edges, and then by cutting across faces), but you can add a Blender-supplied object at any time. See below, **T27, p. 62,** for instructions on how to do this.

Note that you can create an association of one object to another such that each ceases to be a (Blender) object. In such a case, the two together become a single (compound) Blender object which takes the name of one of the original two.

Blender's "datablocks": (It is not essential for the Blender novice to know about datablocks.)

Every Blender object gets its properties from a set of "datablocks", which are just blocks of data in the computer. Every individual datablock has a name. When you create a datablock, Blender will give it a unique name—then you can change the name if you want (see **T21, p. 19**).

An object gets its "**object**" properties (location, scaling, rotation) from its own unique *object* datablock.

The object gets its **geometrical, or shape**, properties from a *geometry* datablock in the computer. A single geometry datablock can give properties to only one object, or to more than one. For instance, as long as a single geometry datablock gives geometry properties to two different objects, the two objects will have the same shape.

An object, or a part of an object, will get its **material properties** (for instance color, shininess, reflectivity, transparency) from a *material* datablock. Any given surface of an object can have only one material datablock; but, a single object can have more than one material datablock because different parts of the object can have their own material datablocks. A single material datablock can give properties to a single object, or to many objects, to one part of an object or to many parts of an object. For instance, as long as a single material datablock gives material properties to two different objects, both objects must always have the same color, etc.

The object gets **texture** properties from *texture* datablocks. These are attached to the material datablocks.

When you change an object's geometrical properties (such as when you transform or extrude part of a mesh, etc.), you are actually modifying the object's geometry datablock. If you have an object whose geometry datablock also gives another object its geometrical properties, when you change the shape of one of the objects, the other object's shape will change in the same way.

When you change a surface's material properties (such as when you change an object's color), you are actually modifying the object's material datablock (or *one* of the object's material datablocks). If you have an object whose material datablock also gives another object its material properties, when you change the color, say, of one of the objects, the other object's color will change in the same way.

An object's geometry datablock is attached to its object datablock.

An object's material datablock can be attached either to the geometry datablock, or directly to the object datablock.

You can replace an object's geometry datablock with another object's geometry datablock, so that both share the same datablock—it is said that the geometrical properties of the two objects are *linked*. Note that if Object A's material datablock is connected to its geometry datablock (and not directly to the object datablock) then if you replace Object A's geometry datablock with Object B's geometry datablock, then Object A's material datablock(s) will also be replaced with the material datablock(s) that are attached to Object B's geometry datablock. When you do this, you are essentially turning an existing object into a "linked" copy of another object. Any change to one will then change the other.

You can replace any of an object's material datablocks with another object's material datablock, so that both objects share the same datablock—it is said that the material properties of the two objects are *linked*. If you change, say, the color of one object, the color of the other will change also.

You can see a diagram of an object's datablocks and how they are related to one another by going to the Outliner window, which is the window with this icon to the left:

(If the Outliner window is not visible, change one of your windows into an Outliner window; see **T1, p. 7.**)

In the Outliner window, you will see a diagram that looks like the image below. (The names of the datablocks in this example are the kind that Blender automatically gives to them.) "Sphere.007" is the object datablock. "Sphere.005" is the geometry datablock. "Material.006" is the material datablock. "Texture.001" and "Texture.002" are texture datablocks:

If you attached the material datablock directly to the object datablock, the diagram would look like this:

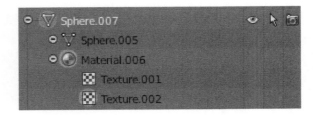

In the "Properties" window:

The **"Object" button**, , displays panels having to do with the **object datablock**.

The **"Object Data" button** has to do with the **geometry datablock**. (This button can look like this:

for mesh objects, or for curves, or for point lamps – or it can have any one of nearly a dozen other icons on it—see **T11, p. 9** for how to find this button)

The **"Material" button**, , has to do with the **material datablock**.

The **"Texture" button**, , has to do with the **texture datablock**.

The diagrams below show different ways that the geometry and material datablocks can be connected to one or two objects:

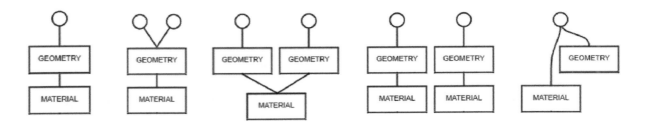

There are two ways of producing a copy of item A: (1) turn an *existing* object, B, into a copy of A; OR: (2) create a *new* item, B, that's a copy of A.

For instructions on how to change an existing object into a linked duplicate of another: see **T31, p. 69**.

You can add a new object or part of an object that is defined by another object's *material* datablock, but with an independent *geometrical* datablock (with identical content) by selecting the existing object and pressing SHIFT + D (see **T30, p. 63**).

You can add a new object that is defined by another object's material *and* geometrical datablocks by selecting the existing object and pressing ALT + D (see **T30, p. 63**).

If you press CTRL+ U and LClick "Save User Settings", you will change your "New" scene. Here's how to restore the factory settings, so that when you LClick "File," then LClick "New," then LClick "Reload Start Up File," you will bring up the original default "primitive" cube: LClick "File" > LClick "Load Factory Settings" > Press CTRL + U > LClick "Save User Settings".

PART ONE: WORKING WITH THE BLENDER INTERFACE TO BUILD YOUR SCENE

T(opic)1: To change one kind of window into another kind of window.

1. In the header of the window that you want to change: LClick the icon at the far left end of the header. In the drop-down menu, LClick the icon for the window you want to change the window to. (If no icon is present, go to the "Info" window's header [the window header with ![icon] to the left] > LClick "Back to Previous".)

T2: To split one window into two.

METHOD 1:

1. Move your mouse cursor over the horizontal (to divide a window vertically) or vertical (to divide a window horizontally) border of the window you want to divide until the double-arrow cursor appears > RClick.

2. LClick "Split Area".

3. Move the vertical or horizontal line to where you want to split one window into two.

4. LClick to split the window.

METHOD 2:

5. LClick and drag on the little triangle at upper right or lower left of an existing window.

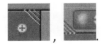

T3: To delete a window.

METHOD 1:

1. When you delete a window, another window will expand to take its place. Move your mouse cursor over the border between the two windows until the little double-arrow cursor appears > RClick.

2. LClick "Join Area".

3. Move your mouse until a big arrow appears to point in the direction of the desired expansion.

4. LClick.

METHOD 2:

5. LClick and drag on the little triangle at upper right or lower left of an existing window.

T4. To cancel an operation in progress:

1. Press ESC

T5. To undo an operation:

METHOD 1:

1. CTRL+Z

2. If you are in Edit mode and there is an error message that there are no more steps to undo, go into another mode and press CTRL+Z again (Blender keeps two different histories: one for Edit mode, and one for all other modes).

METHOD 2:

3. CTRL+ALT+Z

4. LClick the name of the action just before the one(s) you want to undo. (The most recent actions are at the top of the list.)

END OF METHODS.

T6. To redo an undo:

METHOD 1:

1. SHIFT+CTRL+Z

METHOD 2:

2. CTRL+ALT+Z

3. LClick on the name of the action you want to redo.

END OF METHODS.

T7. To enter Edit mode:

Note that every time you enter Edit mode, one and only one object will be "active" and can be worked on. The last object to have been selected in Object mode will be the one that is active upon entering Edit mode.

METHOD 1

1. In the 3D View window's header, look at the Mode button (see **_Introduction_** for its location). If "Edit Mode" is written on this button, stop; you are already in Edit Mode; if "Edit Mode" is not on the button, LClick the button.

2. LClick "Edit Mode".

METHOD 2

3. if "Edit Mode" is not on the Mode button (see **_Introduction_** for its location), press TAB.

END OF METHODS

T8. To enter Object mode:

METHOD 1

1. In the 3D View window's header, look at the Mode button (see **_Introduction_** for its location). If "Object Mode" is written on this button, stop; you are already in Object Mode; if "Object Mode" is not on the button, LClick the button.

2. LClick "Object Mode".

METHOD 2

3. If "Edit Mode" is written on this button, then you can use this method:

4. Press TAB.

END OF METHODS

T9. To find the "Tool Shelf":

The Tool Shelf is a vertical set of panels that is on the left side of the 3D View Window. To make it appear or disappear:

METHOD 1

1. With the mouse cursor in the 3D View window, press T (a toggle).

METHOD 2

2. Go to the 3D View window header (marked by at left) > LClick "View" > LClick "Tool Shelf".

END OF METHODS

T10. To find the "Properties Shelf":

The Properties Shelf is a vertical set of panels that is on the right side of the 3D View Window. To make it appear or disappear:

METHOD 1

1. With the mouse cursor in the 3D View window, press N (a toggle).

METHOD 2

2. Go to the 3D View window header (marked by at left) > LClick "View" > LClick "Properties". (The UV/Image Editor window also has a Properties Shelf, which is accessed in a similar way.)

END OF METHODS

T11. To find The "Object Data" button:

1. Go to the "Properties" window: . If the Modifiers button, , is present, the Object Data button is to its immediate right. If the modifiers button, , is *not* present, you will find the Object Data button to the immediate right of the "Object Constraints" button, . Note that the

"Object Data" button will have an icon on it that corresponds to the kind of object that is active (last selected): [icon] for a mesh, [icon] for a curve, [icon] for a surface, [icon] for a metaball, [icon] for a text, [icon] for an armature, [icon] for a lattice, [icon] for an empty, [icon] for a camera, [icon] for a point lamp, [icon] for a sun lamp, [icon] for a spot lamp, [icon] for a hemi lamp, [icon] for an area lamp.

T12. To turn perspective on or off:

If your model is not in perspective view (i.e., If your model is in "orthographic" ("ortho") view, and things do not appear smaller as they recede into the distance) and you want to show it in perspective OR if your model is in perspective view and you want to show it in orthographic view:
1. Press numpad 5.

T13. To change your point of view as you work on your scene:

1. Notice that this is different from changing an object's orientation or position, and it is different from changing the camera position. (P12 41)
2. Make sure that your mouse pointer is inside the 3D View window (the main modeling window).
3. To allow your number-pad key-presses to work, make sure that the "Num Lock" on your keyboard is set to *off*.
4. To center the object(s) that you've selected: Press numpad-dot (.).
5. To center selected object(s) while hiding all items that are not selected: Press numpad-slash (/). To leave this view: Press numpad-slash (/) again.
6. Do you want to go instantly, with a keystroke, to one or another exact view?
       Yes: Go to **25**.
       No: Go to **7**.
7. Do you want to orbit (move in an arc around, facing, a semi-distant point in model space)?
       Yes: Go to **9**.
       No: Go to **8**.
8. Do you want to pan (to move your viewpoint while looking straight ahead, without moving forward or backward)?
       Yes: Go to **15**.
       No: To zoom (move forward or back), go to **21**.
9. To orbit (around the "center of the view" point in model space—to move this point, see **21**):
METHOD 1
10. MClick & hold. Move mouse to orbit.
METHOD 2
With your mouse pointer in the 3D View window:
11. To orbit **up** 15° (You can change these increments. See below [**note**]): press numpad-8, OR, to orbit **up continuously** in 15° intervals: press & hold numpad-8.

12. To orbit **down** 15°: press numpad-2; OR, to orbit **continuously down** in intervals: press & hold numpad-2.

13. To orbit **counter-clockwise around the global Z axis** (see **T24, p. 32**) 15° : press numpad-4; OR to orbit **continuously left** in intervals: press & hold numpad-4.

14. To orbit **clockwise around the global Z axis** (see **T24, p. 32**) 15° : press numpad-6; OR to orbit **continuously right** in intervals: press & hold numpad-6.

END OF METHODS

note: To change this interval, go to the "User Preferences" window, > LClick "Interface" > Adjust "Rotation Angle".

15. To pan:

METHOD 1

16. SHIFT + MClick & hold. Move mouse to pan.

METHOD 2

With your mouse pointer in the 3D View window:

17. To pan **up**: CTRL + press numpad-8; OR: CTRL + press & hold numpad-8.

18. To pan **down**: CTRL + press numpad-2 ; OR: CTRL + press & hold numpad-2.

19. To pan **left**: CTRL + press numpad-4; OR: CTRL + press & hold numpad-4.

20. To pan **right**: CTRL + press numpad-6; OR: CTRL + press & hold numpad-6.

END OF METHODS

21. To zoom:

In Orthographic view (you can toggle between Orthographic and Perspective views by pressing numpad-5), zooming is simply magnification; in Perspective view, however, zooming moves the viewer through the model space. Note that in Perspective view, zooming moves the viewer toward the "center of the view" and will not move the viewer beyond that point. If this prevents you from zooming as far as you want to go, you will have to move the center of the view to a location that is farther away. To do this,

place the 3D cursor ( ) at the farther-away location; then move the center of the view to the cursor by pressing CTRL + numpad-period(.).

METHOD 1

22. Scroll (mouse scrolling wheel)

METHOD 2

23. (For finer control:) Press CTRL + MClick & hold > Release CTRL > To zoom **in**: drag down. To zoom **out**: drag up > Release MClick.

METHOD 3

24. To zoom **in**: press or press & hold numpad-plus (+). To zoom **out**: press or press & hold numpad-minus (-).

END OF METHODS

25. To go quickly to certain exact views:

METHOD 1

26. In the 3D View window's header (which is, by default, under the 3D View window): LClick "View".

27. For **top view**: LClick "Top".

28. For **bottom view**: LClick "Bottom".

29. For **right side view**: LClick "Right".

30. For **left side view**: LClick "Left".

31. For **front view**: LClick "Front".

32. For **back view**: LClick "Back".

33. For the **camera's view:** LClick "Camera" (toggle). To position the camera, see **41**.

METHOD 2

34. With the mouse cursor in the 3D View window:

35. For **top view**: press numpad-7.

36. For **bottom view**: CTRL + press numpad-7.

37. For **side view**: press numpad-3.

38. For **other side view**: CTRL + press numpad-3.

39. For **front view**: press numpad-1.

40. For **back view**: CTRL + press numpad-1.

41. For the **camera's view:** press numpad-0. (toggle); to adjust the camera view: in Object mode, RClick the border of the camera view.

Shift F

Roll MMB = Zoom

Move Mouse = Pan

Accept = LMB

(a) To roll the camera: Press R > Move the mouse > LClick to fix position.

(b) To pan vertically: Press R > Press X > Press X > Move mouse > LClick to fix positon.

(c) To pan horizontally: Press R > Press Y > Press Y > Move mouse > LClick to fix position.

(d) To dolly forward and back: (i) Press G > MClick (& release) > Move mouse upward and downward > LClick to fix position; OR (ii) Press G > Press Z > Press Z > Move mouse upward an downward > LClick to fix position.

(e) To move the camera to show the current 3D View window view: Press CTRL + ALT + numpad 0.

END OF METHODS

T14. To change the "Viewport Shading Type" in the 3D View window:

1. In this section, I will refer to two buttons: the "**Viewport Shading**" button and the "**Type**" button. The "Viewport Shading" button is in the 3D View window header—go to **_Introduction_** above to see where it

is located. To locate the "Type" button: go to the "Properties" window > > LClick the

"Object" button: ⬜ > Go to the "Display" panel, where you can find the button labeled "Type." To "set" these buttons, LClick them and then LClick your choice.

2. Definitions:

a. The "**Bounding Box**" view presents your object as surrounded by a box.

b. The "**Wireframe**" view is a transparent view that shows only the vertices and edges of your object.

c. The "**Solid**" view shows an object as solid, lit, not by the lamps in your scene, but by the so-called "Open GL" (a kind of standardized lighting which can be re-set in the preference window)

d. The "**Textured**" view allows you to see how the *UV*-textures will look on your models, as lit, not by the lamps in your scene, but by the so-called "Open GL"

e. The "**active**" object is the selected object—if more than one object is selected, the active object is the one that was selected last.

3. To see the active object in **Bounding Box** view and the non-active objects also in **Bounding Box** view: Set the *Viewport Shading* button to "***Bounding Box***" and set the *Type* button to "***Bounds***", "***Wire***", "***Solid***", or "***Textured***".

4. To see the active object in **Bounding Box** view and non-active objects in **Wireframe** view: Set the *Viewport Shading* button to "***Wireframe***" and set the *Type* button to "***Bounds***".

5. To see the active object in **Bounding Box** view and the non-active objects in **Solid** view: Set the *Viewport Shading* button to "***Solid***" and set the *Type* button to "***Bounds***".

6. To see the active object in **Bounding Box** view and the non-active objects in **Textured** view: Set the *Viewport Shading* button to "***Textured***" and set the *Type* button to "***Bounds***".

7. To see the active object in **Wireframe** view and the non-active objects in **Wireframe** view: Set the *Viewport Shading* button to "***Wireframe***" and set the *Type* button to "***Wire***", "***Solid***", or "***Textured***".

8. To see the active object in **Wireframe** view and the non-active objects in **Solid** view: Set the *Viewport Shading* button to "***Solid***" and set the *Type* button to "***Wire***".

9. To see the active object in **Wireframe** view and the non-active objects in **Textured** view: Set the *Viewport Shading* button to "***Textured***" and set the *Type* button to "***Wire***".

10. To see the active object in **Solid** view and the non-active objects in **Solid** view: Set the *Viewport Shading* button to "***Solid***" and set the *Type* button to "***Solid***" or "***Textured***".

11. To see the active object in **Solid** view and the non-active objects in **Textured** view: Set the *Viewport Shading* button to "***Textured***" and set the *Type* button to "***Solid***".

12. To see the active object in **Textired** view and the non-active objects in **Textured** view: Set the *Viewport Shading* button to "***Textured***" and set the *Type* button to "***Textured***".

13. Note that The Viewpoint Shading button will always operate as expected—operating on both active and non-active objects—if you leave the Type button set at its default setting, "**Textured**".

14. hotkeys:

   a. To change the Viewport Shading button setting from **Bounding Box** to **Wireframe**: Press Z.

   b. To change the Viewport Shading button setting from **Bounding Box** to **Solid**: Press ALT + Z.

   c. To change the Viewport Shading button setting from **Wireframe** to **Solid**: Press Z or Alt + Z.

   d. To change the Viewport Shading button setting from **Solid** to **Wireframe**: Press Z.

   e. To change the Viewport Shading button setting from **Solid** to **Textured**: Press ALT + Z.

   f. To change the Viewport Shading button setting from **Textured** to **Wireframe**: Press Z.

   g. To change the Viewport Shading button setting from **Textured** to **Solid**: Press ALT + Z.

15. If you have created a "multires" mesh (see **T54 C, p. 85**) by dividing up your original mesh to produce smaller faces: when you show your object *in Object mode* and in wireframe, it will always take on the general shape that is commensurate with the multires level that you set with the "Preview" button. If "Optimal Display" in the "multires" sub-panel (see **T54 C, step 16, p. 86**) is *not* checked, the size and number of edges in the wireframe will reflect the level you set with the "Preview" button. If "Optimal Display" *is* checked, the number of edges will always reflect the original mesh, before multires subdivisions were made.

16. To superimpose a wireframe over a solid view: go to the "Properties" window > > LClick

the "Object" button: > Go to the "Display" panel > LClick the box next to "Wire" in order to check it.

T15 To open a Blender file:

1. Are you opening Blender and do you want to open the last file you were working on by clicking In the opening panel in the center of the screen?

        Yes: LClick "Recover Last Session". Stop. You are finished.

        No: Go to **2**.

2. Is the file that you want to open a *recent* file?

        Yes: Go to **3**.

        No: Go to **4**.

3. If you are opening Blender, and if the recent file you want is listed under "Recent" in the opening panel in the center of the screen, LClick the name of the file you want to open. Stop. You are finished.

If Blender is already open: go to the "Info" window's header (the window header with   to the left) > LClick "File" > hover over "Open Recent" > LClick the name of the file you want to open. Stop. You are finished.

4. To open a file that has not recently been opened, either (a) go to the "Info" window's header (the window header with   to the left); LClick "File" > LClick "Open", OR (b) press F1, OR (c) press CTRL+O (the letter "O"). The File Browser window will appear. Navigate to the desired file; use the

button at upper left in the File Browser window to move up in the hierarchy. LClick on the desired file's name, then LClick "Open Blender File" at upper right.

5. If you choose not to open a file, LClick "Cancel" at upper right.

T16. To render your scene as an image (more precisely, to render a simple, still 2D camera-view image of any single frame in the 3D View of your scene—not a two-part Compositor render (see **T131, p. 271**) and not a Sequencer render (see **T132, p. 273**)):

1. If you are just beginning to use Blender, just go right to step **9**.

2. Have you worked with the Video Sequence Editor (see **T130, p. 264**) yet?

        Yes: Go to **3**.

        No: Go to **5**.

3. Are there one or more strips in the Video Sequence Editor (see **T130, p. 264**)?

    Yes: Go to **4**.

    No: Go to **5**.

4. Go to the "Properties" window: 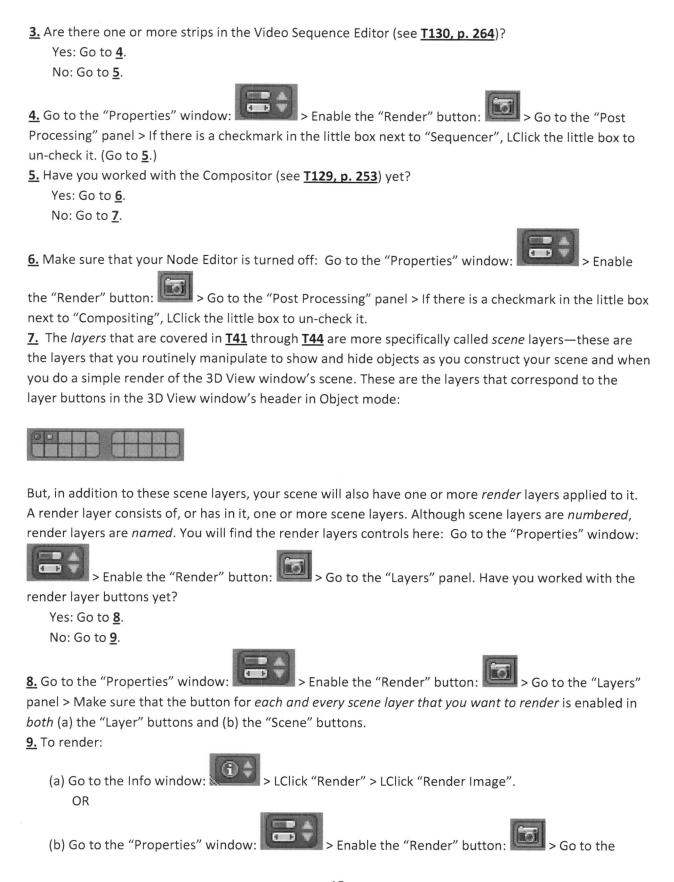 > Enable the "Render" button: > Go to the "Post Processing" panel > If there is a checkmark in the little box next to "Sequencer", LClick the little box to un-check it. (Go to **5**.)

5. Have you worked with the Compositor (see **T129, p. 253**) yet?

    Yes: Go to **6**.

    No: Go to **7**.

6. Make sure that your Node Editor is turned off: Go to the "Properties" window: > Enable the "Render" button: > Go to the "Post Processing" panel > If there is a checkmark in the little box next to "Compositing", LClick the little box to un-check it.

7. The *layers* that are covered in **T41** through **T44** are more specifically called *scene* layers—these are the layers that you routinely manipulate to show and hide objects as you construct your scene and when you do a simple render of the 3D View window's scene. These are the layers that correspond to the layer buttons in the 3D View window's header in Object mode:

But, in addition to these scene layers, your scene will also have one or more *render* layers applied to it. A render layer consists of, or has in it, one or more scene layers. Although scene layers are *numbered*, render layers are *named*. You will find the render layers controls here: Go to the "Properties" window: > Enable the "Render" button: > Go to the "Layers" panel. Have you worked with the render layer buttons yet?

    Yes: Go to **8**.

    No: Go to **9**.

8. Go to the "Properties" window: > Enable the "Render" button: > Go to the "Layers" panel > Make sure that the button for *each and every scene layer that you want to render* is enabled in *both* (a) the "Layer" buttons and (b) the "Scene" buttons.

9. To render:

    (a) Go to the Info window: > LClick "Render" > LClick "Render Image".

       OR

    (b) Go to the "Properties" window: > Enable the "Render" button: > Go to the

"Render" panel > LClick "Image".

  OR

(c) Press F12.

10. (To save the render, see **T18, p. 17**.)

T17. To render *and save* a simple animation of the 3D View (that is, not a two-part Compositor render (see T133, p. 274) and not a Sequencer render (see T134, p. 275)):

1. If you are just beginning to use Blender, just go right to step **9**.

2. Have you worked with the Video Sequence Editor (see **T130, p. 264**) yet?

  Yes: Go to **3**.

  No: Go to **5**.

3. Are there one or more strips in the Video Sequence Editor (see **T130, p. 264**)?

  Yes: Go to **4**.

  No: Go to **5**.

4. Go to the "Properties" window: > Enable the "Render" button: > Go to the "Post Processing" panel > If there is a checkmark in the little box next to "Sequencer", LClick the little box to un-check it. (Go to **5**.)

5. Have you worked with the Compositor (see **T129, p. 253**) yet?

  Yes: Go to **6**.

  No: Go to **7**.

6. Make sure that your Node Editor is turned off: Go to the "Properties" window: > Enable the "Render" button: > Go to the "Post Processing" panel > If there is a checkmark in the little box next to "Compositing", LClick the little box to un-check it.

7. The layers that are covered in **T41** through **T44** are more specifically called *scene* layers—these are the layers that you routinely manipulate to show and hide objects as you construct your scene and when you do a simple render of the 3D View window's scene. These are the layers that correspond to the layer buttons in the 3D View window's header in Object mode:

But, in addition to these scene layers, your scene will also have one or more *render* layers applied to it. A render layer consists of, or has in it, one or more scene layers. Although scene layers are *numbered*, render layers are *named*. You will find the render layers controls here: Go to the "Properties" window: > Enable the "Render" button: > Go to the "Layers" panel. Have you worked with the render layer buttons yet?

16

Yes: Go to **8**.
No: Go to **9**.

8. Go to the "Properties" window:  > Enable the "Render" button: > Go to the "Layers" panel > Make sure that the button for *each and every scene layer that you want to render* in the animation is enabled in *both* (a) the "Layer" buttons and (b) the "Scene" buttons.

9. Go to the "Properties" window: > Enable the "Render" button: > Go to the "Dimensions" panel and make changes if you wish, paying special attention to "Start Frame," "End Frame" and "Frame Rate" (24 frames per second is usual) > Go to the "Output" panel > In the long field at the top, LClick and type in a destination and name for your movie file, if you want to change what's in the field (note that, by default, Blender specifies a *relative*, not an *absolute*, path here; for instance, "//BlueRocket" means "Save in the same folder that the .blend file is in and name the new file BlueRocket"— note also that Blender will add extensions; for instance: "0001-0050.avi" to indicate that the .avi animation runs from frame 1 to frame 50) OR LClick the little button on the right end of this field to browse for a destination > Go down to the next button and LClick it > LClick the name of the file format you want—(a) if you choose an "image" type animation render, Blender will save your animation as a set of image files, one for each frame, and will automatically sequentially name these files; Later, you will want to bring these together into a movie clip in the Video Sequence Editor; to be able to select them all easily, you should put them all by themselves into one folder. To bring these together into a movie clip: bring them into any *empty* VSE as a strip (see **T130, step 7(e), p. 266**), then animation-render the strip using a movie type animation render as described in this step; for shorter animations, you probably don't want to use the image type animation render (but for longer animations, you DO want to) ; (b) If, on the other hand, you use a "movie" type animation render (you might use H.264 for instance) Blender will create a movie file (.avi or .mov) .

10. To render the animation:

(a) Go to the Info window: > LClick "Render" > LClick "Render Animation".
OR

(b) Go to the "Properties" window: > Enable the "Render" button: > Go to the "Render" panel > LClick "Animation".
OR

(c) Press CTRL + F12.

T18. To save a render of a still image:

1. To save a render: With the render displayed and with the mouse cursor in the render window, press F3 > Navigate to where you want to put the image file > LClick the field at upper left, under the long top field > type the name you want to give the file > To choose a file type: Go to the "Save As Image" panel at lower left > LClick on the button at upper left in the panel > LClick a file type > LClick the "Save As Image" button at top right.

T19. To save your scene as a new file:

1. Press F2

        OR

In the "Info" window's header ( ) LClick "File" > LClick "Save As".

        OR

Press SHIFT + CTRL + S*

2. At upper left, in the second long text field from the top, type the name you want to give your file; for instance, **arizona.blend**. (The file name must end in the file extension, ".blend".)

3. Look at top text field. In this field is the name of the folder/directory whose contents are listed in the main field below; the name is preceded by the path, on your hard drive, to this folder.

4. If you want to go up the directory structure, press the button at upper left with the crooked arrow on

it: , or LClick the same kind of arrow, with two dots:  OR , near the top of the list.

5. If you want to go down the directory structure, LClick on a name in the list.

6. If you type in a name after the "/" at the end of the name of the folder/directory whose contents are listed, Blender will create a folder at that place with that name.

7. If you want to refresh the list, LCick the refresh button at upper left: .

8. Find or create a folder where you want to put your new arizona.blend file, and make sure that the name of and path to this folder is shown in the text field at the top.

9. LClick the "Save As Blender File" button at upper right. Your new .blend file will now be saved.

* To return to the window you replaced with the File Browser *without* saving the file, press ESC.

T20. To save your project after you've already saved it at least once:

1. Do you want to overwrite your file:

        Yes: Go to **2**.

        No: Go to **4**.

2. In the "Info" window's header ( ) LClick "File" > LClick "Save" > Go to **5**.

        OR

Press CTRL+W > Go to **3**.

3. In the little window that pops up: LClick the file name under "Save Over". Go to **5**.

4. To save a new version of your project while preserving the current file:

Save the work as a new file (see **T19, p. 18** above) > Go to **5**.

        OR

You can have Blender quickly save a new version with a number automatically added or incremented in order to give progressive versions unique names: press F2 > Press the '+' button at upper right > LClick the "Save As Blender File" button at upper right*. Your new .blend file will now be saved.

5. When you want to close Blender, press CTRL + Q > LClick "Quit Blender".

*To return to the window you replaced with the File Browser without saving, press ESC.

T21 To change the names of the datablocks (see *Introduction*):

1. To change the name of the *object datablock* (that is, to change the name of the object itself), you

must go to the "Properties" window >  > LClick the "Object" button:  > LClick this button, which is at the top:

Type the new name (for instance, "BigTurtle" if you plan to model a big turtle out of it) > Press ENTER.

2. To change the name of the *geometry datablock*: go to the "Properties" window >  > LClick the "Object Data" button (see **T11, p. 9** for how to find it) > LClick this long button that's located at the top of the window:

Type in the new name (for instance, "BigTurtleGeo") > Press ENTER.

3. To change the name of the *material datablock*: go to the "Properties" window >  > LClick

the "Material" button:  > Then LClick this button located near the top of the window:

Type the new name (for instance, "BigTurtleMat") > Press ENTER.

4. To change the name of the *texture datablock*: Go to the "Properties" window:  > LClick the

"Texture" button:  > Go to the row of buttons right below the texture stack & LClick on the field with the Blender-generated or other name in it:

5. Type the name that you want the texture to have > Press ENTER.

PART TWO: GEOMETRICAL PROPERTIES

T22. To select items:

Note that when you select a vertex while keeping an adjacent vertex selected, or when you select two adjacent vertices, Blender will also select the edge between the two vertices. If that edge completes the border of a face, Blender will also select that face.

1. If you are in Object mode (that is, if the Mode button says "Object"),and if no objects are presently selected, and if you want to select all objects, press A.
2. If you are in Edit mode (that is, if the Mode button says "Edit") in the 3D View window, and if none of the object's elements are presently selected, and if you want to select all of the object's elements, press A. (Pressing A similarly selects all elements in the UV/Image Editor window.)
3. Do you want to **select one or more *entire* object(s)**?

> Yes: Go to **4**.
>
> No: Go to **12**.

4. Go into Object mode (see **T8, p. 9**).
5. Do you want to **select *only one* object while de-selecting any already-selected objects**?

> Yes: Go to **6**.
>
> No: Go to **7**.

6. RClick on the object. Stop; you are finished.
7. Do you want to **select *one or more* objects while keeping any already-selected objects selected**?

> Yes: Go to **8**.
>
> No: Go to **10**.

8. SHIFT + RClick on each object
OR
Press (and release) B. Then LClick & hold, to drag a box around the object(s) (or a part of the object(s))
OR
CTRL + LClick & hold, to draw a "lasso" around the object(s) (or large portion of the object(s)) to be selected.
OR
Press C. Then adjust the range of the effect, as shown by the circle, using the mouse wheel. LClick & hold

to drag, to select the items touched by the circle. Press ESC when finished.

9. Stop; you are finished.

10. If you want **to select multiple objects while de-selecting any objects that are already selected**:
RClick on the first object. Then SHIFT+ RClick on each additional object that you want to select

OR

Press A to de-select any already-selected objects. Then Press B. Then LClick & hold, to drag a box around the object(s) (or a part of the object(s)). Press B again and LClick & hold, to draw another box to select more objects, etc.

OR

Press A to de-select any already-selected objects. Press CTRL + LClick & hold, to draw a "lasso" around the object(s) (or large portion of the object(s)) to be selected. CTRL + LClick & hold, to select even more objects, etc.

11. Stop; you are finished.

12. To select a *part* or *parts* of an object; that is, to select one or more points (called "vertices"; singular: "vertex"), one or more lines (called "edges"), or one or more planes (called "faces"):
Make sure the Mode button (see ***Introduction***) is set to "Object Mode" > select the object you want to work on.

13. Go into Edit mode (see **T7, p. 8**).

14. In general, when you make selections in Edit Mode, if you want to **make sure that you are not**

selecting any background geometry, go to the 3D View window header (marked by  at left) >

LClick to enable (darken) this button:  >

15. To select a vertex (without keeping any already-selected items selected):

16. Make sure the "Vertex select mode" button in the 3D View header is activated:

;

if it is not, then:
LClick the button.

      OR

With the mouse cursor in the 3D View window, press CTRL+TAB > LClick "Vertex"

      OR

With the mouse cursor in the 3D View window, press CTRL+TAB > Press 1

17. RClick on the vertex you want to select.

18. To select a vertex while keeping already-selected item(s) selected:

19. Make sure the "Vertex select mode" button in the 3D View header is activated:

;

if it is not, then:

LClick the button.

   OR

With the mouse cursor in the 3D View window, CTRL+TAB > LClick "Vertex"

   OR

With the mouse cursor in the 3D View window, CTRL+TAB > Press 1

METHOD 1

20. Press SHIFT + RClick on the vertex you want to select.

METHOD 2

21. Press B. Then LClick & hold to drag a box around the vertex (or vertices) that you want to select.

METHOD 3

22. Press CTRL+LClick & hold to drag to draw a "lasso" around the vertex (or vertices) that you want to select.

METHOD 4

23. Press C. Then adjust the range of the effect, as shown by the circle, using the mouse wheel. LClick & hold to drag, to select the vertices within the circle. Press ESC when finished.

END OF METHODS

24. **To select an edge (without selecting vertices) without keeping any already-selected items selected:**

25. Make sure the "Edge select mode" button in the 3D View window's header is activated:

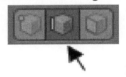
;

if it is not, then:

LClick the button.

   OR

With the mouse cursor in the 3D View window, press CTRL+TAB > LClick "Edge"

   OR

With the mouse cursor in the 3D View window, press CTRL+TAB > Press 2

26. RClick the edge you want to select.

27. **To select an edge and vertices, without keeping any already-selected items selected:**

28. Make sure that the "Vertex select mode" button in the 3D View header is enabled (darkened)—if it is not enabled, LClick it > If the "Edge select mode" button in the 3D View header is not enabled (darkened), Press & hold SHIFT + LClick the button:

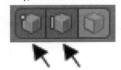

29. RClick the edge you want to select.

30. **To select an edge (without selecting vertices) while keeping already-selected edges and faces selected:**

Make sure the "Edge select mode" button in the 3D View header is activated:

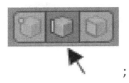

;

if it is not, then:

LClick the button.

    OR

With the mouse cursor in the 3D View window, press CTRL+TAB > LClick "Edge"

    OR

With the mouse cursor in the 3D View window, press CTRL+TAB > Press 2

METHOD 1

31. Press SHIFT + RClick on the edge you want to select.

METHOD 2

32. Press B. Then LClick & hold, to drag a box around the edge(s) that you want to select.

METHOD 3

33. Press CTRL+LClick & hold, to drag to draw a "lasso" around any part of the edge(s) that you want to select.

METHOD 4

34. Press C. Then adjust the range of the effect, as shown by the circle, using the mouse wheel. LClick & hold to drag, to select the edges that touch the circle. Press ESC when finished.

END OF METHODS

Note that when you select an edge that completes the border of a face, Blender will also select that face.

35. **To select an edge and vertices, while keeping already-selected items selected:**

36. Make sure that the "Vertex select mode" button in the 3D View header is enabled (darkened)—if it is not enabled, LClick it > If the "Edge select mode" button in the 3D View header is not enabled (darkened), Press & hold SHIFT + LClick the button:

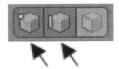

METHOD 1

37. Press SHIFT + RClick on the edge you want to select.

METHOD 2

38. Press B. Then LClick & hold, to drag a box touching the edge(s) that you want to select.

METHOD 3

39. Press CTRL+LClick & hold, to drag to draw a "lasso" around any part of the edge(s) that you want to select.

METHOD 4

40. Press C. Then adjust the range of the effect, as shown by the circle, using the mouse wheel. LClick & hold to drag, to select the items within the circle. Press ESC when finished.

END OF METHODS

41. **To select a face (without selecting vertices) without keeping any already-selected items selected:**

42. Make sure the "Face select mode" button in the 3D View header is enabled (darkened):

 ;

if it is not, then:

LClick the button.

OR

With the mouse cursor in the 3D View window, press CTRL+TAB > LClick "Face"

OR

With the mouse cursor in the 3D View window, press CTRL+TAB > Press 3

43. RClick the face you want to select.

44. To select a vertex, or a face along with its vertices, without keeping any already-selected items selected:

45. Make sure that the "Vertex select mode" button in the 3D View header is enabled (darkened)—if it is not enabled, LClick it > If the "Face select mode" button in the 3D View header is not enabled (darkened), Press & hold SHIFT + LClick the button:

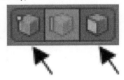

46. RClick the vertex or face that you want to select.

47. To select a face (without selecting vertices) while keeping already-selected faces selected:

Make sure the "Face select mode" button in the 3D View header is activated:

 ;

if it is not, then:

LClick the button.

OR

With the mouse cursor in the 3D View window, press CTRL+TAB > LClick "Face"

OR

With the mouse cursor in the 3D View window, press CTRL+TAB > Press 3

METHOD 1

48. Press SHIFT+RClick on the face you want to select.

METHOD 2

49. Press B.

50. LClick & hold to drag a box over the face(s) that you want to select. You only have to enclose some part of a face in order to select it.

METHOD 3

51. Press CTRL+LClick & hold to drag a "lasso" around the face(s) that you want to select. You only have to enclose some part of a face in order to select it.

METHOD 4

52. Press C. Then adjust the range of the effect, as shown by the circle, using the mouse wheel. LClick & hold to drag, to select the faces touching the circle. Press ESC when finished.

END OF METHODS

53. To select a face and vertices, while keeping already-selected items selected: Make sure that the "Vertex select mode" button in the 3D View header is enabled (darkened)—if it is not enabled, LClick it > If the "Face select mode" button in the 3D View header is not enabled (darkened), Press & hold SHIFT + LClick the button:

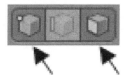

METHOD 1

54. Press SHIFT+RClick on the face you want to select.

METHOD 2

55. Press B.

56. LClick & hold to drag a box over the face(s) that you want to select. You only have to enclose some part of a face in order to select it.

METHOD 3

57. Press CTRL+LClick & hold to drag a "lasso" around the face(s) that you want to select. You only have to enclose some part of a face in order to select it.

METHOD 4

58. Press C. Then adjust the range of the effect, as shown by the circle, using the mouse wheel. LClick & hold to drag, to select the faces touching the circle. Press ESC when finished.

END OF METHODS

59. To select a vertex (without keeping any already-selected items selected); OR: to select an edge or a face, while selecting all adjacent vertices (without keeping any already-selected items selected): Make sure that the "Vertex select mode" button in the 3D View header is enabled (darkened)—if it is not enabled, LClick it:

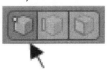

60. If the "Edge select mode" button in the 3D View header is not enabled (darkened), Press & hold SHIFT + LClick the button:

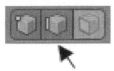

61. If the "Face select mode" button in the 3D View header is not enabled (darkened), Press & hold SHIFT + LClick the button:

62. RClick the vertex, edge, or face you want to select.

63. **To select a vertex, an edge, or a face, while selecting all adjacent vertices (without de-selecting any already-selected items selected):**
Make sure that the "Vertex select mode" button in the 3D View header is enabled (darkened)—if it is not enabled, LClick it:

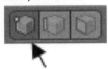

64. If the "Edge select mode" button in the 3D View header is not enabled (darkened), Press & hold SHIFT + LClick the button:

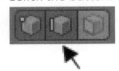

65. If the "Face select mode" button in the 3D View header is not enabled (darkened), Press & hold SHIFT + LClick the button:

66. SHIFT+RClick the vertex, edge, or face you want to select.

67 . **To select the children (and children's children, etc.) of a parent (while deselecting everything else already selected, including the parent):** In Object mode, select the parent; or, if other items are selected, make sure the parent is selected last (i.e., make sure that the parent is the "active" selection).

68. With the mouse pointer in the 3D View window: press SHIFT+G.

69. LClick "Children" OR press C.

70. **To select the children (and _not_ the children's children, etc.) of a parent:**

71. In Object mode, select the parent; or, if other items are selected, make sure the parent is selected last (i.e., make sure that the parent is the "active" selection).

72. With the mouse pointer in the 3D View window: press SHIFT+G.

73. LClick "Immediate Children" OR press (the capital letter) I.

74. **To select a child's parent (while deselecting the child):**

75. In Object mode, select the child; or, if other items are selected, make sure the child is selected last (i.e., make sure that the child is the "active" selection).

76. With the mouse pointer in the 3D View window: press SHIFT+G.

77. LClick "Parent" OR press P.

78. **To select the siblings of a child (leaving the child selected, but without selecting any of the siblings' children or the parent):**

79. In Object mode, select the child; or, if other items are selected, make sure the child is selected last (i.e., make sure that the child is the "active" selection).

80. With the mouse pointer in the 3D View window: press SHIFT+G.

81. LClick "Siblings" OR press S.

82. To select all objects of the same general type (see *Introduction*) as an object, say object A (e.g., if A is a mesh, select all meshes, or if A is a curve, select all curves, etc.):

83. In Object mode, select object A; or, if other items are selected, make sure object A is selected last (i.e., make sure that object A is the "active" selection).

84. With the mouse pointer in the 3D View window: press SHIFT+G.

85. LClick "Type" OR press T.

86. To select all objects on the layers that an object, say object A, is on:

87. In Object mode select object A; or, if other items are selected, make sure object A is selected last (i.e., make sure that object A is the "active" selection).

88. With the mouse pointer in the 3D View window: press SHIFT+G.

89. LClick "Layer" OR press L.

90. To select all objects in the same object group as an object, say, object A:

91. In Object mode, select object A; or, if other items are selected, make sure object A is selected last (i.e., make sure that object A is the "active" selection).

92. With the mouse pointer in the 3D View window: press SHIFT+G.

93. LClick "Group" OR press G.

94. If you're given a choice of groups (i.e., if object A is in more than one group), LClick the name of the group that you want to select.

95. To select an object's "hooks" (see T104, p. 215): Select the object > With the mouse pointer in the 3D View window: SHIFT+G.

96. LClick "Hook" OR press H.

97. To select any objects that have the same "PassIndex" as an object, say object A:

98. Select object A; or, if other items are selected, make sure object A is selected last (i.e., make sure that object A is the "active" selection).

99. With the mouse pointer in the 3D View window: SHIFT+G.

100. LClick "Pass" OR press A.

101. To select an "edge loop"; that is, to select with one click a series of edges sequentially going through 4-way intersections (both ways from the starting edge) following the middle path of each intersection, until a 3-way intersection is reached:

102. In Edit mode (see **T7, p. 8**), go into Edge Select mode: In the 3D View window header, LClick

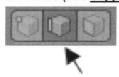

OR

Press CTRL +TAB > LClick "Edge"

103. ALT + RClick on the first edge. (OR SHIFT+ALT+RClick to keep already selected items selected.)

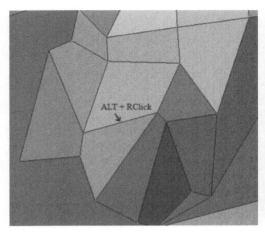 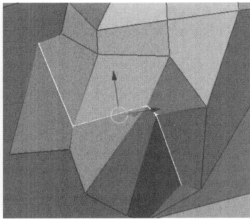

104. To select a "face loop"; that is, to select with one click a series of faces, by clicking on one face, going (both ways from the starting face) automatically through the nearest edge, selecting the next adjacent face, going through that face to its far edge, selecting the next adjacent face, etc.:

105. In Edit mode (see **T7, p. 8**), go into Face Select mode: In the 3D View window header, LClick

OR

Press CTRL +TAB > LClick "Face".

106. ALT + RClick on the face near its border with the next face you want to be selected. In the right-hand picture below, "S" indicates a selected face.

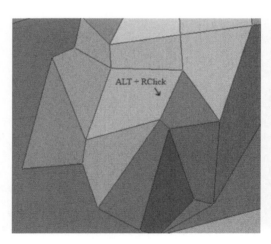 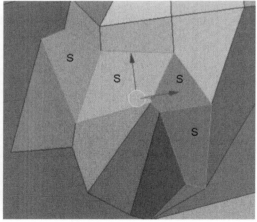

107. To select an "edge ring;" that is, to select with one click a series of edges, by selecting an edge, then going (both ways from the starting edge) through the adjacent face (but not selecting it), selecting this face's far edge, going through the next adjacent face (but not selecting it), selecting that

face's far edge, etc. :

108. In Edit mode (see **T7, p. 8**), go into Edge Select mode: In the 3D View window header, LClick

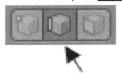

OR

 Press CTRL +TAB > LClick "Edge"

109. CTRL + ALT + RClick on the first edge. In the picture below, "S" indicates a selected edge.

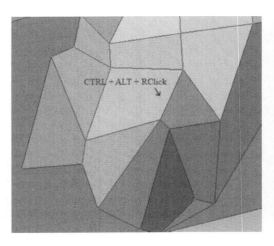
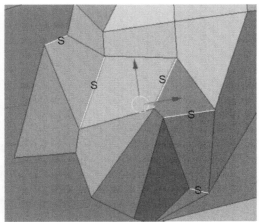

110. **To select a vertex group**:

111. In Object mode (see **T8, p. 9**), select the object that the vertices—the ones in the vertex group that you want to select—belong to.

112. Go to Edit mode (see **T7, p. 8**).

113. In the Properties window header (identified by at the left): LClick the "Object Data"

button: > Go to the "Vertex Groups" panel.

114. From the list (in the large box) of vertex groups assigned to the vertices of the selected object, LClick the name of the vertex group that you want to select.

115. LClick "Select".

116. **To select all elements linked to element E (a vertex, edge, or face)—without deselecting already-selected items:**

117. In Edit mode, LClick the "select mode" button that corresponds to E; suppose, for instance, that E is a vertex:

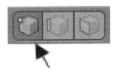

118. Put the mouse cursor near element E > Press L.

T23. To deselect items

1. To deselect all selected items:

Press A

2. To deselect a vertex:

3. Make sure the "Vertex select mode" button in the 3D View header is activated:

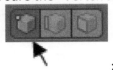

;

if it is not, then:

LClick the button.

      OR

With the mouse cursor in the 3D View window, CTRL+TAB > LClick "Vertex"

      OR

With the mouse cursor in the 3D View window, CTRL+TAB > Press 1

METHOD 1

4. Press SHIFT + RClick on the vertex you want to deselect.

METHOD 2

5. Press B. Then MClick & hold to drag a box around the vertex (or vertices) that you want to deselect.

METHOD 3

6. Press CTRL + SHIFT + LClick & hold to drag to draw a "lasso" around the vertex (or vertices) that you want to deselect.

METHOD 4

7. Press C. Then adjust the range of the effect, as shown by the circle, using the mouse wheel. MClick & hold to drag, to deselect the vertices within the circle. Press ESC when finished.

END OF METHODS

8. To deselect an edge:

Make sure the "Edge select mode" button in the 3D View header is activated:

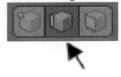

if it is not, then:

LClick the button.

      OR

With the mouse cursor in the 3D View window, press CTRL+TAB > LClick "Edge"

      OR

With the mouse cursor in the 3D View window, press CTRL+TAB > Press 2

METHOD 1

9. Press SHIFT + RClick on the edge you want to deselect.

METHOD 2

10. Press B. Then MClick & hold, to drag a box around some part (or all) of the edge(s) that you want to deselect.

METHOD 3

11. Press CTRL + SHIFT + LClick & hold, to drag to draw a "lasso" around any part (or all) of the edge(s) that you want to deselect.

METHOD 4

12. Press C. Then adjust the range of the effect, as shown by the circle, using the mouse wheel. MClick & hold to drag, to deselect the edges touching the circle. Press ESC when finished.

END OF METHODS

13. To deselect a face:

Make sure the "Face select mode" button in the 3D View header is activated:

if it is not, then:

LClick the button.

      OR

With the mouse cursor in the 3D View window, press CTRL+TAB > LClick "Face"

       OR

With the mouse cursor in the 3D View window, press CTRL+TAB > Press 3

METHOD 1

14. Press SHIFT+RClick on the face you want to deselect.

METHOD 2

15. Press B.

16. MClick & hold to drag a box over the face(s) that you want to select. You only have to enclose some part of a face in order to deselect it.

METHOD 3

17. Press CTRL + SHIFT + LClick & hold to drag a "lasso" around the face(s) that you want to deselect. You only have to enclose some part of a face in order to select it.

METHOD 4

18. Press C. Then adjust the range of the effect, as shown by the circle, using the mouse wheel. MClick & hold to drag, to deselect the faces touching the circle. Press ESC when finished.

END OF METHODS

19. To deselect a vertex group:

20. It is assumed that you are in Edit mode (see **T7, p. 8**) and that a vertex group is selected:

21. In the Properties window header (identified by 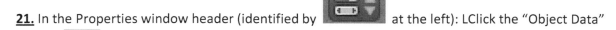 at the left): LClick the "Object Data"

button: > Go to the "Vertex Groups" panel.

22. From the list (in the large box) of vertex groups assigned to the vertices of the selected object, LClick the name of the vertex group that you want to deselect.

23. LClick "Deselect".

24. To deselect all elements linked to element E (a vertex, edge, or face):

25. LClick the "select mode" button that corresponds to E; suppose, for instance, that E is a vertex:

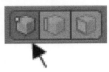

26. Put the mouse cursor near element E > Press SHIFT+L.

T24. The Blender coordinate systems

This picture of a room with translucent walls and floor depicts a coordinate system:

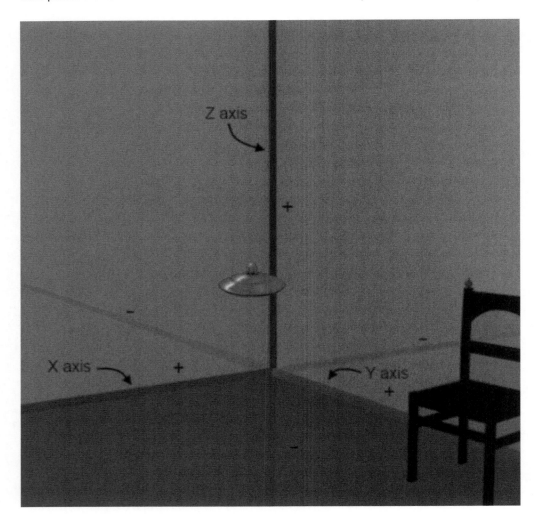

By giving a measurement along each of the three axes, you can describe the position of the tiny alien UFO that's hovering in the room.

The system's *origin* is where the three axes meet – where x=0, y=0 and z=0.

Blender can create any number of such coordinate systems (where X is red, Y is green and Z is blue) for you to use in order to define locations within your model space, but there are only five *kinds* of such coordinate systems in Blender. Here, I'll discuss four of them:

1. In your model, there is only one "**Global**" coordinate system, which is partially imaged as the "base grid" in the scene—this grid represents part of the Global XY plane where Z is zero.

2. There is only one "**View**" coordinate system: as you work on your model, you are *always* looking down the Z axis of this system. The X axis is always horizontal and the Y axis is always vertical.

3. Each object is given a "**Local**" coordinate system, which the object "carries" with it. *The origin of this system (the 0,0,0 point), which is called the "**object origin**", is marked by a tiny orange dot.*

4. Every plane—for instance, a three-sided face—can be given a coordinate system whose Z axis is perpendicular to the plane. Such a system is called a "**Normal**" coordinate system.

5. As you work on your model, you can work with only one kind of coordinate system at a time. Choose which system you want to use by LClicking the "Transform Orientation" button in the 3D View window's header (since different words can appear on this button, I've put a smudged word on it):

OR

OR
Press ALT + Press the SPACEBAR.

6. LClick the name of the system you want to use (View, Normal, Gimbal [which pertains to gyroscope-like or top-like objects], Local or Global)

T25. To move/rotate/scale: transforming

1. Do you want **to move an item or group of items from one place to another, to rotate an item or group of items, or to scale, stretch or compress an item or group of items, and to do so in a way such that no new edges or faces are formed** (i.e., such that any existing connecting edges are distorted to accommodate the change)? In other words, do you want to "transform" an item or group of items?:

       Yes: Go to **2**.

       No: Go to Extruding, **T26, p. 58**, below.

2. Refer to **T24, p. 32** to familiarize yourself with the Blender coordinate systems.

3. To set the pivot point for rotating and scaling: Go to the 3D View window header and LClick the Pivot button (see ***Introduction***).

4. If you are going to rotate or scale around the item that was the last to be selected, LClick "Active Element".

5. If you are in Object mode, and you are going to rotate or scale each selected object around its origin (see **T24, step 3, p. 33**), LClick "Individual Origins".

6. If you are in Edit mode, and have selected one or more sets of faces, and you are going to rotate or scale each separate set around its center (there will be distortion of the faces) LClick "Individual Origins".

7. If you are going to rotate around the center of an edge or face, or around the median of any selected set of items, LClick "Median Point".

8. If you are going to rotate around the 3D cursor (see **T58, p. 98** for how to place this cursor), LClick "3D Cursor".

9. Go to Object Mode (see **T8, p. 9**): select the object you want to work on.

10. Choose a method:

METHOD 1—USE THE "3D TRANSFORM MANIPULATOR" (For **METHOD 2**, go to step **77**.)

11. If you wish, you can bring up a set of "Properties" panels, which may be of some help as you use the transform manipulator:

> (i) With the mouse pointer in the 3D View window, press N
>
> OR:
>
> (ii) Go to the 3D View window's header (this header is marked by at left) > LClick "View" > LClick "Properties").

This will produce a set of "Properties" panels. (To get rid of the Properties panels later, repeat (i) or (ii) above.)

12. Make sure these buttons are visible in the 3D View window header (this header is marked by

 at left):

13. If these three buttons are not visible, (a) LClick this button:

OR

(b) Make sure that your mouse pointer is in the 3D View window and press CTRL+SPACE—This will bring up the three buttons. (It's a toggle.)

14. Choose which coordinate system (see **T24, p. 32**) that you want to use by LClicking the "Transform Orientation" button (since different words can appear on this button, I've put a smudged word on it):

   OR

OR

Press ALT + Press the SPACEBAR.

15. LClick the name of the coordinate system you want to use (View, Normal, Gimbal [which pertains to gyroscopic-type or top-like objects], Local or Global)

16. Do you want to move, rotate, or scale an *entire* object?

> Yes: Go to **17**.
>
> No: To move *part* of an object, go to **20**.

17. Do you want to scale the object? Or, if you want to *move* the object, do you want the *object origin* (see **T24, step 3, p. 33**) to move with it? Or, if you want to *rotate* the object, do you want *the object's* *local coordinate system* (see **T24, step 3, p. 33**) to rotate with it?

> Yes: Go to **24**.

> No: Go to **18**.

18. Go to Edit Mode (see **T7, p. 8**).

19. Select the whole object (see **T22, p. 20**). Go to **24**.

20. Make sure you've selected, in Object Mode (see **T8, p. 9**), the object whose part(s) you want to move, then go into Edit Mode (see **T7, p. 8**) and select the part(s) of the object that you want to move, rotate or scale.

21. Do you want a gradual "falloff" (that is, a gradual transition in size and shape) from the moved, rotated or scaled part(s) to the unchanged part(s)?

> Yes: Go to **22**.

> No: Go to **24**.

22. LClick the "Proportional Edit Tool" (PET) button:

 > LClick "Enable"

OR

Press the letter O key.

23. LClick the PET's curve button:

> LClick on the kind of falloff you want.

> OR

Press & hold SHIFT + press the letter O key repeatedly to cycle through the kinds of falloff until the icon of the one you want appears on the button.

24. Do you want to __MOVE__ the item(s) from one place to another?

> Yes: Go to **25**.

> No: Go to **43**.

25. LClick the "Translate manipulator mode" button (the arrow) in the 3D window header:

This makes the "3D Manipulator" look like this:

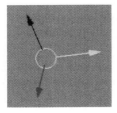

26. Do you want **to move the item in the direction of _only one_ axis**; that is, in the X, in the Y, _or_ in the Z direction (of the coordinate system you chose at steps **14** and **15** above)?

> Yes: Go to **27**.
>
> No: Go to **38**.

27. LClick **& hold** the 3D Manipulator's arrow for the axis whose direction you want to move the item in. (**_Keep holding this button down as you follow the steps below._**)

28. If you are in Edit mode and you clicked the "Proportional Edit Tool" (PET) button at step **22**: SCROLL to adjust the range of the PET's effect (this is generally possible to do, though may take a little dexterity).

29. Do you want to move the item a certain number of units?

> Yes: Go to **30**.
>
> No: Go to **31**.

30.

SUB-METHOD 1

Type the number of units you want the item to move. (Let's say that you type "21": immediately after you type the 2, the selection will move 2 units in the positive direction of the axis; then, when you type the 1, the selection will move 19 more units, for a total of 21.) If you are moving in the View XY plane by dragging the white circle, this sub-method will move the selection in the Global X direction; if you are moving in a Global or Local XZ or XY plane, this will move the selection in the plane's X direction; if you are moving in a Global or Local YZ plane, this will move the selection in the plain's Y direction. Stop. (Release the mouse button.) You are finished.

SUB-METHOD 2

Move the item while watching the indication at the left end of the 3D View window's header which shows how far you've moved the item _in the coordinate system that you chose at steps **14** and **15**_:

Go to **31**.

SUB-METHOD 3

If you brought up the set of "Properties" panels in step **11**: Go to the "Transform" panel.

If you are in **_Object_** mode, look at the **_"Location"_** fields:

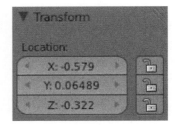

These fields show the coordinates of **the object's origin** in the **Global** coordinate system. Watch these fields to determine how far you've moved the object.

If you are in **Edit** mode, look at the **"Median"** fields (or the **"Vertex"** fields if only a single vertex is selected):

If you enable the "Global" button below these fields, the fields show the coordinates of **the selection's median** (geometrical "center") in the **Global** coordinate system. If you enable the "Local" button below these fields, the fields show the coordinates of the selection's median in the object's **Local** coordinate system. Watch these fields to determine how far you've moved the item. Go to **31**.

END OF SUB-METHODS

31. Do you want to move the item freely?

> Yes: Go to **32**.
>
> No: Go to **33**.

32. Drag the item to where you want it. Release the button. Stop; you are finished.

33. Do you want to move the item in large increments?

> Yes: Go to **34**.
>
> No: Go to **35**.

34. Press & hold CTRL. Move the item to where you want it. Release the button. Release CTRL. Stop; you are finished.

35. Do you want to move the item in small increments?

> Yes: Go to **36**.
>
> No: Go to **37**.

36. Press & hold CTRL and press & hold SHIFT. Move the item to where you want it. Release the button. Release CTRL and release SHIFT. Stop; you are finished.

37. To move the item very slowly, to make fine adjustments: Press & hold SHIFT. Move the item to where you want it. Release the button. Release SHIFT. Stop; you are finished.

38. Do you want **to move the selected item(s) in the XY plane of the View coordinate system** (i.e., such that the item(s) will not move away from nor toward the viewer)?

> Yes: Go to **39**.

No: Go to **41**.

39. LClick & hold the white circle in the middle of the 3D Manipulator.

40. Keep holding the mouse button down. Go to **28**.

41. **To move the selected item in any XY, XZ or YZ plane** (of the axis system you chose at step **14** and step **15** above): SHIFT+LClick & hold on the manipulator arrow that's perpendicular to the plane in which you wish to move. *Release SHIFT.* Move the item.

42. Go to **28**.

43. **Do you want to ROTATE the selected item(s)?**

Yes: Go to **44**.

No: Go to **59**.

44. LClick the "Rotate manipulator mode" button (the little arc):

This makes the "3D Manipulator" look like this:

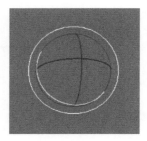

45. Do you want to rotate the selected item(s) in the XY plane of the View coordinate system (i.e., such that no part of the item(s) will move away from nor toward the viewer)?

Yes: Go to **57**.

No: Go to **46**.

46. LClick & hold the red, blue or green arc, on the 3D Manipulator, that you want to use in rotating the item(s). (Keep holding as you follow the steps below.)

47. If you are in Edit mode and you clicked the "Proportional Edit Tool" (PET) button at step **22**: SCROLL to adjust the range of the PET's effect (this is generally possible to do, though may take a little dexterity).

48. Do you want to rotate the item a certain number of degrees?

Yes: Go to **49**.

No: Go to **50**.

49.

SUB-METHOD 1

Type the number of degrees you want the item to rotate. (Let's say that you type "90": immediately after you type the 9, the selection will move 9 degrees; then, when you type the 0, the selection will move 81 more degrees, for a total of 90) Stop. (Release the mouse button.) You are finished.

SUB-METHOD 2

Rotate the item while watching the indication at the left end of the 3D View window's header which shows how far you've rotated the item *in the coordinate system that you chose at steps* ___14___ *and* ___15___:

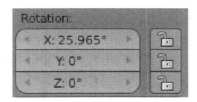

Go to ___50___.

SUB-METHOD 3

If you brought up the set of "Properties" panels in step ___11___, *and are in Object mode*: Go to the "Transform" panel > Look at the "Rotation" fields

Watch these fields to determine how far you've rotated the item. It always shows the rotation on the *Global* coordinate system axes. Go to ___50___.

END OF SUB-METHODS

___50.___ Do you want to rotate the item freely?

      Yes: Go to ___51___.

      No: Go to ___52___.

___51.___ Rotate the item to the desired position. Release the button. Stop; you are finished.

___52.___ Do you want to rotate the item in large increments?

      Yes: Go to ___53___.

      No: Go to ___54___.

___53.___ Press & hold CTRL. Rotate the item to where you want it. Release the button. Release CTRL. Stop; you are finished.

___54.___ Do you want to rotate the item in small increments?

      Yes: Go to ___55___.

      No: Go to ___56___.

___55.___ Press & hold CTRL and press & hold SHIFT. Rotate the item to the desired position. Release the button. Release CTRL and release SHIFT. Stop; you are finished.

___56.___ To rotate the item very slowly, to make fine adjustments: Press & hold SHIFT. Rotate the item to the desired position. Release the button. Release SHIFT. Stop; you are finished.

___57.___ **To rotate the selected item(s) in the XY plane of the View coordinate system** (i.e., such that no part of the item(s) will move away from nor toward the viewer): LClick & hold the big white circle that surrounds the 3D Manipulator.

58. Go to **47**.

59. To SCALE the selected item(s): LClick the "Scale Manipulator mode" button (the little stick with a diamond on the end of it):

This makes the "3D Manipulator" look like this:

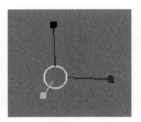

60. Do you want **to scale the object in the direction of *only one* axis**; that is, in the X, in the Y, *or* in the Z direction?

       Yes: Go to **61**.

       No: Go to **72**.

61. LClick & hold the 3D Manipulator's handle for the axis whose direction you want to scale the item in. (Keep holding this button down as you follow the steps below.)

62. If you the clicked the "Proportional Edit Tool" (PET) button at step **22**: SCROLL to adjust the range of the PET's effect (this is generally possible to do, though may take a little dexterity).

63. Do you want to scale the item by a certain number of units?

       Yes: Go to **64**.

       No: Go to **65**.

64.

SUB-METHOD 1

Type the number of units you want the item to scale. (Let's say that you type "2.5" to multiply the dimension(s) by 2.5: immediately after you type the 2, the selection will be scaled by 2 units; then, when you type the .5, the selection will scale by the remaining .5 units, for a total of 2.5) Stop. (Release the mouse button.) You are finished.

SUB-METHOD 2

Scale the item while watching the indication at the left end of the 3D View window's header which shows how far you've scaled the item *in the coordinate system that you chose at steps **14** and **15***:

Scale: 1.7898 global (Smooth) Proportional size: 0.75

Go to **65**.

SUB-METHOD 3

If you brought up the set of "Properties" panels in step **11**, and are in Object mode: Go to the "Transform" panel > Look at the "Scale" and "Dimensions" fields

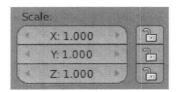

Watch these fields to determine how far you've scaled the item. It always shows the amount of scaling on the *Local* coordinate system axes. Go to **65**.

END OF SUB-METHODS

65. Do you want to scale the item freely?

> Yes: Go to **66**.
>
> No: Go to **67**.

66. Scale the item to the size/proportions you want it to have. Release the button. Stop; you are finished.

67. Do you want to scale the item in large increments?

> Yes: Go to **68**.
>
> No: Go to **69**.

68. Press & hold CTRL. Scale the item to the size/proportions you want it to have. Release the mouse button. Release CTRL. Stop; you are finished.

69. Do you want to scale the item in small increments?

> Yes: Go to **70**.
>
> No: Go to **71**.

70. Press & hold CTRL and press & hold SHIFT. Scale the item to the size/proportions you want it to have. Release the mouse button. Release CTRL and release SHIFT. Stop; you are finished.

71. To scale the item very slowly, to make fine adjustments: Press & hold SHIFT. Scale the item to the size/proportions you want it to have. Release the mouse button. Release SHIFT. Stop; you are finished.

72. Do you want **to scale the selected item(s) in all directions**?

> Yes: Go to **73**.
>
> No: Go to **75**.

73. LClick & hold the white circle in the middle of the 3D Manipulator.

74. Go to **62**. (Note that **SUB-METHOD 1 in step 64** will scale the selection in all three directions by the specified amount.)

75. To scale the selected item in any XY, XZ or YZ plane (of the axis system you chose at step **15**): SHIFT+LClick & hold on the manipulator handle that's perpendicular to the plane in which you wish to scale. Release SHIFT.

76. Go to **62**. (But note that **SUB-METHOD 1 in step 64** will scale the selection by the specified amount in the direction of both of the plane's two axes.)

METHOD 2 – HOTKEYS

77. If you wish, you can bring up a set of "Properties" panels, which may be of some help as you use this method:

> (i) With the mouse pointer in the 3D View window, press N
>
> OR:
>
> (ii) Go to the 3D View window's header (this header is marked by at left) > LClick "View" > LClick "Properties").

This will produce a set of "Properties" panels. (To get rid of the Properties panels later, repeat (i) or (ii) above.)

78. Do you want **to move, rotate, or scale an *entire* object**?

> Yes: Go to **79**.
>
> No: **To move, rotate, or scale *part* of an object**, go to **83**.

79. Do you want to *scale* an object?

> Yes: go to **81** (to scale in Edit mode) or **88** (to scale in Object mode).
>
> No: To move or rotate an object, go to **80**.

80. If you want to **move** the object's geometry, do you want the object origin of the object to move with it? OR, if you want to **rotate** the object, do you want the object's local coordinate system to rotate with it?

> Yes: Make sure you're in Object Mode. Go to **88**.
>
> No: Go to **81**.

81. Go to Edit Mode (see **T7, p. 8**).

82. Select the whole object (see **T22, p. 20**). Go to **88**.

83. Make sure you've selected, in Object Mode, the object whose part(s) you want to move, rotate or scale, then go into Edit Mode (see **T7, p. 8**) and select the part(s) of the object that you want to move, rotate or scale.

84. Do you want a gradual "falloff" (that is, a gradual transition in size and shape) from the moved, rotated or scaled part(s) to the unchanged part(s)?

> Yes: Go to **85**.
>
> No: Go to **88**.

85. LClick the "Proportional Edit Tool" (PET) button:

 > LClick "Enable"

> OR
>
> Press the letter O key.

86. LClick the PET's curve button:

87. LClick on the kind of falloff you want.

OR

Press & hold SHIFT + press the letter O key repeatedly to cycle through the kinds of falloff until the icon of the one you want appears on the button.

88. Do you want to <u>MOVE</u> a selected item (or group of items) from one place to another?

Yes: Go to **89**.

No: Go to **112**.

89. Do you want **to move the selected item (or group of items) in the *View* XY plane**? (Note that, if you use the numpad keys to go to certain exact views [as covered in **T13, step 25, p. 11**], the *View* XY plane can be made to coincide with different *Global* planes. So, for instance, if you want to move the selection around in the Global XZ plane, just press numpad 1, then use this method to move the selection around in the View XY [= Global XZ] plane.)

Yes: Go to **90**.

No: Go to **101**.

90. Press (& release) G.

91. If you the clicked the "Proportional Edit Tool" (PET) button at step **85** above:

SCROLL to adjust the range of the PET's effect

OR

ALT+numpad-plus or numpad-minus to adjust the range of the PET's effect.

92. Do you want to move the item a certain number of units?

Yes: Go to **93**.

No: Go to **94**.

93.

SUB-METHOD 1

Type the number of units you want the item to move. (If you are moving in the View XY plane, this will move the selection in the Global X direction. If you are moving in another XY or XZ plane, this will move the selection in the plane's X direction; if you are moving in a YZ plane, this will move the selection in the plane's Y direction.) LClick. Stop. You are finished.

SUB-METHOD 2

Move the item while watching the indication at the left end of the 3D View window's header which shows how far you've moved the item *in the Global coordinate system*:

D: 0.0362 (0.0362) global (Smooth)   Proportional size: 0.22

Go to **94**.

SUB-METHOD 3

If you brought up the set of "Properties" panels in step **77**: Go to the "Transform" panel.

If you are in **Object** mode, look at the **"Location"** fields:

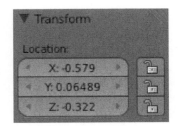

These fields show the coordinates of **the object's origin** in the **Global** coordinate system. Watch these fields to determine how far you've moved the object.

If you are in **Edit** mode, look at the **"Median"** fields (or the **"Vertex"** fields if only a single vertex is selected) :

If you enable the "Global" button below these fields, the fields show the coordinates of **the selection's median** (geometrical "center") in the **Global** coordinate system. If you enable the "Local" button below these fields, the fields show the coordinates of the selection's median in the object's **Local** coordinate system. Watch these fields to determine how far you've moved the item. Go to **94**.

END OF SUB-METHODS

94. Do you want to move the item freely?

    Yes: Go to **95**.

    No: Go to **96**.

95. Move the item to where you want it. LClick. Stop. You are finished.

96. Do you want to move the item in large increments?

    Yes: Go to **97**.

    No: Go to **98**.

97. Press & hold CTRL. Move the item to where you want it. LClick. Release CTRL. Stop. You are finished.

98. Do you want to move the item in small increments?

> Yes: Go to **99**.

> No: Go to **100**.

99. Press & hold CTRL + press & hold SHIFT. Move the item to where you want it. LClick. Release CTRL & SHIFT. Stop. You are finished

100. To move the item very slowly, to make fine adjustments : Press & hold SHIFT. Move the item to where you want it. LClick. Release SHIFT. Stop. You are finished.

101. Do you want **to move the item in the X (or Y, or Z) direction of the *Global* coordinate system**?

> Yes: Go to **102**.

> No: Go to **104**.

102. Press (& release) G. Then press (& release) X (or Y, or Z).

103. Go to **91**.

104. Do you want **to move the item in the X (or Y, or Z) direction of the *Local* coordinate system**?

> Yes: Go to **105**.

> No: Go to **107**.

105. Press (& release) G. Then press (& release) X, then press (& release) X (or press Y then Y, or press Z then Z).

106. Go to **91**.

107. Do you want **to move the item in the *Global* coordinate system's XY (or XZ, or YZ) plane**?

> Yes: Go to **108**.

> No: Go to **110**.

108. Press (& release) G. Then press (& release) SHIFT+Z (or Y, or X).

109. Go to **91**.

110. **To move the item in the *Local* coordinate system's XY (or XZ, or YZ) plane**: Press (& release) G. Then press (& release) SHIFT+Z (or Y, or X). Then press (& release) SHIFT+Z (or Y, or X) again.

111. Go to **91**.

112. **Do you want to ROTATE an item (or group of items)?**

> Yes: Go to **113**.

> No: Go to **130**.

113. Do you want **to rotate a selected item (or group of items) in the *View* XY plane**:

> Yes: Go to **114**.

> No: Go to **125**.

114. Press (& release) R.

115. If you the clicked the "Proportional Edit Tool" (PET) button at step **85** above:

SCROLL to adjust the range of the PET's effect

> OR

ALT+numpad-plus or numpad-minus to adjust the range of the PET's effect.

116. Do you want to rotate the item a certain number of degrees?

> Yes: Go to **117**.

> No: Go to **118**.

117.

SUB-METHOD 1

Type the number of degrees you want the item to rotate > LClick. Stop. You are finished.

SUB-METHOD 2

Rotate the item while watching the indication at the left end of the 3D View window's header which shows how far you've rotated the item:

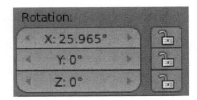

Go to **118**.

SUB-METHOD 3

If you brought up the set of "Properties" panels in step **77**, *and are in Object mode*: Go to the "Transform" panel > Look at the "Rotation" fields

Watch these fields to determine how far you've moved the item. It always shows the rotation on the *Global* coordinate system axes. Go to **118**.

END OF SUB-METHODS

118. Do you want to rotate the item freely?

    Yes: Go to **119**.

    No: Go to **120**.

119. Rotate the item to where you want it. LClick. Stop. You are finished.

120. Do you want to rotate the item in large increments?

    Yes: Go to **121**.

    No: Go to **122**.

121. Press & hold CTRL. Rotate the item to where you want it. LClick. Release CTRL. Stop. You are finished.

122. Do you want to rotate the item in small increments?

    Yes: Go to **123**.

    No: Go to **124**.

123. Press & hold CTRL + press & hold SHIFT. Rotate the item to where you want it. LClick. Release CTRL & SHIFT. Stop. You are finished

124. To rotate the item very slowly, to make fine adjustments : Press & hold SHIFT. Rotate the item to where you want it. LClick. Release SHIFT. Stop. You are finished.

125. Do you want to rotate the item around the X (or Y, or Z) axis direction of the *Global* coordinate system?

    Yes: Go to **126**.

No: Go to **128**.

126. Press (& release) R. Then press (& release) X (or Y, or Z).

127. Go to **115**.

128. To rotate the item in the X (or Y, or Z) direction of the *Local* coordinate system: Press (& release) R. Then press (& release) X, then press (& release) X (or press Y then Y, or press Z then Z).

129. Go to **115**.

130. To SCALE a selected item (or group of items):

131. Do you want to **scale a selected item (or group of items) in *all* directions**?

>   Yes: Go to **132**.

>   No: Go to **143**.

132. Press (& release) S.

133. If you the clicked the "Proportional Edit Tool" (PET) button at step **85** above: SCROLL to adjust the range of the PET's effect

>   OR

ALT+numpad-plus or numpad-minus to adjust the range of the PET's effect.

134. Do you want to scale the item by a certain number of units?

>   Yes: Go to **135**.

>   No: Go to **136**.

135.

>   **SUB-METHOD 1**
>   Type the number of units you want the item to scale > LClick. Stop. You are finished.
>   **SUB-METHOD 2**
>   Scale the item while watching the indication at the left end of the 3D View window's header which shows how much you've scaled the item:

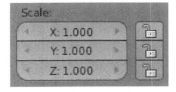

>   Go to **136**.
>   **SUB-METHOD 3**
>   If you brought up the set of "Properties" panels in step **77**, and *are in Object mode*: Go to the "Transform" panel > Look at the "Scale" fields

>   Scale:
>   X: 1.000
>   Y: 1.000
>   Z: 1.000

>   Watch these fields to determine how far you've scaled the item. It always shows the amount of scaling on the *Local* coordinate system axes. Go to **136**.
>   **END OF SUB-METHODS**

136. Do you want to scale the item freely?

>Yes: Go to **137**.

>No: Go to **138**.

137. Scale the item to the proportions you want. LClick. Stop. You are finished.

138. Do you want to scale the item in large increments?

>Yes: Go to **139**.

>No: Go to **140**.

139. Press & hold CTRL. Scale the item to the proportions you want. LClick. Release CTRL. Stop. You are finished.

140. Do you want to scale the item in small increments?

>Yes: Go to **141**.

>No: Go to **142**.

141. Press & hold CTRL + press & hold SHIFT. Scale the item to where you want it. LClick. Release CTRL & SHIFT. Stop. You are finished

142. To scale the item very slowly, to make fine adjustments :   Press & hold SHIFT. Scale the item to where you want it. LClick. Release SHIFT. Stop. You are finished.

143. Do you want to scale the item in the X (or Y, or Z) direction of the *Global* coordinate system?

>Yes: Go to **144**.

>No: Go to **146**.

144. Press (& release) S. Then press (& release) X (or Y, or Z).

145. Go to **133**.

146. Do you want to scale the item in the X (or Y, or Z) direction of the *Local* coordinate system?

>Yes: Go to **147**.

>No: Go to **149**.

147. Press (& release) S. Then press (& release) X, then press (& release) X (or press Y then Y, or press Z then Z).

148. Go to **133**.

149. Do you want to scale the item in the *Global* coordinate system's XY (or XZ, or YZ) plane (scaling simultaneously in both axes of the plane)?

>Yes: Go to **150**.

>No: Go to **152**.

150. Press (& release) S. Then press (& release) SHIFT+Z (or Y, or X).

151. Go to **133**.

152. To scale the item in the *Local* coordinate system's XY (or XZ, or YZ) plane (scaling simultaneously in both axes of the plane) :

153. Press (& release) S. Then press (& release) SHIFT+Z (or Y, or X). Then press (& release) SHIFT + Z (or Y, or X) again.

154. Go to **133**.

METHOD 3 – TO MOVE ALONG, ROTATE AROUND OR SCALE ALONG A SINGLE *GLOBAL* AXIS.

155. If you wish, you can bring up a set of "Properties" panels, which may be of some help as you use this method:

(i) With the mouse pointer in the 3D View window, press N

OR:

(ii) Go to the 3D View window's header (this header is marked by at left) > LClick "View" > LClick "Properties").

This will produce a set of "Properties" panels. (To get rid of the Properties panels later, repeat (i) or (ii) above.)

156. Do you want to move, rotate, or scale an *entire* object?

      Yes: Go to **157**.

      No: To move *part* of an object, go to **160**.

157. Do you want to *scale* the object? OR If you want to *move* the object, do you want to move the center too? OR, if you want to *rotate* the object, do you want to rotate its local coordinate system too?

      Yes: (Make sure you're in Object Mode.) Go to **165**.

      No: Go to **158**.

158. Go to Edit Mode (see **T7, p. 8**).

      OR

press TAB.

159. Select the whole object (see **T22, p. 19**). Go to **165**.

160. Make sure you've selected, in Object Mode, the object whose part(s) you want to move, then go into Edit Mode (see **T7, p. 8**) and select the part(s) of the object that you want to move, rotate or scale.

161. Do you want a gradual "falloff" (that is, a gradual transition in size and shape) from the moved, rotated or scaled part(s) to the unchanged part(s)?

      Yes: Go to **162**.

      No: Go to **165**.

162. LClick the "Proportional Edit Tool" (PET) button:

 > LClick "Enable"

      OR

      Press the letter O key.

163. LClick the PET's curve button:

164. LClick on the kind of falloff you want.

      OR

Press & hold SHIFT + press the letter O key repeatedly to cycle through the kinds of falloff until the icon of the one you want appears on the button.

165. Do you want to <u>MOVE</u> a selected item or items?

Yes: Go to **166**.

No: Go to **179**.

166. Press G.

167. If you the clicked the "Proportional Edit Tool" (PET) button at step **162** above:

SCROLL to adjust the range of the PET's effect

OR

ALT+numberpad-plus or numberpad-minus to adjust the range of the PET's effect.

168. MClick & hold. Drag in the X (or Y, or Z) direction until the movement of the item locks onto that axis direction.

169. Release the middle mouse button.

170. Do you want to move the item a certain number of units?

Yes: Go to **171**.

No: Go to **172**.

171.

SUB-METHOD 1

Type the number of units you want the item to move > LClick. Stop. You are finished.

SUB-METHOD 2

Move the item while watching the indication at the left end of the 3D View window's header which shows how far you've moved the item *in the Global coordinate system*:

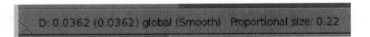

Go to **172**.

SUB-METHOD 3

If you brought up the set of "Properties" panels in step **155**: Go to the "Transform" panel.

If you are in *Object* mode, look at the *"Location"* fields:

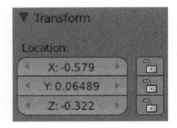

These fields show the coordinates of **the object's origin** in the **Global** coordinate system. Watch these fields to determine how far you've moved the object.

If you are in *Edit* mode, look at the *"Median"* fields (or *"Vertex"* fields if only a vertex is selected):

If you enable the "Global" button below these fields, the fields show the coordinates of **the selection's median** (geometrical "center") in the **Global** coordinate system. If you enable the "Local" button below these fields, the fields show the coordinates of the selection's median in the object's **Local** coordinate system. Watch these fields to determine how far you've moved the item. Stop when you've moved it the desired amount.

Go to **172**.

END OF SUB-METHODS

172. Do you want to move the item freely?

      Yes: Go to **173**.

      No: Go to **174**.

173. Move the item to where you want it. LClick. Stop. You are finished.

174. Do you want to move the item in large increments?

      Yes: Go to **175**.

      No: Go to **176**.

175. Press & hold CTRL. Move the item to where you want it. LClick. Release CTRL. Stop. You are finished.

176. Do you want to move the item in small increments?

      Yes: Go to **177**.

      No: Go to **178**.

177. Press & hold CTRL + press & hold SHIFT. Move the item to where you want it. LClick. Release CTRL & SHIFT. Stop. You are finished

178. To move the item very slowly, to make fine adjustments : Press & hold SHIFT. Move the item to where you want it. LClick. Release SHIFT. Stop. You are finished.

179. **Do you want to __ROTATE__ a selected item or items (around the Global X axis [or Y axis, or Z axis])?**

      Yes: Go to **180**.

      No: Go to **193**.

180. Press R.

181. If you the clicked the "Proportional Edit Tool" (PET) button at step **162** above:

      SCROLL to adjust the range of the PET's effect

      OR

      ALT+numberpad-plus or numberpad-minus to adjust the range of the PET's effect.

182. MClick & hold. Drag in the X (or Y, or Z) direction until the rotation of the item locks onto that axis direction.

183. Release the middle mouse button.

184. Do you want to rotate the item a certain number of units?

> Yes: Go to **185**.
>
> No: Go to **186**.

185.

> **SUB-METHOD 1**
>
> Type the number of degrees you want the item to rotate. LClick. Stop. You are finished.
>
> **SUB-METHOD 2**
>
> Rotate the item while watching the indication at the left end of the 3D View window's header which shows how far you've rotated the item:

> Go to **186**.
>
> **SUB-METHOD 3**
>
> If you brought up the set of "Properties" panels in step **155**, *and are in Object mode*: Go to the "Transform" panel > Look at the "Rotation" fields

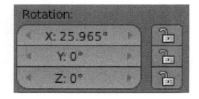

> Watch these fields to determine how far you've rotated the item. It always shows the rotation on the *Global* coordinate system axes.
>
> Go to **186**.
>
> **END OF SUB-METHODS**

186. Do you want to rotate the item freely?

> Yes: Go to **187**.
>
> No: Go to **188**.

187. Rotate the item to where you want it. LClick. Stop. You are finished.

188. Do you want to rotate the item in large increments?

> Yes: Go to **189**.
>
> No: Go to **190**.

189. Press & hold CTRL. Rotate the item to where you want it. LClick. Release CTRL. Stop. You are finished.

190. Do you want to rotate the item in small increments?

> Yes: Go to **191**.

No: Go to **192**.

191. Press & hold CTRL + press & hold SHIFT. Rotate the item to where you want it. LClick. Release CTRL & SHIFT. Stop. You are finished

192. To rotate the item very slowly, to make fine adjustments : Press & hold SHIFT. Rotate the item to where you want it. LClick. Release SHIFT. Stop. You are finished.

193. To SCALE a selected item (or items) along the Global X axis (or Y axis, or Z axis):

194. Press S.

195. If you the clicked the "Proportional Edit Tool" (PET) button at step **162** above:

  SCROLL to adjust the range of the PET's effect

  OR

  ALT+numberpad-plus or numberpad-minus to adjust the range of the PET's effect.

196. MClick & hold. Drag in the X (or Y, or Z) direction until the scaling of the item locks onto that axis direction.

197. Release the middle mouse button.

198. Do you want to scale the item a certain number of units?

  Yes: Go to **199**.

  No: Go to **200**.

199.

  SUB-METHOD 1

  Type the number of units you want the item to scale. LClick. Stop. You are finished.

  SUB-METHOD 2

  Scale the item while watching the indication at the left end of the 3D View window's header which shows how much you've scaled the item:

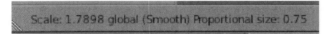

  Go to **200**.

  SUB-METHOD 3

  If you brought up the set of "Properties" panels in step **155**, and *are in Object mode*: Go to the "Transform" panel > Look at the "Scale" fields

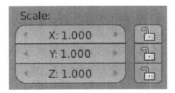

  Watch these fields to determine how far you've scaled the item. It always shows the amount of scaling on the *Local* coordinate system axes (even though you're scaling in the direction of the Global axes). Go to **200**.

  END OF SUB-METHODS

200. Do you want to scale the item freely?

> Yes: Go to **201**.
>
> No: Go to **202**.

201. Scale the item to the size/proportions you want it to have. LClick. Stop. You are finished.

202. Do you want to scale the item in large increments?

> Yes: Go to **203**.
>
> No: Go to **204**.

203. Press & hold CTRL. Scale the item to the size/proportions you want it to have. LClick. Release CTRL. Stop. You are finished.

204. Do you want to scale the item in small increments?

> Yes: Go to **205**.
>
> No: Go to **206**.

205. Press & hold CTRL + press & hold SHIFT. Scale the item to the size/proportions you want it to have. LClick. Release CTRL & SHIFT. Stop. You are finished.

206. To scale the item very slowly, to make fine adjustments : Press & hold SHIFT. Scale the item to the size/proportions you want it to have. LClick. Release SHIFT. Stop. You are finished.

METHOD 4 – USE THE "PROPERTIES" PANELS TO SET LOCATION (IN GLOBAL COORDINATE SYSTEM UNITS), ORIENTATION (IN LOCAL COORDINATE SYSTEM UNITS), OR ROTATION (IN LOCAL COORDINATE SYSTEM UNITS)

207. Bring up the set of "Properties" panels:

> (i) With the mouse pointer in the 3D View window, press N
>
> OR:
>
> (ii) Go to the 3D View window's header (this header is marked by at left) > LClick "View" > LClick "Properties").

This will produce a set of "Properties" panels. (To get rid of the Properties panels later), repeat (i) or (ii) above.

208. To ROTATE the item, go to 210. To SCALE it, go to 211. To MOVE it to a different location, as specified by measurements on the axes of the _Local_ coordinate system, go to 209. To MOVE the item to a different location, as specified by measurements on the axes of the _Global_ coordinate system:

> **SUB-METHOD 1:** In Object mode, go to the Properties panels > Go to the "Transform" panel > Go to the "Location" buttons > Set the "X", the "Y", or the "Z" button to the location to which you want to move the object. LClick in the 3D View window. Stop. You are finished.
>
> **SUB-METHOD 2:** In Edit mode, go to the Properties panels > Go to the "Transform" panel > make sure that "Global" is activated > Go to the "Median" buttons (or the "Vertex" buttons if only a single vertex is selected): Set the "X", the "Y", or the "Z" button to the position to which you want to move the object. Stop. You are finished.
>
> **END OF SUB-METHODS**

209. To MOVE the item by specifying _Local_ measurements: In Edit mode, go to the Properties panels > Go to the "Transform" panel > make sure that "Local" is activated > Go to the "Median" buttons ("Vertex" buttons if only a single vertex is selected): Set the "X", the "Y", or the "Z" button to the position to which you want to move the object. Stop. You are finished.

210. **To <u>ROTATE</u> the item:** In Object mode, go to the Properties panels > Go to the "Transform" panel > Go to the "Rotation" buttons > Set the "X", the "Y", or the "Z" button to the position to which you want to move the object. Stop. You are finished.

211. **To <u>SCALE</u> the item along an axis of the Local coordinate system:** In Object mode, go to the Properties panels > Go to the "Transform" panel > Go to the "Scale" buttons > Set the "X", the "Y", or the "Z" button to adjust the amount of scaling.

<u>METHOD 5</u> – TO MOVE (ENTIRE) OBJECT Obj1 SO THAT VERTEX (POINT) V1 ON THAT OBJECT SNAPS TO VERTEX V2 ON OBJECT Obj2:

212. Make sure the "Mode" button is set to "Object Mode".

213. RClick on object Obj1 to select it.

214. Press TAB (or LClick "Mode" button) to go into Edit mode.

215. RClick vertex v1 (the vertex you want to snap onto the vertex on object Obj2) to select it.

216. Press SHIFT+S (to display the "snap menu").

217. LClick "Cursor to Selected". (This places the 3D cursor onto the selection.)

218. Press TAB (to go to Object mode).

219. In the 3D View window's header, LClick "Object" > hover over "Transform" > LClick "Origin to 3D Cursor". (This deems v1 to be Object Obj1's "object center".)

220. RClick object Obj2 to select it.

221. TAB (to go to Edit mode).

222. RClick vertex v2 (the vertex on Obj2 that you want to snap v1 onto) to select it.

223. SHIFT+S.

224. LClick "Cursor to Selected". (This puts the 3D cursor onto vertex v2.)

225. Press TAB (to go to Object mode).

226. LClick object Obj1 to select it.

227. SHIFT+S.

228. LClick "Selection to Cursor". (This snaps Obj1's object center [v1] onto v2.)

<u>METHOD 6</u> – TO *SLIDE* A SET OF CONNECTED EDGES, WHERE NO TWO EDGES BORDER THE SAME FACE, ALONG THE OTHER EDGES OF THE ADJACENT FACES:

229. In Edit mode, select the edges.

230. Press CTRL + E.

231. LClick "Edge Slide".

232. Move the mouse pointer to position the edges.

233. LClick.

<u>METHOD 7</u> – TO MOVE AN OBJECT'S GEOMETRY SO THAT THE GEOMETRICAL CENTER ("MEDIAN") ALIGNS ITSELF ON THE OBJECT'S ORIGIN (THE ORIGIN OF THE OBJECT'S LOCAL COORDINATE SYSTEM—SEE <u>T24, p. 32</u>):

234. In Object mode (see <u>T8, p. 9</u>), select the object > Go to the 3D View window header (marked by at left): LClick on "Object" > Hover over "Transform" > LClick "Geometry to Origin".

METHOD 8 – TO MOVE AN OBJECT SO THAT THE OBJECT'S ORIGIN (THE ORIGIN OF THE OBJECT'S LOCAL COORDINATE SYSTEM—SEE T24, p. 32) ALIGNS ITSELF ON THE NEAREST POINT ON THE 3D GLOBAL GRID:
235. In Object mode (see **T8, p. 9**), select the object > Press SHIFT + S > LClick "Selection to Grid".

METHOD 9 – TO MOVE AN OBJECT SO THAT THE OBJECT'S ORIGIN (THE ORIGIN OF THE OBJECT'S LOCAL COORDINATE SYSTEM—SEE T24, p. 32) ALIGNS ITSELF ON THE 3D CURSOR:
236. In Object mode (see **T8, p. 9**), select the object > Press SHIFT + S > LClick "Selection to Cursor".

METHOD 10 – TO MOVE A SELECTION ON OBJECT 1 (OR THE SELECTION CAN BE THE ENTIRE OBJECT) SO THAT IT SNAPS ONTO AN ELEMENT (VERTEX, EDGE OR FACE) OF OBJECT 2:
237. In Object mode (see **T8, p. 9**), select the object that you want to move (in whole or in part).
238. Go to Edit mode. Select the geometry that you want to move.

239. Go to the 3D View window header (marked by  at left) > Enable the "Snap during

transform" button (the button whose icon is a magnet): [ ] .
240. To choose which kind of element (vertex, edge, face) *on object 2* that you want to snap *to* (call this element the "target element"), LClick the "Type of element to snap to" button:

(I've blurred the button's icon because the icon can vary—this button is best identified by position.) >
LClick the kind of element that you want to snap to.
241. To specify which part of the selected geometry (on object 1) to snap onto the target, LClick this button which is next to the button you clicked at step **240** :

(I've blurred the button's icon because the icon can vary—this button is best identified by its long shape and its position.) > If you want to snap the last-to-be-selected element onto the target, LClick "Active". If you want to snap the selection's median onto the target, LClick "Median". If you want to snap the selection's center(?) onto the target, LClick "Center". If you want to snap the part of the selection that is closest to your target onto the target, LClick "Closest".
242. Press G > Put your mouse pointer onto the target > LClick.
OR
Enable the "Translate manipulator mode" button (the arrow) in the 3D window header:

LClick & hold onto the white circle at the center of the 3D Manipulator:

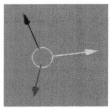

Drag to the target > Release mouse button.

METHOD 11 – TO MOVE, TO SNAP, A MESH SURFACE (ONE THAT IS COMPLEX ENOUGH TO BE SHAPED) FLUSH AGAINST A SURFACE (BELONGING TO THE SAME OR DIFFERENT OBJECT) SUCH THAT THE MOVED SURFACE TAKES ON THE SHAPE OF THE SURFACE THAT IT IS MOVING AGAINST:

243. In Object mode (see **T8, p. 9**), select the object whose geometry (in whole or in part) that you want to snap to the surface. (You might be snapping one selected part of a single object onto another, unselected, part of the same object; or, you might be snapping a selected part of an object onto another object.)

244. Go to Edit mode (see **T7, p. 8**).

245. Select the object, or part of it, that you want to snap to the "target" surface > Go to the 3D View window header (marked by ⬛ at left) > Enable the "Snap during transform" button (the button whose icon is a magnet): ⬛ > LClick the "Type of element to snap to" button:

(I've blurred the button's icon because the icon can vary—this button is best identified by position.)

246. LClick "Face".

247. Still on the 3D View window's header, enable the "Project Individual Elements" button:

248. Will you be snapping a selected part of an object onto another (unselected) part of the same object?

> Yes: Go to **249**.
> No: Go to **250**.

249. Still on the 3D View window's header, enable the "Snap onto itself" button: ⬛ (This button looks just like the "Limit selection to visible" button.) > Make sure that the PET button (see **162**) is *not* enabled > Go to **251**.

250. Still on the 3D View window's header, make sure that the "Snap onto itself" button, , is disabled (That is, make sure it's bright. This button looks just like the "Limit selection to visible" button.) If you wish, you can show your selected geometry in wireframe view while keeping the target in solid view. To do this: Make sure that the Viewport Shading button (see *Introduction*) is set to solid view for

the selection you want to move > Go to the "Properties" window >   > LClick the "Object"

button: > Go to the "Display" panel > LClick the dark "Type" button > LClick "Wire".

251. Position the target surface behind the selected geometry (no geometry other than the target surface should be behind the selected geometry) > press G (this should apply the selected geometry to the surface) > Move the selection to position it where you want it > LClick to set its position > Deselect the "Snap during transform" button (see step **245**) > Use a transform method (see **T24, p. 32**) to move the now "shaped" geometry off of the target.

252. If you enabled the "Wire" button at step **250**, make sure you disable it when you no longer wish to have the snapped geometry in wire frame. Enable "Textured" instead (see **T14, p. 12**).

END OF METHODS

T26. To move/rotate/scale a *face* such that new faces are created to accommodate the change; or to duplicate a *vertex* or an *edge* and Move/Rotate/Scale the duplicate such that new edges and faces are created to accommodate the change: EXTRUDING:

TO MOVE A SELECTED FACE OR GROUP OF FACES FROM ONE PLACE TO ANOTHER, TO ROTATE A SELECTED FACE OR GROUP OF FACES, OR TO SCALE, STRETCH OR COMPRESS A SELECTED FACE OR GROUP OF FACES, AND TO DO SO IN A WAY SUCH THAT NEW EDGES AND FACES ARE FORMED (I.E., SUCH THAT THE ORIGINAL EDGES OF THE FACE ARE KEPT AS THEY WERE AND NEW EDGES AND FACES ARE FORMED TO CONNECT THE MOVED, ROTATED OR SCALED FACE(S) TO THE ORIGINAL EDGES); OR TO CREATE DUPLICATES OF A VERTEX OR GROUP OF VERTICES, OR OF AN EDGE OR GROUP OF EDGES, AND MOVE, ROTATE OR SCALE THE DUPLICATES WHILE CREATING NEW EDGES AND FACES TO CONNECT THE DUPLICATES WITH THE ORIGINALS; IN OTHER WORDS, TO "EXTRUDE" AN ITEM OR GROUP OF ITEMS:

Note that you can extrude vertices, edges, and faces. You can build a mesh by extruding edges. When extruding, do not cancel by simply pressing ESC—that will "double" the selection. Instead, LClick to finish it. Then CTRL+Z to undo it. To undo any doubling: *Press A until everything is selected*, then press W, then LClick "Remove Doubles".

METHOD 1

1. Refer to **T24, p. 32** to familiarize yourself with the Blender coordinate systems.

2. In Object Mode (**T8, p. 9**), make sure you've selected the object (whose part(s) you want to extrude by moving, rotating or scaling) then go into Edit mode (**T7, p. 8**).

3. Select the item(s) you want to extrude.

4. If a face or faces are included in the parts that are selected, the extrusion will occur on the same axes or in the same plane that it would if only the face(s) were selected.

5. To set the pivot point for rotating and scaling while extruding: Go to the 3D View window header and LClick the Pivot button (see ***Introduction***).

a. If you are going to rotate or scale around the item that was the last to be selected, LClick "Active Element".

b. If you will extrude one or more sets of faces, and you are going to rotate or scale each separate set around its center (there will be distortion of the faces) LClick "Individual Origins".

c. If you are going to rotate around the center of an edge or face, or around the median of any selected set of items, LClick "Median Point".

d. If you are going to rotate around the 3D cursor (see **T58, p. 98** for how to place this cursor), LClick "3D Cursor".

6.

a. If you want to extrude along the **GLOBAL X** axis, and

> (i) you are **extruding one or more vertices, one or more edges, or one or more faces**:
> Press E > X > Go to **7**.
>
> OR
>
> (ii) you are **extruding one or more vertices, or one or more edges**:
> Press E > MClick & hold > Move to lock onto the X axis > release the mouse button > Go to step **7**.

b. If you want to extrude along the **GLOBAL Y** axis, and

> (i) you are **extruding one or more vertices, one or more edges, or one or more faces**:
> Press E > Y > Go to **7**.
>
> OR
>
> (ii) you are **extruding one or more vertices, or one or more edges**:
> Press E > MClick & hold > Move to lock onto the Y axis > release the mouse button > Go to **7**.

c. If you want to extrude along the **GLOBAL Z** axis, and

> (i) you are **extruding one or more vertices, or one or more edges**: Press E > Z > Go to **7**;
> OR: Press E > MClick & hold > Move to lock onto the Z axis > release the mouse button > Go to step **7**.
>
> OR
>
> (ii) you are **extruding one or more faces**: Press E > Z > Z > Go to **7**.

d. If you want to extrude along the **LOCAL X** axis, and you are **extruding one or more vertices, or more than one edge**: Press E > X > X > Go to **7**.

e. If you want to extrude along the **LOCAL Y** axis, and you are **extruding one or more vertices, or more than one edge**: Press E > Y > Y > Go to **7**.

f. If you want to extrude along the **LOCAL Z** axis, and you are **extruding one or more vertices, or more than one edge**: Press E > Z > Z > Go to **7**.

g. If you want to extrude along the **NORMAL X** axis, and

> (i) you are **extruding a single edge**: Press E > X > X > Go to **7**.

OR

(ii) you are **extruding one or more faces**: Press E > X > X > Go to **7**; OR: Press E > MClick & hold > Move to lock onto the Normal X axis > Release the mouse button > Go to **7**.

h. If you want to extrude along the **NORMAL Y** axis, and

(i) you are **extruding a single edge**: Press E > Y > Y > Go to **7**.

OR

(ii) you are **extruding one or more faces**: Press E > Y > Y > Go to **7**; OR: Press E > MClick & hold > Move to lock onto the Normal Y axis > Release the mouse button > Go to **7**.

i. If you want to extrude along the **NORMAL Z** axis, and

(i) you are **extruding one edge**: Press E > Z > Z > Go to **7**.

OR

(ii) you are **extruding one face**: Press E > Go to **7**; OR: Press E > MClick & hold > Move to lock onto the Normal Z axis > Release the mouse button > Go To **7**.

OR

(iii) you are **extruding more than one face, along the averaged normal Z**: Press E > Go to **7**; OR: Press ALT+E > LClick "Region" > Go to **7**; OR: Press E > MClick & hold > Move to lock onto the Normal Z axis > Release the mouse button > Go To **7**.

OR

(iv) you are **extruding more than one face, along the individual normal Zs**: Press ALT + E > "Individual faces" > Go To **7**.

j. If you want to extrude in the **VIEW XY** plane, and

(i) you are **extruding one or more vertices, or one or more edges**: Press E > Go to **7**; OR: Press E > SHIFT + Z > SHIFT + Z > SHIFT + Z > Go to **7**.

OR

(ii) you are **extruding one or more faces**: Press E > Z > Go to **7**; OR: Press E > SHIFT + Z > Go to step **7**.

OR

(iii) you are **extruding one or more vertices, one or more edges, or one or more faces**: Press E > SHIFT + X > SHIFT + X > SHIFT + X > Go to **7**; OR: Press E > SHIFT + Y > SHIFT + Y > SHIFT + Y > Go to **7**.

k. If you want to extrude in the **GLOBAL XY** plane, and

(i) you are **extruding one or more vertices, or one or more edges**: Press E > SHIFT + Z > Go to step **7**.

OR

(ii) you are **extruding one or more faces**: Press E > SHIFT + Z > SHIFT + Z > Go to step **7**.

l. If you want to extrude in the **GLOBAL XZ** plane: Press E > SHIFT + Y > Go to **7**.

m. If you want to extrude in the **GLOBAL YZ** plane: Press E > SHIFT + X > Go to **7**.

n. If you want to extrude in the **LOCAL XY** plane, and you are **extruding one or more vertices, or more than one edge**: Press E > SHIFT + Z > SHIFT + Z > Go to **7**.

o. If you want to extrude in the **LOCAL XZ** plane, and you are **extruding one or more vertices, or more than one edge**: Press E > SHIFT + Y > SHIFT + Y > Go to **7**.

p. If you want to extrude in the **LOCAL YZ** plane, and you are **extruding one or more vertices, or more**

than one edge: Press E > SHIFT + X > SHIFT + X > Go to **7**.

q. If you want to extrude in the **NORMAL XY** plane, and you are **extruding one or more faces**: Press E > SHIFT + Z > SHIFT + Z > SHIFT + Z > Go to **7**.

r. If you want to extrude in the **NORMAL XZ** plane, and you are **extruding a single edge, or one or more faces**, Press E > SHIFT + Y > SHIFT + Y > Go to **7**.

s. If you want to extrude in the **NORMAL YZ** plane, and you are **extruding a single edge, or one or more faces**, Press E > SHIFT + X > SHIFT + X > Go to **7**.

7. If you want to rotate the extrusion around the pivot point, press R.

8. If you want to scale the extrusion around the pivot point, press S.

9. Do you want to move the item a certain number of units?

        Yes: Go to **10**.

        No: Go to **11**.

10. Type the number of units you want the item to move (or rotate, or scale). (If you are moving in an XY or XZ plane [unless you are moving in the View XY plane], this will move the selection in the plane's X direction; if you are moving in a YZ plane, this will move the selection in the plane's Y direction; if you are moving in the View XY plane, this will move the selection in the Global X direction.) LClick. Stop. You are finished.

OR

Move the item while watching the indication at the left end of the 3D View window's header, which shows how far you've moved the item and tells you which coordinate system the measurements belong to. Go to **11**.

11. In the 3D View window header, make sure the "Snap During Transform" button is off (light gray), and that the button to its right is set to "Increment": . Do you want to move the item freely?

        Yes: Go to **12**.

        No: Go to **13**.

12. Move the item to where you want it. LClick. Stop. You are finished.

13. Do you want to move the item in large increments?

        Yes: Go to **14**.

        No: Go to **15**.

14. Press & hold CTRL. Move the item to where you want it. LClick. Release CTRL. Stop. You are finished.

15. Do you want to move the item in small increments?

        Yes: Go to **16**.

        No: Go to **17**.

16. Press & hold CTRL + press & hold SHIFT. Move the item to where you want it. LClick. Release CTRL & SHIFT. Stop. You are finished

17. To move the item very slowly, to make fine adjustments : Press & hold SHIFT. Move the item to where you want it. LClick. Release SHIFT. Stop. You are finished.

METHOD 2 – Quick Extrude

18. Select the vertex, edge or face that you want to extrude.

19. CTRL + LClick the point in the View XY plane to which you want to extrude.

T27. To add an object to your scene, (a) keeping it an independent object or (b) turning both it and an existing object into one multi-part object.

The new object will appear with its origin (that is, the origin of its Local coordinate system—see **T24, p. 32**) at the 3D cursor (see **T58, p. 98**)—note that the origin is not always at the object's median (geometrical "center"); for instance, the two do not coincide in the cone.

Note that, although *duplication* of an object involves adding an object to your scene, it is covered separately in **T30, p. 63**.

1. Do you want to add a new entity such that Blender will take it and an already existing object of the same *general* type (mesh, curve, surface, etc.—see ***Introduction***) to be parts of a single object?

        Yes: Go to **2**.

        No: Go to **6**.

2. In Object mode (see **T8, p. 9**), select the object that you want the new entity to be added to.

3. Go to Edit mode (see **T7, p. 8**).

4. Go to the "Info" window's header (the window header with to the left) > LClick "Add" > Hover over the name of the general object type of the object that you want to add (this general type must be the same general type as the general type of the selected object).

OR

Making sure that the cursor is in the 3D View window, press SHIFT + A.

5. LClick to choose the *special* type of the object that you want to add to your scene. (These object types are explained in the ***Introduction***.) Go to **7**.

6. To add a new object such that it is autonomous (not included with any other entity as part of one object):

METHOD 1—to add an object, in Edit mode, that is of a ***different*** general type (see ***Introduction***) than the active (last-selected) object:

        a. In Edit mode, go to the "Info" window's header (the window header with to the left) > LClick "Add" > Hover over the name of the *general* type of the object that you want to add.

        b. LClick to choose the *special* type, of the object that you want to add to your scene. Notice that you have been automatically taken into Object mode.

METHOD 2:

        a. Make sure you are in Object mode.

        b. Go to the "Info" window's header (the window header with to the left) > LClick "Add" > Hover over the name of the *general* type of the object that you want to add.

        OR

        Making sure that the cursor is in the 3D View window, press SHIFT + A. Hover over the *general* type of the object you want to add.

        c. LClick to choose the *special* type of the object that you want to add to your scene.

END OF METHODS

7. Go to the Tool Shelf (see **T9, p. 9**) > A new section will have appeared at the bottom. In this section, you can adjust the properties of the object you have just added to the scene.

(If new objects have been added but cannot be seen: try SHIFT+C, to center the cursor, then try adding objects.)

T28. To separate one mesh object into two:

1. In Object mode (**T8, p. 9**), select the object you want to separate.

2. TAB into Edit mode (**T7, p. 8**).

3. Select the part of the object that you want Blender to consider an independent object.

4. Press P > LClick "Selection."

OR

Go to the 3D View window header (marked by at left): LClick "Mesh"; Hover over "Vertices"; LClick "Separate". LClick "Selection"

5. To move the new object's origin (the origin of its Local coordinate system—see **T24, p. 32**) to its geometrical center: See **T57, p. 98**.

T29. To join two or more objects of the same general type into one (i.e. to have Blender view them as parts of one object):

1. In Object Mode, select one of the objects > Press SHIFT and select the other object(s) (the last one selected is the "active object," the object that the other selected objects will join onto).

2. Press CTRL + J.

T30. To create a *new* object or *new* geometry which is a duplicate of an existing object or geometry (includes making a mirror copy; includes making a series of copies in an "array"):

1. Make sure you are in Object mode.

2. If you will be rotating or scaling the duplicate when the duplication occurs, set your pivot point (see **T25, p. 33, steps 3-8**)

3. If you wish, you can bring up a set of "Properties" panels, which may be of some help when you duplicate an item and move it:

> (i) With the mouse pointer in the 3D View window, press N
>
> OR:
>
> (ii) Go to the 3D View window's header (this header is marked by at left) > LClick "View" > LClick "Properties").

This will produce a set of "Properties" panels. To get rid of the Properties panels, repeat (i) or (ii) above.

4. Do you want to make a mirror duplicate of an object?

> Yes: go to **22**.
>
> No: go to **5**.

5. Do you want to make a series of copies of an object, in an "array"?

Yes: go to **33**.

No: go to **6**.

6. Do you want to duplicate an entire object?

Yes: Go to **7**.

No: Go to **17**.

7. Do you want the original and the copy to be two different objects?

Yes: Go to **8**.

No: To create a copy such that the original and the copy will be two parts of one object, go to step **17**.

8.

(i) If you want **to create a duplicate of an object such that any change in the *material* of one will change the *material* of the other, but such that any change of the *geometry* of one will *not* change the *geometry* of the other** [Speaking in terms of "datablocks" (see ***Introduction***): if you want to duplicate an object such that there is a single material datablock for both, but two geometry datablocks, one for each, the two geometry datablocks having (at least immediately after the operation) identical content]**:** Go to step **9**.

(ii) If you want **to duplicate an object such that any change in the *material* of one will change the *material* of the other, and such that any change of the *geometry* of one will change the *geometry* of the other** [Speaking in terms of "datablocks" (see ***Introduction***): if you want to duplicate an object such that there is a single material datablock for both, and a single geometry datablock for both]**:** Go to step **13**.

9. Select the object that you want to duplicate.

10. Press SHIFT+D.

OR

Go to the 3D View window header (marked by ![icon] at left) > LClick "Object" > LClick "Duplicate Objects".

11. You will now be moving the duplicate as if you were using **METHOD 2** in **T25** above (see **T25, step 90, p. 43**). Use **T25, Methods 2** and **3** as a guide for moving, rotating or scaling the duplicate.

12. When you have the duplicate positioned as you want it, LClick. Stop. You are finished.

13. Select the object that you want to duplicate.

14.

(a) Press ALT+D.

OR

(b) Go to the 3D View window header (marked by ![icon] at left) > LClick "Object" > LClick "Duplicate Linked".

15. You will now be moving the duplicate as if you were using **METHOD 2** in **T25** above (see **T25, step 90, p. 43**).

Use **T24, Methods 2** and **3** as a guide for moving, rotating or scaling the duplicate.

16. When you have the duplicate positioned as you want it, LClick. Stop. You are finished.

17. Select the object that you want to duplicate in whole or in part > Go into Edit mode.

64

18. Select the object or parts of an object that you want to duplicate.

19. (a) Press SHIFT + D; OR

(b) in the 3D View window header:

If the item you have selected is a mesh, LClick "Mesh" > LClick "Add Duplicate".

If the item you have selected is a curve, LClick "Curve" > LClick "Duplicate Curve".

If the item you have selected is a surface, LClick "Surface" > LClick "Duplicate Curve".

If the item you have selected is a metaball, LClick "Metaball" > LClick "Duplicate Metaelements".

(This produces a copy which becomes part of the original object. So, the materials of the duplicated part [or whole] and the copy will be linked [as *any* two parts of the same material are], and the geometries of the original and the copy are not linked [as *any* two parts of the same object are not].)

20. You will now be moving the duplicate as if you were using **METHOD 2** in **T25** above (see **T25, step 91, p. 43**). Use **T25, Methods 2** and **3** as a guide for moving, rotating or scaling the duplicate.

21. When you have the duplicate positioned as you want it, LClick. Stop. You are finished.

22. To make a mirror copy: In Object mode, select the object that you want to mirror-copy.

23. Go to the "Properties" window: > LClick the "Modifiers" button: > Go to the "Modifiers" panel > LClick "Add Modifier" > LClick "Mirror".

24. By default, the center, "mirroring," point between the original geometry and its mirror duplicate is defined by the object's origin (see **T24, p. 32**). To define the mirroring point as the center of another object (such as an Empty): in the Mirror panel (a panel with this icon toward the top left—the lettering will spell part or all of the word "Mirror") that appears, LClick the box labeled "Mirror Object" > LClick the name of the object you want to use to define the mirroring point. (To see what an object's name is, in Object mode select the object. Its name appears at lower left of the 3D View window.)

25. Still in the Mirror panel (a panel with this icon toward the top left) LClick to place a checkmark on X, Y, or Z to choose which of the object's *Local* axes you want to mirror across (you can click more than one axis to mirror across more than one axis at the same time).

26. Do you want to merge vertices across the center seam (by moving the vertices) between the original and the mirror copy?

Yes: Go to **27**.

No: Go to **30**.

27. Also in the Mirror panel, adjust the numbers in the box labeled "Merge Limit:" to set how close together vertices from the original and the mirror copy have to be in order to merge (see the **Introduction** to see the different ways to adjust buttons like this).

28. In Edit mode (**T8, p. 9**), move the original toward and away from the mirror copy in order to merge the vertices you want to merge. If you did not change the default setting (see **25**), mirroring will be done across the object origin (see **T24, p. 32**), and moving the original in Edit mode moves it toward and away from this origin.

29. To lock the merged vertices to the mirror axis, LClick "Clipping".

30. LClick one or more of the three buttons in the center, just under the "Add Modifier" button in order to set the conditions for when the mirroring will be visible. Enable the first button to show the mirror copy in the render. Enable the second button to show the mirror copy in the 3D View window – but note that the third button must also be enabled in order to show the mirror copy in the 3D View window *in Edit mode* (see **T7, p. 8**).

31. If your original object has one or more Vertex Groups (see **T38, p. 73**) applied to it: normally, the vertices in the mirror copy of a Vertex Group will simply be added to the original group when you *apply* the mirror modifier (see **32**). (If you want the original and copy Vertex Groups to be *separate* groups: the original group must have a name ending in ".L" or ".R"—you might have to change the name. For example, suppose that the group is named "Side.L". Create [but don't try to *assign*] a second Vertex Group named "Side.R"; then Go back to the "Mirror" panel and make sure "Vertex Group" is checked.)

32. In general, as long as you do not LClick "Apply", any change to the original object will be mirrored in the copy, and the mirroring can be undone at any time by LClicking the "X" at upper right in the Mirror panel. To make the mirror copy permanent (which will increase the burden on your computer), such that changes can be made to the original and to the copy independently, in Object mode: LClick "Apply". Stop. You are finished.

33. To create a series of copies (in an "array") of an *object*: Make sure that the object you want to duplicate is selected.

34. Go to the "Properties" window: > LClick the "Modifiers" button: > Go to the "Modifiers" panel > LClick "Add Modifier" > LClick "Array".

35. Do you want to fit your array of duplicates to the length of an existing curve – that is, do you want the length of the array (if it is straight or if it were to be straightened out) to be equal to the length of the curve (if the curve were to be straightened out)?

> Yes: Go to **36**.
> No: Go to **38**.

36. In the "Array" sub-panel (identified by this icon toward top left—the lettering spells part or all of the word "Array") that appears, LClick the button to the right of "Fit Type" > LClick "Fit Curve".

37. LClick the field to the right of "Curve" > LClick the name of the curve object that you want to fit the array to. (If you don't know the name of this curve object: In Object mode, select the curve. Its name appears in the 3D View window, lower left.) > Go to **43**.

38. Do you want to fit your array of duplicates into a fixed length--that is, if the array were to be straightened out [if it's not already a straight-line array]?

> Yes: Go to **39**.
> No: Go to **41**.

39. in the Array sub-panel (identified by this icon toward the top left—the lettering spells part or all of the word "Array") that appears, LClick the button to the right of "Fit Type" > LClick "Fit Length".

40. To fix the length, adjust the "Length" button (see ***Introduction*** for instructions on how to adjust buttons like this). Go to **43**.

41. **To create an array of duplicates having a fixed number of duplicates**: in the Array sub-panel (a sub-panel with this icon ![ray icon] toward the top left) that appears, LClick the button to the right of "Fit Type" > LClick "Fixed Count".

42. To fix the count, adjust the "Count" button (see ***Introduction*** for instructions on how to adjust buttons like this).

43. **Do you want the members of your array (series of copies) to be aligned in a straight line (orthogonal or oblique)?**

> Yes: Go to **44**.
>
> No: Go to **47** .

44. **Do you want to place the first copy 1.7 (for example)** *blender units* **away from the original in the original's** *local* **X direction, 1.3** *blender units* **away from the original in the original's local Y direction, and 0** *blender units* **away from the original in the original's local Z direction?** That is, do you want to "offset" the first copy from the original by, for example, X=1.7, Y=1.3, Z=0 -- in blender units -- using the original's local coordinate system?

> **AND**
>
> **do you want the offset from first copy to second copy to be defined the same way**; that is, do you want to "offset" the second copy from the first by X=1.7, Y=1.3, Z=0 -- in blender units -- using the first copy's local coordinate system?
>
> **AND**
>
> **do you want all the remaining offsets to be defined the same way?**
>
> Yes: Go to **45**.
>
> No: Go to **46**.

45. Check the box next to **"Constant Offset"**. Adjust the X, Y, and Z buttons under "Constant Offset" to X=1.7, Y=1.3, Z=0 (see ***Introduction*** for instructions on how to adjust buttons like this). Make sure that "Relative Offset" and "Object Offset" are un-checked. Go to **53**.

46. ***Taking the local X, Y, and Z dimensions (width, length and height) of the original object as units,*** **to place the first copy 11 (for example) units away from the original in the original's** *local* **X direction, 10 units away from the original in the original's local Y direction, and 3 units away from the original in the original's local Z direction,** that is, to "offset" the first copy from the original by X=11, Y=10, Z=3-- in "relative" units -- using the original's local coordinate system

> **AND**
>
> **to have the offset from first copy to second copy to be defined the same way**; that is, to "offset" the second copy from the first by X=11, Y=10, Z=3 -- in relative units -- using the first copy's local coordinate system
>
> **AND**
>
> **to have all the remaining offsets to be defined the same way:** Check the box next to **"Relative Offset"**. Adjust the X, Y, and Z buttons under "Relative Offset" to X=11, Y=10, Z=3 (see ***Introduction*** for instructions on how to adjust buttons like this). Make sure that "Constant Offset" and "Object Offset" are un-checked. Go to **53**.

47. **To make the position, rotation and scaling of another object, an "extraneous" object that's not in the array of copies, define how the first copy will be positioned, rotated and scaled with respect to**

the original – that is, to have the "offset" between the original object in the array and an object not in the array to precisely define the offset between the original object and the array's first copy (the extraneous object and the first copy will be in the same place, and will have the same relative rotation and scaling)-- and, further, to have each pair in the array (first and second copies, second and third copies, etc.) to bear the same relationship to one another as do the original and the first copy: Go to **48**.

48. Do you want to use an *existing* object as the extraneous, offset-defining object?

> Yes: Go to **50**.
>
> No: Go to **49**.

49. Add to your scene the object you wish to use to define the offset (see **T27, p. 62**). Adding an "Empty" (which is just a local coordinate system with no visible geometry attached to it) will work fine.

50. To find the name of the offset-defining object, make sure that the offset-defining object is selected (in Object mode), and then look at the bottom left corner of the 3D View window to find its name (e.g., Empty .001).

51. In Object mode, select the original object of the array. In the "Array" sub-panel (see **54**), check the box next to the "Object Offset" button and make sure that the boxes next to "Constant Offset" and "Relative Offset" are unchecked. LClick the field below "Object Offset" > LClick the name of the offset-defining object.

52. Making sure you are In Object mode: Move, Scale or Rotate the offset-defining object (see **T25 p. 33** above). (You might have to put the array into wireframe view [see **T14, p. 12**] to see this object—or select it in the Outliner.) Since you are in Object mode, you are transforming the object's Local coordinate system, and its position, scale and rotation relative to the array's first object will define the offset from the original to the first array copy, which in turn will be the offset from first copy to second, etc.

53. Do you want to merge adjacent vertices of the original object and the first copy, and adjacent vertices of adjacent copies in the array and/or do you want to merge adjacent vertices of the original object and the last copy in, say, a ring-shaped array where original and last copy are adjacent?

> Yes: Go to **54**.
>
> No: Go to **56**.

54. Still in the "Array" sub-panel (In the "Properties" window: > LClick the "Modifiers" button: ![wrench icon] > Go to the "Modifiers" panel > "Array" sub-panel—a sub-panel with this icon ![array ray icon] toward the top left): to merge original with first copy and to merge all adjacent copies, check the box next to "Merge". To also merge original and last copy, check the box next to "First Last".

55. Adjust the "Distance" button to set how near the adjacent vertices must be in order to be merged.

56. If you want to add a mesh object that's different from the members of the array to the beginning of the array, LClick the field to the right of "Start Cap" > LClick the name of the object that you want to add to the beginning of the array. (To find the name of the object: in Object mode, select it. Its name will appear in the 3D View window, lower left.) To remove this object: RClick the "Start Cap" field > "Reset to Default Value." Note that the object will be added to the start of the array, but any scaling or rotation you made to it will disappear unless you first "set" them by selecting the object, pressing CTRL + A, and applying "Rotation," "Scale" or "Rotation & Scale." The object will take on the material of the array; to change its material qualities, first *apply* the array (see **58**), then give the start cap a different material.

57. If you want to add a mesh object that's different from the members of the array to the end of the array, LClick the field to the right of "End Cap" > LClick the name of the object that you want to add to the end of the array. (To find the name of this object: in Object mode, select it. Its name will appear in the 3D View window, lower left.) To remove this object: RClick the "End Cap" field > "Reset to Default Value." Note that the object will be added to the end of the array, but any scaling or rotation you made to it will disappear unless you first "set" them by selecting the object, pressing CTRL + A, and applying "Rotation," "Scale" or "Rotation & Scale." The object will take on the material of the array; to change its material qualities, first *apply* the array (see **58**), then give the end cap a different material.

58. To make the array permanent, such that changes can be made to the original and to the copies independently, in Object mode: LClick "Apply".

T31. To duplicate the geometry and/or material (not the rotation or scaling) of object A not by creating a new object or new object-like part of the object, but by turning object B into a copy of object A, or to duplicate material A by turning a different material, say, material B, into material A.

METHOD 1:

1. To change the *geometry* (along with a material—with attached textures—if the material datablock is attached to the geometry datablock) of an object into a linked duplicate of another: Select the object

that you want to change > Go to the "Properties" window >  > LClick the "Object Data" button—see **T11, p. 9** for how to find this button > LClick this button near the top of the window:

LClick the name of the geometry datablock (see ***Introduction***) that you want to replace the object's geometry datablock with.

2. To change a *material* of an object (& its textures) into a linked duplicate of another, existing, material:

Select the object > Go to the "Properties" window:  > LClick the "Material" button: > LClick this button near the top of the window:

LClick the name of the material datablock that you want to replace the object's material datablock with.

3. To change a texture of an object into a duplicate of another, existing, texture: Select the object > Go

to the "Properties" window >  > LClick the "Material" button:  > LClick this button near the top of the window:

LClick the name of the texture datablock that you want to replace the object's texture datablock with. **METHOD 2—To turn one or more objects (say, Objects B, C and D) into linked duplicates of another object (say, object A), so that changes to the geometry or material of any of them will produce changes to all. (For instance, if Object A is a blue sphere and Object C is a red square, this operation will turn Object C into a blue sphere, etc.):**
4. In Object mode: In the 3D View window, select objects B, C, D and A (make sure you select A last)— that is: RClick B > SHIFT + RClick C > SHIFT + RClick D > SHIFT + RClick A. Note that all the objects must be of the same *general* type (see **_Introduction_**) for this to work: all meshes, all curves, etc.
5. With the mouse pointer in the 3D View window: Press CTRL+L
6. LClick "Object Data". (This works as expected so long as no material datablock is attached directly to its object datablock—see **_Introduction_**.)

T32. To turn an object that's linked to other objects (as described above) into an independent object.

METHOD 1
1. In Object mode, in the 3D View window, select the object you want to unlink from others.
2. Making sure that the mouse pointer is in the 3D window, press U.
3. Do you want to unlink the selected object's geometrical properties from those of other objects? That is, suppose you have several objects that share a single geometry datablock (see **_Introduction_**), such that when you change the geometry of one you actually change the shared datablock, and so you necessarily change the geometry of all. Do you want to unlink one particular object from the shared geometry datablock and give it its own geometry datablock, which will be, at least until you modify it in some way, a copy of the shared one?

        Yes: LClick "Object & Data" OR press D. Stop. You are finished.
        No: Go to **4**.
4. Do you want to separate an object from linked duplicates of it *in other scenes*?
        Yes: LClick "Object" OR press O. Stop. You are finished.
        No: Go to **5**.
5. Do you want to unlink the object from its shared geometrical and material datablocks and give it its very own geometry and material datablocks, which will be copies of the once-shared ones (so that you can make geometrical and material changes to this object without changing the others)?
        Yes: LClick "Object & Data & Materials+Tex" OR press M. Stop. You are finished.
        No: Go to **6**.

6. If an object has its very own geometry datablock, but shares a material datablock with other objects, you can unlink the object from the shared material datablock and give it its very own material datablock, a copy of the once-shared one by doing this: LClick "Materials+Tex" OR press T. Stop. You are finished.

METHOD 2 – To unlink an object's materials properties from the material properties of other object(s): If an object has its very own geometry datablock (see **_Introduction_**), but shares a material datablock with other objects, you can unlink the object from the shared material datablock and give it its very own material datablock, an independent copy of the once-shared datablock by doing this:

7. In Object mode, RClick on the object to select it.

8. Go to the "Properties" window: 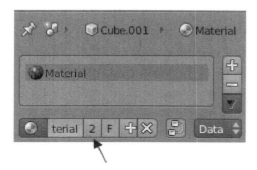 > LClick the "Material" button: > LClick the button that shows how many geometry datablocks are linked to the material datablock in question:

(The absence of a number here means that the material datablock is attached to only one object datablock [see **_Introduction_**]; or, perhaps it is connected to more than one object datablock, but it is attached *by virtue of its being attached to only one geometry datablock, which, in turn, is attached directly to the two object datablocks*.)

END OF METHODS

9. (The above assumes that the material datablock is linked directly to the geometry datablock, but it may be linked directly to the object itself instead.)

T33. To create a parent-children relationship:

In order to create a set of objects (which do not have to be of the same kind) containing one object—called the "parent"—such that when a transformation operation is applied to that parent (that is, it is moved, rotated or scaled), all the other objects of the set—called the "children"—will be transformed along with it, but when a transformation operation is applied to any of the children, neither the parent nor any of the other children will be transformed:

1. In Object mode, select the objects that you want to be part of the set (Note that an object can be the child of only one parent); select the object that you want to be the parent last.

METHOD 1

2. With your mouse pointer in the 3D window: Press CTRL+P

3. LClick "Set Parent To Object"

METHOD 2

Go to the 3D View window header (marked by [icon] to the left) > LClick "Object" > Hover over "Parent" > Hover over "Set" > LClick "Object" > LClick "Set Parent to Object".

T34. To remove a "child" object from its "parent" object (see T33):

1. In Object mode, select the child object that you want to remove from the parent-child relationship.
2. With the mouse pointer in the 3D View window, press ALT+P.
OR

Go to the 3D View window header (marked by [icon] to the left) > LClick "Object" > Hover over "Parent" > Hover over "Clear".

3. Do you want to remove the selected object from the parent-child relationship, while wiping out any transformations (location, rotation or scale) that were made to it via changes to the parent?

        Yes: LClick "Clear Parent". Stop. You are finished.

        No: Go to **4**.

4. To remove the selected object from the parent-child relationship, while preserving any position, rotation and scale transformations that were made to the child via changes to the parent, LClick "Clear and Keep Transformation." Stop. You are finished.

T35. To put object(s) into an *object group*:

(Note that an object can be a member of any number of groups.)
1. Do you want to create a new object group and put one or more objects into it?

        Yes: Go to **2**.

        No: Go to **5**.

2. In Object mode, select the objects you want to put into the new group.
3. (a) With your mouse pointer in the 3D View window, press CTRL+G.

        OR

  (b) Go to the 3D View window header (marked by [icon] to the left) > LClick "Object" > Hover over "Group" > LClick "Create New Group"

4. To name the new group, go to the Tool Shelf (see **T9, p. 9**) > go to the "Create New Group" panel > Blender will have created a name for your group (it may be, simply, "group"). To change this automatically-generated name, LClick in the "Name" field and type in the new name > Press ENTER. Stop. You are finished.

5. Do you want to add one or more objects, say, objects A, B and C, to *all* groups that another object, say, object D, is a member of?

        Yes: Go to **6**.

        No: Go to **7**.

6. In Object mode, select A, B, C and D (be sure to select D last, thus making it the "active" object) > go to the 3D View window header (marked by to the left) > LClick "Object" > Hover over "Group" > LClick "Add Selected To Active Group". Stop. You are finished.

7. To add a single object to an existing group: In Object mode, select the object you want to put into the existing group (or if other objects are also selected, select this object last).

Go to the "Properties" window > > LClick the "Object" button: > Go to the "Groups" panel > LClick "Add to Group" > LClick the name of the group that you want to add the object to. (If the name of this group does not appear in the list, select the text to the right of the magnifying glass at the top of the list and press "Delete." Also, you can use this same text field to search for the name of a group.)

T36. To see what object groups an object is in:

1. In Object mode, select the Object.

2. Go to the "Properties" window > > LClick the "Object" button: > Go to the "Groups" panel > you will see a sub-panel for each group that the object is in.

T37. To remove object(s) from an object group or from all object groups:

1. Do you want to remove an object from a single group?

> Yes: Go to **2**.
> No: Go to **3**.

2. Select the object you want to remove from the group. Go to the "Properties" window > >

LClick the "Object" button: > Go to the "Groups" panel > you will see a sub-panel for each group that the object is in. LClick the X that's next to the name of the group you want to remove the object from. Stop. You are finished.

3. To remove one or more objects from all the groups that they are members of: Select the object(s) you want to remove from the groups; then:

METHOD 1:

In Object mode, go to the 3D View window header (marked by to the left) > LClick "Object" > Hover over "Group" > LClick "Remove from Groups". LClick in the 3D window. Stop. You are finished.

METHOD 2:

In Object mode: press CTRL + ALT+ G.

T38. To create a group not of *objects*, but of *parts* of a *mesh* object; that is, to create a "vertex group".

1. In Object mode: select the mesh object to which the parts that you want to put into a group belong.
2. In Edit mode: select the parts that you want to be in the group.

3. In the Properties window header (identified by at the left): LClick the "Object Data"

button: > Go to the "Vertex Groups" panel > LClick the plus sign (+).
4. Blender will automatically give your new vertex group a name, for instance, "group"; to change this automatically-generated name, LClick the "Name" field > type in the new name > Press ENTER.
5. LClick "Assign"—This puts the selected items into the group.
6. To verify that the group has been created, LClick "Deselect" to deselect the group. If it deselects it, you know that you have successfully created the group. (LClick "Select" to select it again, if you want to.)

T39. To add one or more vertices to a vertex group:

1. In Object mode: select the mesh object to which the parts that you want to put into the group belong.
2. In Edit mode: select the vertex or vertices that you want to be in the group.

3. In the Properties window header (identified by at the left): LClick the "Object Data"

button: > Go to the "Vertex Groups" panel > In the large field, select the name of the vertex group that you want to put the selected vertex or vertices into > LClick "Assign".

T40. To remove one or more vertices from a vertex group:

1. In Object mode: select the mesh object to which the parts that you want to remove from the group belong.
2. In Edit mode: select the vertex or vertices that you want to remove from the group.

3. In the Properties window header (identified by at the left): LClick the "Object Data"

button: > Go to the "Vertex Groups" panel > In the large field, select the name of the vertex group that you want to remove the selected vertex or vertices from > LClick "Remove".

T41. To put one or more objects onto a different *layer*:

1. In Blender, there is a special kind of group, one not covered in **T35-T40**, called a "layer". (The layers discussed here and in **T42-T44** are actually called "scene" layers. *Render* layers, on the other hand, are covered in **T129, step 1, p. 253**.) Confusingly, objects that are in such a layer-group are, because of analogy with layers in 2D graphics programs, said to be "on" the layer, not "in" it—I will say that objects are "in" a layer. Every object is in one or more layers. *In Object mode*:
2. Do you want to take one or more objects *out of* one layer and put it/them into another layer?

Yes: Go to **3**.
No: Go to **6**.

3. (a) If you want to take two or more objects out of a layer and put them into a different layer, select the objects. Go to **4**.

(b) if you want to take a single object out of a layer and put it into a different layer, select the object. If other objects are also selected, make sure that the object that you want to move from one layer to another was selected *last*; that is, make sure it is the "active" object. If only the single object is selected, go to **4** or **5**. If other objects are also selected, and the object that you want to move from one layer to another is the active object, go to **5**.

4. With the mouse pointer in the 3D View window, press M > each square in the pop-up stands for a layer (a darkened square stands for a layer that the selected object is on); LClick the layer that you want to move the object(s) to. Stop. You are finished.

5. Go to the "Properties" window > > LClick the "Object" button: > Go to the "Relations" panel > each square in the twenty-square set of layers buttons stands for a layer (a darkened square stands for a layer that the selected object is in); LClick the layer that you want to move the object to. Stop. You are finished.

6. (a) If you want to put two or more objects into another layer, while keeping them in the layer(s) they are already in: In Object mode (see **T8, p. 9**), select the objects. Go to **7**.

(b) If you want to put a single object into another layer, while keeping it in the layer(s) it is already in, select the object. If other objects are also selected, make sure that the object that you want to put in the different layer was selected last; that is, make sure it is the "active" object. If only the single object is selected, go to **7** or **8**. If other objects are also selected, and the object that you want to put in the different layer is the active object, go to **8**.

7. With the mouse pointer in the 3D View window, press M > Each square in the pop-up stands for a layer (a darkened square stands for a layer that the selected object is in); SHIFT+LClick the layer you want to move the object(s) to. Stop. You are finished.

8. Go to the "Properties" window > > LClick the "Object" button: > Go to the "Relations" panel > each square in the twenty-square set of layers buttons stands for a layer (a darkened square stands for a layer that the selected object is in); SHIFT + LClick the layer you want to move the object to. Stop. You are finished.

T42. To remove an object from one or more layers:

1. See **T41** for a description of layers. Every object is in one or more layer. *So long as the object remains in at least one layer*, you can remove the object from a layer. To do this:
METHOD 1
2. In Object mode, select the object > With the mouse pointer in the 3D View window, press M > Each square in the pop-up stands for a layer (a darkened square stands for a layer that the selected object is on); SHIFT+LClick the layer that you want to remove the object from.
METHOD 2

3. In Object mode, select the object > Go to the "Properties" window >  > LClick the "Object"

button: > Go to the "Relations" panel > each square in the twenty-square set of layer buttons stands for a layer (a darkened square stands for a layer that the selected object is in); SHIFT+LClick the layer that you want to remove the object from.

END OF METHODS

T43. To make layers visible in 3D view and in the render*:

1. In Blender, there is a special kind of group, one not covered in **T35-T40**, called a "layer". Confusingly (because of analogy with layers in 2D graphics programs), objects that are in such a group are said to be *on* the layer, not *in* it—I will say that an object is "in" a layer.

2. To choose which layer(s) will be visible in the 3D View window and in the render: In Object mode, go

to the 3D View window header (marked by to the left) > Go to the set of layer buttons:

.

3. LClick the layer that you want to be visible.

4. To make a layer that's not visible visible, while keeping all visible layers visible: Press SHIFT+ LClick the layer.

*These steps cover only the "scene" layers. It is assumed here that you have not yet worked with the "render layers." For a fuller treatment of layers and rendering, see the section on "render layers": **T129, step 1, p. 253**.

T44. To make layers invisible in 3D view and in the render:

1. In Blender, there is a special kind of group, one not covered in **T35-T40**, called a "layer". Confusingly (because of analogy with layers in 2D graphics programs), objects that are in such a group are said to be *on* the layer, not *in* it—I will say that an object is "in" a layer.

2. Keeping in mind that at least one layer must remain visible, to choose which layer(s) will be invisible in the 3D View window and in the render: In Object mode, go to the 3D View window header (marked

by to the left) > Go to the set of layer buttons: .

3. SHIFT+LClick the shaded layer(s) that you want to be invisible.

T45. To make a copy of an object, or a copy of an Action (see T106, step 5, p. 219), which is in one Blender file (say *london.blend*), and put this copy into another Blender file (say, *paris.blend*), such that the objects in both files can be edited independently—In other words, to *append* an object or Action:

1. Open london.blend.

2.

   (i) If you want to put a copy of an *object* that's in london.blend into paris.blend, go to **3**.

   (ii) If you want to put a copy of an *Action* that's in london.blend into paris.blend, go to **4**.

3. Select the object you want to put into paris.blend. Look at lower left in the 3D View window and find the object's name. Make a note of the name (say it's called "green_cone"). Unlink the object from any Object Actions or a Shapekey Actions that are presently applied to it (see **T109, p. 234**)*. If you want to put copies of these Action into paris.blend, do that separately (see **4**) > Go to **6**.

4. Go to the DopeSheet window > (i) If the Action you want to copy is a Shapekey Action, make sure that the window is in "ShapeKey Editor" mode; (ii) If the Action you want to copy is an Object Action, make sure that the window is in "Action Editor" mode.

5. When the Action is applied to a selected object, look at this button to see the name of the Action:

   >

Make a note of the Action's name (say it's called "cone_animation").

6. (Making sure that london.blend is saved) open paris.blend.

7. Go to the "Info" window's header (with to the left) > LClick "File" > LClick "Append".

OR

SHIFT + F1.

8. To navigate to "london.blend": If you want to go up the directory structure, press the button at upper left with the crooked arrow on it: ⬆, or LClick the same kind of arrow, with two dots: ⬆·· OR

⬆ , near the top of the list.

9. If you want to go down the directory structure, LClick a name in the list.

10. LClick "london.blend".

11. (i) If you are appending the object (green_cone), go to **12**; (ii) If you are appending the Action ("cone_animation"), go to **13**.

12. LClick "Object" > LClick "green_cone" > Go to **14**.

13. LClick "Action" > LClick "cone_animation" > Go to **14**.

14. LClick "Link/Append from Library" at upper right.

15. Save paris.blend.

* If you append an object into paris.blend without unlinking its Actions in london.blend first: in paris.blend, go to the Outliner window, RClick the name of each of these Actions and LClick "Unlink."

T46. To make a copy of an object which is in one Blender file (say, *chicago.blend*), and put this copy into another Blender file (say, *boston.blend*), such that the copy in *boston.blend* can be edited only by editing the original in

chicago.blend.

1. Open chicago.blend. Select the object you want to put into boston.blend. Look at lower left in the 3D View window and find the object's name. Make a note of the name (say it's called "little_car").

2. (Making sure that chicago_blend is saved) open boston.blend.

3. Go to the "Info" window's header (with ![info icon] to the left) > LClick "File" > LClick "Link".

OR

CTRL + ALT + O.

4. Navigate to "chicago.blend": If you want to go up the directory structure, press the button at upper left with the crooked arrow on it: ![arrow up icon] , or LClick the same kind of arrow, with two dots: ![arrow up two dots icon] OR

, near the top of the list.

5. If you want to go down the directory structure, LClick on a name in the list.

6. LClick "chicago.blend".

7. LClick "Object"

8. LClick on "little_car"

9. LClick "Link/Append from Library" at upper right.

10. Save boston.blend.

T47. To import a *reference image* into your scene (any image from your hard drive, to be used as a reference as you build your model):

1. Go to the Properties Shelf (see **T10, p. 9**) – If it is not visible: with the mouse cursor in the 3D View window, press N.

2. Go to the "Background Images" panel. If the panel is collapsed, LClick on the black triangle or on the words "Background Images" to expand it.

3. LClick "Add Image".

4. LClick the button under the white X to specify the view for which the reference image will be visible.

5. LClick the view you want (Left, Right, Front, Bottom, Top, All Views, or Camera).

6. LClick the tiny white triangle to the left of "Not Set" to further expand the panel.

7. To import an image from your hard drive, LClick the "Open" button. (If you want to use an image you've already used in the scene, you can LClick the button to the left of the "Open" button > LClick the desired image.)

8. To have your image files shown as thumbnails, LClick this button at upper left: ![thumbnail icon] .

9. Navigate to the image that you want to use as your reference image. If you want to go up the directory structure, press the button at upper left with the crooked arrow on it: ![arrow up icon] , or LClick the same kind of arrow, with two dots:  OR , near the top of the list.

10. If you want to go down the directory structure, LClick on a name in the list.

11. LClick the file you want to use to select it.

12. LClick "Open Image" at upper right.

13. Go back to the Properties Shelf (see **1**), and to the "Background Images" panel > LClick the little box to the left of the words "Background Images" to put a checkmark in it.

14. To *see* the reference image, (a) you must be in "orthographic" view, not "perspective" view. (numpad5 toggles between these – see **T12, p. 10** above), and (b) depending on which view you chose in step **5**, you must be looking at your scene from the front (numpad1), back (CTRL+numpad1), top (numpad7), bottom (CTRL+numpad7), side (numpad3), or other side (CTRL+numpad3)—see **T13, step 25, p. 11** above.

15. In the Properties Shelf (see **1**), go to the "Background Images" panel > Adjust the "Opacity" button and the "Size" button, and/or adjust the position of the image using the "X" and "Y" buttons (see *Introduction* for instructions on how to adjust buttons of this kind).

16. Following the steps above, you can add different reference images for different views; for instance one for the front view, another for the side view, and a third for the top view.

T48. To merge vertices on a mesh, dragging part of the geometry with the moved vertex/vertices:

(Note: To merge vertices between an object and its mirror copy, see **T30, step 26, p. 65**. To merge vertices in an array, a set of identical items generated by the modifier "Array", see **T30, step 53, p. 68**)

1. In Object mode, select the object that has the vertices that you want to join.

2. Go into Edit mode (**T7, p. 8**).

3. Select the vertices you want to merge into one.

4. Press W.

5. LClick "Merge"

6. LClick to choose where you want the merge to occur (at the first vertex selected: "At First"; at the last vertex selected: "At Last"; between the two: "At Center"; at the 3D cursor: "At Cursor").

T49. To create an edge:

1. In Object mode, select the object that you want to work on.

2. Go into Edit mode (**T7, p. 8**).

3. Extrude a vertex as follows: select the vertex > press E (see **T26, p. 58**).

T50. To create a Face (in Blender versions through 2.62, faces could be only 3- or 4-sided; with 2.63's BMesh system, faces can have any number of sides):

1. In Object mode, select the object that you want to work on.

2. Go into Edit mode (**T7, p. 8**).

METHOD 1

3. Select the vertices that will define the face (If you need to create new vertices to define the new face, you can extrude them from the mesh [see **T26, p. 58**]) > With your mouse pointer is in the 3D View window, press F. (The face will not have to be flat for this to work.)

METHOD 2

4. Duplicate an existing face as follows: select a face > Press SHIFT+D > move it to the desired location > LClick.

METHOD 3

5. Extrude an edge as follows: Select the edge > Press E (see **T26, p. 58**). (Creates one face.)

METHOD 4

6. Extrude a face as follows: Select the face > Press E (see **T26, p. 58**). This creates a number of faces, one for each of the face's edges.

END OF METHODS

T51. To make cuts across face(s), *using Blender versions before 2.63*:

TO MAKE ONE OR MORE STRAIGHT CUTS ACROSS A FACE BY CUTTING ONE OR MORE OF THE FACE'S EDGES—CUTS WILL BE MADE ACROSS THE SURFACE FROM CUT EDGE TO CUT EDGE; OR, IF ONLY ONE OF A FACE'S FOUR EDGES IS CUT, THE CUT WILL BE MADE FROM THE TWO OPPOSITE CORNERS TO THE CUT EDGE.

1. In Object mode (**T8, p. 9**), select the object that you want to work on.

2. Go into Edit mode (**T7, p. 8**).

3. Select the edges that you want to cut (in order to cut the face).

4. Do you want multiple cuts to be automatically generated so that each cut edge will be cut at evenly-spaced points?

        Yes: Go to **8**.

        No: Go to **5**.

5. Do you want to cut the edge(s) at the exact place(s) where you will move your mouse pointer across them?

        Yes: Go to **6**.

        No: Go to **7**.

6. Press & hold K > LClick & hold > Release K > Draw across the edge(s) where you want to make the cut(s) > Release the left mouse button. Stop. You are finished. (This may work only in *ortho* view [**T12**].)

7. To cut the edge(s) at their center(s):

        (a) Press & hold K > LClick & hold > Release K > Draw across the edge(s) where you want to make the cut(s) > Release the left mouse button > Go to the Tool Shelf (press T if it's not visible—see **T9, p. 9**) > LClick the "Type" button > LClick "Midpoints". Stop. You are finished.

        OR

        (b) Press & hold SHIFT and press & hold K > LClick & hold > Release SHIFT and K > Draw across the edge(s) you want to cut (you do not have to draw across their middle points) > Release the left mouse button Stop. You are finished.

8. Press & hold K > LClick & hold > Release K > Draw across the edge(s) where you want to make the cut(s) > Release the left mouse button. Go to the Tool Shelf (press T if it's not visible—see **T9, p. 9**) > LClick the "Type" button > LClick "Multicut". Adjust the "Number of Cuts" button (see **_Introduction_** for instructions on how to adjust buttons of this kind). Stop. You are finished.

T52. To make cuts through face(s), _using Blender versions starting with 2.63_:

A. TO MAKE A SINGLE STRAIGHT CUT THROUGH A FACE, OR TO MAKE AN IRREGULARLY SHAPED CUT COMPOSED OF A SERIES OF SEGMENTS, IN ORDER TO DIVIDE THAT FACE INTO TWO FACES.

1. In Object mode (**T8, p. 9**), select the object that you want to work on.

2. Go into Edit mode (**T7, p. 8**).

3. With the mouse pointer in the 3D View window, press K (a little knife and a green dot will replace the mouse pointer) > (Note that, at any time, if you are hovering above an edge, you can position the knife over the center of that edge by pressing and holding CTRL) > Pick an edge that borders the face that you want to cut into, an edge on which you want to begin the cut > Hover over that edge > Do you want to make a single cut across the face, ending it on another edge?

> Yes: Go to **4**.

> No: Go to **5**.

4. Hover over that edge > Press LClick to fix the end-point of the cut > Press ENTER or SPACEBAR to finish the cut. Stop. You are finished.

5. Move the knife to where you want the first segment of the cut to end; you can end the first segment on another edge or at any point on the face. LClick to fix the end-point of the first segment of the cut > Make further segments of the cut in the same way (keeping in mind that a face in Blender 2.63 can have any number of edges) > End the cut by fixing the end of the last segment on the same edge that you began it on, or on another edge > Press ENTER or SPACEBAR to finish the cut.

B. TO MAKE A "LOOPCUT"; THAT IS, TO AUTOMATICALLY CUT THROUGH A CONNECTED SERIES OF 4-SIDED FACES, BY STARTING ON THE EDGE OF ONE FACE, (GOING BOTH WAYS FROM THE STARTING EDGE) AUTOMATICALLY CUTTING THE ADJACENT FACE FROM THE EDGE TO OPPOSITE EDGE, CUTTING THE NEXT ADJACENT FACE FROM THE EDGE TO OPPOSITE EDGE, ETC.:

1. In Object mode (see **T8, p. 9**), select the object you want to work on.

2. Go into Edit mode (see **T7, p. 8**).

3. Press CTRL + R

4. Move the cursor around, over edges, until the purple line cuts through the faces you want to cut.

5. a. If you want to make multiple, evenly-spaced, cuts through each face: Scroll to produce the number of cuts that you want > LClick > Stop. You are finished.

> b. If you want to make only one cut through each face: Go to **6**.

6. LClick.

7. Do you want to place the cut in the center of the faces?

> Yes: Go to **8**.

> No: Go to **9**.

8. Press ESC. Stop. You are finished.

9. Move the mouse pointer to place the cut exactly where you want it. You can watch the readout in the

3D View window's header area (or "footer") in order to place the loopcut precisely.
10. LClick.

C. TO SUBDIVIDE A FACE OR FACES EACH INTO 4, OR 16, OR 64 FACES:
METHOD 1
1. In Object mode (see **T8, p. 9**), select the mesh object you want to work on.
2. In Edit mode: select the face(s) that you want to subdivide.
3. Go to the Tool Shelf (press T if it's not visible—see **T9, p. 9**) > Go to the "Mesh Tools" panel > Go to the "Add" buttons > LClick the "Subdivide" button.
4. LClick this "Subdivide" button once for each level of subdivision that you want;

     OR

Still in the Tool Shelf, go to the "Subdivide" panel > Adjust the "Number of Cuts" button (see ***Introduction*** for instructions on how to adjust buttons of this kind).
5. To add a smoothing effect: still in the Tool Shelf, go to the "Subdivide" panel > Adjust the "Smoothness" button (see ***Introduction*** for instructions on how to adjust buttons of this kind).
6. To add a random effect: still in the Tool Shelf, go to the "Subdivide" panel > Adjust the "Fractal" button (see ***Introduction*** for instructions on how to adjust buttons of this kind).
METHOD 2
7. In Object mode (see **T8, p. 9**), select the object you want to work on.
8. In Edit mode: select the face(s) that you want to subdivide.
9. Press W.
10. LClick "Subdivide"; OR: press 1; OR: press S.
11. To further subdivide the face(s):
(a) Repeat steps **9** and **10**.

     OR

(b) Go to the Tool Shelf (press T if it's not visible—see **T9, p. 9**) > Go to the "Subdivide" panel. Adjust the "Number of Cuts" button (see ***Introduction*** for instructions on how to adjust buttons of this kind).
12. To add a smoothing effect, go to the Tool Shelf (press T if it's not visible—see **T9, p. 9**) > Go to the "Subdivide" panel > Adjust the "Smoothness" button (see ***Introduction*** for instructions on how to adjust buttons of this kind).
13. To add a random effect, go to the Tool Shelf (press T if it's not visible—see **T9, p. 9**) > Go to the "Subdivide" panel > Adjust the "Fractal" button (see ***Introduction*** for instructions on how to adjust buttons of this kind).
METHOD 3 – TO SUBDIVIDE A FACE OR FACES EACH INTO 4, OR 16 OR 64 FACES, WHILE SMOOTHING THE GEOMETRY:
14. In Object mode (see **T8, p. 9**), select the object you want to work on.
15. In Edit mode: select the face(s) that you want to subdivide.
16. Press W.
17. LClick "Subdivide Smooth"; OR: press 2; OR: press U.
18. To further subdivide the face(s):
(a) Repeat steps **16** and **17**.

     OR

(b) Go to the Tool Shelf (press T if it's not visible—see **T9, p. 9**) > Go to the "Subdivide" panel > Adjust the "Number of Cuts" button (see ***Introduction*** for instructions on how to adjust buttons of this kind).

19. To add an additional smoothing effect, go to the Tool Shelf (press T if it's not visible—see **T9, p. 9**) > Go to the "Subdivide" panel > Adjust the "Smoothness" button (see ***Introduction*** for instructions on how to adjust buttons of this kind).

20. To add a random effect, go to the Tool Shelf (press T if it's not visible—see **T9, p. 9**) > Go to the "Subdivide" panel > Adjust the "Fractal" button (see ***Introduction*** for instructions on how to adjust buttons of this kind).

D. TO SUBDIVIDE AND SMOOTH – SEE T50 [SUBSURF; MULTIRES]

T53. To reposition object A's *object origin* onto a vertex on object B, without moving object A's *geometry*:

1. In "Object Mode" (see **T8, p. 9**), RClick Object B.

2. Go into Edit mode (see **T7, p. 8**).

3. Select the vertex on Object B to which you want to move Object A's Object Origin.

4. Press SHIFT+S (to display the "snap menu").

5. LClick "Cursor to Selected". (This places the 3D cursor onto the selected vertex.)

6. Go to Object mode (see **T8, p. 9**).

7. Select Object A > Go to the 3D View window header (marked by  at left): LClick on "Object" > Hover over "Transform" > LClick "Origin to 3D Cursor."

T54. To subdivide an object's faces while adjusting the faces to smooth its shape; for the *Subsurf* method, go to A; for the *"Subdivide Smooth"* method, go to B; for the *Multires* method, go to C.:

A. TO SUBDIVIDE AN OBJECT'S FACES SUCH THAT (UNLESS THE "APPLIED" BUTTON IS CLICKED) THE ORIGINAL SHAPE PERSISTS IN EDIT MODE AS THE OBJECT'S SO-CALLED "CAGE", AND SUCH THAT TRANSFORMATIONS WILL BE ABLE TO BE DONE ONLY ON THE "CAGE"—I.E. TO USE THE SUBSURF MODIFIER. THE SUBSURF MODIFIER IS TEMPORARY UNLESS THE "APPLIED" BUTTON IS CLICKED:

1. In Object mode (see **T8, p. 9**) select the object.

2. In Object mode (see **T8**) or Edit mode (see **T7, p. 8**) > Go to the "Properties" window:  > LClick the "Modifiers" button:  > Go to the "Modifiers" panel > LClick "Add Modifier".

3. LClick "Subdivision Surface".

4. In the "Subsurf" panel, a panel with this icon

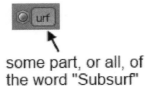

some part, or all, of
the word "Subsurf"

toward the top left: make sure that "Catmull-Clark" is enabled (that is, is colored blue).

5. So that you will be able to see the object as subdivided and smoothed in the 3D View window and in *Object* mode, make sure that this button

in the top part of the Subsurf panel is enabled (darkened).

6. To be able to see the object as subdivided and smoothed in the 3D View window and in *Edit* mode, make sure that both of these buttons

in the top part of the Subsurf panel are both enabled (darkened).

7. To see, in the 3D View window and in *Edit* mode, both the original shape, as an ephemeral "cage," and the object as subdivided and smoothed at the same time, make sure that these buttons

in the top part of the Subsurf panel are both enabled (darkened) and that this button

next to them is not enabled (not darkened).

8. To see, in the 3D View window and in *Edit* mode, only the object as subdivided and smoothed, and not the "cage," (though the cage will still be editable—see step **13**) make sure that these buttons

in the top part of the Subsurf panel are all enabled (darkened).

9. So that you will be able to see the object as subdivided and smoothed in the render, make sure that this button

in the top part of the Subsurf panel is enabled (darkened).

10. Still in the Subsurf panel, to choose the level of subdivision that will be visible in the 3D View window: adjust the "View" button (see ***Introduction*** for instructions on how to adjust buttons of this kind).

11. To choose the level of subdivision that will be used for the render: adjust the "Render" button (see ***Introduction*** for instructions on how to adjust buttons of this kind). (Many Blender artists use level 1 for the 3D window, while using level 2 or 3 for the render.)

12. To hide—in the 3D View window in Object mode, when in wireframe view (see **T14, p. 12**) —the edges that the subsurf produces, while giving the original edges the general shape that correlates with the subsurf level that you set in step **10**, LClick "Optimal Display".

13. As long as you do not LClick "Apply", Edit mode editing can be made only to the persisting, and possibly ephemeral (depending on your settings at **6-7** above) original shape (the "cage") , and the subdividing can be undone at any time by LClicking the "X" to the right of the "Subsurf" label. To make the subdividing permanent (which will increase the burden on your computer), such that changes can be made to the subdivisions themselves, in Object mode: LClick "Apply".

14. Note that you don't need both Subsurf *and* Multires (see **C** below).

B. TO SUBDIVIDE ONE OR MORE FACES OF AN OBJECT WITHOUT THE OBJECT'S ORIGINAL SHAPE PERSISTING:

1. In Edit mode: Select the face(s).

2. Press W.

3. LClick "Subdivide Smooth".

4. To further subdivide and smooth, repeat steps **2 and 3**, etc.

C. TO SUBDIVIDE AN OBJECT'S FACES SUCH THAT THE ORIGINAL SHAPE PERSISTS IN EDIT, BUT NOT AS A "CAGE", AND SUCH THAT SCULPTING WILL BE ABLE TO BE DONE ON THE SUBDIVIDED GEOMETRY— I.E. TO USE "MULTIRES":

1. Note that, if you are working with multires meshes, you will be able to move vertices as you sculpt; but, you will not be able to add (e.g. by extruding) or delete vertices, edges, or faces unless you *apply* the multires. Also, to add smoothness to the edges, see **T55, p. 87**.

2. In Object mode (see **T8, p. 9**), select the object.

3. Do you want to add multires subdivision to a square or rectangular *mesh plane* while retaining its square or rectangular shape?

> Yes: Go to **4**.
>
> No: Go to **5**.

4. Go to Edit mode, use CTRL + R (see **T52, B, p. 81**) to put a thin frame around the plane > Go to Object mode (after step **10** the divisions will be there, though they will not be visible) > Go to **5**.

5. Go to the "Properties" window: ![icon] > LClick the "Modifiers" button: ![icon] > Go to the "Modifiers" panel > LClick "Add Modifier".

6. LClick "Multiresolution".

7. In the Multires sub-panel, a sub-panel with this icon

toward the top left: make sure that "Catmull-Clark" is enabled (that is, is colored blue).

8. So that you will be able to see the subdivisions in the 3D View window, make sure that this button

in the top part of the Multires panel is enabled (darkened).

9. So that you will be able to see the subdivisions in the render, make sure that this button in the top part of the Multires panel is enabled (darkened).

10. To add a level of subdivision: In ***Object*** mode, still in the Multires panel, LClick "Subdivide." LClick it again to add another level, etc. (Only the power of your computer will limit the number of levels you can add.)

11. So long as you do not LClick on "Apply", you can choose, at any time, which level you want to appear in the 3D View window in Object and Sculpt modes, and in the render:

12. To specify which of the levels that you created at step **10** are to be visible in object mode (the subdivisions will not be visible in Edit mode),in the 3D View window, adjust the "Preview" button (see ***Introduction*** for instructions on how to adjust buttons of this kind).

13. To specify which of the levels that you created at step **10** are to be visible in Sculpt mode in the 3D View window, adjust the "Sculpt" button (see ***Introduction*** for instructions on how to adjust buttons of this kind).

14. To specify which of the levels that you created at step **10** are to be visible in the render, adjust the "Render" button (see ***Introduction*** for instructions on how to adjust buttons of this kind).

15. Note that a higher number of levels allows you to make detailed, fine-grained, changes using Sculpt mode, but increases the computing burden on your computer. You can choose a high level so that you can transform or sculpt in a detailed way; then, you can choose to view a lower level—to which the changes will be automatically transferred with as much detail is as possible—as you continue to work on the object or on other parts of the model. The edited higher level will be preserved—it simply will not be visible until you choose to make it visible using the "Preview", "Sculpt", and "Render" buttons.)

16. When you show your multires-modified object in wireframe (see **T14, steps 7-9, p. 13**), it will, in Object mode and in Sculpt mode, always take on the general shape that correlates with the multires level that you set with the "Preview" button (for Object mode) and with the "Sculpt" button (for Sculpt mode). If "Optimal Display" in the "multiresolution" panel is *not checked*, the size and number of edges in the wireframe will reflect the level you set with the "Preview" and "Sculpt" buttons. If "Optimal Display" *is* checked, the number of edges will always reflect the original mesh, before multires subdivisions were made.

17. To superimpose a wireframe, as described in step **16** above, over a solid view: With Viewport Shading Type set to "solid" view in Object or Sculpt mode (see **T14, p. 12**) go to the "Properties" window > [image] > LClick the "Object" button: [image] > Go to the "Display" panel > LClick the box next to "Wire" in order to check it.

18. To permanently delete all multires levels above the one presently showing in the 3D View window:

In the "Properties" window: [image] > Enable the "Modifiers" button: [image] > Go to the "Modifiers" panel > Go to the "Multires" sub-panel > LClick the "Delete Higher" button.

19. To make the multires level which is presently showing in the 3D View window permanent, that is, to delete all levels above and below it, and allow the object to be fully editable (allowing not just sculpting, but also allowing the transforming of—and the adding and deleting of—vertices, edges and faces, and so, for instance, allowing extruding): in the "Multiresolution" panel, LClick the "Apply" button.

T55. **To smooth edges:**

 (To smooth while subdividing faces, see **T54, p. 83**)
1. (In Object or Edit mode,) select the object.
2. Go to the Tool Shelf (see **T9, p. 9**) – if it is not visible, press T.
3. Go to the "Shading" buttons.
4. LClick "Smooth".

T56. **To sculpt your mesh object using the sculpting "brushes":**

The sculpting brushes work best on a greatly subdivided mesh, for instance use multires (see **T54, C, p. 85**).
1. A SCULPTING-BRUSH OVERVIEW:

In Blender, you sculpt with a sculpting "*brush.*" Every sculpting brush has a set of properties, *all of which can be changed*:

(a) At any given time, a brush will have what I call a single, specific *tooling functionality*—that is, the brush will affect the object's surface in a certain way. For instance, If the brush has a "Draw" type tooling functionality (with the "add" button enabled) it will pull up on the mesh's vertices; if it has a "Fill" type tooling functionality (with the "Deepen" button enabled), it will deepen a crevice on the object's surface; etc.
(b) A brush will have a set size, called its *radius*.
(c) A brush will have a set *strength*.
(d) A brush will be configured to have a certain kind of *stroke*—for example, a series of dots, or an airbrush stroke, etc.
(e) A brush can be given what I call a *texturing functionality*, which will cause the brush to produce a stroke that is textured in one way or another.

At any time, you will have available to you, in Sculpt mode, a set of sculpting brushes. You can create brushes and add them to the set, and you can throw brushes away. In Sculpt mode, in the Tool Shelf, look at the big picture at the top of the "Brush" panel. Think of this big picture as the door to your sculpting brush cabinet. LClick it to open the cabinet and view your brushes. If you are opening the cabinet for the first time, you will see that Blender has supplied you with a set of brushes. Notice that each brush has a name: "Blob" is a name for one of your brushes—as its picture indicates, this brush presently has a "Blob" type tooling functionality, "Brush" is another brush in your cabinet—it has a "Draw" type tooling functionality, etc. It's good to keep at least one brush for each tooling functionality in this "cabinet," so that you can change tooling functionality quickly while sculpting.

In Sculpt mode, in the Tool Shelf, in the "Texture" panel: look at the big picture at the top. Think of this as the door to a cabinet within which can be stored a collection of textures that can be used by your brush's texturing functionality (see **1(e)** above). You can LClick this big picture at any time, in Sculpt mode, to see what textures are in there.

2. If the object that you want to sculpt is not already selected: In Object Mode (see **T8, p. 9**), select the object. (Note that if a non-mesh object, such as a curve, is selected, you won't be able to get into Sculpt Mode. Also, note that, in Sculpt mode, if your brush will not move across the object's surface, check to make sure that you have that object selected.)

3. Get into Sculpt Mode; in general, here's how to get into Sculpt Mode:

METHOD 1:

4. Go to the Mode button (see ***Introduction***). If "Sculpt Mode" is on this button, you are ready to sculpt; if "Sculpt Mode" is not on the button, LClick the button, then LClick "Sculpt Mode".

METHOD 2:

5. You can use this method only if "Edit Mode" is on the Mode button (see ***Introduction***), and only if you were in Sculpt Mode just before going into Edit Mode: Press TAB.

END OF METHODS

6. When you go into Sculpt mode, one of the brushes available to you will be "active"—it will be the "current" brush. In the Tool Shelf, go to the "Brush" panel. The big image at the top portrays the current brush. Underneath this big image, you will see a row of buttons that pertain to the current brush, the brush you are using now. Its name is written on the far-left button (If your Tool Shelf is very narrow, only a part of the name might be visible on the button; in order to see the whole name, you may have to expand the Tool Shelf horizontally: hover over its edge until the double-headed arrow appears and then drag.)

7. To create a new brush: Still in Sculpt mode, in the Tool Shelf, in the "Brush" panel, go to the row of buttons just below the big image at the top > LClick the button with the plus sign (+) on it. You have now created a brush—the brush you have been using has been saved (put back into the brush "cabinet"), and the brush you have just created has, until you change them, all the same properties that the previous brush had.

8. To retrieve a brush from your set of available brushes: (a) Still in Sculpt mode, go to the "Brush" panel > LClick the big picture at the top (to open the "door" to your sculpting-brush "cabinet", see **1** above) > If you want to choose a stored brush depending on its tooling functionality, but you are not sure which tooling function is appropriate for what you want to do, use step **12** to decide > Get the brush by LClicking its image; OR **(b)** If you want to choose a stored brush depending on what tooling functionality it has, but you are not sure exactly which tooling function is appropriate for what you want to do, use step **12** to decide > Use a **hotkey**: For instance, to retrieve a brush that has a "Draw" type tooling functionality, press D—if more than one stored brush has a Draw type tooling functionality, you can retrieve one after the other by pressing D repeatedly.

Preset hotkeys are:
  Draw = D
  Smooth = S
  Pinch = P
  Inflate = I
  Grab = G
  Layer = L
  Flatten = SHIFT+T
  Clay = C
  Crease = SHIFT+C

You can customize these hotkeys. To set a hotkey to a tooling functionality: Go to "User Preferences" by pressing CTRL+ALT+U (OR: File > "User Preferences") > LClick the "Input" tab > LClick the little triangle to the left of "3D View" to expand it > LClick the little triangle to the left of "Sculpt" to expand it > LClick the little triangle to the left of any "Brush Select" to expand it > LClick the button to the right of "Sculpt Tool" > LClick the name of the tooling functionality that you want to set a hotkey to > Make sure that the first button at the top is set to "Keyboard" > LClick the button to the right > On your keyboard, press the key that you want to be the hotkey.

9. **To save a brush** (that is, to put a new brush into the sculpting-brush "cabinet" or put a brush you took from the "cabinet" back into the "cabinet," saving whatever property-changes you might have made to it): Save your Blender file (see **T19, p. 18** and **T20, p. 18**) OR create a new brush (see **7**) OR retrieve a brush from your set of brushes (see **8**)—brush size will not be saved.

10. **To rename a brush**: In Sculpt mode, in the "Brush" panel, look underneath the big image, you will see a row of buttons that pertain to the current brush, the brush you are using now. The brush's name is written on the far-left button (If your Tool Shelf is very narrow, only a part of the name might be visible on the button; in order to see the whole name, you may have to expand the Tool Shelf horizontally: hover over its edge until the double-headed arrow appears and then drag) > LClick this far-left button > Type the new name > Press ENTER.

11. **To change to a different tooling functionality as you sculpt:** (a) (Recommended:) Retrieve a stored brush that has the tooling functionality that you want; see step **8** for how to do this—use hotkeys whenever possible; OR: (b) Change your brush's tooling functionality—see step **14**.

12. **To choose the right tooling functionality:**
  (a) If you want to raise or lower the surface of your object as you draw on it by moving a group of faces in the direction of their average normal (a face's "normal" is the direction 90 degrees from the surface, choose "**Draw**." (Note that "**Clay**" is much like "Draw", with some additional controls.)
  (b) If you want to lay clay strips onto the material, choose "**Clay Strips.**"
  (c) If you want to smooth the surface, choose "**Smooth**."
  (d) If you want to pull vertices toward, or push them away from, the center of the brush, choose "**Pinch**."
  (e) If you want to raise or lower the surface of your object as you draw on it by moving each face in a group of faces in the direction of its own normal (a face's "normal" is the direction perpendicular to the surface plane), choose "**Inflate**."

(f) If you want to grab and pull a group of vertices on your object's surface, choose "**Grab**."

(g) If you want to raise or lower the surface of your object as you draw on it such that the process will tend to leave a *flatter* raised or lowered surface than when using the Draw functionality, choose "**Layer**."

(h) If you want to either flatten the surface of your object as you move your sculpt tool over it or enhance the contrast of the surface irregularities, choose "**Flatten**."

(i) If you want to put a ridge on, or a crease in, the surface of your object, choose "**Crease**".

(j) If you want to fill in, or deepen, a dip or crease in the surface of your object, choose "**Fill**".

(k) If you want to move vertices in the direction of the brush strokes, choose "**Nudge**".

(l) If you want to pull the mesh out, creating a spherical "blob", or push it in, creating a spherical cavity, choose "**Blob**".

13. **To work with the tooling functionalities:**

(a) Draw: If the brush is set to *raise* the surface of your object as you draw on it (the default setting), and you want to set it to *lower* the surface: still in the Tool Shelf, go to the "Brush" panel and LClick "Subtract" (that is, turn this button blue);

      OR

Press and hold CTRL while drawing.

If the brush is set to *lower* the surface of your object as you draw on it, and you want to *raise* the surface of your object as you draw on it: still in the Tool Shelf, go to the "Brush" panel and LClick "Add" (that is, turn it blue);

      OR

Press and hold CTRL while drawing.

(b) Clay Strips: If you want the brush to *lower* the surface of your object as you draw on it: Press and hold CTRL while drawing.

(c) Pinch: If the brush is actually set to pinch the mesh, that is, if it is set to pull vertices toward the center of the brush (the default setting), and you want to set it to push vertices *away* from the center: still in the Tool Shelf, go to the "Brush" panel and LClick "Magnify" (that is, turn this button blue);

      OR

Press and hold CTRL while drawing.

If the brush's Pinch functionality is set to push vertices away from the center of the brush, and you want to set it to pull vertices toward the center: still in the Tool Shelf, go to the "Brush" panel and LClick "Pinch" (that is, turn this button blue);

      OR

Press and hold CTRL while drawing.

(d) Inflate: If the brush is actually set to inflate the mesh, that is, if it is set to *raise* the surface of your object as you draw on it (the default setting), and you want to set it to *lower* the surface: still in the Tool Shelf, go to the "Brush" panel and LClick "Deflate" (that is, turn this button blue);

      OR

Press and hold CTRL while drawing.

If the brush is set to *lower* the surface of your object as you draw on it, and you want to *raise* the surface of your object as you draw on it: still in the Tool Shelf, go to the "Brush" panel and LClick "Inflate" (that is, turn this button blue);

OR

Press and hold CTRL while drawing.

(e) Layer: If the brush is set to *raise* the surface of your object as you draw on it (the default setting), and you want to set it to *lower* the surface: still in the Tool Shelf, go to the "Brush" panel and LClick "Subtract" (that is, turn this button blue);

OR

Press and hold CTRL while drawing.

If the brush is set to *lower* the surface of your object as you draw on it, and you want to *raise* the surface of your object as you draw on it: still in the Tool Shelf, go to the "Brush" panel and LClick "Add" (that is, turn this button blue);

OR

Press and hold CTRL while drawing.

(f) Flatten: If the brush is actually set to flatten the surface of your object as you draw on it (the default setting), and you want to set it to *enhance the contrast* of the surface irregularities instead: still in the Tool Shelf, go to the "Brush" panel and LClick "Contrast" (that is, turn this button blue);

OR

Press and hold CTRL while drawing.

If the brush is set to *enhance the contrast* of the surface irregularities of your object as you draw on it, and you want to *flatten* the surface of your object as you draw on it instead: still in the Tool Shelf, go to the "Brush" panel and LClick "Flatten" (that is, turn this button blue);

OR

Press and hold CTRL while drawing.

(g) Crease: If the brush is set to *put a ridge on* the surface of your object as you draw on it, and you want to set it to *put a crease in* the surface: still in the Tool Shelf, go to the "Brush" panel and LClick "Subtract" (that is, turn this button blue);

OR

Press and hold CTRL while drawing.

If the brush is set to *put a crease in* the surface of your object as you draw on it, and you want to *put a ridge on* the surface of your object as you draw on it: still in the Tool Shelf, go to the "Brush" panel and LClick "Add" (that is, turn this button blue);

OR

Press and hold CTRL while drawing.

(h) Fill: If the brush is set to *fill in dips or creases* of the surface of your object as you draw on it (the default setting", and you want to set it to *deepen a dip or crease* in the surface: still in the Tool Shelf, go to the "Brush" panel and LClick "Deepen" (that is, turn this button blue);

OR

Press and hold CTRL while drawing.

If the brush is set to *deepen dips or creases* of the surface of your object as you draw on it, and you want to *fill in a dip or crease on* the surface of your object as you draw on it: still in the Tool Shelf, go to the "Brush" panel and LClick "Fill" (that is, turn this button blue);

OR

Press and hold CTRL while drawing.

(i) Blob: If the brush is set to *pull the mesh out* as you draw on it (the default setting), and you want to set it to *push the mesh in*: still in the Tool Shelf, go to the "Brush" panel and LClick "Subtract" (that is, turn this button blue);

OR

Press and hold CTRL while drawing.

If the brush is set to *push the mesh in* as you draw on it, and you want to *pull the mesh out*: still in the Tool Shelf, go to the "Brush" panel and LClick "Add" (that is, turn this button blue);

OR

Press and hold CTRL while drawing.

(j) When using any tooling functionality: To smooth the surface, press SHIFT + LClick and drag.

To change one or more properties of a brush:

14. **To change your brush's tooling functionality** (see **1**), in Sculpt mode, go to the 3D View window header > LClick "Brush" > Hover over "Sculpt Tool" > LClick the name of the tooling functionality that you want to use. **For guidance on deciding which tooling functionality to use**, see step **12**.

15. AIRBRUSH. (The following, steps **15-17**, pertains to all of the tooling functionalities except Grab:) By default, when you LClick & hold to operate the brush, it will quickly stop working unless you move it across the surface. If you want it to keep working as long as you hold the left mouse button down, even if you aren't moving the brush, you will have **to turn on the "Airbrush"** stroke method:

16. Still in the Tool Shelf, go to the "Stroke" panel > LClick the "Stroke Method" button > LClick "Airbrush";

OR

With the cursor in the 3D View window, press A > (a) LClick "Airbrush" OR (b) press I (as in airbrush).

17. To disable Airbrush and return to the standard, default brush stroke: Still in the Tool Shelf, go to the "Stroke" panel > LClick the "Stroke Method" button > LClick "Space" > Set "Spacing" to 10%;

OR

With the cursor in 3D View window, press A > LClick "Space" OR press S > Go to the Tool Shelf > go to the "Stroke" panel >Set "Spacing" to 10%.

18. To create a sculpting brush effect at a place on the mesh, and then to resize the effect by moving closer to or farther from the brush's center: Still in the Tool Shelf, go to the "Stroke" panel > LClick the "Stroke Method" button > LClick "Anchored";

OR

With the cursor in the 3D View window, press A > (a) LClick "Anchored" OR (b) press A.

19. To create a sculpting brush effect and then drag it around on the surface: Still in the Tool Shelf, go to the "Stroke" panel > LClick the "Stroke Method" button > LClick "Drag Dot";

OR

With the cursor in the 3D View window, press A > (a) LClick "Drag Dot" OR (b) press R.

20. To produce an intermittent effect of the sculpting brush as you move it along the surface, and set the distance of the intervals: Still in the Tool Shelf, go to the "Stroke" panel > LClick the "Stroke Method" button > LClick "Space" (this is the default setting);

OR

With the cursor in the 3D View window, press A > (a) LClick "Space" OR (b) press S.

21. To set the spacing: In the Tool Shelf, go to the "Stroke" panel > set the "Spacing" button (the default setting, 10%, produces a continuous effect).

22. To produce a kind of standard, continuous effect: Still in the Tool Shelf, go to the "Stroke" panel > LClick the "Stroke Method" button > LClick "Dots";

> OR

With the cursor in the 3D View window, press A > (a) LClick "Dots" OR (b) press D.

23. In Sculpt mode, vertices are pushed and pulled in the direction of the normal of a plane; you choose which plane to use by going to the "Brush" panel and LClicking the dark button with one of the following words on it: "Z Plane", "Y Plane", "X Plane", "View Plane", or "Area Plane". (a) **To choose the plane derived from the average face-planes within the area of the brush**, LClick "Area Plane"; (b) **To choose the View XY plane**, LClick "View Plane"; (c) **To choose the plane perpendicular to the object's Local X axis**, LClick "X Plane"; (d) **To choose the plane perpendicular to the object's Local Y axis**, LClick "Y Plane"; (e) **To choose the plane perpendicular to the object's Local Z axis**, LClick "Z Plane".

24. Do you want to change the size of your sculpting brush?

> Yes: Go to **25**.
>
> No: Go to **32**.

25. (Still in Sculpt mode,) to change the size of your sculpting brush:

METHOD 1:

26. Still in the Tool Shelf, go to the "Brush" panel.

27. Adjust the "Radius" button. After you've set the size, go to **32**.

METHOD 2:

28. With the cursor in the 3D View window, press F.

29. Move the cursor toward and away from the center of the circle to make the brush the size you want it. (Note that if you've applied a texture to the brush's texture functionality, this texture should be visible within the circle.)

30. LClick. After you've set the size, go to **32**.

METHOD 3:

31. Note that if you are using a pressure sensitive tablet, you can use pen pressure as you sculpt to control the brush size by enabling the pressure sensitivity button to the right of the "Radius" button:

 > Go to **32**.

END OF METHODS

32. Do you want to change the strength of your sculpting brush? (Note that you cannot change the strength of the *Grab* tooling functionality.)

> Yes: Go to **33**.
>
> No: Go to **39**.

33. (Still in sculpt mode,) **to change the strength of your brush**:

METHOD 1:

Still in the Tool Shelf, go to the "Brush" panel >

34. Adjust the "Strength" button. After you've set the strength, go to **39**.

METHOD 2:

35. With the cursor in the 3D View window, SHIFT + F.

36. Move the cursor toward and away from the center of the circle to give the brush the strength you want it to have: making the circle smaller increases the strength; making the circle larger decreases the strength. (Note that if you've applied a texture to the brush's texture functionality, this texture should be visible within the circle.)

37. LClick. After you've set the strength, go to **39**.

METHOD 3:

38. Note that if you are using a pressure sensitive tablet, you can use pen pressure to control the brush strength as you sculpt by enabling the pressure sensitivity button to the right of the "Strength" button:

 . > Go to **39**.

END OF METHODS

39. To make sure that your sculpting will affect only the front part of the mesh, that is, the part that is visible: Still in the Tool Shelf, go to the "Brush" panel > check "Front Faces Only".

40. Symmetry: Do you want whatever you do with your brush on the *positive* side of your object's *local* X (and/or Y and/or Z) axis to be replicated on the *negative* side of the same axis, OR: do you want whatever you do with your brush on the *negative* side of your object's local X (and/or Y and/or Z) axis to be replicated on the *positive* side of the same axis? (See **T24, p. 32**.)

     OR

do you want to *stop* such symmetrical replication from happening?

     Yes: Go to **41**.

     No: Go to **43**.

41. Still in the Tool Shelf, go to the "Symmetry" panel > LClick the "X" button, and/or the "Y" button, and/or the "Z" button, to make sure that all, and only, the axes that you want to have symmetry along are checked.

42. To blend two symmetrical brush strokes where they meet: Still in the Tool Shelf, go to the "Symmetry" panel and check "Feather".

43. Do you want to prevent vertices from moving in the direction of selected axes in the object's Local coordinate system? (With respect to the *Grab* tooling functionality: by default, it moves vertices in the *View* coordinate system's XY axis. But constraining movement in accord with step **44** below will actually allow the Grab functionality to move vertices in the directions of any unconstrained axis of the object's local coordinate system)

     Yes: Go to **44**.

     No: Go to **45**.

44. Still in the Tool Shelf, go to the "Options" panel: Go to the X, the Y, and the Z "Lock" buttons. LClick on any axis or axes that you want to prevent vertices from moving in the direction of as you use your sculpting brush.

45. Do you want **to change how gradually or abruptly your brush's effect falls off**, outward from the center of the brush?

     Yes: Go to **46**.

No: Go to **49**.

46. Still in the Tool Shelf, go to the "Curve" panel:

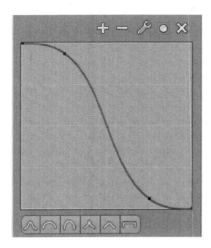

47. You can change how your brush's effect falls off by changing the curve shown in this panel. To do this, you can adjust the curve by LClicking & holding the curve itself, and dragging its nodes.

48. To set the curve in accord with certain basic shapes, LClick one of the "Set brush shape" buttons beneath the curve.

49. Do you want to modify your active sculpting brush's texturing functionality so that it will texture its strokes, or, if it already textures its strokes, do you want to change (or remove) this texturing?

Yes: Go to **50**.

No: Go to **70**.

50. Is your active sculpting brush non-texturing, and do you want to modify it so that it will texture its strokes?

Yes: Go to **51**.

No: To change or remove your sculpting brush's existing texture: Go to **60**.

51. Do you want to use a texture that you've already used in the scene?

Yes: Go to **52**.

No: Go to **53**.

52. (a) Still in Sculpt mode, go to the Tool Shelf (see **T9, p. 9**) > Go to the "Texture" panel (LClick the black triangle to the left of "Texture" to expand the panel if necessary—you might have to drag in the vertical scrollbar to see this panel) > LClick the large image > LClick the texture you want to use. Go to step **66**.

OR

(b) Still in Sculpt mode > Go to the "Properties" window: > LClick the "Texture" button:

 > Make sure the "Show Brush Textures" button is enabled: ![icon] > LClick the checker-board

button ![icon] near the upper left of the "Properties" window > LClick the texture you want to use. Go to step **66**.

53. (a) Still in Sculpt mode, go to the Tool Shelf (see **T9, p. 9**) > Go to the "Texture" panel (LClick the black triangle to the left of "Texture" to expand the panel if necessary—you might have to drag in the vertical scrollbar to see this panel) > LClick the "New" button below the large image.

OR

(b) Go to the "Properties" window: > Make sure that the "Texture" button is enabled

> Make sure the "Show Brush Textures" button is enabled: > LClick "New".

54. In the "Properties" window: > Make sure that the "Texture" button is enabled >

Make sure the "Show Brush Textures" button is enabled: > LClick the "Type" button at the top > LClick the type of texture you want.

55. Did you just choose "image or movie"?

       Yes: Go to **56**.

       No: Go to **65**.

56. Go to the "Image" panel > LClick "Open" > To have your image files shown as thumbnails, LClick this

button at upper left: .

57. Navigate to the image that you want to use as your image texture. If you want to go up the directory

structure, press the button at upper left with the crooked arrow on it: , or LClick the same kind of

arrow, with two dots: OR , near the top of the list.

58. If you want to go down the directory structure, LClick on a name in the list.

59. LClick the file you want to use to select it > LClick "Open Image" at upper right. Go to **65**.

       OR

Double LClick the file you want to use. Go to **65**.

60. Do you want to remove all texturing from your current brush?

       Yes: Go to **61**.

       No: To change your current brush's texturing, go to **62**.

61. In Sculpt mode, in the Tool Shelf, in the "Texture" panel: Go to the row of buttons below the big image > LClick the button with "X" on it, at the far right end of the row. Go to **70**.

62. Do you want to change your brush's texture to a texture that you've already used in the scene?

       Yes: Go to **63**.

       No: Go to **64**.

63. (a) Still in Sculpt mode, go to the Tool Shelf > Go to the "Texture" panel > LClick the large picture > LClick to choose the texture you want > Go to **66**.

OR

(b) Still in Sculpt mode > Go to the "Properties" window: > LClick the "Texture" button: > Make sure that the "Show Brush Textures" button is enabled: > LClick the checker-board button at the left end of the line of buttons above the "Type" button:

LClick the name of the texture you want > Go to **66**.

64. (a) Still in Sculpt mode, go to the Tool Shelf > Go to the "Texture" panel > Go to the row of buttons under the big image > LClick the button with a plus sign (+) on it > Go to **54**.

OR

Go to the "Properties" window: > Make sure that the "Texture" button is enabled >

Make sure the "Show Brush Textures" button is enabled: > In the row of buttons above the "Type" button, LClick the plus sign (+):

> Go to step **54**.

65. To name your texture:

(a) In Sculpt mode, in the Tool Shelf, in the "Texture" panel: Go to the row of buttons just under the big image > LClick the first of these buttons > Type the new name > Press ENTER.

OR

(b) in the "Properties" window: , with the "Texture" button enabled, and with the

"Show Brush Textures" button enabled: go to the row of buttons above the "Type" button > LClick the word in the longest of these buttons > Type the new name > Press ENTER.

66. To specify how the texture will align with the surface, still in Sculpt mode, in the Tool Shelf (**T9, p. 9**), go to the "Texture" panel > Go to the "Brush Mapping" buttons:

(a) To start applying the texture anew with each stroke (so that separate strokes will not necessarily align), LClick "Fixed" > Go to **67**.

(b) To apply the texture so that it is tiled across the surface and such that it is positioned in accord with where the tool stroke occurs, LClick "Tiled" > Go to **67**.

(c) To apply the texture so that it is aligned with the surface itself and not the sculpt tool position, LClick "3D". Go to **68**.

67. To specify the rotation angle of the Sculpting brush as it applies the texture: still in Sculpt mode, in the Tool Shelf (**T9, p. 9**), go to the "Texture" panel > LClick the top button of the two "Angle" buttons:

(a) To be able to set the angle by adjusting the bottom button of the two "Angle" buttons, LClick "User".

(b) To make the angle follow the direction of brush movement, LClick "Rake".

(c) To randomize the angle, LClick "Random".

68. To adjust the positioning of the texture, adjust the "Offset" buttons.

69. To adjust the size of the texture, adjust the "Size" buttons.

70. LClick & hold, and drag the brush across the surface to apply the sculpting stroke.

T57. To position an object's origin (see T24, p. 32) without moving the object's geometry:

1. To move the object's origin to the object's geometrical center: In Object mode, go to the 3D View window's header (this header is marked by at left) > LClick "Object" > Hover over "Transform" > LClick "Origin to Geometry".

2. To move the object's origin to the 3D cursor, without moving the object's geometry: In Object mode, go to the 3D View window's header (this header is marked by at left) > LClick "Object" > Hover over "Transform" > LClick "Origin to 3D cursor".

T58. To position the 3D cursor:

METHOD 1:

1. To change the View XY coordinates (see **T24, p. 32**) of the 3D cursor : LClick where you want to re-position the 3D cursor. (the View Z coordinate of the cursor will not change.)

Note that using this method, you can place the 3D cursor in the 3D space: press numpad-7 for top view > LClick where you want to position the 3D cursor in the View XY plane (which, since you're in top view, is the same as the Global XY plane) > press numpad-1 for front view > LClick above or below the 3D cursor to place it on the View Y axis (which, since you're in front view, is the same as the Global Z axis).

METHOD 2:

2. (In Object or Edit mode,) If the Properties Shelf (**T10, p. 9**) is not visible: with the mouse pointer in the 3D View window, (a) go to the 3D View window header (marked by to the left) > LClick "View" > LClick "Properties" OR (b) press N.

3. In the Properties Shelf, go to the "View" panel > Adjust the "3D Cursor Location" buttons.

METHOD 3:

4. To put the 3D cursor on the nearest (visible or invisible) point on the Global grid: in Object or Edit mode, with the mouse pointer in the 3D View window, press SHIFT+S > (a) LClick "Cursor to Grid" OR (b) press G.

METHOD 4:

5. To put the 3D cursor on the origin of the active (that is, the last-selected) object, or the center of the active edge, or face, or on the active vertex: with the mouse pointer in the 3D View window, press SHIFT+S > (a) LClick "Cursor to Active" OR (b) press A.

METHOD 5:

6. To put, in Object mode, the 3D cursor on the origin of the selected object (or median of a multiple selection), or to put, in Edit mode, the 3D cursor on the center of a selection (or median of a multiple selection): with the mouse pointer in the 3D View window, press SHIFT+S > (a) LClick "Cursor to Selected" OR (b) press C.

METHOD 6:

7: To put the 3D cursor on the origin of the Global coordinate system: with the mouse pointer in the 3D View window, press SHIFT+S > (a) LClick "Cursor to Center" OR (b) press U.

T59. To retrieve a lost 3D cursor:

If your 3D cursor () disappears, it may have acquired far-out coordinates somehow; to get it back: Go to the "Properties Shelf" (see **T10, p. 9**) > Go to the "3D Cursor" panel > "Location" buttons to change extreme coordinates to normal ones.

T60. To shape a Bezier curve, to shape a Nurbs curve, a Bezier circle, or a Nurbs circle:

1. Note that, by default, the control- and end-points of a new curve or circle can be moved in three dimensions, allowing you to create a curve that curves in 3D space. At any time, you can **transform a 3D curve into a 2D curve, flattening it into two dimensions and changing its control- and end-points into ones that can be moved only in the curve's or circle's local XY axis.** Here is how you can do this:

2. With the curve or circle having been selected in Object mode: in Object or Edit mode, go to the "Properties" window: > Enable the "Object Data" button: > Go to the "Shape" panel > enable the 2D button.

3. To allow the control- and end-points to be moved in 3D (that is, in the curve's or circle's local Z axis, as well as in the local X and Y axes), do this:

With the curve or circle having been selected in Object mode: in Object or Edit mode, go to the "Properties" window: > Enable the "Object Data" button: > Go to the "Shape" panel > enable the "3D" button.

4. (If you enable the "3D" button, and the curve has been closed and extruded, the top and bottom surfaces will disappear.)

5. To change the resolution of your curve (number of straight lines in a segment) in the 3D View window or in the render: Go to the "Properties" window: > Enable the "Object Data" button: >

Go to the "Shape" panel > Go to the "Resolution" buttons > Adjust the "Preview U" button for the 3D View window or the "Render U" button for the render.

6. To change a curve or circle into a mesh at any time: Go into Object mode (see **T8, p. 9**) > Press ALT + C > LClick "Convert to Mesh from Curve/Meta/Surf/Text". The resolution of the mesh will match the number set by the "Preview U" button (see step **5** above). So, if you change a closed and extruded curve or an extruded circle (see below) into to a mesh, the number of faces around the extruded surface will match the number that is set by the "Preview U" button.

7. To give a (closed or open) curve or a circle depth at any time:

METHOD 1: A SIMPLE EXTRUSION

8. With the curve or circle having been selected in Object mode: in Object or Edit mode, go to the "Properties" window: > Enable the "Object Data" button: > Go to the "Geometry" panel > Adjust the "Extrude" button. (See the **Introduction** for how to adjust buttons like this.) You can think of this as a "thick" curve or circle, whose shape can be changed (aside from further changing its thickness, and so long as the "3D" button has not been enabled) only within its local XY plane. Note that you cannot make a simple extrusion of this type if the "Bevel Object" controls have been activated. To deactivate them: RClick the "Bevel Object" field > LClick "Reset to Default Value".

METHOD 2: A COMPLEX EXTRUSION USING "BevObj":

9. You can extrude and shape a curve or circle (here we'll call it the "original" curve or circle) by using a second curve (which we'll call a "bevel object", or "BevObj", curve). Here's how:

10. After you have created and edited a curve (or circle), which may be flat and without thickness, that is, after you have created and edited what we are calling the "original" curve, go into Object Mode (see section **T8, p. 9** above). (If you start with a curve which has been extruded using **METHOD 1** above, following these steps in **METHOD 2** will delete the previous extrusion and will treat the original curve as if it had never been extruded using **METHOD 1**.)

11. Add another curve (see **T27, p. 62** above)—this will be the "BevObj" curve. Make it 2D (see step **2**).You can make sure that the curve is oriented correctly with respect to its own local axes this way: Select the curve in Object mode > Go to Edit mode > LClick the "Transform Orientation" button (since different words can appear on this button, I've put a smudged word on it):

OR

> LClick "Local" > Rotate the curve to align it to its local X and Y axes as shown below.

12. Still in Edit Mode:

13. Using the directions below, shape the BevObj curve with the following in mind:

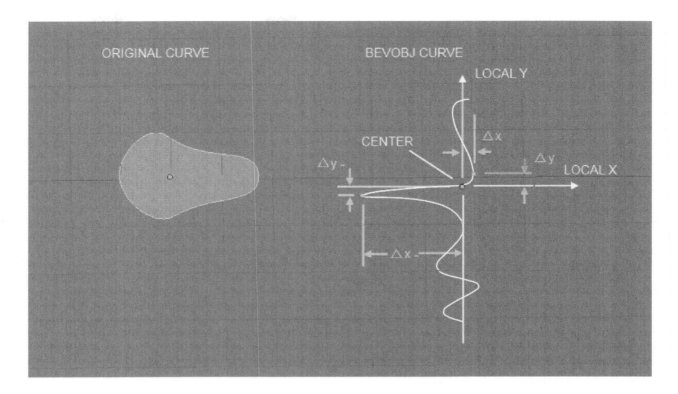

This picture shows the flat original curve, in this case a closed curve (see step **29**), and the BevObj curve (the undulating line on the right—a curve made up of several curve segments [see steps **26-28**]), with axes, etc. added for illustration purposes. Note the following:

• BevObj's positive local X will correspond to the moving of points on the original curve (that is, on the edge of the flat original shape) toward the original curve's center.

• BevObj's negative local X will correspond to the moving of points on the original curve away from the original curve's center.

• BevObj's positive local Y will correspond to the original curve's positive local Z.

• BevObj's negative local Y will correspond to the original curve's negative local Z.

Here, in this example, when you activate the "Bevel Object" control, the BevObj will extrude the flat original curve a distance of △y in the original curve's local positive Z direction and, on that plane, pulls every point on the original curve in toward the original curve's center a distance of △x. The BevObj extrudes the original curve a distance of △y- in the original curve's local negative Z direction and, on that plane, pushes every point on the original curve away from the original curve's center a distance of △x-. And so on for every point on the BevObj curve. In this example, the extruded original curve will look like this:

To activate the "Bevel Object" controls in order to extrude the original curve in line with the BevObj curve's shape:

14. When the BevObj curve is selected, look at bottom left in the 3D View window to see and remember its name. Let's say its name is "Curve.001".

15. Go into Object Mode and select the original curve.

16. Go to the "Properties" window: ▭ > Enable the "Object Data" button: ▭ > Go to the "Geometry" panel > Go to the "Bevel Object" field > (a) LClick the field & LClick the name of the curve you want to use as a bevel object, OR (b) type in the name of the curve you want to use as a bevel object; in this case, you will type in "Curve.001" > Press ENTER.

17. To *de*activate the "Bevel Object" controls (so that, for example, you can do a "simple extrude" [**step 7, METHOD 1**]): RClick the "Bevel Object" field > LClick "Reset to Default Value".

END OF METHODS

18. If you want to shape a Bezier curve, go to **19**.

If you want to shape a NURBS curve, go to **36**.

If you want to shape a Bezier circle, go to **46**.

If you want to shape a NURBS circle, go to **47**.

TO SHAPE A BEZIER CURVE:

19. Right after you add a Bezier curve (see section **T27, p. 62**), go to Edit view (see **T7, p. 8**), and if you then press numpad-7 for a top view, the curve will look like this (labels added):

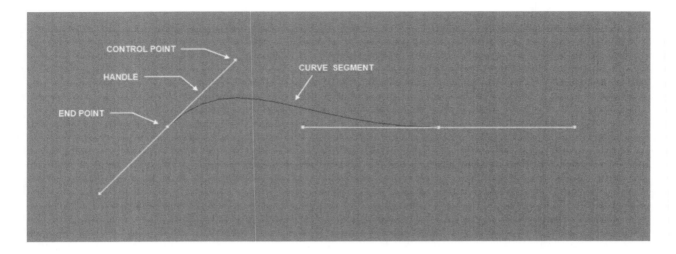

An "end point" may not be at the end of the curve (as it is in the illustration), but it always marks the end of a curve *segment*.

20. To change the shape of any Bezier curve you will move the control points and the end points. There are four different kinds of handles:

21. An "**aligned**" handle-pair will move as one rigid handle. Its handles are pink.

To change any pair of handles into aligned handles, select the end point between the pair and press V > LClick "Aligned".

22. The handles of a "**free**" handle-pair move independently.

To change any pair of handles into free handles, select the end point between the pair and press V > LClick "Free"; OR: if a pair of handles is vectored (yellow-green), select and move one of the control points.

 23. A "**vector**" handle (which is yellow-green) is a handle which always points toward the end point of any adjacent handle-pair. To change one or more handles into vector handles, select the control point of the handle(s) (either directly or by selecting the related end point[s]; or by pressing A) and press V > LClick "Vector".

24. An "**auto aligned**" handle pair is a handle pair whose angle changes to reflect the shape of the curve. Auto aligned handles are yellow. To change any handle-pair into an auto aligned handle-pair, select the end point between the pair and press V > LClick "Automatic"

25. To move the selected control points: use any method that is described in section **T25, p. 33** above (To select both control points, select the end point between them). For instance, if the curve is still in the Global XY plane (as it is when you first add it to your scene) and you have pressed numpad-7 for the top view, and the 3D Manipulator is in "translate" mode (with the arrows) (a) LClick & drag on the white circle on the 3D Manipulator OR (b) RClick on the point and press G > Move the control points > LClick to confirm placement.

26. To add a new segment end-point and another pair of handles on the curve, in between two existing segment end-points: select both of the existing end-points; then press W; LClick "Subdivide". (To add new end-points and handles between several pairs of existing segment end-points, select all the relevant existing end-points; then press W and LClick "Subdivide".)

27. **To add a segment to an end of a curve** (adding another end-point and another pair of handles): In Edit mode: select the curve end-point, or one of its associated control points (whose handles may be free, aligned, vectored or auto aligned), onto which you want to add the new segment. Then extrude: Press E; OR: Press CTRL + LClick at the place to which you want to extrude the new end-point.

28. **To join an end-point of one (2D or 3D) curve to the end-point of another (2D or 3D) curve with a new connecting curve, thus producing a single long curve** (this can be done only if the second of the two curves was created in Edit mode when the first had been selected in object mode; that is, only two separate curves which are part of the same object can be joined this way): In Edit mode: select the two points to be joined. Then press F.

29. **To close the (2D or 3D) curve.** In Edit mode (**T7, p. 8**), select at least one of the end-points or control points; then press Alt + C. (If, and only if, the curve is 2D, closing the curve will create a surface, a fill.)

30. **To cut a hole in the surface of a closed 2D curve:** In Edit mode, position the 3D cursor above the plane of the closed curve (it does not have to be on that plane) > add another curve (Bezier or NURBS) and close it, or add a Bezier or NURBS circle, and scale it and/or move it until it fits within the surface. (Note that, since the new curve is added in Edit mode, the new curve or circle will be created in the same plane as the original curve-- they are both parts of the same object.)

31. **If you want to put a bevel around the extruded (or even around a non-extruded) open or closed curve's edges** (including any edges bordering internal openings): In Object mode (**T8, p. 9**), select the curve > In Object or Edit mode: Go to the "Properties" window: > Enable the "Object Data" button: > Go to the "Geometry" panel > Go to The "Bevel" buttons > adjust the "Depth" button (see the ***Introduction*** for how to adjust buttons of this kind).

32. **If you want to adjust the sharpness or smoothness of the bevels** that you made in step **31** above: In Object mode (**T8, p. 9**), select the curve > In Object or Edit mode: Go to the "Properties" window: > Enable the "Object Data" button: > Go to the "Geometry" panel > Go to The "Bevel" buttons > adjust the "Resolution" button (see the ***Introduction*** for how to adjust buttons of this kind).

33. **To remove or add an extruded closed curve's top and/or bottom surface**, in Object mode (**T8, p. 9**), select the curve > In Object or Edit mode: Go to the "Properties" window: > Enable the "Object Data" button: > Go to the "Shape" panel > LClick the "Fill" button > LClick to choose which surface(s) to show .

34. **To increase or decrease the number of surfaces around the extruded sides of the curve, *in 3D View***, in Object mode (**T8, p. 9**), select the curve > In Object or Edit mode: Go to the "Properties" window: > Enable the "Object Data" button: > Go to the "Shape" panel > Go to the "Resolution" buttons > Adjust the "Preview U" button. (See the ***Introduction*** for how to adjust buttons of this kind).

35. **To increase or decrease the number of surfaces around the extruded sides of the curve, *in the***

rendered image, in Object mode (**T8 p. 9**), select the curve > In Object or Edit mode: Go to the

"Properties" window: 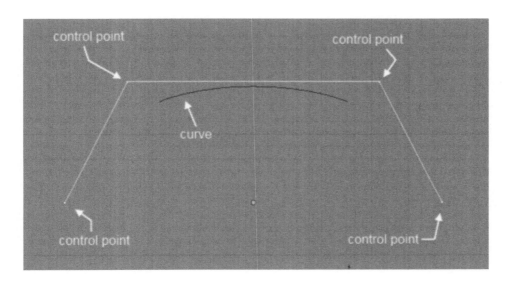 > Enable the "Object Data" button: > Go to the "Shape" panel > Go to the "Resolution" buttons > Adjust the "Render U" button. (see the *Introduction* for how to adjust buttons of this kind). (Note that if the "Render U" button is set to zero, the render will reflect the "Preview U" button's setting.)

TO SHAPE A "NURBS" CURVE:

36. To shape a "NURBS" curve: Right after you add a NURBS curve (see section **T27, p. 62**), go to Edit mode (see section **T7, p. 8**), and if you then LClick numpad-7 for a top view, the curve will look like this (labels added):

37. You can choose among three different so-called "knot" settings:

If you choose the **Uniform** setting, your curve will float; it will not be attached to the control points.

If you choose the **Endpoint** setting, the ends of your curve will be attached to the first and last control points, and these two control points will not be affected by "order" and "weight" settings (see below).

The **Bezier** setting only works if the "order" is set to 3 or 4 (see below). If you choose the Bezier setting: if the order is set at 3: Every 3rd control point connects to the curve. If the order is 4: Every 4th control point connects to the curve.

To choose your knot setting:

38. In Object mode, select your NURBS curve > Go to Edit mode > Go to the "Properties" window:

> Enable the "Object Data" button: > Go to the "Active Spline" panel.

39. To choose the **uniform** setting, leave the "Cyclic", "Bezier" and "Endpoint" boxes unchecked.

To choose the **endpoint** setting, LClick the "Endpoint" box to put a check mark into it. Make sure that the other two boxes are unchecked.

To choose the **Bezier** setting, LClick the "Bezier" box to put a check mark into it. Make sure that the other two boxes are unchecked.

40. You can choose an "order" which adjusts the "pull" of *all* control points *at the same time* such that the curve fits more or less snugly to the handles. The minimum order value is 2, the maximum is 6. When order 2 is chosen, each control point has maximum "pull" on the curve. When order 6 is chosen, each control point has minimum "pull" on the curve. If your curve has exactly 4 control points, you can set the order up to 4. If your curve has exactly 5 control points, you can set the order up to 5. If your curve has 6 or more control points, you can set the order up to 6.

41. To set the order number: In Object mode, select your NURBS curve > Go to Edit mode > Go to the "Properties" window: > Enable the "Object Data" button: > Go to the "Active Spline" panel > Adjust the "Order" button (see the ***Introduction*** for how to adjust buttons of this kind).

42. You can set the so-called "weight" of *individual* control points. "Weight" might better be called "pull strength": The higher the "weight", the more the control point will pull on the curve. A weight of .01 will set the pulling-strength of the control point to a minimum. A weight of 100 will set the pulling-strength of the control point to maximum. To set the weight of a control point:

43. In Edit mode, select the control point.

44. Go to the "Properties Shelf" (see **T10, p. 9**) > Go to the "Transform" panel > Go to the "Vertex" buttons > Adjust the "W" button. (See the ***Introduction*** for how to adjust buttons of this kind.)

45. Go to **25-35**. above.

TO SHAPE A BEZIER CIRCLE:

46. To change the shape of any Bezier circle you will move the control points and the segment end points. There are four different kinds of handles: do steps **21-26** above, then do **30-35**.

TO SHAPE A NURBS CIRCLE:

47. Do **37-44** above; then do **25-26**; then do **30-35**.

PART THREE: MATERIAL PROPERTIES

OVERVIEW:

Material properties include (what I call) a **"substance color"** (which is a kind of base color for the object), **shading properties, specular highlights, transparency, mirror-reflectivity, texture, "vertex paint"** (see below), and **"ramps"** (see below).

For an object to have any material properties at all—beyond a very light gray color and simple shading—what I call **a "base material"** must be applied to the entire object. (That is, the *object datablock* or the *geometry datablock* must have at least one *material datablock* [see ***Introduction***] attached to it).

The initial cube that Blender gives you, by default, when you open a new scene has a base material already applied to it, but whenever, in object mode, you add an object to your scene, that new object will possess no base material until you give it one. (That is, it has no *material datablock* [see ***Introduction***] until you give it one.)

At some point, you might want to change the material properties of some *part* of an already-applied material. In many cases (if, for instance, you want the part to have a different substance color), in order to do this you will have to transform that part of the material into a totally different material. (This is how your object acquires a plurality of *material datablocks* [see **_Introduction_**].)

T61. The *base material* is the material that has to be applied to your entire object before you can give the object any material properties beyond a very light gray color and simple shading. Also, a base material must have already been applied before you can apply a material to a *part* of the object. The cube that Blender gives you, by default, when you first open a new scene already has a base material, but any other object that you add to your scene will have no base material until you give it one. To determine whether or not the object has a base material:

1. In Object mode (see section **T8, p. 9** above), RClick the object in question.

2. Go to the "Properties" window: ![properties icon] > LClick the "Material" button: ![material icon] .

3. If you see a large set of panels with many buttons, then your object has at least one material, a base material, already applied to it. But, if you just see a single large box and a small number of buttons, one with the word "New" on it, then your object has no base material applied to it yet. To give it a base material, go to **T62**.

T62. To give your object a *base material*:

1. In Object mode (see section **T8, p. 9** above), RClick the object in question, to select it.

2. Go to the "Properties" window: ![properties icon] > LClick the "Material" button: ![material icon] .

3. (For most purposes, you can ignore this step—just go to step **4**.) If you want to attach your base material's *material datablock* directly to your object's *object datablock* (see **_Introduction_**), LClick the "+" button in the group of three buttons at top right:

   >

LClick the little, dark, button with the word "Data" on it. LClick "Object".

4. Do you want to assign to your object a material that is already assigned to another object in your scene? (That is, do you want to attach, to this object also, a material datablock [see **_Introduction_**], along with any attached texture datablock[s], that's already attached to another object in your scene?)

      Yes: Go to **5**.
      No: Go to **7**.

5. LClick the button to the left of the "New" button near the top:

6. LClick the name of the existing material that you want to apply to your object. Stop. You are finished.
7. Assign a material (one that is not already being used in your scene) to the whole object: LClick the "New" button.
8. Note that you have now assigned a material *to the whole object*, a **base material**. This material is light gray, non-mirror-reflective, and opaque.
9. You can see the name (which you can change), which was automatically given to the new material in the large box at the top and also on this long button underneath the box:

To change this automatically-created name: LClick the long button > Type in the name that you want your material to have > Press ENTER.

T63. To find the name of a face's (or surface's) material:

1. In Object mode, select the object that the face is on.
2. Go to Edit mode > Select the face.

3. Go to the "Properties" window: > LClick the "Material" button: .
4. You will find the name highlighted in the large box at the top, and you will find it on the long button in the set of buttons near the top that looks like this:

T64. To change the name of a material:

1. In Object mode: Select an Object that has that material applied to it.

2. Go to the "Properties" window: > LClick the "Material" button: .
3. In the large box at the top, select the name of the material, the name that you want to change.
4. LClick the long button in this set of buttons near the top:

5. Type the new name > Press ENTER.

T65. To replace *all* (not just part) of material *myMaterial1* with (for instance) existing material *myMaterial2*:

1. In Object mode, select the object that has *myMaterial1* applied to it.

2. Go to the "Properties" window:  > LClick the "Material" button: .

3. In the materials-list box at the top, select the name *myMaterial1*.

4. LClick the small button at the left end of the set of buttons near the top:

5. LClick the name *myMaterial2* (you may have to scroll to find the name).

T66. To replace *part* of an existing material *myMaterial* (for instance) with another material:

1. See whether the object has a *base material* applied to it yet; if it does not, make sure that it gets one. (See **T61** and **T62, p. 107** for how to do this.)

2. In Object mode, select the object.

3. In Edit mode (see section **T7, p. 8**) select the entire part of *myMaterial* where you want to replace *myMaterial* with the other material.

4. Go to the "Properties" window: > LClick the "Material" button: .

5. LClick the "+" button in the group of three buttons at top right:

6. (a) If you want to have the datablock of the material that will replace *myMaterial* connect with the geometry datablock (the usual, default connection—see **Introduction**), go to the dark button with either "Data" or "Object" on it > If it has "Data" on it, leave it alone; but, if it has "Object" on it, LClick it > LClick "Data"> Go to **7**.

(b) If you want to have the datablock of the material that will replace *myMaterial* connect directly to the object datablock, and not to the geometry datablock, go to the dark button with either "Data" or "Object" on it > If it has "Object" on it, leave it alone; but, if it has "Data" on it, LClick it > LClick "Object".

7. LClick "Assign".

8. Do you want to replace the part of *myMaterial* with a material that already exists in the scene?

      Yes: Go to **9**.

      No: Go to **10**.

9. LClick the little button to the left of the "New" button:

                                                                    >

LClick the name of the material that you want to replace *myMaterial* with (you may have to scroll to find the name). Stop. You are finished.

10. LClick "New". You have now replaced part of *myMaterial* with a new material. This material is light gray, non-mirror-reflective, and opaque.

T67. To give material *myMaterial1* (for instance) the properties of material *myMaterial2*, while *myMaterial1* remains *myMaterial1*. (That is, to turn material datablock *myMaterial1* into a copy of datablock *myMaterial2*, while maintaining its identity as *myMaterial1*):

1. In Object mode, select the object that has *myMaterial2* applied to it.

2. Go to the "Properties" window:  > LClick the "Material" button: .

3. In the large materials-list box at the top, find the name *myMaterial2*. LClick the name *myMaterial2* in order to highlight it.

4. LClick the bottom button in the group of three buttons at top right:

5. LClick "Copy Material"

6. (Still in Object mode,) select the object that has *myMaterial1* applied to it.

7. Go to the "Properties" window: > LClick the "Material" button: .

8. In the large materials-list box at the top, find the name *myMaterial1*. LClick the name *myMaterial1* in order to highlight it.

9. LClick the bottom button in the group of three buttons at top right:

10. LClick "Paste Material".

T68. To change the *substance color* of any material:

1. In Object mode, select the object that has the material applied to it.

2. Go to the "Properties" window:  > LClick the "Material" button: .

3. In the large materials-list box at the top, select the name of the material whose color you want to change.

4. Go to the "Diffuse" panel ("Diffuse" just refers to the general, basic color of the material; that is, not to the color of the highlights nor of the mirror-type reflections) > LClick in the color-swatch box (which *may* be just a white or light gray rectangle) on the left to bring up the palette.

5.

METHOD 1:

The artist thinks of a color as a blended mixture of a hue component (red, yellow, blue, etc.), a white component, and a black component (any one or two of these may be absent in a color).

Here's a way to use the palette to choose a color: first, go to the (default) color wheel: choose a **hue** by LClicking, holding and dragging around the edge of the circle. Note that the Blender circle presents the hues in a different way than does the artist's traditional circle of hues. The traditional, and long-respected, "color wheel" represents the perceptual distances between hues this way:

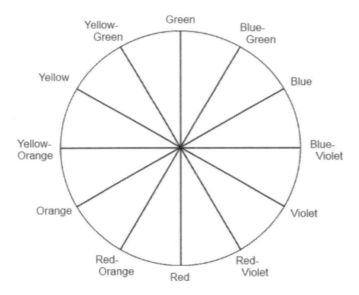

This traditional diagram shows that we perceive, for instance, that red is about as far from red-orange as blue-green is from blue. But the default* Blender circle is more like this:

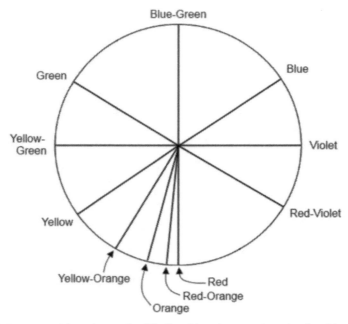

The artist may not be pleased with the Blender version: in the Blender circle, for instance, the span of Blue-Green (from Green to Blue) is roughly seven times greater than the span of Red-Orange (from Red to Orange), even though perceptually these spans are about the same.

(*You can switch to a square in "User Preferences" window [see **T1, p. 7**] > System > Color-Picker Type > Choose Circle, Square (HV+S), Square (HS+V) or Square (SV+H) > If you wish, you can "Save as Default".)

Now specify the ratio of pure hue to pure white in the hue+white component by dragging the mouse pointer toward and away from the center of the circle. As you move straight toward the center (that is, as you move along a radius toward the center), you add more and more white to the hue without changing the hue. In Blender terminology, this is called "changing the **saturation**" of the hue+white component of the color.

Release the mouse at the desired point. The following illustration shows how the saturation of the hue+white component changes as you move along a radius, without changing the hue (which is *orange* here).—pure hue is on the circumference, pure white at the center. The squares show the ratios diagrammatically (gray represents pure orange); under "Color" are the descriptions of the actual color:

112

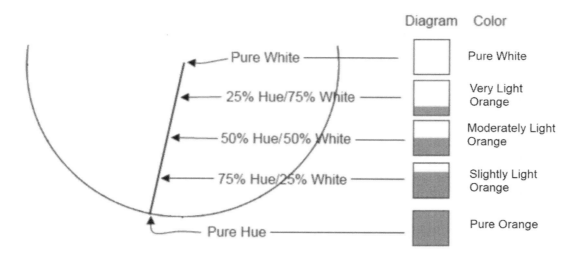

Let's say you choose 75% Hue/25% White.

Then specify the ratio of the hue+white component (which you set above to 75/25) to the **black** component by adjusting the "**Value**" slider:

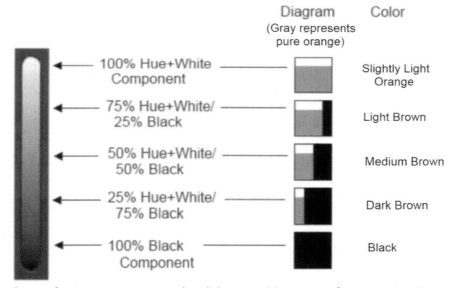

Let's say, for instance, you set the slider, roughly, to 50%/50%. As the illustration shows, your color is now set to a kind of warm brown. (In the Blender palette, the Value slider confusingly looks like a black-to-white slider).

METHOD 2:

6. LClick the "RGB" button.

7. LClick & hold to drag horizontally in each of the three sliders to produce the color you want. (If you LClick and release the mouse button in a slider—see below—you will not be able to slide it until you press ENTER, or until you LClick outside the button.) Sliding one slider with one of the others at minimum and the other at maximum produces the pure hues. A general minimizing of the sliders darkens the colors. 0 ,0, 0 produces black. 1, 1, 1 produces white. .5, .5, .5 produces a medium gray. OR

LClick and release the mouse button in a slider button and type in a number to change its setting > Press ENTER, or LClick outside the button.

METHOD 3:

8. LClick the " HSV" button.

9. LClick & hold to drag horizontally in the H, S, and V sliders to produce the color you want. "H", Hue, moves the dot around the center of the color-circle (see **METHOD 1** above), "S", saturation, moves the dot in the color-circle toward and away from the center (see **METHOD 1** above). "V", value, moves the dot up and down in the "Value" slider (see **METHOD 1** above). (If you LClick and release the mouse button in a slider—see below—you will not be able to slide it until you press ENTER or until you LClick outside the button.)

OR

LClick and release the mouse button in a slider button and type in a number to change its setting > Press ENTER, or LClick outside the button.

METHOD 3:

10. To use a color that already exists in your scene, LClick the color-sampler: ![icon] > LClick in the scene on the color you want to use. The color-sampler treats the entire Blender window as if it were a color photograph: If you LClick on a dark, shaded part of a light-colored object, the color it picks up will be dark; if you LClick on the green arrow of the 3D Manipulator, it will pick up the green color, etc.

T69. To change the color of the highlights of a material's specular color:

To change the color tint (which by default is white) of the highlights of a material—that is, to change the material's "specular" color:

1. In Object mode, select the object.

2. Go to the "Properties" window: ![icon] > LClick the "Material" button: ![icon] .

3. In the large materials-list box at the top, LClick the name of the material.

4. Go to the "Specular" panel > LClick in the color-swatch box (which may be just a white or light gray rectangle) on the left to bring up the palette > follow the instructions in **T64, step 5, p. 111**.

T70. To change the lit-to-unlit gradation across the surface--SHADERS:

1. The "shader" setting determines how light falling on your material creates lit-to-unlit gradation across the surface. To change the shader setting: In Object mode (see section **T8, p. 9** above), select the object you want to work on.

2. Make sure that the object has at least one material applied to it (see **T61** and **T62, p. 107** above).

3. Go to the "Properties" window: ![icon] > LClick the "Material" button: ![icon] .

4. In the large materials-list box at the top, LClick the name of the material.

5. Do you want to change the setting of the shader for the material's "diffuse" color (that is, the substance color, the texture, the vertex paint, or the ramp—the color created by light scattering off of the surface, not the "specular" color of the highlight)?

       Yes: Go to **6**.

       No: Go to **11**.

6. To change the setting of the material's "diffuse" shader:

7. Go to the "Diffuse" panel. LClick the "diffuse shader" button—this is the dark button to the right of the color-swatch box (which shows the diffuse color of the material, which may be white, or any other color).

8. LClick one of the Shaders' names:

       a. To give the material a kind of **standard appearance**: LClick "**Lambert**", which is **the default shader**.

       OR

       b. To give the material an appearance that is **affected by the object's surface roughness**, LClick "**Oren-Nayar**." To adjust the roughness, adjust the "Roughness" button (see **_Introduction_** for how to adjust buttons of this kind).

       c. To give the material **a cartoon shading**, LClick "**Toon**." To adjust the size of the color patches, adjust the "Size" button (see **_Introduction_** for how to adjust buttons of this kind). To adjust smoothness of the shading transition, LClick and drag in the "Smooth" button.

       d. To **lighten the edges of the object or darken the parts of the object that are facing the viewer**, LClick "**Minnaert**". To make the edges lighter, adjust the "Darkness" button to a setting below 1. To darken the parts of the object facing the viewer, adjust the "Darkness" button to a setting above 1 (see **_Introduction_** for how to adjust buttons of this kind).

       e. **To darken the parts of the material that face the light**, LClick "**Fresnel**". To adjust the effect, adjust the "Fresnel" button; to intensify the Fresnel setting, adjust the "Factor" button (see **_Introduction_** for how to adjust buttons of this kind).

9. In order to adjust the amount of light the material will reflect: still in the "Diffuse" panel, LClick and drag in the "Intensity" button (0 is minimum, 1 is maximum).

10. To see the results of modifying the material using the shader, press F12 to render the scene.

11. To change the material's "specular" highlight shader:

12. Go to the "Specular" panel. LClick the "specular shader" button—this is the dark button to the right of the color-swatch box (which shows the specular (highlight) color of the material, which may be white, or any other color).

13. LClick one of the Shaders' names:

       a. To choose Blender's **default specular shader**, LClick "**CookTorr**". To reduce or enlarge the highlight, adjust the "Hardness" button (see **_Introduction_** for how to adjust buttons of this kind). A lower number produces a larger highlight.

       b. To choose a specular shader that's **like CookTorr, but softer**, LClick "**Phong**"; To reduce or enlarge the highlight, adjust the "Hardness" button (see **_Introduction_** for how to adjust buttons of this kind). A lower number produces a larger highlight.

       c. To choose a specular shader that's **more refined and accurate than CookTorr and Phong**, LClick "**Blinn**"; To reduce or enlarge the highlight, adjust the "Hardness" button. To soften(?) the highlight, adjust the "IOR" button. (See **_Introduction_** for how to adjust buttons of this kind.)

       d. To give the highlight **a cartoon look**, LClick "**Toon**". To adjust the size of the color patches, adjust the "Size" button (see ***Introduction*** for how to adjust buttons of this kind). To adjust smoothness of the shading transition, LClick and drag in the "Smooth" button.

    e. To give the highlight **a metallic or very shiny look**, LClick "**WardIso**" ("Iso" as in "Isotropic"); To change the highlight's sharpness, LClick and drag in the "Slope" button.

14. To change the highlight brightness: in the "Specular" panel, LClick and drag the "Intensity" button.

T71. A short overview of transparency, mirror reflectivity, and the non-geometrical layers—vertex paint, texture, and ramp. For fuller instructions, see the sections below:

1. The non-geometrical properties of your material (essentially, the color properties, the transparency and the reflectivity of it) are applied, in Blender, in layers:

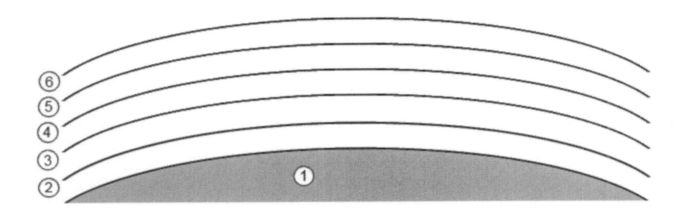

① **The material itself**. The material is given a **substance color** (See **T68, p. 111** for full instructions on how to change this color). The material's **transparency/opacity** *in the render* is controlled in two ways: "Z Transparency" and "Ray Transparency". For transparency (see **T72, p. 117** below for full instructions):

In the "Properties" window: [image] > LClick the "Material" button: [image] > Go to the "Transparency" panel > Put a check next to "Transparency"; then (a) for Z Transparency, enable the "Z Transparency" button > LClick and drag in the "Alpha" button to make the material more or less transparent. (b) For Ray Transparency, enable the "Raytrace" button > LClick and drag in the "Alpha" button for more or less transparency. The effect of both kinds of transparency goes through all layers, even opaque ones. The material can also be made **mirror reflective** (see **T73, p. 118** for full

instructions): Go to the "Properties" window: [image] > LClick the "Material" button: [image] > Go to the "Mirror" panel > Put a check next to "Mirror" > adjust the "Reflectivity" button for more or less mirror reflectivity. The effect of this kind of mirror reflectivity also goes through all layers. There's another kind of mirror reflectivity, "Environment Map", which is a kind of texture (see ③,④,⑤ below)—its effect does not go through the higher layers unless they are translucent or transparent. (See **T74, p. 120** below)

② **The Vertex Paint layer**. (See **T80, p. 167** for full instructions.) If no texture or ramp covers it, you can make this surface layer visible: go to the "Properties" window: > LClick the "Material" button: > Go to the "Options" panel > Put a check in the little box next to "Vertex Color Paint"; to make the layer invisible, uncheck the box. Note that Vertex Painting is done to the surface of the entire object, not just the single material.

③,④,⑤ **Layers of textures**. (For a fuller account, see **T74, p. 120**.) Their transparency/opacity in the render is controlled this way: Go to the "Properties" window: > Make sure that the "Texture" button is enabled: > Go to the texture stack at the top. In order to make a texture visible on your rendered material, you must make sure that it appears in this stack of texture channels, and it must be checked to the right, and it must not be occluded by another texture. Also, the transparency/opacity controls for textures are in the "Influence" panel; for instance, one such control is one of the "Diffuse" buttons: the "color" button. A lower texture in the stack will cover a higher one.

⑥ **The Ramps layer**. (See **T79, p. 165** below.) A ramp's transparency/opacity in the render is controlled this way: go to the "Properties" window: > LClick the "Material" button: > Go to the "Diffuse" panel or to the "Specular" panel > Put a check mark into the little square next to "Ramp" > Slide the "Factor" slider.

T72. To make a material transparent:

1. Make sure that the object has at least one material applied to it (see **T61, p. 107** above).
2. In Object mode, select the object.

3. Go to the "Properties" window: > LClick the "Material" button: .
4. In the large materials-list box at the top, LClick the name of the material that you want to make transparent.
5. Go to the "Transparency" panel > LClick the small box to the left of the word "Transparency" to put a check mark in it.
6. If you want to use a fast-rendering method for creating transparency or translucency, one where what's behind the object simply becomes visible, go to step **7**.
If you want to use a slower-rendering method, one that uses ray-tracing to produce accurate transparency and translucency, taking into account an index or refraction, etc., go to step **9**.
7. To make your material "Z-Transparent":
Enable the "Z Transparency" button > LClick and drag in the "Alpha" button: zero is full transparency, 1

is full opacity.

8. You can get an idea of how it will look if you look at the image in the "Preview" panel; but, of course, the best way to see what it looks like is to render it (F12). Stop. You are finished.

9. To make your material "Ray Transparent":
Enable the "Raytrace" button > LClick and drag in the "Alpha" button: zero is full transparency, 1 is full opacity.

10. At any time, you can get an idea of how it will look if you look at the image in the "Preview" panel; but, of course, the best way to see what it looks like is to render it (F12). If the transparency cannot be

seen in the render, still in the "Properties" window, , LClick the "Render" button: > Go

to the "Shading" panel > Make sure that "Ray Tracing" is checked > Go back to  >

"Transparency" panel.

11. If you want to adjust the index of refraction of the material (the degree to which light rays will bend when entering and exiting the material), adjust the "**IOR**" button (see **_Introduction_** for how to adjust buttons of this kind).

12. If you want to specify how many surfaces of transparent materials, one behind the other, the viewer (the camera) will be able to see through, adjust the "**Depth**" button (see **_Introduction_** for how to adjust buttons of this kind).

13. If you want to give your transparent material more or less of the coloring (see **T62, p. 107** and **T68, p. 111**) of the material, adjust the "**Filter**" button and the "**Limit**" button (see **_Introduction_** for how to adjust buttons of this kind).

14. If you want to adjust how quickly light is absorbed when going through the material, adjust the "**Falloff**" button (see **_Introduction_** for how to adjust buttons of this kind).

15. If you want to make the specular areas (areas reflecting highlights) more or less opaque, LClick and drag in the "**Specular**" button.

16. If you want the material's coloring (see **T62, p. 107** and **T68, p. 111**) to tint the transparent material more intensely where the surface is more oblique to the camera (for instance, at the edges of a sphere), adjust the "**Fresnel**" button—the lower the number is, the greater will be the effect (see **_Introduction_** for how to adjust buttons of this kind).

17. If you want to give your material a more or less matte, or frosted, appearance (with less or more transparency), go to the "**Gloss**" buttons > LClick and drag in the "**Amount**" button.

18. To adjust a threshold for stopping Blender's sampling of rays in the creation of gloss, LClick and drag in the "**Threshold**" button.

19. To set the number of rays to be sampled in the creation of gloss, adjust the "**Samples**" button. More samples will produce a smoother result but will render more slowly. (See **_Introduction_** for how to adjust buttons of this kind.)

T73. To make the selected material mirror-reflective:

1. Make sure that the object has at least one material applied to it (see **T61, p. 107** above).

2. In Object mode, select the object.

3. Go to the "Properties" window: > LClick the "Material" button: > In the large materials-list box at the top, LClick the name of the material that you want to make mirror-reflective.

4. (a) If you want to use a fast-rendering method for creating an approximation of mirror reflectivity, a method that simply creates an image of the objects surrounding the selected material and then applies that image, as a texture, onto that material, go to **T74, p. 120**, below, and apply an "EnvMap" texture. OR

(b) If you want to use a slower-rendering method, one that uses ray-tracing to produce accurate reflections, go to **5**.

5. To make your material "ray mirror-reflective":

6. Go to the "Mirror" panel > LClick the small box to the left of the word "Mirror" to put a check mark in it. (This turns on ray-mirror-reflectivity for the selected material.)

7. To adjust the degree of the material's mirror-reflectivity, LClick and drag in the "**Reflectivity**" button. 1.00 is full reflectivity, 0.00 is no reflectivity.

8. At any time, you can get an idea of how it will look if you look at the image in the "Preview" panel; but, of course, the best way to see what it looks like is to render it (F12). If the reflectivity cannot be

seen in the render, still in the "Properties" window, , LClick the "Render" button: > Go

to the "Shading" panel > Make sure that "Ray Tracing" is checked > Go back to > > "Mirror" panel.

9. Do you want to apply a color tint to the reflections, to change the material's "mirror" color?

       Yes: Go to **10**.

       No: Go to **11**.

10. To apply a color tint to the reflections, LClick in the color-swatch box (which may be just a white or light gray rectangle—it's under the "Reflectivity" button) to bring up the palette > follow the instructions in **T68, p. 111**. (Go to **11**.)

11. To make surface areas that face the camera (such as the center of a sphere) less reflective than those that are more oblique to the camera (such as the edges of a sphere)**,** adjust the "**Fresnel**" button (see ***Introduction*** for how to adjust buttons of this kind) .

12. To adjust the blending between reflective and non-reflective areas, LClick and drag in the "**Blend**" button.

13. To set the maximum number of surfaces off of which a single light ray will be reflected, adjust the "**Depth**" button. A setting of 4 or 5 is usually good. (See ***Introduction*** for how to adjust buttons of this kind.)

14. To set the distance, in Blender units, away from the camera at which ray-tracing will fade out (see next step), adjust the "**Max Dist**" button (see ***Introduction*** for how to adjust buttons of this kind).

15. Ray tracing will fade out in the distance (see above step) in one of two ways: it will fade to the material's color (usually best for indoor scenes), or it will fade to the sky color (usually best for outdoor scenes). To change this color, LClick the "**Fade To**" button > LClick your choice.

16. To make the reflection more grainy (to look more like a fogged mirror), go to the "**Gloss**" buttons > LClick and drag in the "**Amount**" button.

17. To adjust a threshold for stopping Blender's sampling of rays in this creation of gloss, LClick and drag in the "**Threshold**" button.

18. To set the number of rays to be sampled in the creation of gloss, adjust the "**Samples**" button. More samples will produce a smoother result but will render more slowly. (See ***Introduction*** for how to adjust buttons of this kind.)

19. If the little "Tangent Shading" box in the "Shading" panel is checked (thus creating something called a "tangent vector" on the material), Blender automatically will render a blurry reflection (as set in step **16** above) as a stretched "anisotropic" reflection (that is, as a reflection that has different properties associated with different directions). To set the amount that a reflection is stretched like this in the "tangent" direction: (Still in the "Mirror" panel) LClick and drag in the "**Anisotropic**" button.

T74. To add a *texture* to your selected material such that the texture can appear in the render:

Note that there are four kinds of textures that you can apply to your material:

> (a) ***procedural*** textures. These are textures that are mathematically generated and supplied by Blender.
> (b) ***EnvMap*** texture. This applies a simulated mirror reflective surface onto your material.
> (c) what I call ***"simple projected"*** image textures, where image files from your hard drive are "projected" onto the material.
> (d) the so-called ***"UV"*** image textures, where image files from your hard drive are carefully "mapped" onto the faces of your material.

Any of these kinds of textures can be applied to put color (or black and white) patterns or shapes onto the material's overall surface, to give pattern to the material's reflective qualities, to produce simulated "tactile" roughness (raised and lowered areas) in the patterns and shapes defined by the particular texture, or to produce other effects. (see **T77, step 8, p. 130** below.)

Note also that a texture must always be applied to an existing material (see **T61, p. 107 -T66, p. 109** above for how to apply a material to an object or to part of an object) and in that material's entirety. To apply a texture to only part of a material, you must select that part, apply a new material to that part (see **T66, p. 109** above), and then apply the texture to that new material.

1. Make sure that the object has at least one material applied to it (see **T61, T62, p. 107** above).

2. In Object mode, select the object.

3. Go to the "Properties" window: [icon] > LClick the "Material" button: [icon] . In the large materials-list box at the top, LClick the name of the material that you want to add a texture to.

4. Still in the "Properties" window: [icon] > LClick the "Texture" button: [icon] > Make sure that the "Show Material Textures" button at upper left (in the group of 3 buttons) is enabled (bright):

5. At the top of the window: look at the "texture channel stack"; let's say it looks like this (or there may be no texture names in it at all):

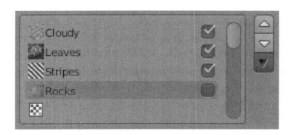

        This stack governs which textures appear in the render. In order to make a texture visible on your rendered material (the stack lists all textures on your selected *material*; the *object* that the material is on may have textures that do not appear in the stack), you must make sure that it appears in this stack of texture channels, and it must be checked to the right, and it must not be occluded by another texture. Also, the transparency/opacity controls for textures are in the "Influence" panel; for instance, one such control is one of the "Diffuse" buttons: the "color" button--see below. A lower texture in the stack will cover a higher one (unless the lower one is a "Normal" type texture—see **T77, step 8(m), p. 131** below). Here, four textures are in the stack, a "procedural" texture called "Cloudy", a simple image texture called "Leaves," a procedural texture of type *wood*, called "Stripes," and a simple image texture called "Rocks". The first (the top) texture, "Cloudy", will be the first texture layer covering your material. The second texture, "Leaves" will cover the first texture, so that the first texture will not appear in the render. The third Texture, "Stripes", will cover the second texture—but because "Stripes" is a procedural texture of type *wood*, and the *wood* procedural texture has transparent gaps in its pattern, you will be able to see parts of the "Leaves" layer through the "Stripes" layer in the render. The fourth texture, "Rocks", is not checked, so will be invisible (100% transparent) in the render. If you want to work on a texture, you can select it by LClicking its name in the stack.

You can move a texture up or down in the stack by LClicking its name and using these buttons to the

right of the stacks: .

6. Is the stack empty, with no textures in it at all?

      Yes: Go to **8**.

      No: Go to **7**.

7. LClick In the highest empty channel in the stack:

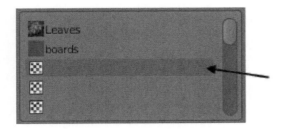

8. Do you want to apply a texture that's already existing somewhere in your scene to the material*?

> Yes: Go to **9**.

> No: Go to **11**.

(*Note: It is not recommended that you use an existing environment map texture, because if you use an existing environment map texture that is applied to another object, it will produce reflections from the viewpoint of that other object.)

9. LClick the little button on the left end of the row of buttons beneath the textures stack:

10. LClick the name of the existing texture that you want to apply to the material. (a) If the texture is a UV image texture, go to **30**. (b) If the texture is a procedural texture or is a simple projected image, you have applied your texture. Stop. You are finished—to modify this texture, see **T77, p. 128**.

11. LClick the "New" button. When you add this new texture, Blender names it for you.

12. Choose a texture type:

In the "Properties" window: [icon] > LClick the "Texture" button: [icon] > LClick the "Type" button:

(a) If you want your new texture to be a **procedural** texture, LClick the name of the procedural texture type that you want to use (all texture types in the drop down list are procedural except for "Image or Movie" and "Environment Map"). Stop. You have added a procedural texture to your material. To modify this texture, see **T77, p. 128**.

(b) If you want your new texture to be an **Environment Map** texture, simulated mirror-reflectivity done without ray tracing, LClick "Environment Map". Go to **13**.

(c) If you want your new texture to be a **simple projected image** texture, LClick "Image or Movie". Go to step **14**.

(d) If you want your new texture to be a **UV image** texture, that is, if you want to carefully "map" an image from your hard drive onto the faces of your material, LClick "image or Movie". Go to **22**.

13. Environment Map: After you LClicked "Environment Map", two new panels (with buttons that control the Environment Map texture) will appear: "Environment Map" and "Environment Map Sampling". Go to the "Environment Map" panel > Make sure that "Static" or "Animated" is enabled > LClick the "Viewpoint Object" button > LClick the name of the object that has the material applied to it to which you are applying the Environment Map texture > Go to the "Mapping" panel > LClick the "Coordinates" button > LClick "Reflection." Stop. You have added an Environment Map texture to your material. (To modify this texture, see **T77, p. 128**).

14. Go to the "Image" panel .

15. In creating your new texture, do you want to use an image that you've already applied as a texture to some material on your object?

        Yes: Go to **16**.

        No: Go to **17**.

16. LClick the button to the far left:

LClick the name of the image that you want to use. Stop. You have added a simple projected image texture to your material. (To modify this texture, see **T77, p. 128**).

17. To use an image on your hard drive: LClick the "Open" button:

18. To have your image files shown as thumbnails, LClick this button at upper left:  .

19. Navigate to the image that you want to use. If you want to go up the directory structure, press the button at upper left with the crooked arrow on it: , or LClick the same kind of arrow, with two

dots: OR , near the top of the list.

20. If you want to go down the directory structure, LClick on a name in the list.

21. LClick the file you want to use to select it > LClick "Open Image" at upper right.

Stop. You've added a simple projected image texture to your material. (To modify this texture, see **T77, p. 128**).

22. Go to the "Image" panel.

23. In creating your new UV Image texture, do you want to use an image that you've already applied as a texture to some material in your scene?

Yes: Go to **24**.

No: Go to **25**.

24. LClick the button to the far left:

LClick the name of the image that you want to use. Go to **30**.

25. To use an image on your hard drive: LClick the "Open" button:

26. To have your image files shown as thumbnails, LClick this button at upper left: .

27. Navigate to the image that you want to use. You should use a square image whose dimensions conform to a power of 2; for instance: 512 (= 2^9) x 512, 1024 (= 2^{10}) x1024, 2048 (= 2^{11}) x 2048; If you want to go up the directory structure, press the button at upper left with the crooked arrow on it:

, or LClick the same kind of arrow, with two dots: OR , near the top of the list.

28. If you want to go down the directory structure, LClick on a name in the list.

29. (a) LClick the file you want to use to select it > LClick "Open Image" at upper right.

OR

(b) Double LClick the file you want to use.

30. Go to the "Mapping" panel (In the "Properties" window: 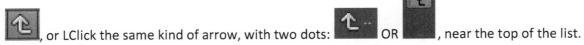 > Make sure that the "Texture"

button is enabled: > "Mapping" panel).

31. LClick the "Coordinate" button > LClick "UV" > LClick the "Projection" button > LClick "Flat".

32. A UV image texture is a texture that is carefully "mapped" onto the faces of your material. For the texture to be mapped onto the material, there must, of course, be a *map*. So when we are dealing with a UV image texture, we are dealing with three things: (a) the "**UV image texture**" (the image used as a texture), which you have just created, (b) what I call a "**UV map-framework**", which is a split and flattened version of the mesh—just vertices, edges and transparent faces, and (c) the union of texture and map-framework, which I'll call the "**UV map**" itself. (This 2D map's two axes are U and V – not X and

Y, because X and Y are used in Blender's 3D space.)

UV image texture

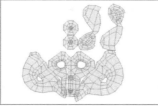
UV map-framework

UV map

You have just created the UV image texture. Now you have to pair it with a UV map-framework in the render.

33. Have you already applied **one and only one** UV map-framework to this same material?*

      Yes: go to **34**.

      No: Go to **35**.

(* To see a list of the selected material's UV map-frameworks, still in the "Properties" window:

 > LClick the "Object Data" button: [icon] > Go to the "UV Maps" panel (I would've named it the "UV Map-Frameworks" panel) > Check the list > To go back to the Texture panels: LClick the

"Texture" button: [icon] .)

34. If the UV image texture is in the texture stack, checked, etc. (see **step 5**) so that it is visible in the render, Blender will pair the UV image texture with that UV map-framework in the render. Are you satisfied to use that UV map-framework with your UV image texture?

      Yes: Stop. You have finished creating your UV map (to modify it, see **T77, p. 128**).

      No: You will have to create a new UV map-framework for your material, a UV map-framework that you want to pair with your UV image texture in order to create the UV map. Go to **39**.

35. Have you already applied **more than one** UV map-framework to this same material?

      Yes: Go to **36**.

      No: Go to **38**.

36. Go to the "Properties" window: [icon] > LClick the "Object Data" button: [icon] > Go to the "UV Maps" panel > Go to the name of the UV map-framework that you want to use, in the list of UV map-frameworks > Find the line whose camera icon (at the right end) is enabled (brightened). The name on this line is the name of the UV map-framework that will be paired with the UV image texture when it is visible in the render. Are you satisfied to use that UV map-framework with your UV image texture?

      Yes: Stop. You have finished creating your UV map (to modify it, see **T77, p. 128**);

      No: Go to **37**.

37. Do you wish to use any of the other UV map-frameworks listed there?

      Yes: Look at the line that the name of that UV map-framework is on and LClick the camera icon at the far right end of that line. Stop. You've created your UV map (to modify it, see **T77, p. 128**).

No: You will have to create a new UV map-framework for your material, a UV map-framework that you want to pair with your UV image texture. Go to **39**.

38. If you have not yet applied even one UV map-framework to your material, you have to create a UV map-framework for your material, a UV map-framework that you want to pair with your UV image texture in order to create your UV map. Go to **39**.

39. To create a UV map-framework to be paired with your UV image texture:

A *UV map-framework* is (as I am defining it here) a flattened and spread-out *wireframe image* of your material's surface that will be aligned over the *UV image (texture)* to form a *UV map*. You can unwrap a very complex object, for instance, a character, such that a set of UV mapping "islands" will be created in the map; and you can then create a complex UV image for it such that the whole object will be mapped to this single image.

40. Will this be a first UV map-framework for your material?

Yes: Go to **42**.

No: Go to **41**.

41. Go to the "Properties" window:  > LClick the "Object Data" button: > Go to the

"UV Maps" panel > LClick the "Add UV Map" button: ⊞ .

42. To unwrap your material's mesh to create a UV map-framework: first, create seams: If your material is on a simple cube, cylinder or sphere, you can create a map without specifying seams. For a more complex shape, you should specify seams. **Do you want to specify where seams should be** on your material so that when the UV map-framework of the selected material is created and spread out flat, and then laid on top of the UV image, there will be minimal distortion of the texture on the rendered material?

Yes: Go to **43**.

No: Go to **45**.

43. In the 3D View window header, in Edit mode: LClick the edge select button:

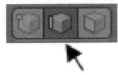

In the 3D View window header, still in Edit mode: If there are any unwanted seams already defined on the material, select these seams (RClick, or SHIFT + RClick) > press CTRL + E > "Clear Seam". (This operation will not destroy the previously-created UV map-framework.) Deselect all edges that you don't want to be seams in the new map-framework. Then make sure that all the edges that you want to make into seams are selected (RClick; SHIFT+RClick, OR select edge loops [see **T22, step 101, p. 27**]). (It's best to put the seams in places that will be more or less hidden from view in the render.)

44. With the mouse pointer in the 3D View window, (a) press CTRL+E > LClick "Mark Seam"; OR (b) in the 3D View header, LClick "Mesh" > Hover over "Edges" > LClick "Mark Seam"; OR (c) Go to the Tool Shelf (see **T9, p. 9**) > Go to the "Mesh Tools" panel > Go to the "UV Mapping" buttons > LClick "Mark Seam". The seams will appear orange. (To remove a seam: do (a), (b) or (c) above, but LClick "Clear Seam" instead of "Mark Seam.") Go to **46**.

45. *In Edit mode*, in the 3D View window, make sure that *all (and only)* the faces of the material you want to apply the UV texture to are selected. (a) Press U > LClick "Cube Projection", "Cylinder Projection", or "Sphere Projection"; OR (b) in the 3D View header, LClick "Mesh" > hover over "UV Unwrap. . ." > LClick "Cube Projection", "Cylinder Projection", or "Sphere Projection"; OR (c) Go to the Tool Shelf (see **T9, p. 9**) > Go to the "Mesh Tools" panel > Go to the "UV Mapping" buttons > LClick "Unwrap" > LClick "Cube Projection", "Cylinder Projection", or "Sphere Projection".
Stop. You have finished creating your UV map (to modify it, see **T77, p. 128**);

46. In Edit mode, in the 3D View window, make sure that *all (and only)* the faces of the material you want to apply the UV texture to are selected. (a) Press U > LClick "Unwrap"; OR (b) in the 3D View header, LClick "Mesh" > hover over "UV Unwrap. . ." > LClick "Unwrap"; OR (c) Go to the Tool Shelf (see **T9, p. 9**) > Go to the "Mesh Tools" panel > Go to the "UV Mapping" buttons > LClick "Unwrap" > LClick "Unwrap".

47. If this is your first UV map-framework for this material, Blender will automatically give your new UV map-framework a unique name. (To change it, see **T77, step 2, p. 129**.) (In general, to modify your UV image texture, see **T77, p. 128**.)

T75. To see or render your textured material:

1. To have a texture, including a UV image texture, appear in the render, in the "Properties" window: > LClick the "Texture" button: > you must make sure that the texture appears in this stack of texture channels, and it must be checked to the right, and it must not be occluded by another texture (a lower texture in the stack will cover a higher one—unless the lower one is a "Normal" type texture— see **T77, step 8(m), p. 131**). Also, its transparency/opacity control (in the "Influence" panel; for instance: the "Diffuse" buttons > the "color" button--see below) cannot be set to full transparency.

2. To have a UV map-framework appear in the render, paired with a UV image texture (made visible in the render in accord with step **1** above) which the UV map-framework maps to the material: Go to the

"Properties" window: > LClick the "Object Data" button: > Go to the "UV Maps" panel > In the list of UV map-frameworks, go to the line that the name of the UV map-framework that you want to appear in the render is on > Make sure that the camera icon at the right end of the line is enabled (brightened).

3. To have a particular UV image texture that's applied to the object appear in the UV/Image Editor window so that you can edit a UV map: Go to the UV/Image Editing window > LClick the "Browse Image to be linked" button:

LClick the name of the image file that you want to appear in the UV/Image Editor window. (It can be a different image than the one that appears in the render.) If the UV image disappears from the UV/Image

Editor window, try selecting a face on the object in 3D View.

4. To have a particular one of the UV map-frameworks that you've applied to the material appear in the UV/Image Editor window so that you can edit a UV map: Make sure the mesh in the 3D View window is selected > Go to the UV/Image Editor window's header > LClick the "Active UV Texture" button:

LClick the name of the UV map-framework that you want to map the UV image texture in the UV/Image Editing window. (It can be a different UV map-framework than the one that maps the UV image texture in the render.)

5. To have the mapped UV image texture, as specified in the UV/Image Editor, appear in the 3D View window: Make sure that the mapped UV image texture appears in the UV/Image Editing window (see step **3**) > Go to the 3D View window's header > LClick the Viewport Shading button > LClick "Textured". (See **T14, p. 12**.) *Note that what appears in the 3D View window matches what appears in the UV/Image Editor, not necessarily what appears in the render.*

6. To get a *rough* idea of what your textured material looks like: In the "Properties" window: > LClick the "Texture" button: ▨ > LClick the texture's name in the texture stack at the top > Go to the "Preview" panel > Enable the "Texture" button. To see, roughly, what your material looks like with its textures applied, still in the "Preview" panel, LClick the "Material" button.

T76. To set up an existing UV map (existing UV image texture + existing UV map-framework [see T74, step 32, p. 124 for definitions of these terms]) in the UV/Image Editor window, with the 3D View showing in another window, so that you can edit the UV map:

1. Go to the "Info" window's header (the window header with ⊙ to the left) > LClick the "Choose Screen lay out" button: ▦ > LClick "UV Editing". (Alternatively, use the directions in **T1 and T2, p. 7** to create a layout where a UV/Image Editor window is side-by-side with a 3D View window.)

2. Put the UV image texture that you want to use into the UV/Image Editor window (see **T75, step 3, p. 127**) and put the UV map-framework that you want to use into the UV/Image Editor window (see **T75, step 4, p. 128**).

3. To see the UV map-framework in the UV/Image Editor window: In Edit mode, in the 3D View window, select the faces of the material—only what's selected in the 3D View window will appear in the UV/Image Editor window.

T77. To change the properties of a material's texture [including: *changing* the name of new textures, of new UV map-frameworks, etc.; and including Texture

Painting]:

1. To re-name a texture: To change the name of a texture: Go to the "Properties" window: >

LClick the "Texture" button:  > In the textures stack, LClick the name of the texture, the name you want to change > Go to the row or buttons right below the texture stack > LClick on the field with the existing name in it:

Type in the name you want the texture to have > Press ENTER.

2. To re-name a UV map-framework: Go to the "Properties" window: > LClick the "Object

Data" button: > Go to the "UV Maps" panel > In the list of UV map-frameworks, LClick the name of the UV map-framework, the name that you want to change > LClick the "Name" box > Type in the name you want the UV map-framework to have > Press ENTER.

3. (Always keep in mind that if your texture datablock [see ***Introduction***] is applied to more than one material, if you change the texture on one material, it will change on the other(s) as well [except that, where two materials share a procedural texture, changes in the "Influence" and "mapping" panels for the texture of one of the materials will not change the texture of the other].)

4. To change a texture in some way: In Object mode, select the object to which is applied the material to which the texture is applied.

5. Go to the "Properties" window: > LClick the "Material" button: . In the large materials-list box at the top, LClick the name of the material to which the texture is applied that you want to change.

6. Still in the "Properties" window: > LClick the "Texture" button: > Make sure that the "Show Material Textures" button at upper left (in the group of 3 buttons) is enabled (bright):

.

7. At the top of the window: look at the "texture channel stack"; let's say it looks like this:

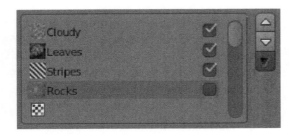

LClick the name of the texture you want to change, to highlight it.

8. To change which property or properties of the *material* that you want to apply the texture's pattern (or shapes) to, and/or to adjust the intensity of the effect :

(a) Go to the "Properties" window:  > LClick the "Texture" button: > Go to the "Influence" panel.

(b) You can activate one or any number of these buttons at the same time.

Applying a texture to a material's *color* properties and/or adjusting the intensity of the effect:

(c) To specify that the material's so-called "diffuse" color (that is, its *substance* color, the *primary* or *main* color), is to be covered up by the colors and shapes of the texture (this is the default setting for new textures), go to the "**Diffuse**" buttons > Make sure that there is a check mark in the little box next to the "**Color**" button. LClick and drag in the "Color" button to make the texture's covering-layer more transparent or less transparent—this works for procedural, simple projected image, UV image and environment map textures.

(d) To specify that the material's "specular" color (see **T69, p. 114, and T70, step 11, p. 115** above) is to be changed to match the chosen texture, go to the "**Specular**" buttons > Make sure that there is a check mark in the little box next to the "**Color**" button. LClick and drag in the "Color" button to increase or decrease the intensity of the texturing.

(e) To specify the degree to which the material's "specular" reflectivity (see **T69, p. 114, and T70, step 11, p. 115**) is to be patterned in accord with the chosen texture, go to the "**Specular**" buttons > Make sure that there is a check mark in the little box next to the "**Intensity**" button. LClick and drag in the "Intensity" button to increase or decrease the intensity of the texturing.

(f) To specify that the texture will be superimposed on any reflectivity that the material may have, go to the "**Shading**" buttons > Make sure that there is a check mark in the little box next to the "**Mirror**" button. LClick and drag in the "Mirror" button to increase or decrease the effect.

(g) To specify that the material's ability to receive ambient light is to be patterned across the surface in accord with the pattern of the chosen texture, go to the "**Shading**" buttons. Make sure that there is a check mark in the little box next to the "**Ambient**" button. LClick and drag in the "Ambient" button to increase or decrease the effect.

(h) To specify that the amount of the material's specular hardness is to be patterned in accord with the pattern of the chosen texture, go to the "**Specular**" buttons. Make sure that there is a check mark in the little box next to the "**Hardness**" button. LClick and drag in the "Hardness" button to adjust the hardness.

(i) To specify that the degree of transparency of the material across its surface is to be patterned in accord with the pattern of the chosen texture, go to the "**Diffuse**" buttons. Make sure that there is a check mark in the little box next to the "**Alpha**" button. LClick and drag in the "Alpha" button to increase or decrease the effect.

(j) To specify that the amount of light emitted by the material across its surface is to be patterned in accord with the pattern of the chosen texture, go to the "**Shading**" buttons. Make sure that there is a check mark in the little box next to the "**Emit**" button. LClick and drag in the "Emit" button to increase or decrease the effect.

(k) To specify that the amount of translucency of the material across its surface is to be patterned in accord with the pattern of the chosen texture, go to the "**Diffuse**" buttons. Make sure that there is a check mark in the little box next to the "**Translucency**" button. LClick and drag in the "Translucency" button to increase or decrease the effect.

(l) To specify that the color of any raytraced mirror reflections on the material is to be affected across the surface in accord with the pattern of the chosen texture, go to the "**Shading**" buttons > Make sure that there is a check mark in the small box to the left of the "**Ray Mirror**" button > LClick and drag in the "Ray Mirror" button to increase or decrease the intensity of the effect.

Applying a texture to a material's simulated or real *sculptural* properties and/or adjusting the intensity of the effect :

(m) Still in the "Properties" window: 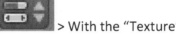 > With the "Texture" button still enabled:

> Go to the "Influence" panel > To specify that the material will appear to take on simulated raised and lowered areas in accord with the patterns or shapes of the chosen texture, go to the "**Geometry**" buttons > Make sure that there is a check mark in the little box next to the "**Normal**" button. To increase or decrease the intensity of the texturing, go to the "Colors" panel and LClick and drag in the "Contrast" button. (In Blender-speak, since adding ridges and valleys would change the direction to which some number of the surface's faces are oriented, it is said that the "Normal" button appears to change these faces' "normals"—where a face's "normal" is a line perpendicular to the face.)

(n) To specify that the actual displacement of vertices across the material's surface—in the render, but not in the 3D View window—is to be patterned in accord with the pattern of the chosen texture, go to the "**Geometry**" buttons. LClick the little box next to the "**Displace**" button. LClick and drag in the "Displace" button to increase or decrease the effect.

9.

If the texture you want to modify is a **procedural texture**, go to **10**;

if it is an **Environmental Map texture**, go to **23**;

if it is a **simple projected image texture**, go to **24**.

if it is a **UV Image texture**, go to **60**.

10. Procedural textures: In most cases, after you have LClicked the name of a procedural texture, as you did in **T74, step 12(a), p. 122**, a new panel (with buttons that control that particular texture) having the name of the chosen texture will appear. Experiment with these buttons to adjust your texture.

11. Note that if, in, **step 8 (c)-(n)** above, in this section, you LClicked one of the buttons that apply the texture to color—for instance, if you checked the little box next to "Color" at **step 8 (c)**—and if the texture you chose in **T74, step 12(a), p. 122** is a "colorless" texture (that is, if it is a procedural texture other than "Magic"), the intense parts of the texture will appear purple.

12. This color can be changed in two ways:

METHOD 1:

13. With the texture selected in the texture stack: go to the "Influence" panel > LClick the color swatch under the words "RGB to Intensity" > Set the color using the methods described in **T68, step 5, p. 111**.

METHOD 2:

14. With the texture selected in the texture stack: change the color using the texture "ramp" (note that if you set the color using **METHOD 1** and if you then enable the ramp, following the directions below, the ramp-generated color will replace the color that you set in **METHOD 1**):

To change the procedural texture's color using the texture's "ramp":

In the "Properties" window: ▭ > Make sure that the "Texture" button is enabled: ▦ .

15. With the texture selected in the texture stack, go to the "Colors" panel > LClick the little square next to "Ramp".

16. The "ramp" that appears *represents* on the left the least intense part of the procedural texture, through a gradual transition to, on the right, the most intense part of the texture. The ramp opens with opaque white on the right, and completely *transparent* black on the left, with gradations from one to the other across the ramp. Against the far right edge is a vertical line that marks the position on the ramp of the pure white, and against the far left edge is a vertical line that marks the position on the ramp of the pure (transparent) black. When you open the ramp, the texture you just applied to the material will take on the coloring of the ramp: the transparent areas will gradually transition into white pattern elements.

17. To add a color to the center of the ramp, LClick the "Add" button. The new color will be the same as the color that is at the center of the ramp, and will transition gradually into the colors to left and right (so, there will not yet be any color change to the ramp). You will be able to change all of these colors, and their positions on the ramp (see below).

18. To select any color on the ramp, LClick the vertical line that marks its position on the ramp; OR: Go to this button above the ramp:

Using this button, you can select a color on the ramp this way: keeping in mind that the colors are numbered left to right across the ramp, starting with 0, choose the number of the color you want to select. (See **_Introduction_** for how to adjust buttons of this kind.)

19. Note that the selected color's vertical line will be dashed. The currently selected color will appear in the color swatch below the ramp.

20. To change the position of a color on the ramp (thus changing its position in the transition, on your actual material, from the least to most intense parts of the texture), LClick & hold on the vertical line that marks the color's position and drag.

21. To change a color on the ramp, select the color on the ramp (see **18** above) and LClick the color swatch under the ramp > Choose your color using to the methods described in **T68, step 5, p. 111**, above.

22. To change the transparency of a texture's color using the ramp: select the color on the ramp (see **step 18**) > LClick the color swatch under the ramp > LClick and drag in the "A" button ("A" stands for "Alpha" which means "transparency"). 1 is full opacity, zero is full transparency.

END OF METHODS

Suppose that the material shares a texture with another material (that is, suppose that it uses the same texture datablock [see **_Introduction_**] as another material): if you used **METHOD 1** above: **METHOD 1** will *not* change the other material's procedural texture's color; but if you used **METHOD 2**, then a change in one *will* produce a similar change in the other. (Changes in the "Colors" panel will change the texture datablock, but changes in the "Influence" panel will not.) Go to **32**.

23. Changing an Environment Map Texture: (If this texture doesn't appear in the render, make sure that, with the texture selected in the texture stack, the little square next to "Ramp" in the "Colors" panel is unchecked.) Experiment with the buttons in the "Environment Map" and the "Environment Map Sampling" panels to adjust your texture. (Recall [see **8 (c)**] that you can make the "reflections" more or less visible by adjusting a button in the "Influence" panel: "Diffuse" buttons > the "Color" button.) Go to step **30**.

24. Changing a simple projected image texture: (If this texture doesn't appear in the render, make sure that, with the texture selected in the texture stack, the little square next to "Ramp" in the "Colors" panel is unchecked.) You can specify that the image will be "projected" onto the material much like a real projected image would, or you can specify that it be "projected" such that it will wrap around the object in different ways. Do you want to specify how the image will be "projected" onto the object?

> Yes: Go to **25**.

> No: Go to **30**.

25. "Projecting" the image texture onto the material in different ways: Go to the "Mapping" panel > LClick the "Projection" button.

26. If you want to make the projected image land on the object much like a real-world projected image (an image being projected from a slide projector, for instance) will land on a flat or curved object, LClick "**Flat**".

27. If you want to make the projected image land on the object as if it splits into six duplicate images with each image landing on the object as if landing on all six sides of a cube (which the object might be), LClick "**Cube**".

28. If you want to make the top edge and the bottom edge of the projected image each shrink to a point while wrapping the rest of the texture around the object, with left and right edges joining behind the back of the object (good for putting the texture onto a sphere), LClick "**Sphere**".

29. If you want to make the projected image wrap around the object's sides with left and right edges joining in back (good for projecting a texture onto a tube), LClick "**Tube**".

30. In this section, **T77, p. 128, steps 8 (c)-(n)**, did you LClick at least one of the buttons that apply the texture to *color*—for instance, you might have LClicked (or left active) one of the "Color" buttons— and do you want to change the overall color cast of that texture?

> Yes: Go to **31**.
> No: Go to **32**.

31. **To change the overall coloring of your *image* or *environment map* texture [if the material uses the same image texture as another material, changing one changes both]:** Go to the "Colors" panel > Adjust the "R", "G", "B", "Brightness", "Contrast", and "Saturation" buttons. (See ***Introduction*** for how to adjust buttons of this kind.)

32. Do you want to adjust the orientation or position or size of your texture?

> Yes: Go to **33**.
> No: Stop. You are finished.

33. Make sure that the texture whose positioning you want to change is selected in the texture stack (see steps **4-7** above for how to do this).

34. Do you want to adjust either your texture's orientation or its position?

> Yes: Go to **35**.
> No: To change your texture's size, go to **54**.

35. **To change your texture's orientation or position:**

36. Just as an object does, a texture carries with it its own coordinate system. A procedural texture (any of the textures mathematically generated by Blender—see **10** above) is 3D, having X, Y and Z axes; a simple, projected image texture (not a "UV" image texture) has only X and Y axes. When a texture is applied to a material, the texture's own axes must be aligned with the axes of some already-existing coordinate system, or to other "vectors" (directed lines) in the scene. When you apply a texture to an object's material, Blender, by default, will align the texture's X axis with the object's **local X** axis, the texture's Y axis with the object's **local Y** axis, and the texture's Z axis (if it has one) with the object's **local Z** axis (see **T24, p. 32** above). Any alignment where the axes of the texture are aligned with the **local** axes of the object (& note that X need not be aligned with X, Y with Y, nor Z with Z) is called a "Generated" alignment (see **41** below), and this alignment can be changed.

37. So, your selected texture's axes are necessarily aligned to the axes of some other coordinate system, or to some existing vector, in your scene. You can *change* your texture's position or rotation by aligning it to a *different* coordinate system, or vector (see **METHOD 1** below), or by keeping it aligned with the same coordinate system or vector, but changing which axes are aligned with which (for instance, instead of aligning the texture's X axis with the object's local X axis, you might align the texture's X axis with the object's local Z axis—see **METHOD 2** below). You can also use SHIFT + T (**METHOD 3**) or the Offset buttons (**METHOD 4**). *These methods can be used together* to align a single texture:

METHOD 1:

38. To change which coordinate system or vector you want to align your texture's axes to: Go to the

"Mapping" panel (In the "Properties" window: > Make sure that the "Texture" button is

enabled: > Make sure that the "Show Material Textures" button at upper left (in the group of 3 buttons) is enabled (bright):

> "Mapping" panel).

39. To align the coordinates of a texture that is on Object A with Object B's coordinates:

    a. For instance, Object B might be an "empty" named "MyEmpty". (Let's say you created it this way: In Object mode: SHIFT + A > LClick "Empty"—Blender gave it the name "Empty.001" but you re-named it MyEmpty"—see **T21, step 1, p. 19** for how to change an object's name.)

    b. Select the texture on Object A that you want to align (see **4-7**).

    c. In the "Mapping" panel > LClick the "Coordinates" button > LClick "**Object**".

    d. LClick the "Object" button > LClick "MyEmpty" .

    e. You can adjust the positioning, rotation of your texture by positioning, rotating the empty in Object mode. (You can also scale the texture by scaling the empty.)

40. **OR:** You can "project" a tiled version of the texture, where one of the tiles is centered on the global coordinates, 0,0,0. To align the texture this way, in the "Mapping" panel > LClick the "Coordinates" button > LClick "**Global**".

41. **OR:** To aim the projected texture, as if it is projected from a place in space on the object's local positive Y axis, toward the origin (0,0,0) of the object's local coordinate system, LClick "**Generated**".

42. **OR:** To have the texture "projected" onto the object (and perhaps wrapping around it) that it's assigned to, from the camera position, first press numpad 0 to go into Camera view > press SPACEBAR >

Type "Sticky" > LClick "Add Sticky" > "Properties" window: > Make sure that the "Texture"

button is enabled: ![checkerboard icon] > "Mapping" panel > LClick "Coordinates" button > LClick "**Sticky**".

43. **OR:** To have the texture "projected" onto the object (and perhaps wrapping around it) that it's assigned to, from the camera position such that if the object that the texture's assigned to is moved across the camera's field (in successive renderings) the surface will pick up different parts of the tiled whole: still in the "Mapping" panel > LClick "Coordinates" button > LClick "**Window**".

44. **OR:** To direct the projected texture [somehow] along axes defined by the surface's normal vectors (lines perpendicular to the planes): still in "Mapping" panel > LClick "Coordinates" button > LClick "**Normal**".

45. **OR:** To direct the projected texture [somehow] along axes defined by the "reflection vector": still in the "Mapping" panel > LClick "Coordinates" button > LClick "**Reflection**".

METHOD 2:

46. To reposition your texture's axes while keeping it aligned to the same coordinate system: If your texture's axes are aligned with the axes of some other coordinate system—which I'll call a *reference system*—in your scene (that is, if **Global** or **Generated** is set [see **40** and **41** above]), you can reposition each of the texture's axes onto a different axis of the reference system. For instance, an image texture might be aligned with the global coordinate system, that is, the global coordinate system will be the texture's *reference* system. Furthermore, the texture's X axis might be aligned with the global X axis and its Y axis might be aligned with the global Y axis. You can re-position your texture by changing which of the texture's axes are aligned with which of the reference system's axes. To do this:

47. Go to the "Mapping" panel > Look at the three buttons under the "Projection" button:

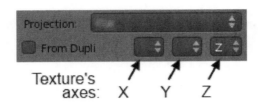

48. Specify which of the texture's axes will be aligned with which of the reference system's axes:

for instance, suppose that you LClick the first, X, button and then LClick "Y" in the menu that pops up; then LClick the second, Y, button, then LClick "X" in the menu. Suppose also that in this example, the Reference system is the Gobal coordinate system (that is, let's suppose that at **METHOD 1, step 40** above, you LClicked "Global," before applying this method). Here, then, the texture's X axis is now aligned with the Global system's Y axis, the texture's Y axis is aligned with the Global system's X axis, and the texture's Z axis is (by default) aligned with the Global system's Z axis.

METHOD 3—for procedural and simple projected image textures, when, in the "Properties" window:

button says "Generated":

49. With the mouse pointer in the 3D view window, press SHIFT + T > Move the texture by moving the "texture space" (a line-drawing of a box that you can move around) > LClick to fix the position > To move it again, press SHIFT + T again. To turn off the display of the texture space: still in the "Properties" window > [icon] > LClick the "Object" button: [icon] > Go to the "Display" panel > LClick the box next to "Texture Space" in order to uncheck it. To continue with the steps below, LClick the "Texture"

button:  .

METHOD 4:

50. Every texture has its own coordinate system. To move the texture (any texture except for UV textures (see **T74, step 12(d), p. 122**)) along its X, Y or Z axis:

51. Go to the "Mapping" panel (In the "Properties" window: [icon] > Make sure that the "Texture"

button is enabled: [icon] > "Mapping" panel).

52. Adjust the three "Offset" buttons. (See ***Introduction*** for how to adjust buttons of this kind.)

END OF METHODS

53. Go to **54**.

54. To adjust the size of a texture: To adjust the size of a texture that has been applied to an object's material: Select the texture whose size you want to change (see **4-7** above for how to select the texture; for another method of scaling the texture, see **39e**).

METHOD 1:

55. To make the texture smaller or larger in the texture's X, Y or Z direction:

56. Go to the "Mapping" panel (In the "Properties" window: > Make sure that the "Texture" button is enabled: > "Mapping" panel).

57. Adjust the three "Size" buttons. (See ***Introduction*** for how to adjust buttons of this kind.)

METHOD 2—this method is for procedural textures, when, in the "Properties" window

with the "Texture" button **enabled: in the "Mapping" panel, the "Coordinates" button says "Generated":**

58. With the mouse pointer in the 3D view window, Press SHIFT + T > Press S > Scale the texture by turning on and scaling the "texture space" > LClick to fix the size> To scale it again, press SHIFT + T >

Press S again. To turn off the display of the texture space, still in the "Properties" window >

> LClick the "Object" button: > Go to the "Display" panel > LClick the box next to "Texture Space"

in order to uncheck it. To go back to the texture controls, LClick the "Texture" button: .

END OF METHODS

59. Stop. You are finished.

60. To modify a UV image texture:

61. Suppose that you have created one or more UV image textures and one or more different UV map-frameworks for your material (see **T74, step 32, p. 124**): At any time, you can put any one of these textures together with any one of these map-frameworks to produce a map to texture your material in the ***render***. See **T75, p. 127, steps 1 & 2** for how to do this.

62. Suppose that you have created one or more UV image textures and one or more different UV map-frameworks for your material (see **T74, step 32, p. 124**): At any time, you can put any one of these textures together with any one of these map-frameworks to produce a map to show in the ***UV/Image Editor window*** (the window where you edit the map). See **T75, p. 127, steps 3 & 4** for how to do this.

63. If you have set up your UV map in the UV/Image Editor window (see **T76, p. 128**), and if you are working with a symmetrical model and have applied the seams in a symmetrical way, and want to straighten out a lopsided UV map of the model: in the UV/Image Editor window, select the edges that constitute the lopsided vertical median line > press S > X > 0 (to scale to zero)—this should straighten the center vertical line; press P (to pin – so that this line will stay put when the same mesh is unwrapped again); put your mouse pointer in the 3D View window; press U; LClick "Unwrap". This should make the image symmetrical.

64. Do you want to adjust the way that the image is being mapped onto the faces of the material?

Yes: Put the image into a UV layout as directed in step **65**.

No: Go to **114**.

65. To adjust the mapping of any UV image texture to the material, using your UV map: Set up your UV map in the UV/Image Editor window (see **T76, p. 128**). (Check to see if you can select parts of the map

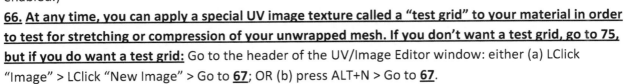

by RClicking. If you cannot select these parts, make sure the "Image Paint" button is not enabled.)

66. At any time, you can apply a special UV image texture called a "test grid" to your material in order to test for stretching or compression of your unwrapped mesh. If you don't want a test grid, go to 75, but if you do want a test grid: Go to the header of the UV/Image Editor window: either (a) LClick "Image" > LClick "New Image" > Go to **67**; OR (b) press ALT+N > Go to **67**.

67. LClick the name to the right of "Name" and type a name for your grid image (for instance, type *mygrid*) > LClick out of the "Name" field.

68. LClick the little square next to "UV Test Grid" to put a check mark into it.

69. LClick "OK"

70. If the grid did not appear in the UV/Image Editor window when you LClicked "OK" in step **69**: in the UV/Image Editor window header, LClick the "Browse Image" button:

Then LClick the grid name (in this example, *mygrid*). You've not yet applied the grid image to your material—it will not yet appear *in the render* (you've got to put it into the stack for that [see **T70, p. 114**]). But since whatever's in the UV map will appear in the 3D View window (so long as you are in Edit mode and so long as you LClicked the Viewport Shading button (see ***Introduction*** for instructions on how to locate this button) and LClicked "Textured" (see **T14, step 1, p. 12**)), you can adjust the mapping of the grid to the faces of your material.

71. Now the UV layout has "mapped" the checkerboard pattern to each of the material's faces. Note that only what's selected in the 3D View window will appear in the UV map.

72. If any of the grid squares on the object in the 3D View window is distorted, there has been stretching or compression of the unwrapped mesh in the UV map. To reduce this distortion, you can edit the UV map in the UV/Image Editor window by LClicking vertices, pressing G, moving the vertices, then LClicking to set the position.

73. When you are finished with your grid, put your UV image texture's image back into the UV/Image Editor window: In the UV/Image Editor window header, LClick the "Browse Image" button:

74. LClick the name of your UV image texture's image.

75. To adjust the way the UV map-framework is aligned with the UV image in the

UV map: in adjusting this alignment, you move the points, edges, and faces in the UV/Image Editor window—this does not change the position of the vertices in your model space; it only changes how your image is mapped to the faces. If you are not presently showing the UV/Image Editor screen layout, go to the "Info" window's header (the window header with ![info icon] to the left) > LClick the "Choose Screen lay out" button: ![screen layout icon] > LClick "UV Editing." (Alternatively, you can use the directions in **T1** and **T2 p. 7** to create a layout where a UV/Image Editing window is side-by-side with a 3D View window.)
76. If the UV image disappears from the UV/Image Editor window, try selecting a face on the object in the 3D View window.
77. If you will be rotating or scaling your UV map-framework or some part of it, you might want to set the pivot point, around which you will rotate or scale; to set the pivot point for rotating and scaling selected parts of your UV map: Go to the UV/Image Editor window header and LClick the Pivot button,

which may look like  OR ![pivot icon] OR ![pivot icon] > (a) If you are going to move an item from place to place, or to rotate around, or scale from, the center of an edge or face, or around the median of any selected set of items, LClick "Median Point". (b) If you are going to rotate around the 2D cursor (the 2D cursor is moved in much the same way as is the 3D View window's 3D cursor—see **T58, p. 98**--but the choices are more limited), LClick "2D Cursor". Go to step **78**.

78. Do you want **to select and transform (move, rotate, or scale) UV map items in the usual way**?
>   Yes: Go to **79**.
>   No: Go to **81**.

79. To select the item(s), make sure that the SyncSelection button, ![syncselection icon] , is **off** (bright) > Find the "Sticky Selection Mode" button, which is the button that has one of these 3 icons on it:

 , ![icon] or ![icon]

If the Sticky Selection Mode" button is not displaying the ![shared location icon] icon ("Shared Location"), LClick the button > LClick "Shared Location". Use the basic selection techniques covered in **T22, p. 20**. But note that the "lasso" (CTRL + LClick & drag) is not available in the UV/Image Editor window. Also note that the selection-type buttons look different:

![selection-type buttons]

LClick the first button if you will want to select vertices on the UV map-framework; LClick the second if you are going to select edges; LClick the third if you will want to select faces; LClick the fourth if you will want to select entire "islands" (islands are separate parts, isolated from one another, of the UV map—these might or might not exist in your map, depending on how you placed your seams before unwrapping the mesh) > Select the item(s).

80. To transform (move, rotate or scale) the selection, go to **94**.

81. Note that *two or more* points on a UV map, in the UV/Image Editor window, may correspond to a *single* vertex on the corresponding mesh in the 3D View window; that is, they were the same point before they were separated when the seam opened up. For instance, these two points in the UV map correspond to the same mesh-vertex:

Do you want **to select all of the UV map points (OR edges) that correspond to a single mesh-vertex (OR edge) in the 3D View window by selecting only one of these map points (OR edges)**?

       Yes: Go to **82**.

       No: Go to **85**.

82.

METHOD 1:

83. To select the items: In the UV/Image Editor header, make sure that the SyncSelection button,

, is **off** (bright)> Find the "Sticky Selection Mode" button, which is the button that has one of these 3 icons on it:

If the "Sticky Selection Mode" button is not displaying the   icon ("Shared Vertex"), LClick the button > LClick "Shared Vertex" > Go to these buttons:

140

LClick the first button if you will want to select points on the UV map; LClick the second if you are going to select edges; LClick the third if you will want to select faces. To select an item or items, RClick (to deselect any existing selections when you select the item) or SHIFT + RClick (to leave existing selections selected). > To transform (move, rotate or scale) the selection, go to **94**.

METHOD 2:

84. To select the items: In the UV/Image Editor header, make sure that the SyncSelector button,

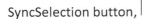

, is **on** (that is, that it's dark) > Use the basic selection techniques covered in **T22, p. 20**. But note that the "lasso" (CTRL + LClick & drag) is not available in the UV/Image Editor window.> To transform (move, rotate or scale) the selection, go to **94**.

END OF METHODS

85. Do you want to select all components of an "island" (islands are separate parts, isolated from one another, of the UV map-framework —there may or not be islands in your particular UV map, depending on how you placed your seams before unwrapping the mesh)?

> Yes: Go to **86**.
>
> No: Go to **90**.

86. To select all components of an "island": In the UV/Image Editor header, make sure that the

SyncSelection button,  , is **off** (bright) > Go to these buttons:

METHOD 1:

 87. With any one of the first three buttons enabled: Hover the mouse over the island > Press L.

METHOD 2:

88. With the fourth button enabled, select any of the island's components.

END OF METHODS

89. To transform (move, rotate or scale) the selection, go to **94**.

90. To separate faces from adjoining faces in the UV map-framework (you will not be able to see that they've been separated until you transform [move, rotate or scale] them):

METHOD 1—ENTIRE SEPARATION OF FACES:

91. In the UV/Image Editor header: Make sure that the "Proportional Edit" button ![button] is disabled > Using the technique described in **79**, select the face(s) you want to separate > Press ALT + L >

Then, to transform (move, rotate or scale) the selection, go to **97**.

The pictures below illustrate how methods 2 and 3 work ("S" next to a vertex or edge, or on a face indicates that that element is selected):

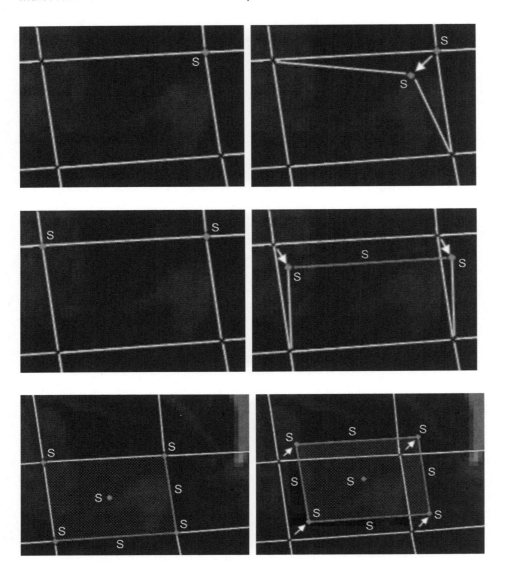

METHOD 2—ENTIRE OR PARTIAL SEPARATION OF FACES:

92. In the UV/Image Editor header: make sure that the SyncSelection button, , is **off** (bright) >

Find the "Sticky Selection Mode" button, which is the button that has one of these 3 icons on it: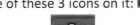

, or > If the Sticky Selection Mode" button is not displaying the icon ("Disabled"), LClick the button > LClick "Disabled" > Make sure that the "Proportional Edit" button

 is disabled > Use the basic selection techniques covered in **T22, p. 20**. But note that the "lasso" (CTRL + LClick & drag) is not available in the UV/Image Editor window. Also note that the selection-type buttons look different:

LClick the first button if you will want to select points on the UV map-framework; LClick the second if you are going to select edges; LClick the third if you will want to select faces; LClick the fourth if you will want to select entire "islands" (islands are separate parts, isolated from one another, of the UV map-framework —these islands might or might not exist, depending on how you placed your seams before unwrapping the mesh) > Select the item(s) > To transform (move, rotate or scale) the selection, go to **97**.
METHOD 3—ENTIRE SEPARATION OF FACES:

93. In the UV/Image Editor header: make sure that the SyncSelection button, , is **on** (dark) >

Make sure that the "Proportional Edit" button  is disabled > Select the face(s), using the basic selection techniques covered in **T22, p. 20**. But note that the "lasso" (CTRL + LClick & drag) is not available in the UV/Image Editor window > To transform (move, rotate or scale) the selection, go to **97**.
END OF METHODS.

94. If you choose to use the Proportional Edit Tool (PET) to adjust the UV map, when you move one vertex or face, you will also move neighboring elements; the extent to which more distant neighboring elements are moved is called "falloff" and can be controlled with the mouse wheel (see below). Do you want to use the Proportional Edit Tool?

      Yes: Go to **95**.

      No: Go to **97**.

95. (a) In the 3D View window or in the UV/Image Editor window: LClick the "Proportional Edit Tool" (PET) button:

Then LClick "Enable".

      OR

(b) With the mouse cursor in the UV/Image Editor window or in the 3D View window, press the letter O key.

96. (a) LClick the PET's curve button:

LClick on the kind of falloff you want.

OR

(b) With the mouse cursor in the UV/Image Editor window or in the 3D View window, press & hold SHIFT + press the letter O key repeatedly to cycle through the kinds of falloff until the icon of the one you want appears on the button.

97. Do you want to move the selected part of the UV map-framework from one position to another?

Yes: Go to **98**.

No: Go to **101**.

98. To **move** the selected part of the UV map-framework from one place to another, (a) Press G to move the selected part in the XY plane, OR (b) Press G > Press X OR Y to move it in the X OR Y direction, OR (c) Press G > MClick & hold, start to drag and lock onto an axis > Release MClick .

99. If you enabled the Proportional Editing Tool at steps **94** through **96**, while you are moving the elements of the UV map around, you can change the radius of the proportional editing effect by moving the wheel on your mouse.

100. Move the selected part to where you want it > LClick. Go to **108**.

101. Do you want to rotate the selected part of the UV map?

Yes: Go to **102**.

No: Go to **105**.

102. To **rotate** the selected part of the UV map, press R.

103. If you enabled the Proportional Editing Tool at steps **94** through **96**, while you are rotating the elements of the UV map-framework, you can change the radius of the proportional editing effect by moving the wheel on your mouse.

104. Rotate the selection to where you want it > LClick. Go to **108**

105. To **scale** the selected part of the UV map-framework, (a) Press S to scale the selected part in the XY plane, OR (b) Press S > Press X OR Y to scale it in the X OR Y direction, OR (c) Press S > MClick & hold, start to drag and lock onto an axis > Release MClick .

106. If you enabled the Proportional Editing Tool at steps **94** through **96**, while you are scaling the elements of the UV map-framework, you can change the radius of the proportional editing effect by moving the wheel on your mouse.

107. Scale it to where you want it > LClick.

108. To **save your UV map-framework as an image file**, in 3D View, press A once or twice to select the whole map-framework > go to the UV/Image Editor window's header > LClick "UVs" > LClick "Export UV Layout" > If you want to go up the directory structure, press the button at upper left with the crooked arrow on it: ![arrow icon], or LClick the same kind of arrow, with two dots: ![arrow two dots icon] OR ![folder icon], near the top of the list.

109. If you want to go down the directory structure, LClick a name in the list.

110. LClick the name of the folder that you want to put the UV map-framework into > To change the name of the map-framework image file, select the name (to the left of the dot) in the lower of the two long fields at the top > type the name you want to file to have > Press ENTER—the file will be saved as a PNG file > LClick "Export UV Layout" at upper right.

111. To quickly save your UV image texture, in the UV/Image Editor window header, (a) LClick "Image"> LClick "Save Image" OR (b) press ALT + S.

112. To save your UV image texture, putting it in a different folder or renaming it, in the UV/Image Editor window header, (a) LClick "Image"> LClick "Save As Image" OR (b) press F3 > If you want to go up

the directory structure, press the button at upper left with the crooked arrow on it: , or LClick the

same kind of arrow, with two dots: OR , near the top of the list.

113. If you want to go down the directory structure, LClick on a name in the list.

114. LClick the name of the folder that you want to put the image into > To change the name of the image file, select the name (to the left of the dot, if you don't want to change the file format) in the lower of the two long fields at the top > type the name you want the file to have > Press ENTER > LClick "Save As Image" at upper right.

115. To work on your UV texture in your graphics program: Since the UV map-framework is saved as a PNG file, you can make all areas other than the edges transparent (you can, for instance, select these areas using the "Magic Wand" and then move the selection out of the image). Put the saved UV image texture together with your saved UV map-framework on two different layers.

116. To return to the default window layout, go to the "Info" window's header (the window header

with to the left) > LClick the "Choose Screen lay out" button: > LClick "Default". (Alternatively, set up the window layout as you want it, following the directions in **T1, T2, and T3, p. 7**.)

TEXTURE PAINTING:

117. (Although you can do texture painting in the 3D View window without the UV/Image Editor window showing, you may need to use the Property Shelf in the UV/Image Editor window; therefore, these steps will direct you to have both windows showing while texture painting.)

118. (i) Blender allows you to paint directly on a UV image texture that's been mapped to your object's material. You can paint on the UV image either (a) in the UV/Image Editor window (where the UV image texture is displayed with the UV map-framework, as a complete map [see **T74, step 32, p. 124**], or (b) in the 3D View window (where the image is displayed on the object itself as a texture).

(ii) To view the painted UV image texture in render, make sure it's been put into the texture stack (see **T75, steps 1 & 2, p. 127**). When you make a change, the change will appear in the next render.

119. To do Texture Painting: If you are not presently showing the UV Editing screen layout (which displays both the UV Editing window and the 3D View window), go to the "Info" window's header (the

window header with to the left) > LClick the "Choose Screen lay out" button: >

LClick "UV Editing". (Alternatively , use the directions in **T1 and T2, p. 7** to create a layout where a UV/Image Editor window is side-by-side with a 3D View window.) Make sure that your second main window is the 3D View window.

120. If the Tool Shelf is not visible on the left side of the 3D View window, (a) press T; OR (b) in the 3D View window's header, LClick "View" > LClick "Tool Shelf".

121. If the Properties Shelf is not visible on the left side of the UV/Image Editor window, (a) press N; OR

(b) in the UV/Image Editor's header, LClick "View" > LClick "Properties".

122. (a) If you want to paint in the UV/Image Editor window, while watching the effect in the 3D View window, go to **123**.

(b) If you want to paint in the 3D View window while watching the effect on the UV map in the UV/Image Editor window, go to **125**.

123. Make sure there is an image in the UV/Image Editor window (see **T75, step 3, p. 127**). In the UV/Image Editor's header, LClick the "Image Painting" button (you may have to scroll in the header for it to appear):

OR

In the UV/Image Editor's header, LClick "Image" > LClick "Image Painting".

124. To see the UV map-framework in the UV/Image Editor window as you paint, make sure that the Mode button in the 3D View window (see **Introduction** for the location of this button) is set to "Edit" mode (**T7, p. 8**). Go to step **126**.

125. In the 3D View window's header, LClick the Mode button (see **Introduction** for the location of this button) > LClick "Texture Paint" > (In order to have the UV/Image Editor's Property Shelf available to you:) In the UV/Image Editor's header, (a) LClick the "Image Painting" button (you may have to scroll in the header for it to appear):

OR

(b) LClick "Image" > LClick "Image Painting".

126. To paint, at any time, LClick and drag..

127. A TEXTURE-PAINTING BRUSH OVERVIEW:

Every texture-painting brush has a set of properties, *all of which can be changed*:

(a) At any given time, a brush will have what I call a single, specific *brushwork functionality*—that is, the brush will apply the paint in a certain way. For instance, If the brush has been given a "Draw" type brushwork functionality it will paint in the usual way; if you've given it a "Smear" type brushwork functionality, it will smudge the existing paint; etc.

(b) A brush will be loaded with paint of a specified *color*.

(c) A brush will have a set size, called its *radius*.

(d) A brush will have a set *strength*—a weak brush's paint will be applied as a transparent wash while a strong brush will apply paint as an opaque coat.

(e) A brush will be configured to have a certain kind of *stroke*—It can have an airbrush stroke, a "space" stroke, or a "wrap" stroke.

(f) A brush can be given what I call a *texturing functionality*, which will cause the brush to produce a stroke that is textured in one way or another.

At any time, you will have available to you, in Image Paint/Texture Paint mode, a set of texture-painting brushes. You can create brushes and add them to the set, and you can throw brushes away. (a) In the UV/Image Editor window, in Image Painting mode (see **123**), in the Properties Shelf, in the "Paint" panel, or (b) in the 3D View window, in Texture Paint mode (see **125**), in the Tool Shelf, in the "Brush" panel:, Look at the big picture at the top of the panel. Think of this big picture as the door to your texture-painting brush cabinet. LClick it to open the cabinet and view your brushes. If you are opening the cabinet for the first time, you will see that Blender has supplied you with a set of brushes. Notice that each brush has a name: "Brush" is a name for one of your brushes—this brush presently has a "Draw" type brushwork functionality, "Clone" is another—it has a "Clone" type brushwork functionality, etc.

(a) In the UV/Image Editor window, in Image Painting mode (see **123**), in the Properties Shelf, in the "Texture" panel, OR (b) in the 3D View window, in Texture Paint mode (see **125**), in the Tool Shelf, in the "Texture" panel: Look at the big picture at the top of the panel. Think of this big picture as the door to a cabinet within which can be stored a collection of textures that can be used by your brush's texturing functionality (see **127(f)** above). You can LClick this big picture at any time to see what textures are in there.

When you go into Image Paint/Texture Paint mode, one of the brushes available to you will be "active"—it will be the "current" brush. (a) In the UV/Image Editor window, in Image Painting mode (see step **123**), in the Properties Shelf, in the "Paint" panel, OR (b) in the 3D View window, in Texture Paint mode (see **125**), in the Tool Shelf, in the "Brush" panel: The big image at the top portrays the current brush. Underneath this big image, you will see a row of buttons that pertain to the current brush, the brush you are using now. Its name is written on the far-left button (If your Properties or Tool Shelf is very narrow, only a part of the name might be visible on the button; in order to see the whole name, you may have to expand the Properties or Tool Shelf: hover over its edge until the double-headed arrow appears and then drag.)

128. You can add any number of brushes, and give each its own settings: color, strength, etc. **To create a new brush**:

i. (a) Go to the UV/Image Editor window, in Image Painting mode (see **123**) > Go to the Properties Shelf > Go to the "Paint" panel, OR (b) Go to the 3D View window, in Texture Paint mode (see **125**) > Go to the Tool Shelf > Go to the "Brush" panel.

ii. Go to the row of buttons underneath the big image at the top > LClick the button with the plus sign (+) on it. You have now created a brush. Blender will give the new brush a name, and its settings will be the same as the last brush you were using. You can re-name the new brush (see **132**), and you can change its settings all you want. The brush you had been using, with all its current settings except for brush size, has been saved (put back into the brush "cabinet").

129. To retrieve a brush from your set of available brushes:

METHOD 1:

i. (a) Go to the UV/Image Editor window, in Image Painting mode (see **123**) > Go to the Properties Shelf > Go to the "Paint" panel, OR (b) Go to the 3D View window, in Texture Paint mode (see **125**) > Go to the Tool Shelf > Go to the "Brush" panel.

ii. LClick the big picture at the top to open the "door" to your texture-painting brush "cabinet". (See step **127** above) > Get the brush by LClicking its image. Once retrieved, you can change its settings all you want. The brush you have been using, with all its current settings except for brush size, has been saved (put back into the brush "cabinet").

METHOD 2:

130. On the main keyboard (not the number pad), press 1, or 2, or 3, etc.

END OF METHODS

131. To save a brush (that is, to put a new brush into the texture-painting brush "cabinet" or put a brush you took from the "cabinet" back into the "cabinet," saving whatever property-changes—except for brush size—you might have made to it): Save your Blender file (see **T17, p. 16** and **T18, p. 17**) OR create a new brush (see **128**) OR retrieve a brush from your set of brushes (see **129**).

132. To rename your current brush:

i. (a) Go to the UV/Image Editor window, in Image Painting mode (see **123**) > Go to the Properties Shelf > Go to the "Paint" panel, OR (b) Go to the 3D View window, in Texture Paint mode (see **125**) > Go to the Tool Shelf > Go to the "Brush" panel.

ii. Look at the big image at the top > Go to the row of buttons underneath this big image > The brush's name is written on the far-left button (If your Property Shelf or Tool Shelf is very narrow, only a part of the name might be visible on the button; in order to see the whole name, you may have to expand the Property Shelf or Tool Shelf: hover over its edge until the double-headed arrow appears and then drag)

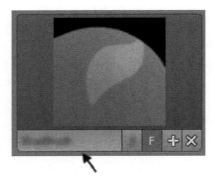

> LClick this far-left button > Type the new name > Press ENTER.

133. To get rid of a brush:

i. (a) Go to the UV/Image Editor window, in Image Painting mode (see **123**) > Go to the Properties Shelf > Go to the "Paint" panel, OR (b) Go to the 3D View window, in Texture Paint mode (see **125**) > Go to the Tool Shelf > Go to the "Brush" panel.

ii. Look at the big image at the top > Go to the row of buttons underneath this big image > Make sure that the name of the brush that you want to throw out is written on the far-left button (If your Property

Shelf or Tool Shelf is very narrow, only a part of the name might be visible on the button; in order to see the whole name, you may have to expand the Property Shelf or Tool Shelf: hover over its edge until the double-headed arrow appears and then drag) > LClick the button with "X" on it.

To change the properties (including paint color) of a texture-painting brush (your current brush in the UV/Image Editor will also be the current brush in the 3D View window) :

134. To change your brush's brushwork functionality:
(i) In the UV/Image Editor window, in Image Painting mode (see **123**): Go to the Properties Shelf > Go to the "Tool" panel (If you have to expand it, LClick the little black triangle—and you might have to drag the vertical scrollbar to see the whole panel) > LClick the main button.
    OR
(ii) In the 3D View window's header, in Texture Paint mode (see **125**): LClick "Brush" > Hover over "Image Paint Tool."
135. LClick one of the four brushwork functionalities (Blender calls them "image paint tools." I find it confusing to think of these brush functionalities as separate tools—RC): (a) if you want to set the brush to paint in the usual manner: LClick "**Draw**"and go to **147** OR (b) to use a different brushwork functionality, go to **136**.
136. If you want to blend the edges between two colors: LClick "**Soften**" and go to **147**; if not, go to **137**.
137. If you want to smudge colors: LClick "**Smear**" > go to **147**; to use the Clone brushwork functionality instead, go to **138**.
138. You can lay a second image over your image in the UV/Image Editor window and paint (*clone*) parts of the second image onto the first, then remove the second image, leaving the "cloned" areas on the first. To do cloning like this, LClick "**Clone**" > Go to the UV/Image Editor window > Go to the Properties Shelf (see **121**) > Go to the "Paint" panel > LClick the "Image" button. Is the name of the image that you want to use as the second image in the list of images?
       Yes: Go to **145**.
       No: Go to **139**.
139. Go to the UV/Image Editor window > Look at the image that is showing in that window (the image that you want to clone the second image onto) > The name of the image can be found in the UV/Image Editor window's header:

> Take note of that name.
140. In the UV/Image Editor window's header, LClick "Image"> LClick "Open Image" > navigate to the image file you want to clone onto your texture image: to have your image files shown as thumbnails,

LClick this button at upper left: ▦ . If you want to go up the directory structure, press the button at

upper left with the crooked arrow on it: ⬆, or LClick the same kind of arrow, with two dots: ⬆..

OR ![folder icon], near the top of the list. If you want to go down the directory structure, LClick on a name in the list > Find the image file that you want to use; remember the name of the file.

141. LClick the file you want to use > LClick "Open Image" at upper right.

142. in the UV/Image Editor window header, LClick the "Browse Image" button:

143. (To restore the original image to the UV/Image Editor window,) LClick the name that you noted in step **139**.

144. Go to the Properties Shelf of the UV/Image Editor window (see **121**) > Go to the "Paint" panel > LClick the "Image" button > LClick the name of the image file that you opened at step **141**. Go to **146**.

145. LClick the name of the file.

146. If you want to position the cloning image, RClick and drag. To clone onto the original image a part of the image that you just opened, LClick and hold, and drag over the area you want to clone. In the "Paint" panel, adjust the "Strength" button to adjust the transparency of the cloning effect. To stop cloning, go back to the "Tool" panel, LClick the main button, and choose another brushwork functionality (another so-called "tool").

Wrap:

147. You can turn on the "Wrap" mode, which has this effect: when you are painting in the UV/Image Editor window, if you run your brush off an edge of the image, the mark will pick up at the opposite edge, and you can continue to paint on the image with your brush off the image. To turn on this mode, go to the UV/Image Editor window > Go to the Properties Shelf > Go to the "Paint Stroke" panel > LClick the little box next to "Wrap" to put a check mark in it. To turn Wrap mode off, uncheck the little box.

148. Do you want to change the color of the paint that your brush is loaded with?

>Yes: Go to **149**.

>No: Go to **152**.

Change the color of the paint that your brush is loaded with:

149. Do you want to use a color that's already in your scene?

>Yes: In the UV/Image Editor window or in the 3D View window (if it's in "Texture Paint" mode) RClick the color *where it appears in the window*. Go to **152**.

>No: Go to **150**.

150. (a) Go to the UV/Image Editor window > Go to the Properties Shelf (see **121**) > Go to the "Paint" panel or, (b) if the 3D View window is in "Texture Paint" mode (see **125**), go to the Tool Shelf of the 3D View window (see step **120**) > Go to the "Brush" panel.

151. To quickly adjust the paint color, adjust the color-picker circle and value slider, or, for more control, LClick the color swatch under the color-picker > adjust the color-picker in the pop-up panel. Use **T68, step 5, p. 111** as a guide.

152. Do you want to specify how the paint you are applying will be affected (or not) by the colors it paints over; OR do you want to make the areas where you paint become transparent or become

<u>opaque?</u>

> Yes: Go to **153**.

> No: Go to **163**.

153. (a) In the UV/Image Editor window, in "Image Paint" mode (see **123**), go to the window's Properties Shelf (see **121**) > In the "Paint" panel, LClick the "Blend" button, the button that says "Mix" by default. OR (b) In the 3D View window, in "Texture Paint" mode, go to the window's Tool Shelf (see step **120**) > In the "Brush" panel, LClick the "Blend" button—this is the button that says "Mix" by default.

154. If you want just to paint over the existing colors: LClick "**Mix**".

155. if you want to mix the paint you're applying with the color you're painting over, and mix them together in the way that colored lights mix In the real world, LClick "**Add**".

(Note that, in the real physical world, combining colored lights is not like mixing paints. For instance, mixing red and green lights produces yellow, but mixing red and green paints produces black or dark gray.)

156. If you want to subtract the paint you're applying from the color you're painting over, as you would subtract a colored light (by dimming it) from a mixture of colored lights (so that, for instance, red over yellow makes green), LClick "**Subtract**".

157. If you want to "multiply" the underlying color with the brush color (where, for example, if the underlying color is R = .8, G = .2, B = .3, and if the brush color is R = .3, G = .5, B = .9, then the resulting color will be R = (.8 x .3) = .24, G = (.2x.5) = 1, B = (.3 x .9) = .27) LClick "**Multiply**".

158. (?)If and only if the underlying color is darker than the brush color, to paint with the brush color, LClick "**Lighten**".

159. (?)If and only if the underlying color is darker than the brush color, to paint with the brush color, LClick "**Darken**".

160. If you want the areas where you paint to become transparent, LClick "**Erase Alpha**"; then, to see the painted area as transparent *in the UV/Image Editor window*, enable this button in the window's header (you might have to scroll in the header to see it):

then paint with your brush. To view, in the UV/Image Editor window, *only* what's transparent, in the UV/Image Editor window's header, enable this button:

To see the painted transparency *in the render*, change one of your windows to the "Properties" window (see **T1. p. 7**): > Make sure that the "Texture" button is enabled: > Go to the "Image Sampling" panel > Go to the "Alpha" boxes > LClick "Use" to check it. Change your window back to what it was (so that the UV/Image Editor window and the 3D View window are both showing).

161. If you want to undo parts of what you painted in **160**: (a) go to the "Properties Shelf" in the UV/Image Editor window > go to the "Paint" panel OR (b) go to the "Tool Shelf" in the 3D View window (in Texture Paint mode—see step **125**) > go to the "Brush" panel.

162. LClick the "Blend" button > LClick "Add Alpha" > Paint on the image in the UV/Image Editor.

163. To turn your brush into an airbrush so that it will paint continually when you LClick and hold, instead of only when the mouse is moving:

Go to the UV/Image Editor window, in Image Painting mode (see **123**) > Go to the Properties Shelf > Go to the "Paint Stroke" panel; OR Go to the 3D View window, in Texture Paint mode (see **125**) > Go to the Tool Shelf > Go to the "Stroke" panel.

164. LClick the little box next to "Airbrush" to put a check mark into it.

165. To turn your brush from an airbrush into a regular brush:

166. Go to the UV/Image Editor window, in Image Painting mode (see **123**) > Go to the Properties Shelf > Go to the "Paint Stroke" panel; OR Go to the 3D View window, in Texture Paint mode (see **125**) > Go to the Tool Shelf > Go to the "Stroke" panel.

167. LClick the little box next to "Airbrush" to remove the check mark.

168. Do you want to change the size of your texture-painting brush?

        Yes: Go to 169.

        No: Go to 176.

169. (Still in Image Paint/Texture Paint mode,) to change the size of your texture-painting brush:
METHOD 1:

170. In the UV/Image Editor window, in "Image Paint" mode (see **123**), go to the window's Properties Shelf (see **121**) > Go to the "Paint" panel OR (b) In the 3D View window, in "Texture Paint" mode, go to the window's Tool Shelf (see **120**) > Go to the "Brush" panel.

171. Adjust the "Radius" button. After you've set the size, go to **176**.
METHOD 2:

172. With the cursor in the 3D View window, press F.

173. Move the cursor toward and away from the center of the circle to make the brush the size you want it. (Note that if you've applied a texture to the brush's texture functionality, this texture should be visible within the circle.)

174. LClick. After you've set the size, go to **176**.

METHOD 3:

175. Note that if you are using a pressure sensitive tablet, you can use pen pressure as you paint to control the brush size by enabling the pressure sensitivity button to the right of the "Radius" button:

 > Go to **176**.

END OF METHODS

176. Do you want to change the strength of your texture-painting brush?

        Yes: Go to **177**.

        No: Go to **184**.

177. (Still in Image Paint/Texture Paint mode,) **to change the strength (opacity) of your brush's strokes:**
METHOD 1:

178. In the UV/Image Editor window, in "Image Paint" mode (see **123**), go to the window's Properties Shelf (see **121**) > Go to the "Paint" panel OR (b) In the 3D View window, in "Texture Paint" mode, go to the window's Tool Shelf (see **120**) > Go to the "Brush" panel.

179. Adjust the "Strength" button. After you've set the strength, go to **184**.

METHOD 2:

180. With the cursor in the 3D View window, press SHIFT + F.

181. Move the cursor toward and away from the center of the circle to give the brush the strength you want it to have: making the circle smaller increases the strength; making the circle larger decreases the strength. (Note that if you've applied a texture to the brush's texture functionality, this texture should be visible within the circle.)

182. LClick. After you've set the strength, go to **184**.

METHOD 3:

183. Note that if you are using a pressure sensitive tablet, you can use pen pressure to control the brush strength as you paint by enabling the pressure sensitivity button to the right of the "Strength" button:

 . > Go to **184**.

END OF METHODS

184. Do you want **to change how gradually or abruptly your brush's effect falls off**, outward from the center of the brush?

      Yes: Go to **185**.

      No: Go to **189**.

185. (a) In the UV/Image Editor window, in "Image Paint" mode (see **123**), go to the window's Properties Shelf (see **121**) > Go to the "Paint Curve" panel OR (b) In the 3D View window, in "Texture Paint" mode, go to the window's Tool Shelf (see **120**) > Go to the "Curve" panel.

186. Look at the curve diagram:

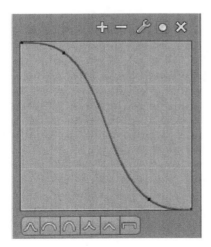

187. You can change how your brush's effect falls off by changing the curve shown in this panel. To do this, you can adjust the curve by LClicking & holding the curve itself, and dragging its nodes.

188. To set the curve in accord with certain basic shapes, LClick one of the "Set brush shape" buttons beneath the curve.

189. To adjust how close together the paint spurts are as you drag your brush, (a) Go to the UV/Image Editor > Go to the "Properties Shelf" > Go to the "Paint Stroke" panel > LClick the little box to the left of "Space" > Adjust the "Distance" button; OR (b) Go to the 3D View window > Go to the "Tool Shelf" > Go to the "Stroke" panel > LClick the little box to the left of "Space" > Adjust the "Spacing" button.

190. Do you want to modify your active texture-painting brush's texturing functionality so that it will texture its strokes, or, if it already textures its strokes, do you want to change (or remove) this texturing?

> Yes: Go to **191**.

> No: You are finished adjusting your settings. Just LClick and drag to texture-paint your texture.

191. Is your active texture-painting brush non-texturing, and do you want to modify it so that it will texture its strokes?

> Yes: Go to **192**.

> No: To change or remove your texture-painting brush's existing texture: Go to **208**.

192. Do you want to use a texture that you've already used in the scene?

> Yes: Go to **193**.

> No: Go to **197**.

193. Use a texture that you've already used in the scene:

METHOD 1:

194. Go to the UV/Image Editor window, in Image Painting mode (see **123**) > Go to the Properties Shelf OR Go to the 3D View window, in Texture Paint mode (see **125**) > Go to the Tool Shelf.

195. Go to the "Texture" panel. (LClick the black triangle to the left of "Texture" to expand the panel if necessary—you might have to drag in the vertical scrollbar to see this panel) > LClick the large image > LClick the texture you want to use. Go to step **224**.

METHOD 2:

196. Change one of your windows to the "Properties" window (see **T1. p. 7**): > Make sure that the "Texture" button is enabled: > Make sure that the "Show Brush Textures" button is enabled (bright):

> LClick the checker-board button near the upper left of the "Properties" window > LClick the texture you want to use. > Change your window back to what it was (so that the UV/Image Editor window and the 3D View window are both showing) > Go to step **224**.

END OF METHODS.

197. Apply a brand new texture to your brush:

METHOD 1:

198. Go to the UV/Image Editor window, in Image Painting mode (see **123**) > Go to the Properties Shelf OR Go to the 3D View window, in Texture Paint mode (see **125**) > Go to the Tool Shelf.

199. Go to the "Texture" panel. (LClick the black triangle to the left of "Texture" to expand the panel if necessary—you might have to drag in the vertical scrollbar to see this panel).

200. LClick the "New" button below the large image > Change one of your windows to the "Properties"

window (see **T1. p. 7**): > Make sure that the "Texture" button is enabled: > Make sure that the "Show Brush Textures" button is enabled (bright):

 > Go to **202.**

METHOD 2:

201. Change one of your windows to the "Properties" window (see **T1. p. 7**): > Make

sure that the "Texture" button is enabled: > Make sure that the "Show Brush Textures" button is enabled (bright):

> LClick "New" > Go to **202.**

END OF METHODS.

202. LClick the "Type" button at the top > LClick the type of texture you want.

203. Did you just choose "image or movie"?

       Yes: Go to **204**.

       No: Change your window back to what it was (so that the UV/Image Editor window and the 3D

       View window are both showing) > Go to **220**.

204. Go to the "Image" panel > LClick "Open" > To have your image files shown as thumbnails, LClick

this button at upper left:  .

205. Navigate to the image that you want to use as your image texture. If you want to go up the

directory structure, press the button at upper left with the crooked arrow on it: , or LClick the

same kind of arrow, with two dots: OR , near the top of the list.

206. If you want to go down the directory structure, LClick on a name in the list.

207. LClick the file you want to use to select it > LClick "Open Image" at upper right. Change your window back to what it was (so that the UV/Image Editor window and the 3D View window are both showing) > Go to **220**.

208. Do you want to remove all texturing from your current brush?

> Yes: Go to **209**.

> No: To change your current brush's texturing, go to **211**.

209. To remove all texturing from your current brush, go to the UV/Image Editor window, in Image Painting mode (see **123**) > Go to the Properties Shelf OR Go to the 3D View window, in Texture Paint mode (see **125**) > Go to the Tool Shelf.

210. Go to the "Texture" panel. (LClick the black triangle to the left of "Texture" to expand the panel if necessary—you might have to drag in the vertical scrollbar to see this panel) > Go to the row of buttons below the big image > LClick the button with "X" on it, at the far right end of the row. You are finished adjusting your settings. Just LClick and drag the brush to texture-paint your texture.

211. Do you want to change your brush's texture to a texture that you've already used in the scene?

> Yes: Go to **212**.

> No: Go to **216**.

212. Use a texture that you've already used in the scene:

METHOD 1:

213. Go to the UV/Image Editor window, in Image Painting mode (see **123**) > Go to the Properties Shelf OR Go to the 3D View window, in Texture Paint mode (see **125**) > Go to the Tool Shelf.

214. Go to the "Texture" panel. (LClick the black triangle to the left of "Texture" to expand the panel if necessary—you might have to drag in the vertical scrollbar to see this panel) > LClick the large image > LClick the texture you want to use. Go to step **224**.

METHOD 2:

215. Change one of your windows to the "Properties" window (see **T1. p. 7**): > Make sure

that the "Texture" button is enabled: > Make sure that the "Show Brush Textures" button is enabled (bright):

> LClick the checker-board button near the upper left of the "Properties" window

> LClick the texture you want to use > Change your window back to what it was (so that the UV/Image Editor window and the 3D View window are both showing) > Go to step **224**.

END OF METHODS.

216. Apply a brand new texture to your brush:

METHOD 1:

217. Go to the UV/Image Editor window, in Image Painting mode (see **123**) > Go to the Properties Shelf OR Go to the 3D View window, in Texture Paint mode (see **125**) > Go to the Tool Shelf.

218. Go to the "Texture" panel. (LClick the black triangle to the left of "Texture" to expand the panel if necessary—you might have to drag in the vertical scrollbar to see this panel) > Go to the row of buttons under the big image > LClick the button with a plus sign (+) on it > Change one of your windows to the

"Properties" window (see **T1. p. 7**):  > Make sure that the "Texture" button is enabled:

> Make sure that the "Show Brush Textures" button is enabled (bright):

 > Go to **202.**

METHOD 2:

219. Change one of your windows to the "Properties" window (see **T1. p. 7**): 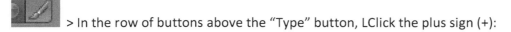 > Make sure

that the "Texture" button is enabled > Make sure the "Show Brush Textures" button is enabled:

> In the row of buttons above the "Type" button, LClick the plus sign (+):

> Go to step **202.**

END OF METHODS

220. To name your texture:

METHOD 1:

221. Go to the UV/Image Editor window, in Image Painting mode (see **123**) > Go to the Properties Shelf OR Go to the 3D View window, in Texture Paint mode (see **125**) > Go to the Tool Shelf.

222. Go to the "Texture" panel. (LClick the black triangle to the left of "Texture" to expand the panel if necessary—you might have to drag in the vertical scrollbar to see this panel) > Go to the row of buttons under the big image > LClick the first of these buttons > Type the new name > Press ENTER.

METHOD 2.

223. Make sure that one of your windows is the "Properties" window (see **T1. p. 7**): > Make

sure that the "Texture" button is enabled > Make sure the "Show Brush Textures" button is

enabled: > In the row of buttons above the "Type" button, LClick the word in the longest of these buttons > Type the new name > Press ENTER > Change your window back to what it was (so that the UV/Image Editor window and the 3D View window are both showing).

END OF METHODS

224. To specify how the texture will align with the surface:

225. Go to the UV/Image Editor window, in Image Painting mode (see **123**) > Go to the Properties Shelf

OR Go to the 3D View window, in Texture Paint mode (see **125**) > Go to the Tool Shelf.

226. Go to the "Texture" panel. (LClick the black triangle to the left of "Texture" to expand the panel if necessary—you might have to drag in the vertical scrollbar to see this panel) > To "drag" the texture with your brush as you paint, leave the little square next to "Fixed Texture" unchecked; but to keep the texture fixed as you paint, LClick the little square to put a check mark into it.

227. _**Warning: The painted texture will not be saved unless you save it in the following way:**_ In the UV/Image Editor window's header, LClick "Image"; then (a) LClick "Save Image" or press ALT+S, OR (b) LClick "Save As Image" or press F3 (to save it using "Save As," so as not to save over your original image, if there is one).

T78. **To do projection painting:**

1. If you have modeled an object—a human head, say—and have given it a base material (see **T62, p. 107**), and have photographic image files of a roughly similar head from different angles, say from the front and from one side—on your hard drive (these photos should be as free from shadow and highlights as possible), then you can map the colors from the photographic images onto your model using a process called "projection painting." First, if the 3D View window is in _perspective_ view, such that things appear smaller as they recede into the distance, press numpad 5 to put it into _ortho_ view.

2. (Assuming you have already prepared the two photographic image files:) Make sure you are displaying the "default" layout: go to the "Info" window's header (the window header with to the left) > LClick the "Choose Screen lay out" button: > LClick "Default". (If "Default" does not appear in the list that appears, use the directions in **T1 and T2, p. 7** to create a layout where your main window is the 3D View window, and where the "Properties" window,   , is also showing.)

3. The "base" map-framework is just a UV map-framework (representing the unwrapped mesh) that will end up mapping the projection painting to the mesh. Have you already created a UV map-framework for your model that you want to use as a base map?

> Yes: Let's say that, for some reason, you named it "MyBaseMap" (though it can have any name at all). Go to **5**.

> No: Go to **4**.

4. Create a base map-framework for your model—name it (for instance) "MyBaseMap"—and unwrap your mesh (see **T74, step 39, p. 126 – step 47**).

5. To create a "3D" map-framework for the front view (note that you don't need to view these maps as you create them): Go to the "Properties" window: > LClick the mesh "Object Data" button: > Go to the "UV Texture" panel > To create another map-framework, LClick the button with a plus sign on it: .

6. LClick the "Name" field > Type in the field to change the name that Blender automatically gave to your new map-framework. Name it, say,"Front" (since you will use it for the front view) > Press ENTER.

7. (With "Front" highlighted in the list of UV map-frameworks in the "UV Texture" panel:) In Edit mode, in the 3D View window, change your point of view so that you are looking at your model from the front. Press "A" one or more times until the whole mesh is selected > With the mouse pointer in the 3D View window. press U > LClick "Project From View".

8. To create a "3D" map-framework for the side view: Still in the "UV Texture" panel > To create yet another map-framework, LClick the button with a plus sign on it:  .

9. LClick the "Name" field > Type in the field to change the name that Blender automatically gave to your new map-framework. Name it, say, "Side" (since you will use it for the side view) > Press ENTER.

10. (With "Side" highlighted in the list of UV map-frameworks in the "UV Texture" panel:) In Edit mode, in the 3D View window, change your point of view so that you are looking at your model from the side. Press "A" until the whole mesh is selected > With the mouse pointer in the 3D View window, press U > LClick "Project From View".

You now have three map-frameworks—a 2D one named "MyBaseMap" and two "3D" ones, one named "Front" and the other named "Side"—to use in your projection painting.

11. Go to the "Info" window's header (the window header with [icon] to the left) > LClick the "Choose Screen lay out" button: [icon] > LClick "UV Editing". (Alternatively, use the directions in **T1 and T2** to create a layout where a UV/Image Editor window is side-by-side with a 3D View window.) Make sure that your second main window is the 3D View window. In the UV/Image Editor's header, look to see if the "Image Paint" button [icon] is there (you may have to scroll in the header for it to appear). If it is in the header, make sure that it is *not* enabled (that is, make sure it is bright, not dark).

12. In the UV/Image Editor window's header, LClick the "Active UV texture" button (you may have to put your mouse pointer in the header and scroll in order to see this button—also, make sure that the *3D View* window is not in Texture Paint mode):

[image: button]

LClick "Front", to put the "Front" map that you created into the UV/Image Editor window.

13. To put the photographic image of the person's face as viewed from the front into the UV/Image Editor window: in the UV/Image Editor window's header, LClick "Image"; LClick "Open Image"; navigate to the person's-face-from-the-front file that you want to open in the window: to have your image files shown as thumbnails, LClick this button at upper left: [icon] . If you want to go up the directory structure, press the button at upper left with the crooked arrow on it: [icon] , or LClick the same kind of arrow, with two dots:  OR , near the top of the list. If you want to go down the directory structure, LClick on a name in the list.

14. (a) LClick the file you want to use to select it > LClick "Open Image" at upper right.

OR

(b) Double LClick the file you want to use.

15. Making sure that the 3D View window is in Edit mode and that your model is viewed from the front, press "A" one or more times until the whole mesh is selected > look in the UV/Image Editor window. If the aspect ratio of the "Front" 3D map-framework in that window is different from that of the image (for instance, if the 3D map-framework looks squashed), you can put your mouse pointer in the 3D View window, press U, and LClick "Project From View" again, to re-make the map-framework.

16. *In the 3D View window*, press "A" to deselect everything > Make sure that this button: is enabled (dark) so that you can't see the back part of the mesh > Press "B" and select all the faces that are visible from the front.

17. By selecting various parts of the 3D map-framework in the UV/Image Editor window, and using G, S, and R (see **T25, METHOD 2, p. 42**), and using Proportional Editing (see **T25, steps 84-87, p. 42**), carefully align all parts of the 3D map-framework with the analogous parts of the image.

18. In the 3D View window header, go into "Texture Paint" mode > Set the "Viewport Shading" button [see **Introduction** for the location of this button] to "solid" > examine your model to see how well the image was mapped to it.

19. If you are not satisfied with the results, in the 3D View window, go back into "Edit" mode > Go back to step **17**; if you are satisfied, go to step **20**.

20. In the 3D View window, go to "Edit" mode. With the mouse cursor in the 3D View window Press A one or more times until the whole mesh is selected.

21. To show the Base map-framework in the UV/Image Editor window: in the UV/Image Editor window's header, LClick the "Active UV texture" button:

(You may have to put your mouse pointer in the header and scroll to see this button—if you can't find it

at all, make sure that, in the UV/Image Editor's header, the "Image Paint" button is not enabled—you may have to scroll in the header to find this button.) > LClick "MyBaseMap" (see **steps 3 and 4**), to put the "MyBaseMap" map-framework, that you created, into the UV/Image Editor window. (This base map-framework won't appear in the UV/Image Editor window unless the *3D View* window is in Edit mode, and the geometry of the model is selected.)

22. To create a UV image texture for the Base map-framework (that is, to *create* a black UV image texture that you will paint on; not to *open* an *existing* UV image texture) and put it in the UV/Image

Editor window: In the UV/Image Editor window, LClick "image" > LClick "New Image" > Name it, say, "basemap_image" (and remember its name). Give it a fairly large size, such as 2048 x 2048. LClick "OK".

23. In the 3D View window's header: Go into "Texture Paint" mode. Your model should be black.

24. Go to the 3D View window's header > LClick "Brush" > Hover over "Image Paint Tool" > LClick "Clone" > Go to the Tool Shelf > Go to the "Brush" panel > Set the "Strength" button all the way to the right.

25. Still in the Tool Shelf, go to the "Project Paint" panel > Make sure that the little square next to "Project Paint" is checked > Make sure that "Occlude", "Cull", "Normal", "Stencil", and "Clone" are all checked > LClick the button to the right of "Clone" > LClick "Front" (the name of your map-framework for the front view—the name you gave it in **6**).

26. *In the 3D View window*, paint directly on your model. (You are painting [cloning] the "Front" UV image texture onto the "MyBaseMap" map-framework, and thus onto the model.)

27. When you're finished, **to save the .blend file:** with your mouse cursor still in the 3D View window, (a) press CTRL+S; then LClick the path and filename under "Save over"

OR:

(b) Go to the "Info" window's header (the window header with ![icon] to the left); LClick "File" > LClick "Save As…" > If you want to go up the directory structure, press the button at upper left with the

crooked arrow on it: ![icon], or LClick the same kind of arrow, with two dots: ![icon] OR ![icon], near the top of the list.

28. If you want to go down the directory structure, LClick on a name in the list.

29. LClick the name of the folder that you want to put the .blender file into > LClick "Save As Blender File" at upper right.

30. But **the newly painted-on basemap image has not been saved yet. To save it:** In the UV/Image Editor window header, (a) LClick "Image"> LClick "Save As Image" OR (b) press F3 > If you want to go up

the directory structure, press the button at upper left with the crooked arrow on it: ![icon], or LClick the

same kind of arrow, with two dots: ![icon] OR ![icon], near the top of the list.

31. If you want to go down the directory structure, LClick on a name in the list.

32. LClick the name of the folder that you want to put the image into > To change the name of the image file, select the name (to the left of the dot) in the lower of the two long fields at the top > type the name you want to file to have > You can choose the file format by going to the "Save As Image" panel and LClicking the "File Type" button, and then LClicking the desired file type > LClick "Save As Image" at upper right.

33. Go to the 3D View window > position your viewpoint so that you are looking at the model from the side.

34. Make sure that the 3D View window is in Edit mode > Press A one or more times untill you have selected the whole mesh > In the UV/Image Editor window's header, LClick the "Active UV texture" button:

(You may have to put your mouse pointer in the header and scroll to see this button—if you can't find it at all, make sure that, in the UV/Image Editor's header, the "Image Paint" button is not enabled—you may have to scroll in the header to find this button.) > LClick "Side", to put the "Side" map-framework that you created into the UV/Image Editor window.

35. To put the photographic image of the person's face as viewed from the side into the UV/Image Editor window, in the UV/Image Editor window's header, LClick "Image"; LClick "Open Image"; navigate to the person's-face-from-the-side file that you want to open in the window: to have your image files shown as thumbnails, LClick this button at upper left: . If you want to go up the directory structure, press the button at upper left with the crooked arrow on it: , or LClick the same kind of

arrow, with two dots: OR   , near the top of the list. If you want to go down the directory structure, LClick on a name in the list.

36. (a) LClick the file you want to use to select it > LClick "Open Image" at upper right.
 OR
(b) Double LClick the file you want to use.

37. Making sure that the 3D View window is still in Edit mode and that your model is still in side view, and that the whole mesh is still selected > look in the UV/Image Editor window. If the aspect ratio of the "Side" 3D map-framework in that window is different from that of the image (for instance, if the 3D map looks squashed), you can put your mouse pointer in the 3D View window, press U, and LClick "Project From View" again, to re-make the map.

38. *In the 3D View window,* press "A" to deselect everything > Make sure that this button: is enabled (dark) so that you can't see the other side of the mesh > Press "B" and select everything that's visible from the side.

39. By selecting various parts of the 3D map in the UV/Image Editor window, and using G, S, and R (see **T25, METHOD 2, p. 42**), and using Proportional Editing (see **T25, steps 84-87, p. 42**), carefully align all parts of the 3D map-framework with the analogous parts of the side image.

40. In the 3D View window header, go into "Texture Paint" mode > Set the "Viewport Shading" button [see ***Introduction*** for the location of this button] to "solid" > examine your model to see how well the image was mapped to it.

41. If you are not satisfied with the results, in the 3D View window, go back into "Edit" mode > Go back to step **39**; if you are satisfied, go to step **42**.

42. In the 3D View window, go to "Edit" mode. With the mouse cursor in the 3D View window Press A one or more times until the whole mesh is selected.

43. Make sure that the Base map-framework (MyBaseMap) is showing in the UV/Image Editor window; if it is not : in the UV/Image Editor window's header, LClick the "Active UV texture" button:

(You may have to put your mouse pointer in the header and scroll to see this button—if you can't find it

at all, make sure that, in the UV/Image Editor's header, the "Image Paint" button [image] is not enabled—you may have to scroll in the header to find this button.) > LClick "MyBaseMap" (see **steps 3 and 4**) to put the "MyBaseMap" map-framework, that you created into the UV/Image Editor window. (This base map-framework won't appear in the UV/Image Editor window unless the 3D window is in Edit mode, and the geometry of the model is selected.)

44. In the UV/Image Editor window header, LClick the "Browse Image" button:

If it is not already selected, LClick the name of the UV image you created at step **22**; that is, in this example: LClick "basemap_image".

45. In the 3D View window's header: Go into "Texture Paint" mode.

46. Go to the 3D View window's header > LClick "Brush" > Hover over "Image Paint Tool" > LClick "Clone" > Go to the Tool Shelf > Go to the "Brush" panel > Set the "Strength" button all the way to the right.

47. Still in the Tool Shelf, go to the "Project Paint" panel > Make sure that the little square next to "Project Paint" is checked > Make sure that "Occlude", "Cull", "Normal", "Stencil", and "Clone" are all checked > LClick the button to the right of "Clone" > LClick "Side" (the name of your map-framework for the side view, the name you gave it at step **9**).

48. *In the 3D View window*, draw directly on the side of the model head, blending the side coloring into the front coloring. If the side and front colors don't quite match, you can go to the "Brush" panel and turn down the "Strength" button. (You are painting (cloning) the "Side" UV map onto the "MyBaseMap" map-framework, and thus onto the model.)

49. When you're finished, **save the .blend file:** Go to the "Info" window's header (the window header

with [image] to the left) > LClick "File" > LClick "Save;" OR: Press CTRL + S > LClick the little window that pops up.

50. To save the newly-painted-on basemap image: In the UV/Image Editor window header, (a) LClick "Image"> LClick "Save Image" OR (b) press ALT + S.

51. To be able to *render* the image you just painted as a texture on the model, you have to put basemap_image as a texture into the texture stack. Go to the "Info" window's header (the window header with 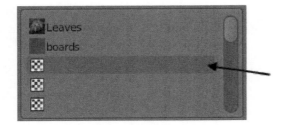 to the left) > LClick the "Choose Screen lay out" button: 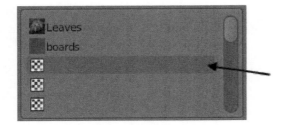 > LClick "Default". (Alternatively, use the directions in **T1 and T2** to create a layout where your main window is

the 3D View window, and where the "Properties" window, , is also showing.)

52. Go to the "Properties" window: > LClick the "Texture" button:

53. At the top of the window: look at the "texture channel stack": Do you see a "New" button right under the stack?

        Yes: Go to **55**.

        No: Go to **54**.

54. LClick In the highest empty channel in the stack:

55. LClick the "New" button under the stack:

56. LClick the "Type" button:

57. LClick "Image or Movie" > Go to the "Image" panel > LClick the little button to the left of the "New" button:

58. LClick the name you gave to the base map image in step **22**; in this example, LClick "basemap_image". (If you cannot find it in the list, hover over the lowest or highest name in the list and scroll down or up).

59. Go to the "Mapping" panel > LClick the "Coordinate" button > LClick "UV" > LClick the "Projection" button > LClick "Flat".

60. LClick the "Object Data" button: > Go to the "UV Texture" panel > Make sure that the little camera icon to the right of the name of the map-framework that you want to use (in this example, MyBaseMap") is enabled.

61. Render your model (F12).

T79. To apply a ramp:

1. Using the "Ramp Shader", you can throw color casts over different parts of one gradient or another that exists across your model's surface; for instance, you might want to throw a purple cast over the low-lit parts of the object's surface, a blue cast over the moderately lit parts of the surface, and a reddish cast over the more brightly lit parts of the surface. Or, you might want to throw a yellow cast over the central parts of a sphere's surface, an oranger cast over the off-center parts of the surface, and a reddish cast over the parts of the surface that lie near the sphere's edge. You can do all this using the Ramp Shader. The color casts generated by the Ramp Shader will lie on top of all your textures (except those which mimic raised and lowered, or bumpy, surfaces), which, in turn lie on top of your material's substance color.

2. Make sure that the object has at least one material, a base material, applied to it (**T61 and T62, p. 107** above).

3. Go to the "Properties" window: > LClick the "Material" button: .

4.

> a. If you want to throw color casts over some gradient *across the whole surface* (for instance, see the two examples in **1** above): Go to the "Diffuse" panel > LClick the little box to the left of "Ramp" to put a check mark in it.
>
> b. If you want to throw color casts over the gradient that spans the least-lit parts and most-lit parts of your object's *specular highlight(s)* (for instance, you might want the highlight to be bluish around the edges and yellowish near and at the center): Go to the "Specular" panel > LClick the little box to the left of "Ramp" to put a check mark in it.

5. LClick the "Input" button:

6.

> a. If you want to throw color casts over the surface, casts that are correlated to the "least-lit to most-lit" gradient, (see the first example in **1** above)—such that if the light source itself is set to a dimmer setting, the color sequence of the color casts won't change—LClick "Shader".
>
> b. If you want to throw color casts over the surface, casts that are correlated to the "low-lit to high-lit" gradient—such that if the light source itself is set to a dimmer setting, the color casts will change—LClick "Energy".
>
> c. If you want to throw color casts over the surface, casts that are correlated to the "surface-facing-camera to surface-more-oblique-to-camera" gradient, (see the second example in step **1** above), LClick "Normal".

7. If you clicked "Shader" in step **6**, this colorband *represents* on the left the least well-lit parts of the surface, through a gradual transition to, on the right, the most well-lit parts of the surface.

If you clicked "Energy" in step **6**, this colorband *represents* on the left the dark parts of the surface, through a gradual transition to, on the right, the bright parts of the surface.

If you clicked "Normal" in step **6**, this colorband *represents* on the left the most oblique parts of the surface, through a gradual transition to, on the right, the least oblique parts of the surface.

The colorband opens (at step **4**) with opaque white on the right, and completely transparent black on the left, with gradations from one to the other across the colorband. Against the far right edge is a vertical line that marks the position on the colorband of the pure white, and against the far left edge is a vertical line that marks the position on the colorband of the pure (transparent) black. When you open the colorband, your object's surface will take on the coloring of the colorband: the transparent areas will gradually transition into white.

8. To add a color to the center of the colorband, LClick the "Add" button. The new color will be the same as the color that was in the center of the colorband when you clicked, and will transition gradually into the colors to left and right. At this point, the transparent areas of your texture will transition gradually to the middle color, then to white. You will be able to change all of these colors, and their positions on the colorband (see below).

9. To add a new color anywhere in the colorband, press CTRL + LClick at the position on the colorband where you want it to appear. The new color will be the same as the color that was under your mouse pointer when you clicked—you will be able to change the color (see below).

10. To select any color on the colorband, LClick the vertical line that marks its position on the colorband; OR:

Go to this button above the ramp:

Using this button, you can select a color on the ramp this way: keeping in mind that the colors are numbered left to right across the colorband, starting with 0, choose the number of the color you want to select. (See ***Introduction*** for how to adjust buttons of this kind.)

11. Note that the selected color's vertical line will be dashed. The currently selected color will appear in the color swatch.

12. To change the position of a color on the colorband, LClick & hold on the vertical line that marks the color's position > Drag the line.

13. To change a color on the colorband, select the color (see **10**) and LClick the color swatch to the right of the "Pos" button. Choose your color using to the methods described in **T68, step 5, p. 111**.

14. To change the transparency of a color on the colorband: select the color on the colorband (see **10**) > LClick the color swatch to the right of the "Pos" button > Adjust the "A" (for "Alpha," which means "transparency") button: LClick & drag in the button; 1 is full opacity, zero is full transparency.

15. To specify how the color casts will be influenced by the colors underneath them: LClick the "Blend" button > LClick "Mix" to produce the Ramp layer as straightforwardly indicated by the colorband; OR: try the different settings (Add, Multiply, Subtract, Screen, Divide, Difference, Darken Lighten, Overlay, Dodge, Burn, Hue, Saturation, Value, Color, Soft Light, Linear Light) while looking at the Preview panel for different color effects.

16. Transparency/opacity of the ramp layer is controlled by the "Factor" button.

T80. To apply Vertex Paint:

1. Whereas using *Texture* Painting (see above, **T77, step 117, p. 145**) you paint the texture, using Vertex Painting, which works only on meshes, you can paint directly onto the mesh in the 3D View window (in the render, the Vertex Paint layer is beneath the texture layers—see **T71, p. 116**). (Actually, you are painting vertices, and for each face whose vertices you paint, Blender fills in the entire face by blending together the colors of all the face's vertices.)

The vertex-painting brushes work best on a greatly subdivided mesh, but vertex painting will not work with the "Subsurf" modifier or the "multires" (multi-resolution meshes) modifier unless they have been applied (see **T54, p. 83, A and C**).

2. A VERTEX-PAINTING BRUSH OVERVIEW:

Every vertex-painting brush has a set of properties, *all of which can be changed*:

(a) At any given time, a brush will have what I call a single, specific *overpaint functionality*—that is, the brush's paint application to the object's surface will be affected by the underlying paint in a certain way. For instance, If the brush has a "Mix" type overpaint functionality, it will lay down a translucent or opaque wash; if it has an "Add" type overpaint functionality, your paint will mix together with the color underneath in the way that colored lights mix together; etc.

(b) A brush will have a set size, called its *radius*.

(c) A brush will have a set *strength*.

(d) A brush will be configured to have a certain kind of *stroke*—for example, a series of dots, or an airbrush stroke, etc.

At any time, you will have available to you, in Vertex Paint mode, a set of vertex-paint brushes. You can create brushes and add them to the set, and you can throw brushes away. In Vertex Paint mode, in the Tool Shelf, look at the big picture at the top of the "Brush" panel. Think of this big picture as the door to your vertex-paint brush cabinet. LClick it to open the cabinet and view your brushes. If you are opening the cabinet for the first time, you will see that Blender has supplied you with a set of brushes. Notice that each brush has a name (which may be hard to read): "Add" is the name of one of your brushes— this brush has (unless and until you change it) an "Add" type overpaint functionality. "Brush" is the name of another of your brushes—this brush has a "Mix" type overpaint functionality, etc.

3. Make sure that the object has at least one material applied to it (see **T61 and T62, p. 107** above).

4. In the 3D View window, In Object mode, select the object that you want to vertex paint. (Your painting surface will be the whole object, not just a material.)

5. Make sure that the "Viewport Shading" button (see ***Introduction*** for how to locate this button) is set to "Solid".

6. To go into Vertex Paint mode: (a) with your mouse pointer in the 3D View window and in Object mode, press V, OR (b) go to the 3D View window's header and LClick the Mode button (see **_Introduction_** for how to locate this button) > LClick "Vertex Paint".

7. By default, the Vertex Paint layer (see **T71, p. 116**, ②) will be white.

8. If the Tool Shelf is not visible in the 3D View window: with your mouse in the 3D View window, press T.

9. When you go into Vertex Paint mode, one of the brushes available to you will be "active"—it will be the "current" brush. In the Tool Shelf, go to the "Brush" panel. The big image at the top portrays the current brush. Underneath this big image, you will see a row of buttons that pertain to the current brush, the brush you are using now. Its name is written on the far-left button (If your Tool Shelf is very narrow, only a part of the name might be visible on the button; in order to see the whole name, you may have to expand the Tool Shelf: hover over its edge until the double-headed arrow appears and then drag.)

10. To create a new brush: Still in Vertex Paint mode, in the Tool Shelf, in the "Brush" panel, go to the row of buttons just below the big image at the top > LClick the button with the plus sign (+) on it. You have now created a brush—the brush you have been using has been saved (put back into the brush "cabinet"), and the brush you have just created has all the same properties that the previous brush had.

11. To retrieve a brush from your set of available brushes: Still in Vertex Paint mode, (a) go to the Tool Shelf > Go to the "Brush" panel > LClick the big picture at the top (to open the "door" to your vertex-paint brush "cabinet", see **1** above) > Get the brush by LClicking its image; OR (b) On the main keyboard (not the number pad), press 1, or 2, or 3, etc.

12. To save a brush (that is, to put a new brush into the vertex-painting brush "cabinet" or put a brush you took from the "cabinet" back into the "cabinet," saving whatever property-changes you might have made to it): Save your Blender file (see **T19, p. 18** and **T20, p. 18**) OR create a new brush (see **7**) OR retrieve a brush from your set of brushes (see **14**)—brush size will not be saved.

13. To rename a brush: In Vertex Paint mode, in the Tool Shelf, in the "Brush" panel, look underneath the big image, you will see a row of buttons that pertain to the current brush, the brush you are using now. The brush's name is written on the far-left button (If your Tool Shelf is very narrow, only a part of the name might be visible on the button; in order to see the whole name, you may have to expand the Tool Shelf: hover over its edge until the double-headed arrow appears and then drag) > LClick this far-left button > Type the new name.

14. To paint, LClick and drag over the surface of the object in the 3D View window.

To change the properties of a vertex paint brush:

15. To choose a color for your brush: Go to the Tool Shelf > Go to the "Brush" panel:
> (a) Adjust the (default) hue+saturation circle and the value slider (see **T68, step 5, p. 111**);
> OR
> (b) LClick the color swatch box (which may be white) under the hue+saturation circle and the value slider > Adjust the color (see **T68, step 5, p. 111** for how to use the color picker).

16. To change the opacity/translucency of your paint at any time, go to the Tool Shelf > Go to the "Brush" panel > adjust the "Strength" button.

17. To change the size (radius) of your brush at any time, go to the Tool Shelf > Go to the "Brush" panel

> adjust the "Radius" button.

18.   Do you want to show the edges and vertices of your object, so that you can see which vertices you're painting?

> Yes: Go to **19**.

> No: Go to **20**.

19. In the "Properties" window > > LClick the "Object" button: > Go to the "Display" panel > LClick the box next to "Wire" in order to check it.

20. To change your brush's overpaint functionality, that is, to change how your vertex paint will be affected (or not) by the underlying color(s) **in one of the ways, a-g, below, first, In the 3D View window, go to the 3D View window's header > LClick "Brush" > Hover over "Vertex/Weight Paint Tool."**

> a. To put a wash of translucent or opaque paint over existing colors: LClick **"Mix"**.

> b. if you want to mix the paint you're applying with the color you're painting over, and mix them together in the way that colored lights mix In the real world, LClick **"Add"**. (Note that, in the real physical world, combining colored lights is not like mixing paints. For instance, mixing red and green *lights* produces yellow, but mixing red and green *paints* produces black or dark gray.)

> c. If you want to, in some sense, subtract the paint you're applying from the color you're painting over, LClick **"Subtract"**.

> d. If you want to "multiply" the underlying color with the brush color (where, for example, if the underlying color is R = .8, G = .2, B = .3, and if the brush color is R = .3, G = .5, B = .9, then the resulting color will be R = (.8 x .3) = .24, G = (.2x.5) = 1, B = (.3 x .9) = .27) LClick **"Multiply"**.

> e. If you want to mix together all the vertices within the brush's radius, LClick **"Blur"**.

> f. ?If you want the paint to be applied only where it's lighter than the color that's being painted over, LClick **"Lighten"**.

> g. ?If you want the paint to be applied only where it's darker than the color that's being painted over, LClick **"Darken"**.

21. To be able to create a "**mask**," that is, to be able to select faces such that only those faces can be vertex painted: still in Vertex Paint mode, and with your mouse pointer in the 3D View window, press M; select the faces you want to paint; paint them (you will see that you cannot paint the un-selected faces); when you're finished, press M again (it's a toggle).

22. To *render* the Vertex Paint layer (see **T71, p. 116**, ②): Go to the "Properties" window: >

LClick the "Material" button: > Go to the "Options" panel > LClick the little box to the left of "Vertex Color Paint" to put a check mark in it. This will make the vertex paint layer visible in the render (unless it's covered by a texture or a ramp).

23. When you leave Vertex Paint mode, go to the "Properties" window > > LClick the

"Object" button: > Go to "Display" panel > Make sure the little box next to "Wire" is unchecked.

PART FOUR: LIGHTING AND ENVIRONMENT

T81. Lighting 1: How to arrange your lamps: (The light source itself is normally not rendered)

1. A good, basic lighting arrangement is: (a) place the strongest lamp a little to left or right of the camera and a little above the object. This is called the **"Key"** lamp. (b) Place a second lamp, called the **"fill"** lamp on the other side of the camera (about 90 degrees from the key lamp, with the object at the apex of the right angle), and (c) place a third lamp, called the **back"** (or **"rim"**) lamp on the side of the object opposite to the camera. You can add additional lights to illuminate objects other than the main object. Note that the ambient light can be controlled, and is independent of the lamps themselves.

T82. Lighting 2: How to add a new lamp to your scene or to change an existing lamp into another kind of lamp:

1. Do you want to add a new lamp to your scene?

> Yes: Go to **2**.

> No: To change an existing lamp into another kind of lamp, go to **3**.

To add a new lamp to your scene:

2. In Object mode (see **T8, p. 9**):

(a) press SHIFT + A > Hover over "Lamp" > Go to **5**;

> OR

(b) go to the "Info" window's header (the window header with ![info icon] to the left) > LClick "Add" > Hover over "Lamp" > Go to **5**.

To change an existing lamp to another kind of lamp:

3. In Object mode (see **T8, p. 9**), select (RClick) the lamp whose lamp-type you want to change.

4. Go to the "Properties" window: ![properties icon] > LClick the "Object Data" button—see **T83, step 4, p. 171** for how to identify this button > Go to the "Lamp" panel.

5.

> a. To choose a **point** lamp, whose light rays are emitted in all directions from a single point and which makes a good fill light, LClick "Point".

> b. To choose the **sun** lamp, which produces parallel light rays and which is good as an outdoor key light, LClick "Sun".

> c. To choose a **spot** lamp, which produces a cone of light from a point source and which makes a great key lamp, LClick "Spot".

> d. To choose a **hemi** lamp, whose light is produced as if by a glowing hemisphere surrounding the scene and which is good as a fill or back light, LClick "Hemi".

> e. To choose an **area** lamp, whose light is produced from an array of point lamps and which is a good key lamp, LClick "Area".

T83. Lighting 3: To position, to aim, or to otherwise modify a lamp in some way; or to create & control ambient light:

1. To change an existing lamp into a different kind of lamp: go to **T82, p. 170**.

2. Do you want to modify a **Point lamp** in some way (other than changing its type)?

> Yes: Go to **3**.
>
> No: Go to **6**.

To modify a Point lamp in some way:

3. First, make sure that your lamp, which you assume to be a Point lamp, is, in fact, a Point lamp: In Object mode (see **T8, p. 9**), select (RClick) the lamp that you want to adjust.

4. Go to the "Properties" window: > Find the "Object Data" button—this button's appearance will vary in accord with what kind of lamp is selected. for a **Point** lamp: ; for a **Sun** lamp: ; for a **Spot** lamp: ; for a **Hemi** lamp: ; for an **Area** lamp: > If the picture on the "Object Data" button shows that your lamp is not a Point lamp, but you want it to be one, LClick the "Object Data" button > Go to the "Lamp" panel > LClick "Point."

To position the Point lamp:

5. Since the **Point lamp** emits light in all directions, you don't *aim* the Point lamp; to *position* it, however, use the methods described in **T25, p. 33**. Go to **40**.

6. Do you want to modify a **Sun lamp** in some way (other than changing its type)?

> Yes: Go to **7**.
>
> No: Go to **10**.

To modify a Sun lamp in some way:

7. First, make sure that your lamp, which you assume to be a Sun lamp, is, in fact, a Sun lamp: In Object mode (see **T8, p. 9**), select (RClick) the lamp that you want to adjust.

8. Go to the "Properties" window: > Find the "Object Data" button (see **4** for how to identify this button) > If the picture on the "Object Data" button shows that your lamp is not a Sun lamp, but you want it to be one, LClick the "Object Data" button > Go to the "Lamp" panel > LClick "Sun."

To aim the Sun lamp:

9. If you want to aim a **Sun lamp**, first note that since the sun is likely to be millions of miles away from your scene, the Sun lamp icon in the 3D View does not actually mark the location of the Sun lamp; rather, This icon, together with the dotted line that's attached to it, simply serves to indicate the direction of the parallel light rays in your model space:

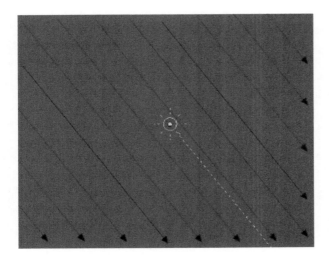

So, you only have to pay attention to *aiming* your Sun lamp, since changing its location in the 3D View window makes no difference at all. To aim it, rotate it (see **T25, p. 33**). Go to **40**.

10. Do you want to modify a **Spot lamp** in some way (other than changing its type)?

>Yes: Go to **11**.

>No: Go to. **28**.

To modify a Spot lamp in some way:

11. First, make sure that your lamp, which you assume to be a Spot lamp, is, in fact, a Spot lamp: In Object mode (see **T8, p. 9**), select (RClick) the lamp that you want to adjust.

12. Go to the "Properties" window: > Find the "Object Data" button (see **4** for how to identify this button) > If the picture on the "Object Data" button shows that your lamp is not a Spot lamp, but you want it to be one, LClick the "Object Data" button > Go to the "Lamp" panel > LClick "Spot."

To position and/or aim the Spot lamp:

13. To position and/or aim a **Spot lamp**, use the methods described in **T25, p. 33**.

To make another modification to the Spot lamp:

14. To make another modification to the Spot lamp: Go to the "Properties" window: > LClick the "Object Data" button (see **4** for how to identify this button) > Go to the "Spot Shape" panel .

15. To change the size, in degrees, of the spot's light cone (maximum is 180°), adjust the "Size" button (see **_Introduction_** for how to adjust buttons of this kind).

16. To soften the light's edges, increase the "Blend" button's value.

17. To show the light cone, as if the air is dusty, LClick the little box to the left of "Halo" in order to put a check mark in it. To hide the light cone, LClick the box to uncheck it.

18. To make the Spot light square instead of round, LClick the little box to the left of "Square" in order to put a check mark in it.

19.

(a) If you want realistic, slower rendering, shadows, go to **40**.

(b) If you want less realistic, but faster rendering, shadows, go to the "Shadow" panel > LClick "Buffer

Shadow." If no shadow appears, go to the "Properties" window, , LClick the "Render" button: > Go to the "Shading" panel > Make sure that "Shadows" is checked. If there is still no shadow, go to the 3D View window, select the object that should be casting the shadow > Go to the "Properties" window: > LClick the "Material" button: > Go to the "Shadow" panel > Make sure that the little box next to "Cast Buffer Shadows" is checked. In the 3D View window, select your lamp > Go to the "Properties" window: > LClick the "Object Data" button (see **4** for how to identify this button) > Go to **20**.

20. To change rendering speed in a way that is said to make the shadow more or less crisp, go to the "Shadow" panel > adjust the "Size" button (see ***Introduction*** for how to adjust buttons of this kind).

21. To change rendering speed in a way that is said to make the shadow softer or harder, go to the "Shadow" panel > adjust the "Samples" button (see ***Introduction*** for how to adjust buttons of this kind).

22. To offset the shadow slightly from the object that's casting it, in order to get rid of small irregularities, go to the "Shadow" panel > adjust the "Bias" button (see ***Introduction*** for how to adjust buttons of this kind). (It's usually best to leave "Bias" at its default setting.)

23. To soften the shadow's edges, go to the "Shadow" panel > adjust the "Soft" button (see ***Introduction*** for how to adjust buttons of this kind) .

24. Using the Spot lamp, suppose that you want item(s) A to cast a shadow: to specify that A will cast a shadow onto surface S: go to the "Shadow" panel > (a) make sure that the "Clip Start" value is smaller than the "Clip End" value, and that S is closer to the lamp than the "Clip End" value, and that A is farther from the lamp than the "Clip Start" value. (A line representing the span between the Clip Start and the Clip End distances can be seen in the 3D View window; both the shadow-casting item(s) and the shadow-receiving surface(s) should be within the span indicated by this line.) (b) If you want A *not* to cast a shadow on S, make sure that A is closer to the lamp than the Clip Start value.

25. It is said that to render fur and hair better, you should go to the "Shadow" panel > LClick the "Sample Buffers" button > LClick a number to increase the value.

26. If you enabled "Halo" in step **17**, and if you want to adjust the visibility of the object's shadow *in the air* within the light cone that's made visible by "Halo," go to the "Spot Shape" panel > adjust the "Step" button (zero: no shadow in the air; 12: a fuller shadow in the air) (see ***Introduction*** for how to adjust buttons of this kind).

27. Go to **41**.

28. Do you want to modify an **Area lamp** in some way (other than changing its type)?

> Yes: Go to **29**.

> No: Go to **37**.

To modify an Area lamp in some way:

29. First, make sure that your lamp, which you assume to be an Area lamp, is, in fact, an Area lamp: In Object mode (see **T8, p. 9**), select (RClick) the lamp that you want to adjust.

30. Go to the "Properties" window:  > Find the "Object Data" button (see **4** for how to identify this button) > If the picture on the "Object Data" button shows that your lamp is not an Area lamp, but you want it to be one, LClick the "Object Data" button > Go to the "Lamp" panel > LClick "Area."

To position and/or aim the Area lamp:

31. If you want to position and/or aim an **Area lamp**, use the methods described in **T25, p. 33**.

32. LClick the "Object Data" button > To have the area lamp produce shadows, go to the "Shadow" panel > LClick the "Ray Shadow" button.

33. To change the shape of the lamp, go to the "Area Shape" panel > LClick the "Square" button or the "Rectangle" button.

34. To change the size of the lamp, go to the "Area Shape" panel > adjust the "Size" button if the lamp is square, or the "Size X" and "Size Y" buttons if it is rectangular.

To make another modification of the Area lamp:

35. To change the number of lamps in the Area lamp's array, go to the "Shadow" panel > Go to the "Sampling" buttons > if the lamp is square, adjust the "Samples" button. Choosing 3, for instance, will produce an array with 3 columns of lamps horizontally, and 3 rows of lamps vertically, for a total of 9 lamps. If the lamp is rectangular, adjust the "Samples X" button to specify the number of columns and "Samples Y" button to specify the number of rows in the array.

36. Go to **40**.

To modify a Hemi lamp in some way:

37. To modify a **Hemi lamp** in some way (other than changing its type), first, make sure that your lamp, which you assume to be a Hemi lamp, is, in fact, a Hemi lamp: in Object mode (see **T8, p. 9**), select (RClick) the lamp that you want to adjust.

38. Go to the "Properties" window:  > Find the "Object Data" button (see **4** for how to identify this button) > If the picture on the "Object Data" button shows that your lamp is not a Hemi lamp, but you want it to be one, LClick the "Object Data" button > Go to the "Lamp" panel > LClick "Hemi."

To aim the Hemi lamp:

39. As with the Sun lamp (see **7** above) you only have to pay attention to *aiming* your Hemi lamp, since changing its location in the 3D View window makes no difference at all. To aim it, rotate it (see **T25, p. 33**).

To make further modifications to your point, sun, spot, area or hemi lamp:

40. For *all lamps except the Hemi*, to use ray-tracing to create shadows: Go to the "Shadow" panel >

LClick "Ray Shadow." If no shadows appear, go to the "Properties" window, , LClick the

"Render" button:  > Go to the "Shading" panel > Make sure that "Shadows" and "Ray Tracing" are both checked. If there are still no shadows, in the 3D View window, in Object mode, select the object

that should be receiving the shadow > Go to the "Properties" window:  > LClick the

"Material" button: > Go to the "Shadow" panel > Make sure that the little box next to "Receive" is checked. (For all lamps other than the Hemi:) If shadows still do not appear, in the 3D View window, select the lamp > Go to the "Properties" window: > LClick the "Object Data" button (see **4** for how to identify this button) > Go to the "Shadow" panel > Try setting the "Samples" button to a lower value.)

41. To further modify a lamp *of any kind*: Select the lamp > Go to the "Properties" window: > LClick the "Object Data" button (see **4** for how to identify this button). Go to **42**.

To adjust brightness:

42. To adjust the brightness of a lamp of any kind, go to the "Lamp" panel > adjust the "Energy" button (see ***Introduction*** for how to adjust buttons of this kind).

To change the color of the light:

43. To change the color of the light that the lamp emits, go to the "Lamp" panel > LClick the color swatch (which might be white, or any color) underneath the first row of buttons > Choose a color using the methods presented in **T68, step 5, p. 111**.

To adjust a lamp's effective distance:

44. For a Spot lamp or an Area lamp: to specify a distance, say 20 units, from the light beyond which the light will begin to diminish, go to the "Lamp" panel > adjust the "Distance" button to 20.

45. For a Point lamp: to specify a distance, say 20 units, from the light beyond which the light will begin to diminish, in the "Lamp" panel: make sure that the little box next to "Sphere" is unchecked and adjust the "Distance" button to 20; but to specify that the light starts at maximum at the lamp, and gets weaker gradually until it reaches zero at a certain distance, say 20 units, make sure that, in the "Lamp" panel, the little box next to "Sphere" is checked and adjust the "Distance" button to 20.

46. To see, in the 3D View window, how far the light's full intensity will extend from the lamp (see **44** and **45**): (a) for the Area lamp, look at the line that points in the direction that the light is aiming; (b) for the Spot lamp: Look at the length of the cone; (c) for the Point lamp, if the little square next to "Sphere" is checked (see **45**), you will see a circle that represents the "Distance" distance.

47. In the "Shadow" panel: If Ray Shadow is enabled, note the button that has "Adaptive QMC" on it, and the button that has "Constant QMC" on it. These labels refer to methods Blender uses to create ray-traced shadows. Adaptive QMC is faster than Constant QMC. LClick the button for the method you want to use.

48. If your lamp is a Point lamp, a Sun lamp, or a Spot lamp, and if Ray Shadow is enabled, to specify the number of raytracings to use for the shadows, go to the "Shadow" panel > adjust the "Samples" button (see ***Introduction*** for how to adjust buttons of this kind). A higher number increases accuracy, but also increases render-time.

49. If your lamp is a Point lamp, a Sun lamp, or a Spot lamp, and if Ray Shadow is enabled, to control blurriness of the shadow's edge, go to the "Shadow" panel > Make sure that the "Samples" button is set to a value greater than 1 > adjust the "Soft Size" button   (A higher value produces a blurrier edge) > Adjust the "Samples" button to reduce/increase the graininess of the shadow's edge. (See ***Introduction***

for how to adjust buttons of this kind.)

50. If your lamp is a Point lamp, a Sun lamp, a Spot lamp, or an Area lamp, and if Ray Shadow is enabled, and if you chose Adaptive QMC at step **47**, you can shorten render time while maintaining shadow accuracy: Go to the "Shadow" panel > adjust the value of "Threshold".

51. If your lamp is a Point lamp, a Sun lamp, a Spot lamp, or an Area lamp, and if Ray Shadow is enabled, to change the color of the shadow, Go to the "Shadow" panel > LClick the color swatch (which may be white, black or any color) and adjust the color as shown in **T68, step 5, p. 111**.

52. The Hemi lamp does not cast shadows. If a lamp is a Point lamp, a Sun lamp, a Spot lamp or an Area lamp, you can prevent it from casting shadows by going to the "Shadow" panel and LClicking "No Shadow".

To illuminate only on the same layer:

53. For any lamp: to make your lamp illuminate only objects that are on the same layer (see **T41, p. 74-T44, p. 76**) as your lamp, go to the "Lamp" panel > LClick the little box next to "This Layer Only" to put a check mark in it.

Only shadows:

54. For any lamp other than a Hemi lamp: to cast shadows without adding light, make sure that "Ray Shadow" (or "Buf Shadow") is enabled and go to the "Shadow" panel > LClick "Only Shadow". (Note that with "Only Shadow" enabled for a lamp, there must be at least one other lamp, or ambient lighting, supplying the light; otherwise, the render will be black—but if ambient lighting is the only other lighting, the shadow will not be visible.)

To shine darkness:

55. To shine darkness onto your scene: Go to the "Lamp" panel > LClick the little box next to "Negative" to put a check mark in it. (Note that with "Negative" enabled for a lamp, there must be at least one other lamp, or ambient lighting, supplying the light; otherwise, the render will be black—but if ambient lighting is the only other lighting, the "negative lighting" will not be visible.)

No diffuse light:

56. To prevent the lamp from producing diffuse light, that is, to have your lamp produce only specular highlights: Go to the "Lamp" panel > Make sure that the little box next to "Specular" is checked and that the little box next to "Diffuse" is not checked.

No specular highlights:

57. To prevent the lamp from producing specular highlights, that is, to have your lamp produce only diffuse light: Go to the "Lamp" panel > Make sure that the little box next to "Diffuse" is checked and that the little box next to "Specular" is not checked. (This is a good setting for a "fill" light.)

To add a texture to the light:

58. You can add a texture to the lamp (to the lamp's light). To do this: *with the lamp selected*, go to the

"Properties" window: > LClick the "Texture" button: to add a texture as you would add a usual material texture (see **T74, p. 120**), though your options will be a little more limited.

To create and control AMBIENT LIGHT in your scene:

59. Ambient light is produced in the real world as individual light rays bounce many times off of objects, thus lighting even the parts of objects which do not receive the direct rays from the light source(s). In ambient light, surfaces near one another tend to cast shadows on one another. Blender can simulate this effect. Follow the steps below to enable Blender's simulated ambient light and shading.

60. In the real world, you cannot have ambient light without there being a primary light source. But in Blender, you can light your scene with ambient light alone; that is, without using a lamp of any kind. Of course, using a lamp *together with* ambient light gives more realistic results than using ambient light alone. Do you want to use ambient lighting *alone* to light your scene?

> Yes: Go to **61**.

> No: Go to **62**.

61. Delete or de-energize all lamps from your scene. Go to **63**.

62. Make sure that you have one or more lamps operating in your scene.

To enable ambient light and shadow:

63. Go to the "Properties" window >  > LClick the "Render" button: > Go to the "Shading" panel: Make sure that the little box next to "Shadows" is checked.

64. To put ambient light and shading into your scene: go to the "Properties" window:  > LClick the "World" button: > you can use Method 1 or Method 2, or both together:

METHOD 1:

65. Go to the "Ambient Occlusion" panel – LClick the little box next to "Ambient Occlusion".

66. Adjust the "Factor" slider to change the intensity of the ambient light.

METHOD 2:

67. Go to the "Envronment Lighting" panel – LClick the little box next to "Environment Lighting".

68. LClick the right-hand button:

> If you want your ambient light to be white, LClick "White".

> If you want your ambient light to be the sky color (as set at **T84, p. 179**), LClick "Sky Color".

> If you want your ambient light to be a color derived from the sky texture (**T84**), LClick "Sky Texture".

69. Adjust the "Energy" slider to change the intensity of the ambient light.

END OF METHODS

To set the ambient light's color:

70. To change the color of your scene's ambient light, go to the "Properties" window: > LClick the "World" button: > Go to the "World" panel > LClick the "Ambient Color" swatch > Adjust the color, as shown in **T68, step 5, p. 111**. Making the ambient light's color "blacker" (by minimizing the setting of the Value slider) actually makes it whiter, in the sense that, as with white light in the real world, it will cause all materials to show their true colors. Making the ambient light's color "whiter" (by dragging the pointer toward the center of the color circle) adds a white cast to all material colors; for the most realistic lighting, use colors that lie at the edge of the color circle and adjust the values slider.

Making the ambient light's color, say, red or yellow gives material colors a pink or yellow cast. To adjust the R, G, and B sliders for a sunny day, try .9, .9, .8 (with a very low value-slider setting).

To choose Raytrace or Approximate for creating ambient light:

71. Do you want to use a method for creating ambient light which is fast and not grainy, but less accurate?

>Yes: Go to **78**.

>No: To use a method which is slow (unless you don't care if it's grainy) but is more accurate, go to **72**.

72. Go to the "Properties" window >  > LClick the "Render" button: > Go to the "Shading" panel: Make sure that the little box next to "Ray Tracing" is checked > Still in the "Properties" window: > LClick the "World" button: > Go to the "Gather" panel > LClick **Raytrace** > LClick the "Sampling" button:

>(a) To use a kind of ray tracing where the rays are evenly and randomly sampled, LClick "Constant QMC". Go to **75**.

>(b) To use a better kind of ray tracing, LClick "Adaptive QMC". Go to **73**.

>(c) To use an older kind of ray tracing which can cause certain unwanted "artifacts", LClick "Constant jittered". Go to **74**.

73. To experiment with a control that influences the appearance of the ambient light's shadows, adjust the "Threshold" button. Go to **75**.

74. Using "Constant jittered", some edges may become visible on smoothed objects. To deal with this, you can adjust the "Bias" button.

75. To increase the accuracy and smoothness in the creation of the ambient light shadows: still in the "Gather" panel, increase the value of the "Samples" button.

76. To simulate ambient light shadows, Blender's raytracing determines when two surfaces are close to each other. To control the length of these rays, still in the "Gather" panel, adjust the "Distance" value. Longer rays will allow mutual shading to occur on more distant pairs of surfaces, but will slow the render.

77. Go to **83**.

78. Go to the "Properties" window: > LClick the "World" button: > Go to the "Gather" panel > LClick **"Approximate"**.

79. To set a tolerance for error between approximate and fully computed, adjust the "Error" button (see *Introduction* for how to adjust buttons of this kind). A lower setting is slower but more accurate. (0-10; default: .25)

80. To speed up rendering, usually without noticeable quality loss, LClick the little box next to "Pixel Cache".

81. It is said that to set the number of "pre-processing" passes, or calculations, adjust the "Passes" button (see **_Introduction_** for how to adjust buttons of this kind).

82. It is said that to correct for a specific kind of possible over-shading error, adjust the "Correction" button (see *__Introduction__* for how to adjust buttons of this kind).

83. To change the size of the ambient-light's shadows: LClick the little box next to "Falloff" > adjust the "Strength" button (see *__Introduction__* for how to adjust buttons of this kind). Setting "Strength" to a higher number is said to create more subtle shadows.

To change the amount of ambient light a material will receive:

84. To change the amount of ambient light, as set at **step 64, Method 2** above, that a material in your scene will receive: Select the object that has the material applied to it > Go to the "Properties" window:

> LClick the "Material" button: > In the large box at the top, select the name of the material > Go to the "Shading" panel > Adjust the "Ambient" slider (0.0 for no ambient light; 1.0 for all the ambient light).

T84. To set up your scene's environment—Part One: To create a sky:

METHOD 1 – Use an *image texture* of a sky (mountains, etc.) as a background: Go to **T87, p. 182 below.**

METHOD 2 – Use a Blender-generated sky:

1. Go to the "Properties" window: > LClick the "World" button: > Go to the "World" panel.

To set the horizon color:

2. To set the sky's horizon color: LClick the "Horizon Color" swatch (which may be white, black or any color) > pick the color using the methods covered in **T68, step 5, p. 111**.

To set the zenith color:

3. To set the sky's zenith color: LClick the "Zenith Color" swatch (which may be white, black or any color) > pick the color using the methods covered in **T68, step 5, p. 111**.

To set the horizon/zenith arrangement:

4. To create a sky such that the horizon color will always be at the bottom of the rendered image, blending to the zenith color at the top (regardless of where the camera is aiming): Make sure that "Paper Sky" is checked (for a more intense zenith color) or unchecked, "Blend Sky" is checked, and "Real Sky" is unchecked.

5. To create a **natural sky**, that is, to place the pure horizon color at the global grid plane and the pure zenith color straight up (and straight down) in the global Z direction, make sure that "Paper Sky" is unchecked, "Blend Sky" is checked, and "Real Sky" is checked.

6. To create a sky such that the horizon color is always at the center of the render, and such that this horizon color blends to the zenith color when the camera is aimed horizontally, but blends toward a color that is a mixture of horizon and zenith color as the camera aims up or down, with horizon color dominating more and more until, when the camera is aiming straight up or down (in the global Z direction) the sky uniformly takes on the horizon color, make sure that "Paper Sky", "Blend Sky" and "Real Sky" are all checked.

7. To create a sky that is uniformly the horizon color, make sure that "Paper Sky", "Blend Sky" and "Real Sky" are all unchecked.

8. If you have a Sun lamp in your scene, you can change the sky by selecting and adjusting your Sun lamp: In Object mode (see **T8, p. 9**), select (RClick) the Sun lamp that you want to adjust.

9. Go to the "Properties" window: > LClick the "Object Data" button (see **T83, step 4, p. 171** for how to identify this button) > Go to the "Lamp" panel > Make sure that you have "Sun" selected, so that your lamp will *be* a Sun lamp.

10. Go to the "Sky & Atmosphere" panel > LClick the little box next to "Sky" to put a check mark in it. [I admit that I do not fully understand exactly how the controls discussed in **11-13** are supposed to work. If you wish to create a sky for a photorealistic image and have difficulty operating these controls, consider using Method 1 above; that is, consider importing an image texture into your scene—RC]

11. Adjust "Turbidity" for sky color effects which vary with the direction of the Sun lamp's parallel light rays – for instance, when the Sun's rays are not much inclined with respect to the Global XY plane (simulating a rising or setting sun), a turbidity setting might make the horizon red; whereas when the Sun's rays are more nearly perpendicular to the plane (as around noon in the tropics), with the same turbidity setting, the horizon may be pink.

12. Also in the "Sky & Atmosphere" panel, and with the Sun lamp still selected, you can get other sky-color effects by adjusting the two "Horizon" buttons, "Brightness" and "Spread".

13. The settings you make in **11** and **12** above can be modified by LClicking the top "Blending" button and LClicking a mixing method in the drop down list—that is, (it seems true to say), by choosing a method by which the colors created in **8-13** above will be mixed with the colors created in steps **1-7** above.

14. To add stars to any sky, go to the "Properties" window: > LClick the "World" button: > Go to the "Stars" panel > LClick the little box to the left of "Stars" to put a check mark in it > LClick on the little black arrow if you need to expand the panel > Adjust the buttons to change the appearance of the stars.

15. You can add a texture to the sky; for instance, you might add a Marble texture to put clouds in your sky. To do this, go to the "Properties" window: > LClick the "World" button: > Go to the "World" panel > Make sure that "Paper" and "Blend" are checked > LClick the "Texture" button at the top: . (Now you will be applying a texture not to a material, but to the "World"; in this case, to the sky) > Choose a texture much as you would do when applying a texture to a material (see **T74**). (If you can't see your textured sky, select your lamp > Go to the "Properties" window: > LClick the "Object Data" button (see **T83, step 4, p. 171** for how to identify this button) > Go to the "Sky & Atmosphere" panel > If the little box next to "Sky" is checked, try experimenting with the settings of the button to the right of "Sky" and with the settings of the upper "Blending" button.)

END OF METHODS

T85. To set up your scene's environment—Part Two: to show and modify the sun itself:

1. When you use a Sun lamp, the model space is filled with parallel rays of sunlight. To make the camera image the Sun itself, place the camera, or adjust the Sun lamp's rays, so that the camera is looking more or less directly into one of these oncoming parallel rays. Note that because the Sun lamp *icon*

does not stand for the Sun (lamp) itself, but is only there as an indicator of the direction of the Sun's rays (see **T83, step 9, p. 171**), the position of the Sun lamp icon is not important in this regard—the camera can be facing the sun, and can image it, even when the Sun lamp icon is in back of the camera.

2. To modify the Sun's appearance: in object mode (see **T8, p. 9**), in the 3D View window, select (RClick) the icon for the Sun lamp.

3. Go to the "Properties" window: [image] > LClick the "Object Data" button (see **T83, step 4, p. 171** for how to identify this button) > Go to the "Lamp" panel > Make sure that you have "Sun" selected, so that your lamp will *be* a Sun lamp.

4. Go to the "Sky & Atmosphere" panel > LClick the little square next to "Sky" to put a check mark in it > adjust the "Turbidity" button, the "Horizon" button called "Brightness," and the "Sun" button called "Size"", to give the Sun the appearance you want it to have > Make further modifications by LClicking the top button under "Blending" and then LClicking a mixing method in the drop down list—that is (it seems true to say), by choosing a method by which the colors created here will be mixed with the colors that were created in **T84, steps 1-7, p. 179**.

T86. To set up your scene's environment—Part Three: to specify atmospheric properties:

To add mist to your scene:

1. In the 3D View window, select your camera > , go to the "Properties" window: [image] > LClick the

"Object Data" button, which, because the camera is selected, looks like this: [image] > Go to the "Display" panel > LClick the little box next to "Mist" to put a check mark in it. This will add to the camera icon what I'll call a "mist-fade-in line," a line that starts at the distance from the camera at which the mist will begin to increase from minimum and ends at the distance beyond which the mist will completely hide objects. Note that as long as the box next to "Mist" is checked, a minimal mist will exist between the camera and the "Start" distance of the mist-fade-in line.

2. To add mist, go to the "Properties" window: [image] > LClick the "World" button: [image] > Go to

181

the "Mist" panel > LClick the little box to the left of "Mist" to put a check mark in it > LClick on the little black arrow to expand the panel > Watching the "mist-fade-in line" (see **1** above), adjust the buttons to change the appearance of the mist. The "Minimum" button controls the intensity of the mist minimum—if "Minimum" is set to zero, the mist will increase from zero mist to maximum (completely hiding objects) along the mist-fade-in line's distance. The "Depth" button controls the distance over which the mist gradually becomes maximized. If "Height" is set to zero, the mist extends to a maximum height; when it is not zero, a lower setting produces a lower height.

3. You can add a texture to the mist; for instance, you might add a Cloud texture to make your mist

patchy. To do this, go to the "Properties" window:  > LClick the "World" button: >

LClick the "Texture" button: . (Now you will be applying a texture not to a material, but to the "World"; in this case, to the mist) > Choose a texture much as you would do when applying a texture to a material (see **T74, p. 120**).

To change atmospheric conditions in ways that require there to be a Sun lamp in your scene:

4. There are ways to change the atmosphere that require there to be a Sun lamp in your scene: First, in object mode (see **T8, p. 9**), select (RClick) the Sun lamp.

5. Go to the "Properties" window: > LClick the "Object Data" button (see **T83, step 4, p. 171** for how to identify this button) > Go to the "Lamp" panel > Make sure that you have "Sun" selected, so that your lamp will, in fact, *be* a Sun lamp.

6. Go to the "Sky & Atmosphere" panel > LClick the little box next to "Atmosphere" to put a check mark in it.

7. It is said that to modify the atmosphere to reflect a more or less intense sun, adjust "Sun."

8. It is said that to modify the atmosphere to reflect the scattering of sunlight in it, adjust "Inscattering".

9. It is said that to change the amount of something called "light extinction", you should adjust "Extinction".

10. It is said that to give the atmosphere a yellower cast, you should increase "Distance".

T87. To set up your scene's environment—Part Four: to put a background image into your scene:

1. To put a background image, say, of trees, hills and a sky, into your scene, go to the "Properties"

window: > LClick the "World" button: > LClick the "Texture" button: . (Now you will be applying a texture not to a material, but to the "World" .)

2. Is the texture stack empty, with no textures in it at all?

      Yes: Go to **4**.

      No: Go to **3**.

3. LClick In the highest empty channel in the stack:

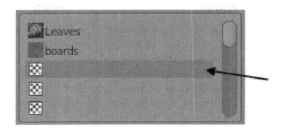

4. Do you want to apply a texture that's already existing somewhere in your scene to the material?

Yes: Go to **5**.

No: Go to **7**.

5. LClick the little button on the left end of the row of buttons beneath the textures stack:

6. LClick the name of the existing texture that you want to apply to the material. You have applied your texture. Go to **19**.

7. LClick the "New" button.

8. Re-name your newly-added texture: When you add this new texture, Blender names it for you. To change this name, go to the row or buttons right below the texture stack > LClick on the field with the Blender-generated name in it:

9. Type the name you want the texture to have > Press ENTER.

10. Choose the "Image or Movie" texture type:

LClick the "Type" button:

LClick "Image or Movie".

11. Go to the "Image" panel .

12. In creating your new texture, do you want to use an image that you've already applied as a texture to some material in your scene?

Yes: Go to **13**.

No: Go to **14**.

13. LClick the button to the far left:

LClick the name of the image that you want to use. Go to **19**.

14. To use an image on your hard drive: LClick the "Open" button:

15. To have your image files shown as thumbnails, LClick this button at upper left: 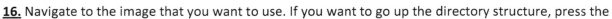 .

16. Navigate to the image that you want to use. If you want to go up the directory structure, press the

button at upper left with the crooked arrow on it: 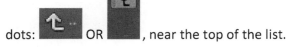, or LClick the same kind of arrow, with two

dots: OR , near the top of the list.

17. If you want to go down the directory structure, LClick a name in the list.

18. (a) LClick the file you want to use to select it > LClick "Open Image" at upper right.

　　　OR

(b) Double LClick the file you want to use.

19. Go to the "Influence" panel > Put check marks in the little boxes next to "Horizon", "Zenith Up", and "Zenith Down" (so that the texture will cover up all parts of the "Sky") > Go to the "Mapping" panel > Look at the "Coordinates" button : if it does not say "View" on it, LClick it and then LClick "View" > Adjust the size of the image by adjusting the "Size" buttons (see ***Introduction*** for how to adjust buttons of this kind). *Increasing a size button's value decreases the image's size* > Adjust the image's position by adjusting the "Offset" buttons. If you have more than one background image texture in the stack, the lowest in the stack will be the one that renders. Use the arrows to the right of the stack to change the order of these textures.

PART FIVE: TOOLS THAT ARE OF GENERAL USE—THAT IS, TOOLS THAT CAN BE USED IN CREATING BOTH STILL IMAGES AND ANIMATION—BUT THAT ARE PRIMARILY FOR USE IN ANIMATION

T88. Rigging a mesh model—Part One: Overview and general procedures for working with an armature (for directions for building an armature for a human-shaped mesh in particular, go to T89):

1. Rigging a model—An Overview

Animating, or even posing, a figure, a human-shaped mesh for instance, is made much easier if you put a skeleton-like, posable *armature* inside it.

First, *in Edit mode*, amid the other objects in your scene, or all by itself in a scene, you can (using the methods covered in the other sections of this book—see PARTS ONE through THREE) build the mesh model in a kind of standardized pose—for instance, your mesh person might be built in a standing position with arms held straight out to the sides along the Global X axis. Whatever pose you use at this stage, it is called the "rest pose".

Then, without changing the rest pose at all, you can build the armature (see **T89**) inside the mesh, and, in a process called "skinning" the mesh, attach the armature's bones (see **T90**) to the mesh "skin", so that the "skin" moves with the bones.

Then, in order to *pose* the mesh + armature figure, which I'll call a "rigged model," you have to put the scene into **Pose mode**. No matter how you change the pose in Pose mode—let's say you raise the figure's arms straight up—if you go back into Edit mode, the model will snap back into the rest pose. Then, keeping the model in rest pose, you can edit the mesh (see PARTS TWO and THREE) and edit the armature (see this Topic [**T89**], below, & **T91**); for instance, you can lengthen the arms. If you then go into Pose mode again, the model, now with longer arms, will snap back to its "arms-straight-up" pose.

When you are finished editing your mesh and its armature in Edit mode, and if you intend to animate the model, you can create your *keyframes* (see **T107, step 20, Example 2, p. 227**) in Pose mode.

Note that you will be able to bring your rigged mesh, and its actions (see **T45, p. 76**) into any scene by using File > Append, and importing the mesh along with the armature, and Actions.

The armature is made up of *bones*. When I refer to the parts of a bone, in its octahedron form, I will use these terms:

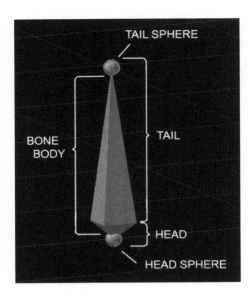

By default, the **armature**'s origin (see **T24, p. 32**) is in the center of the first **bone**'s head sphere. Each bone has its own coordinate system also, as you will see below.

To add an armature to your scene:

2. When adding an armature, it is often beneficial to add it with its origin at the Global origin (X=0, Y=0, Z=0), and to have already positioned your model accordingly (for instance, you should have positioned your human-shaped mesh such that the Global origin is located within the abdomen). If you want to add an armature so that the new armature's origin will be at the Global origin, first place your 3D cursor there: With your mouse cursor in the 3D View window: Press SHIFT+S > LClick "Cursor to Center." Now, when you add your armature—it will be added in the form of a single bone—and the armature's origin (see **T24**), which will be at the center of this bone's head sphere, will be at the position of the Global origin. To add an armature: *Make sure you are in Object mode* > Press SHIFT+A > Hover over "Armature" > LClick "Single Bone." (This Topic is general; for directions on how to add an armature to a *human-shaped mesh* in particular, see **T89** below.)

3. If your armature is inside your mesh, you will want to make the armature visible. **To make your armature visible:** Still in Object mode, still in the 3D View window, the new armature (at this point a single bone) should still be selected; if you have deselected it for any reason, select it again (since you may not be able to see the armature inside the mesh in the 3D View window, you might have to select it

in the Outliner window) > Go to the "Properties" window: ⬚ > Enable the "Object Data" button: ⬚ > Go to the "Display" panel > Put a check inside the little box next to "X-Ray". If the armature

does not become visible, select the mesh > Go to the "Properties" window: ⬚ > Enable the

"Object" button: ⬚ > Go to the "Display" panel > If the little box next to "X-Ray" is checked, uncheck it.

To add a bone to an existing armature, use one of these METHODS:
METHOD 1—Extrude.
4. If you use this method to add a bone, and if you extrude from the *tail* sphere of a bone, your extruded bone will be the child (see **T33, p. 71**) of the bone whose tail sphere it was extruded from, and so, *in Pose mode*, will move, rotate or scale when its parent is moved, rotated or scaled (but not vice versa); but, if you extrude from the *head* sphere of a bone, your extruded bone will not (automatically) be the child of the bone you extruded it from. (Note that a bone, which is a *part* of the armature *object*, can have a parent/child relationship with another bone even though, normally, this relationship occurs only between *objects*.)

5. To **extrude** a bone from a bone's sphere:
Do you want to extrude a bone to the right (or left) such that you will also extrude a mirror-copy of the bone to the left (or right)?

> Yes: Go to **6.**

> No: Go to **7.**

6. Suppose that you want to extrude the new bone from the tail sphere of a bone called "Bone1". For this mirroring to work, Bone1 must be aligned with the Global Z axis—its origin must be at Global X = 0 and Y = 0 > In Object mode, select the armature with Bone1 in it > Go to Edit mode > Select the tail sphere of Bone1 > Go to front view: Press numpad1 > Press E > Pull the bone out to the right to some arbitrary size > LClick > Go to the "Properties" window: > Enable the "Bone" button: > LClick the long field at the top (this field has the name in it that Blender has given the new bone) > Type a name that ends in ".R"—"'ArmBone.R" for instance > Press ENTER > RClick Bone1's tail sphere again, to select it > Press E > Extrude a new bone to the left, making it the size that you want both new bones to be > LClick > Go to the "Properties" window: > Enable the "Bone" button: > LClick the long field at the top (this field has the name in it that Blender has given the second new bone) > Type "ArmBone.L" > Press ENTER > Go to the Tool Shelf (if it's not there, press T) > Go to the "Armature Options" panel > Put a check into the little square next to "X-Axis Mirror" > Press G. ArmBone.R will snap to the same size as ArmBone.L and to an orientation which is a mirror image of ArmBone.L's orientation > Press ESC. Now when you extrude a new bone from ArmBone.L or from ArmBone.R, you will be extruding a mirror copy from the other bone automatically, and so on along a chain of new bones starting with ArmBone.L and ArmBone.R. If you re-name the new bones, make sure to preserve the .L and .R endings. (For another way to create a symmetrical armature, see **T89, step 13, p. 193**.)

7. In Object mode, select the armature > Go to Edit mode > Select the bone's sphere that you want to extrude a new bone from > (a) Press E > Extrude the new bone, OR (b) If the sphere you selected was the tail sphere of a bone: place the mouse cursor at the point to which you want to extend the tail sphere of the new bone > Press CTRL+LClick.

METHOD 2—Duplicate.
8. To **duplicate** a bone: In Object mode, select the armature > Go to Edit mode, select the bone body of the bone you want to duplicate > With the mouse cursor in the 3D View window, press SHIFT + D >

Move the duplicate where you want it > LClick. The duplicate will be the child of the bone that the original bone is the child of, and will have the same constraints (see **T94, p. 207** through **T102, p. 213**) as the original.

METHOD 3—Subdivide.

9. To **subdivide** a bone: In Object mode, select the armature > Go to Edit mode, select the bone body of the bone you want to subdivide > With the mouse cursor in the 3D View window, press W > LClick "Subdivide" > Go to the Tool Shelf (if it's not there, press T) > Go to the "Subdivide Multi" panel > Adjust the "Number of Cuts" button to stipulate the number of cuts you want. The new bones will have the parent/child relationships that the original bone had.

METHOD 4—Use SHIFT+A.

10. **To add a bone to the armature, a bone that will have no parent/child relationships with the rest of the armature**: In Object mode, select the armature > Go to Edit mode > With the mouse cursor in the 3D View window, Press SHIFT+A .

END OF METHODS

11. **To subdivide a bone**: See **step 9** above.

12. **To reverse the direction of one or more bones:** In Object mode, select the armature > Go to Edit mode > Select the bone(s) whose direction you want to reverse > (a) Press W > LClick "Switch Direction" OR (b) Press ALT+F. Reversing a bone will sever connections and parent/child relationships that it has with adjacent bones.

13. Blender automatically sets up a parent/child relationship when you extrude a new bone (see **5**), but you might want **to make,say, BoneA the child of, say, BoneB, and you might at the same time want to have BoneA's head sphere connect to BoneB's tail sphere**. To do this, in Object mode, select the armature > Go to Edit mode > Select BoneA

METHOD 1—if you opt to connect BoneA's head sphere to BoneB's tail sphere, and the two bones are visually separated, this method moves BoneA, in its entirety, over to BoneB:

14. Press SHIFT+RClick to select BoneB > Press CTRL+P.

15.

    (a) If you want to connect BoneA's head sphere to BoneB's tail sphere, LClick "Connected".

    (b) If you do not want to connect BoneA's head sphere to BoneB's tail sphere, LClick "Keep Offset".

METHOD 2—if you opt to connect BoneA's head sphere to BoneB's tail sphere, and the two bones are visually separated, this method moves BoneA's head sphere to BoneB's tail sphere but leaves BoneA's tail sphere where it is, thus rescaling boneA:

16. Go to the "Properties" window: > Enable the "Bone" button: > Go to the "Relations" panel >

    (a) If you want to connect BoneA's head sphere to BoneB's tail sphere, Make sure that the little box next to "Connected" is checked.

    (b) If you do not want to connect BoneA's head sphere to BoneB's tail sphere, Make sure that the little box next to "Connected" is not checked.

17. LClick the "Parent" button (field) > LClick the name of BoneB in the drop-down list. (You may have to scroll in this list to find the name.)

END OF METHODS

18. Remember that the parenting relationships only work as expected in *Pose* mode (and in the render).

19. To clear a parenting relationship between, and to separate, bones: In Object mode, select the armature > Go to Edit mode > Select the child bone > Press ALT+P > LClick "Clear Parent".

20. To disconnect a child from its parent while preserving the parent/child relationship: In Object mode, select the armature > Go to Edit mode > Select the child bone > Press ALT+P > LClick "Disconnect Bone".

21. Remember that the parenting relationships only work as expected in *Pose* mode (and in the render).

22. To change your armature's name: In Object mode, select the armature > Go to the "Properties"

window: > Enable the "Object" button: > LClick the long field at the top (inside which is the armature's present name) > Type the new name > Press ENTER.

23. To change a bone's name: In Object mode, select the armature > Go into Edit mode > Select the

bone whose name you want to change > Go to the "Properties" window: > Enable the "Bone"

button: > LClick in the long field at the top (the field with the bone icon to its left and with the selected bone's present name in it) > Type the new name > Press ENTER.

24. To be able to see the bones' names in the 3D View window: > Go to the "Properties" window:

> Enable the "Object Data" button: > Go to the "Display" panel > Put a check inside the little box next to "Names".

25. To be able to see the bones' individual coordinate systems: Even though they are not objects (the armature is the object), bones have their own individual coordinate systems. To show these systems in the 3D View window: In Object mode, in the 3D View window, select the armature > Go to the

"Properties" window: > Enable the "Object Data" button: > Go to the "Display" panel > Put a check inside the little box next to "Axes".

26. "Bone layers" overview: I'll call the layers that were covered in **T41-T44** "scene" layers. These are layers that you can put objects (such as an armature) into. An armature's *bones*, on the other hand, can be put into "bone" layers. All of the bone layers are in the *scene* layer that the armature is in—the bone layers can be thought of as "sublayers". Every armature has 32 bone layers in the scene layer it's in.

27. To put the active bone (= the only selected bone or the last-to-be-selected one) into a bone layer: In Object mode > Select the armature > Go into Edit mode > Select the bone > Go to the "Properties"

window: > Enable the "Bone" button: > Go to the "Relations" panel > Go to the "Layers" buttons > (a) to put the bone into, say, the 3rd bone layer while taking it out of any layers it is already in: LClick the 3rd button from top left; OR (b) to put the bone into, say, the 3rd bone layer while keeping it in any layers it is already in: SHIFT+LClick the 3rd button from top left.

28. To make one or more bone layers of a given armature visible: Go to Object mode > (assuming the scene layer that the armature is on is visible—see **T41, p. 74**) Select the armature > Go to the "Properties" window: ▨ > Enable the "Object Data" button: ⍟ > Go to the "Skeleton" panel > Go to the "Layers" buttons > (a) To make a bone layer visible while making currently visible bone layers invisible: LClick the button for the layer that you want to make visible; OR (b) To make a bone layer visible while keeping the bone layers that are currently visible visible: SHIFT+LClick the button of the layer that you want to make visible.

29. To make a bone curve when its joint with another bone is flexed: Go to the "Properties" window: ▨ > Enable the "Bone" button: ⍟ > Go to the "Deform" panel > Put a check mark in the check box next to "Deform." Adjust the "Segments" button. To make adjustments on the curve, adjust the "Ease In" and "Ease Out" buttons. When the skin has been attached to the bone ("skinned"), you will see the effect of the curved bone on the mesh, but you will not be able to see the bone's curve unless you have enabled the B-Bone bone visualization (see step **30(c)**).

30. To give your amature's bones a different appearance, depending on what features of the bones that you want to see: In Object mode, select the armature > Go to the "Properties" window: ▨ > Enable the "Object Data" button: ⍟ > Go to the "Display" panel.

(a) If you want to see the bones' direction and "roll", enable the "**Octahedral**" button (this is the default appearance).

(b) If you want a clear view of your model, enable "**Stick**".

(c) If you have curved one or more bones (see **29**): to see, in Object or Pose mode, the bones' curve, enable "**B-Bone**".

(d) If you want to see the envelopes (see **T90, step 3(b), p. 194**) of your armature's bones, enable "**Envelope**".

(e) If you want the bones to look like wires, enable "**Wire**".

31. A note about _bone groups_: a bone can be in only one bone group. If a bone is in Group1, say, and you put it into Group2, say, then it will be taken out of Group1.

32. To create a bone group with selected bones in it:

33. In Object mode > select the armature > Go to Pose mode.

34. Do either **(a)** or **(b)**:

(a) Press CTRL+G > "Add Bone Group"

(b) Go to the "Properties" window: ▨ > Enable the "Object Data" button: ⍟ > Go to the "Bone Groups" panel > LClick the "Plus" sign: ⊞ .

35. Go to the 3D View window > Select the bones that you want to be in the new group.

36. > Go to the "Properties" window: ▨ > Enable the "Object Data" button: ⍟ > Go to the "Bone Groups" panel > LClick "Assign" > LClick the "Name" button > Type to change the name that

Blender has given to the group > Press ENTER.

37. To remove a bone group:

38. In Object mode > select the armature > Go to Pose mode.

39. Go to the "Properties" window:  > Enable the "Object Data" button: > Go to the "Bone Groups" panel > In the list of bone groups in the large field, select the name of the bone group that you want to remove. Either (a) LClick the button with the "Minus" sign on it; OR (b) Put the mouse cursor in the 3D View window > Press CTRL+G > "Remove Bone Group".

40. To add a bone or bones to an existing bone group: In Object mode, select the armature > Go to Pose mode > Select the bone(s) that you want to add to the group > Go to the "Properties" window:

 > Enable the "Object Data" button: > Go to the "Bone Groups" panel > In the list of bone groups in the large field, select the name of the group that you want to add the selected bone(s) to > LClick "Assign".

41. To remove a bone or bones from a bone group: In Object mode, select the armature > Go to Pose mode > Select the bone(s) that you want to remove from the group > Go to the "Properties" window:

 > Enable the "Object Data" button: > Go to the "Bone Groups" panel > LClick "Remove".

42. To give all the bones of a bone group the same distinctive color—(Of course, the armature is always invisible in the render): In Object mode, select the armature > Go into Pose mode > Go to the

"Properties" window: > Enable the "Object Data" button: > Go to the "Display" panel > Make sure that the little box next to "Colors" is checked > Go to the "Bone Groups" panel > In the list of bone groups in the large field, select the name of the group whose bones you want to color (or whose color you want to change) > LClick the "Color Set" button. (You may have to expand the "Properties" window horizontally to read the full name of this button.) A color set is a set of three colors; you will see in the next step the three color swatches that represent these colors: the first represents the bone's color, the second is the color of the outline around non-active selected bones, and the third is the color of the outline around the active selected bone.

METHOD 1

43. LClick one of the Blender-supplied "Theme Color Sets."

METHOD 2

To give the group a custom color: LClick "Custom Color Set" > LClick the part of the long, three-part color swatch that you want to change > Use the palette to change the color (see **T68, step 5, p. 111**).

END OF METHODS

T89. Rigging a Mesh Model—Part Two: To build an armature inside your human-shaped mesh (if you want to practice rigging a simple human-shaped model, T92

gives steps for creating one):

1. To build an armature inside your human-shaped mesh: Start with the mesh figure standing with his arms straight out from his sides—this is known as the "T" position. The figure should be facing you when you're in Front View (Press numpad 1 to get into front view), and his abdomen should be centered on the Global origin (X = 0, Y = 0, Z = 0)—most importantly, the mesh should be centered on the Z axis, and facing you when in Front View. Put your 3D cursor at the Global origin (X=0. Y=0, Z=0): With your mouse cursor in the 3D View window: Press SHIFT+S > LClick "Cursor to Center."

2. In Object mode: Press numpad 1 to go into Front View > SHIFT+A > Hover over "Armature" > LClick "Single Bone". This will add an armature, in the form of a single bone to your mesh.

3. To make your armature visible: Still in Object mode, still in the 3D View window, the new armature (at this point a single bone) should still be selected; if you have deselected it for any reason, select it again (since you may not be able to see the armature inside the mesh in the 3D View window, you might have to select it in the Outliner window) > Go to the "Properties" window: 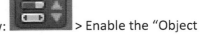 > Enable the "Object Data" button: > Go to the "Display" panel > Put a check inside the little box next to "X-Ray". If the armature does not become visible, select the mesh > Go to the "Properties" window: > Enable the "Object" button: > Go to the "Display" panel > If the little box next to "X-Ray" is checked, uncheck it.

4. Position the bone so that its head sphere is at the crotch > Go to Edit mode > RClick the bone's tail sphere > Press G > Press Z > Stretch the bone's tail up to the top of the head > LClick.

5. If the Tool Shelf is not showing, press T to show it > RClick the body of the bone to select the bone > Press W > LClick "Subdivide": This should divide the single bone into two > Go to the Tool Shelf > Go to the "Subdivide Multi" panel > Adjust the "Number of Cuts" button to 4—this produces 5 bones > scale all the bones, by selecting bones' spheres and pressing G then Z, then making the adjustment, then LClicking, so that the *head* bone is large, the *neck* bone is tiny, the *ribs* bone is large, and the bottom two, the *spine* bones, are small.

6. To rename the bones: RClick the body of the bottom bone to select it > Go to the "Properties" window: > Enable the "Bone" button: > LClick the top field > type, say, "spine_1" > Press ENTER > In a similar way: rename the next bone, say, "spine_2", the next one "ribs", the next one "neck", and the top bone, say, "head." To show the names in the 3D View window: Enable the "Object Data" button: > Go to the "Display" panel > Put a check inside the little box next to "Names."

7. Select the body of the *neck* bone > Make sure that you are still in front view by pressing numpad 1 > Press SHIFT+D > Place the new bone with its head sphere at the position of the figure's left shoulder socket (the figure should be facing you in front view) > LClick > Rename (see **5**) the new bone "upper_arm.L". (You can name it anything you want, so long as you end it with ".L". The ".L" stands for "Left". Actually, you could have ended it with ".R", meaning "Right"—but we'll stick with ".L".) **Since the**

neck bone is a child (see **T33, p. 71**) of the *rib* bone, the *neck* bone's duplicate, *upper_arm.L* will also be a child of the *ribs* bone: when you move *ribs* (not in Edit mode, but in *Pose* mode), you will automatically move *upper_arm.L* also—but not vice versa.

8. Still in Edit mode, select the tail sphere of *upper_arm.L* > (Still in Front View:) Press G > rotate *upper_arm.L* and stretch it out so that it fits into the character's upper left arm > LClick

9. With the tail sphere of *upper_arm.L* still selected, press E > Extrude a bone into the character's lower left arm > LClick > Rename the bone "lower_arm.L".

10. Select the body of the *spine_1* bone > Press SHIFT+D > Place the head sphere of the new bone at the position of the character's leg socket > LClick > Select the tail sphere of the new bone > Press G > Rotate the new bone so that the tail points downward and extend the tail of the bone down to the knee > LClick > Rename the new bone "upper_leg.L".

11. To make *upper_leg.L* a child of the *spine_1* bone: Still in Edit mode, RClick the body of *upper_leg.L* > Press SHIFT+RClick the *spine_1* bone to select it also > Press CTRL+P > LClick "Keep Offset". (The parenting relationship will be apparent only in *Pose* mode; that is, if, *in Edit mode,*you select only spine_1 and move it, upper_leg.L will not move with it; but if you are *in Pose mode* and if you select only spine_1 and move it, upper_leg.L *will* move with it.)

12. Still in Edit mode, select the tail sphere of *upper_leg.L* > Press E > Press Z > Extrude the new bone down to the foot > LClick > Rename the lower leg bone "lower_leg.L"

13. To create the figure's right-side bones as a mirror image of those on the left: Press A once or twice to deselect everything > Select all 4 of the arm and leg bones > Press SHIFT+D (and don't move your mouse at all) > Press ESC (The new duplicates are in the same positions as the originals, and are selected) > To make the 3D cursor your pivot point: Press the period [.] key on the main, alphanumeric part of the keyboard (not the period in the number pad). > To put the 3D cursor at the Global origin: Press SHIFT+S > LClick "Cursor to Center" > To place the new bones, the duplicates, into a position where they will mirror the originals: Press CTRL+ M > Press X > LClick > To make the median point the pivot point again: Press CTRL+ comma [,] > To get the figure's right-side bones named correctly: Press W > LClick "Flip Names" > Press A to deselect everything. (For another way to create a symmetrical armature, see **T88, step 6, p. 187**.)

T90. Rigging a Mesh Model—Part Three: To set things up so that the mesh will move along with the armature; that is, to "skin" the mesh to the armature:

1. This topic shows how to make vertices in the mesh move along with the bones of the armature in Pose mode and for the render. For instance, you might want to have the vertices that constitute your mesh character's right arm move along with the right-arm bones of the armature.

2. Below, I will refer to the "**Vertex Groups checkbox**" and the "**Bone Envelopes checkbox**"; here's how

to find these checkboxes: In Object mode, select the mesh > Go to the "Properties" window:

> Enable the "Modifier" button: > Go to the "Armature Modifier" panel, which has the armature icon and part or all of the word "Armature" at the top (you might have to expand the Properties window

to see the whole word): [icon] ature (when you do the two steps described in **step 4** below, Blender will automatically create this modifier for your mesh) > You will find both the "Vertex Groups" checkbox and the "Bone Envelopes" checkbox here.

3. There are **two mechanisms** by means of which a vertex, say V1, can be made to follow a bone, say, a bone named "ArmBone2":

(a) MECHANISM 1: FONDNESS
("Fondness" is my term for what Blender calls—confusingly, I think—"weight")
Vertex V1 can have *fondness* for ArmBone2, so that when you move ArmBone2, V1 will follow it.

There are different degrees of fondness; these degrees are associated with *colors*. The degrees of fondness, from lowest to highest are BLUE-GREEN, GREEN, YELLOW, ORANGE, RED. Note that BLUE is not a degree of fondness; it is no fondness at all.

If V1 has fondness only for ArmBone2, it will follow its beloved ArmBone2's movements exactly—whether it has green-fondness or red-fondness will make no difference at all. But if V1 has fondness for both ArmBone2 and another bone, say, ArmBone3, then the degree of fondness it has for each becomes important: if V1 has, for instance, red-fondness for ArmBone2 and yellow-fondness for ArmBone3, then V1 will follow both, but (assuming no envelopes are involved—see below) it will follow ArmBone2 more diligently than it will follow ArmBone3.

Importantly, no vertex can have a fondness for a bone unless the vertex is in a *vertex group* within the mesh, a vertex group with the same name as the bone. So, for V1 to be able to have fondness for ArmBone2, V1 *must* be in the mesh's vertex group named "ArmBone2". (But V1 can be in this vertex group without having fondness for ArmBone2.)

For fondness to have any effect, the "Vertex Groups" checkbox (see step **2**) for the mesh must be checked.

(b) MECHANISM 2: ENVELOPES
Every bone has an envelope. ArmBone2's envelope will *capture* vertex V1 (so that V1 will move with it) if and only if

(i) V1 is inside ArmBone2's envelope,
(ii) the "Bone Envelopes" checkbox (see step **2**) for the mesh is checked.
(iii) V1 does not belong to any vertex group associated with any bone AND/OR the "Vertex Groups" checkbox (see step **2**) for the mesh is unchecked.

4. The skinning procedure itself, the procedure that joins your mesh to the armature so that the mesh can follow the movements of the armature, consists of *two steps*: CTRL+P, followed by clicking one of three options (see below). After you finish these two steps, you will have produced one of **three different initial set-ups,** depending on which of the three options you chose. Your initial set-up can then be adjusted—for instance, if you think you chose the wrong option, you can, without re-doing the two steps, simply re-arrange things to match one of the other two initial set-ups.

It's important to note that the two mechanisms discussed in step **2** above will always work as described there, regardless of which of the three options for creating the *initial* set-up you choose.

194

(Also note that each of the three methods below automatically creates vertex groups and an armature modifier.)

5. <u>SKINNING THE MESH TO THE ARMATURE—THREE OPTIONS:</u>

<u>OPTION 1:</u>

6. <u>To have Blender automatically create, in the mesh, *a vertex group for each bone, each group having the same name as the bone it's associated with* (when I talk about vertex groups of this special kind, I will talk about the mesh's *"bone-associated vertex groups"*), but such that these groups will be absolutely empty, with not a single vertex in any of them</u> (In a sense, or strictly speaking, these "empty groups" are not *really* groups but are empty containers for groups—but call them groups.): In Object mode, select the mesh > Press SHIFT+RClick to select the armature > Press CTRL+P > LClick **"with Empty Groups"**.

<u>7.</u> Note that unless and until you put one or more vertices into one or more of the mesh's bone-associated vertex groups, any bone envelope will be able to capture every vertex that's inside the envelope. (For how to put a vertex into a mesh's bone-associated vertex group, see **<u>T91, step 9, p. 198</u>**.) And, of course, since, in this initial set-up, there's no vertex in any of the mesh's bone-associated vertex groups, no vertex will have fondness for any bone. Unless you make changes, **only the *envelope* mechanism will work**.

<u>OPTION 2:</u>

8. <u>To have Blender create, in the mesh, *a vertex group for each bone*, and put all and only the vertices that are inside its envelope into the group, and instill these particular vertices with varying degrees of fondness for the bone:</u> In Object mode, select the armature > Go to Edit or Pose mode > Go to the

"Properties" window: > Enable the "Object Data" button: > Go to the "Display" panel > Enable "Envelope" to change the visualization style of the bones (so that you can see the envelopes) >

Enable the "Bone" button: .

<u>9.</u> For each bone: RClick to select the bone > Go to the "Deform" panel > Make sure the little box next to "Deform" is checked > LClick on the panel if you need to expand it > The bones may be very fat; you can adjust the thickness of the bone by adjusting the "Radius" buttons > Adjust the bone's envelope so that it encloses the vertices that you want to be in it by adjusting the "Distance" button.

<u>10.</u> After doing step **<u>9</u>** for each bone, go to Object mode > Select the mesh > Press SHIFT+RClick to select the armature > Press CTRL+P > LClick **"with Envelope Weights"**.

<u>11.</u> The envelopes, since (if the "Vertex Groups" checkbox [see **<u>2</u>**] is checked) they can capture only vertices that are not in groups, will have no effect whatsoever on any vertex that was inside an envelope when you clicked "with Envelope Weights" (unless and until you remove it from all groups—see **<u>T91, step 12, p. 198</u>**, or unless the "Vertex Groups" checkbox [see step **<u>2</u>**] is unchecked), but they *will* be able to capture any vertex that was not in an envelope (unless and until you put that vertex into a group—see **<u>T91, step 9, p. 198</u>**). (So long as the "Vertex Groups" checkbox [see step **<u>2</u>**] is checked) any vertex that has fondness for a bone will, of course follow that bone. (To give fondness to a vertex that *doesn't* have it, see **<u>T91, step 17, p. 199</u>**). In this initial set-up, **both the *envelope* and the *fondness* mechanism can work**.

OPTION 3:

12. **To have Blender automatically create, in the mesh, *a vertex group for each bone,*and fill each group with vertices (whether or not the vertices are enclosed in envelopes) and instill the vertices with degrees of fondness for the bone**, In Object mode, select the mesh > Press SHIFT+RClick to select the armature > Press CTRL+P > LClick "**with Automatic Weights**".

13. Note that if you chose this option to initialize the skinning, then (if the "Vertex Groups" checkbox – see step **2**—is checked) the envelopes will not work on the vertices which are in the mesh's bone-associated vertex groups. To get the envelopes to be able to capture one of these vertices, you will have to (a) remove the vertex from *all* the bone-associated vertex groups that it is in OR (b) uncheck the Vertex Groups checkbox (see **2**), which turns off the fondness of *all* the vertices that are in the bone-associated vertex groups, and which allows *all* vertices to be influenced by the envelopes.

T91. Rigging a Mesh Model—Part Four: Making changes to the rigging *after* you've skinned the model (see T90):

1. To see a bone's envelope: In Object mode, select the armature > Go to Edit or Pose mode > Select the bone > Go to the "Properties" window: [icon] > Enable the "Object Data" button: [icon] > Go to the "Display" panel > Enable "Envelope". If you can't see the envelope: In Edit mode > Select the bone > Go to the "Properties" window: [icon] > Enable the "Bone" button: [icon] > Go to the "Deform" panel > Make sure the little box next to "Deform" is checked. If you still can't see the envelope, try expanding the envelope using the "Distance" button: see step **6**.

2. If, at any time, you find that none of the bone envelopes are capturing any of the mesh's vertices but you want them to: First, Make sure that you are not trying to capture vertices that are in any of the mesh's bone-associated vertex groups—(so long as the Vertex Groups checkbox [see **T90, step 2, p. 193**] is checked) a bone's envelope will not capture a vertex that is in *any* of the vertex groups that are associated with the bones. (To remove a vertex from a vertex group, see **12**.) If the vertices that you want your envelopes to capture are not in any of the mesh's bone-associated vertex groups: In Object mode, select the mesh > Go to the "Properties" window: [icon] > Enable the "Modifier" button: [icon] > Go to the "Armature Modifier" panel, which has the armature icon and part or all of the word "Armature" at the top (you might have to expand the Properties window to see the whole word): [icon] (when you did the two steps described in **T90, step 4, p. 194** above, Blender created this modifier for your mesh) > Make sure that the little box next to "Bone Envelopes" is checked.

3. If your envelopes are capturing vertices, and you want, say, Bone3's envelope to capture vertex V1, but it's not: (a) if the envelope is not enveloping V1, enlarge the envelope (see **6**) so that it does. If that isn't the problem, check to make sure that V1 is not in any vertex group: In Object mode, select the mesh > Go to Edit mode > Press A to deselect all > Go to the "Properties" window: > Enable the "Object Data" button: > Go to the "Vertex Groups" panel > Do the following for *each* of the vertex groups which has the same name as a bone: In the large box containing the list of these vertex groups, select the name of the vertex group > LClick "Select" > (a) If the vertex is among the selected vertices, remove it from the vertex group by doing this: Press A to deselect all > Select V1 > Go back to the "Vertex Groups" panel > LClick "Remove" > Press A to deselect all. (b) If the vertex is not among the selected vertices, press A to deselect all.

4. To make the envelopes unable to capture the vertices within them: In Object mode, select the mesh > Go to the "Properties" window: > Enable the "Modifier" button: > Go to the "Armature Modifier" panel, which has the armature icon and part or all of the word "Armature" at the top (you might have to expand the Properties window to see the whole word): (when you did either step **6**, step **10** or step **12** in **T90**, Blender created this modifier for your mesh) > uncheck the little box next to "Bone Envelopes."

5. To make a bone's envelope, along with its power to capture vertices, disappear/appear: In Object mode, RClick the armature to select it > Go to Edit mode > Select the bone > Go to the "Properties" window: > Enable the "Bone" button: > Go to the "Deform" panel > Make sure the little box next to "Deform" is unchecked/checked.

6. To change the size of a bone's envelope: In Object mode, RClick the armature to select it > Go to Edit or Pose mode > Select the bone whose envelope you want to change > (a) Go to the "Properties" window: > Enable the "Bone" button: > Go to the "Deform" panel > If the panel is collapsed, LClick the little black triangle to expand it > Adjust the "Distance" button; OR (b) Press CTRL+ALT+S > Move the mouse to make the envelope the size you want it to be.

7. To see how much fondness every vertex of the mesh has for a given bone, say, a bone whose name is "ArmBone1": In Object mode, RClick the mesh to select it > LClick the Mode button in the 3D View header > LClick "Weight Paint" > Go to the "Properties" window: > Enable the "Object Data" button: > Go to the "Vertex Groups" panel > You want to image the fondness-level that every vertex in the mesh has for ArmBone1, so, in the big box, select the vertex group with the same name as the bone; that is, select the vertex group named "ArmBone1" (all vertices not in this group will be imaged as blue, but some vertices *in* the group might be blue also). See step **18** for the meaning of the colors.

8. To see which vertices are in a mesh's bone-associated vertex group—suppose, for example, that the group is called *ArmBone1*: In Object mode, RClick the mesh to select it > Go into Edit mode > Press A to

deselect everything > Go to the "Properties" window: > Enable the "Object Data" button:
> Go to the "Vertex Groups" panel > In the vertex groups list, select "ArmBone1" > LClick "Select".
This should select the vertices in the *ArmBone1* vertex group.

9. To put a vertex (or vertices) into a mesh's bone-associated vertex group: In Object mode, select the
mesh > Go to the "Properties" window: > Enable the "Object Data" button: > Go to the
"Vertex Groups" panel > In the big box with the list of vertex groups in it, LClick to select the vertex
group with the name of the bone.

METHOD 1
10. Go to Edit mode > Select the vertex (or vertices) > LClick "Assign." If you use this method, the vertex
(or vertices) you add to the group will automatically be given red-fondness for the bone (see **T90, step
3(a), p. 194**).
METHOD 2
11. Apply weight paint to the vertex (or vertices) (see **17** below). If you use this method, the vertex (or
vertices) will be given the fondness color that is loaded on your brush.
END OF METHODS

12. To take a vertex out of a mesh's bone-associated vertex group: In Object mode, select the mesh >
Go to Edit mode > Select the vertex (or vertices) > Go to the "Properties" window: > Enable
the "Object Data" button: > Go to the "Vertex Groups" panel > In the big box with the list of
vertex groups in it, LClick to select the vertex group that you want to remove the vertex from > LClick
"Remove".

**13. If, at any time, you find that the mesh's vertices are not following a bone or bones that they have
fondness for, but you want them to:** (a) If the vertices are not following any bone: In Object mode,
select the mesh > Go to the "Properties" window: > Enable the "Modifier" button: >
Go to the "Armature Modifier" panel, which has the armature icon and part or all of the word
"Armature" at the top (you might have to expand the Properties window to see the whole word):
(when you did either step **6**, step **10** or step **12** in **T90**, Blender created this modifier for
your mesh) > Make sure that the little box next to "Vertex Groups" is checked. (b) If vertices follow
some bones, but will not follow a certain bone: In Object mode, select the armature > Go to Edit mode >
select the bone > Go to the "Properties" window: > Enable the "Bone" button: > Go
to the "Deform" panel > Make sure that the little box next to "Deform" is checked.
14. (Assuming that the relevant bone envelopes have been minimized [see step **6**] or that "Bone
Envelopes" is unchecked [see step **4**]): **To make the vertices *not* follow the bone(s) that they have
fondness for:**

METHOD 1

15. To make no vertices follow the bones: In Object mode, select the mesh > Go to the "Properties" window: [icon] > Enable the "Modifier" button: [icon] > Go to the "Armature Modifier" panel, which has the armature icon and part or all of the word "Armature" at the top (you might have to expand the Properties window to see the whole word): [icon] (when you did either step **6**, step **10** or step **12** in **T90**, Blender created this modifier for your mesh) > uncheck the little box next to "Vertex Groups."

METHOD 2

16. For an individual bone: In Object mode, select the armature > Go to Edit mode > select the bone > Go to the "Properties" window: [icon] > Enable the "Bone" button: [icon] > Go to the "Deform" panel > Make sure that the little box next to "Deform" is unchecked.

END OF METHODS

WEIGHT PAINTING:

17. To change the degree of *fondness* (the Blender term is "weight") that one or more vertices have for a given bone, say, a bone whose name is "ArmBone1":

18. Keep in mind that red symbolizes a higher intensity of fondness than yellow, and that yellow symbolizes a higher intensity of fondness than green, and that blue symbolizes zero fondness (see **T90, step 3(a), p. 194**). So from least fondness to more: blue → green → yellow → red.

19. To go into Weight Painting mode: In Object mode, RClick the mesh to select it > LClick the Mode button in the 3D View header > LClick "Weight Paint."

20. If you've set up X-Axis Mirroring (see **T88, step 6, p. 187**—and suppose the bone is named, not "ArmBone1," but "ArmBone1.L"), and if the left and right sides of your mesh are identical, **you can set things up so that your weight paint will be applied symmetrically**. To do this: Go to the Tool Shelf (press T if it's not there) > Go to the "Options" panel > LClick the little box next to "X Mirror" to put a check mark into it. (If you apply paint to, say, vertices in the ArmBone1.L group, you will have to select the ArmBone1.R group in the "Vertex Groups" panel [see step **7**] to see that the paint has, in fact, been applied symmetrically.)

21. Here is the next step you must take in order to change the degree of fondness that one or more vertices have for ArmBone1: Go to the "Properties" window: [icon] > Enable the "Object Data" button: [icon] > Go to the "Vertex Groups" panel > **You need to image the fondness-level that every vertex in the mesh has for ArmBone1**; so, in the big box, select the vertex group with the same name as the bone; that is, select the vertex group named "ArmBone1" (some vertices in this group will likely be imaged as blue, and all vertices *not* in this group will be imaged as blue—Note that when you weight-paint any vertex that's not in the selected vertex group, you will thereby put that vertex into the group).

22. If the Tool Shelf is not visible in the 3D View window: with your mouse in the 3D View window, press T.

23. A "WEIGHT-PAINTING" BRUSH OVERVIEW:
Every weight-painting brush has a set of properties, *all of which can be changed*:

(a) At any given time, a weight-painting brush will have what I call a single, specific *brushwork functionality*— that is, the brush will change the fondness (weight) paint in a certain way. For instance, If the brush has a "Mix" type brushwork functionality (the default setting), it will bring the color it paints closer and closer to the color it's loaded with (the setting of the "weight" button determines what color, what fondness degree, the brush is loaded with); if it has an "Add" type brushwork functionality, your paint will bring the color it's painting over closer and closer to red; etc.
(b) A brush will have a particular size, called its *radius*.
(c) A brush will have a particular *strength*.
(d) A brush will be configured to have a certain kind of *stroke*—for example, a series of dots separated by this or that distance, or an airbrush stroke, etc.

At any time, you will have available to you, in Weight Paint mode, a set of weight-paint brushes. You can create brushes and add them to the set, and you can throw brushes away. In Weight Paint mode, in the Tool Shelf, look at the big picture at the top of the "Brush" panel. Think of this big picture as the door to your weight-paint brush cabinet. LClick it to open the cabinet and view your brushes. If you are opening the cabinet for the first time, you will see that Blender has supplied you with a set of brushes. Notice that each brush has a name: "Add" is the name of one of your brushes—this brush has (unless and until you change it) an "Add" type brushwork functionality. "Brush" is the name of another of your brushes—this brush has a "Mix" type brushwork functionality, etc.
24. When you go into Weight Paint mode, one of the brushes available to you will be "active"—it will be the "current" brush. In the Tool Shelf, go to the "Brush" panel. The big image at the top portrays the current brush. Underneath this big image, you will see a row of buttons that pertain to the current brush, the brush you are using now. Its name is written on the far-left button (If your Tool Shelf is very narrow, only a part of the name might be visible on the button; in order to see the whole name, you may have to expand the Tool Shelf: hover over its edge until the double-headed arrow appears and then drag.)
25. To create a new brush: Still in Weight Paint mode, in the Tool Shelf, in the "Brush" panel, go to the row of buttons just below the big image at the top > LClick the button with the plus sign (+) on it. You have now created a brush—the brush you have been using has been saved (put back into the brush "cabinet"), and the brush you have just created has all the same properties that the previous brush had. Blender will automatically give the new brush a unique name, which you can change (see **28**).
26. To retrieve a brush from your set of available brushes: Still in Weight Paint mode, (a) go to the Tool Shelf > Go to the "Brush" panel > LClick the big picture at the top (to open the "door" to your weight-paint brush "cabinet", see **23** above) > Get the brush by LClicking its image; OR (b) On the main keyboard (not the number pad), press 1, or 2, or 3, etc.
27. To save a brush (that is, to put a new brush into the weight-painting brush "cabinet" or put a brush you took from the "cabinet" back into the "cabinet," saving whatever property-changes you might have made to it): Save your Blender file (see **T19, p. 18** and **T20, p. 18**) OR create a new brush (see **25**) OR retrieve a brush from your set of brushes (see **29**)—brush size will not be saved.

28. To rename a brush: In Weight Paint mode, in the Tool Shelf, in the "Brush" panel, look underneath the big image, you will see a row of buttons that pertain to the current brush, the brush you are using now. The brush's name is written on the far-left button (If your Tool Shelf is very narrow, only a part of the name might be visible on the button; in order to see the whole name, you may have to expand the Tool Shelf: hover over its edge until the double-headed arrow appears and then drag) > LClick this far-left button > Type the new name > Press ENTER.

29. To paint, LClick and drag over the surface of the object in the 3D View window.

TO CHANGE THE PROPERTIES OF A WEIGHT PAINT BRUSH:

30. To change the size (radius) of your brush at any time:

METHOD 1:

31. Go to the Tool Shelf > Go to the "Brush" panel > adjust the "Radius" button.

METHOD 2:

32. With the cursor in the 3D View window, press F > Move the cursor toward and away from the center of the circle to make the brush the size you want it.

33. Do you want to **show the hidden edges and vertices of your object**, so that you can see which vertices you're painting? Or do you want to hide the visible edges and vertices?

Yes: In the "Properties" window > > LClick the "Object" button: > Go to the "Display" panel > LClick the box next to "Wire" in order to check it. Go to **34**.

No: Go to **34**.

34. To change your brush's *brushwork functionality*—that is, to make a change in one of the ways listed (**a-g**) below:

a. To give your brush a specific color (degree of fondness, or "weight") setting, and then to set things up so that, when you use the brush to paint the mesh, you will, as you paint, bring the color that you're painting over closer and closer to the loaded color: Go to the Tool Shelf > Go to the "Brush" panel > To load your brush with minimum fondness (blue) paint, set the "Weight" button to the far left; to load your brush with maximum fondness (red) paint, set the "Weight" button to the far left; to load your brush with an intermediate degree of fondness (green, yellow, orange), give the "Weight" button an intermediate setting > In the 3D View window, go to the 3D View window's header > LClick "Brush" > Hover over "Vertex/Weight Paint Tool"> LClick "**Mix**."

To change your brush's brushwork functionality in one of the ways, b-g, below, first, In the 3D View window, go to the 3D View window's header > LClick "Brush" > Hover over "Vertex/Weight Paint Tool."

b. To change a color toward red as you apply the paint (that is, to increase the vertices' fondness for the bone in question), for instance, to change blue to green, then yellow, then red (gradually or quickly depending on the brush-strength setting), LClick "**Add**".

c. To change a color toward blue as you apply the paint (that is, to decrease the vertices' fondness for the bone in question), for instance, to change red to yellow, then green, then blue (gradually or quickly depending on the brush-strength setting), LClick "**Subtract**".

d. If you want to "multiply"(?) the underlying color with the brush color, LClick "**Multiply**".

e. If you want to mix together the colors within the brush's radius, LClick "**Blur**".

Re f and g below: Artists conceive of the sequence blue to green to yellow to orange to red as a sequence of "cool" to "warm"; on the other hand, Blender sees it as a sequence of dark to light—Blender's view is confusing because (pure) yellow is most definitely not darker than (pure) orange or (pure) red!

    f. If you want to bring colors that are cooler than the color that is set by the "Weight" button (see step **a** above) closer to the color set by the "Weight" button, LClick "**Lighten**" (When you read "Lighten", think "make warmer").

    g. If you want to bring colors that are warmer than the color that is set by the "Weight" button (see step **a** above) closer to the color set by the "Weight" button, LClick "**Darken**" (When you read "Darken", think "make cooler").

35. **To specify the type of brush stroke:** Go to the Tool Shelf > Go to the "Stroke" panel >

    a. **To paint with an ordinary brush:** Make sure that all three check boxes in the "Stroke" panel are unchecked.

    b. **To paint with an airbrush** so that the brush will paint continually when you LClick and hold, instead of only when the mouse is moving: Put a check mark in the "Airbrush" check box > Make sure that both the "Smooth Stroke" and the "Space" check boxes are unchecked.

    c. **To paint in spurts and to adjust how close together the paint spurts are** as you drag your brush: Put a check mark in the "Space" check box > Make sure that the "Smooth Stroke" checkbox is unchecked > Adjust the "Spacing" button.

    d. **To paint a stroke where the stroke lags behind the brush and paints along a smoother path:** Put a check mark in the "Smooth Stroke" check box > Make sure that the "Space" checkbox is unchecked.

36. Do you want to change the size of your weight-painting brush?

        Yes: Go to **37.**

        No: Go to **44.**

37. (Still in Weight Paint mode,) **to change the size of your weight-painting brush:**

METHOD 1:

38. In the 3D View window, in "Weight Paint" mode, go to the window's Tool Shelf (if it's not there, press T) > Go to the "Brush" panel.

39. Adjust the "Radius" button.

METHOD 2:

40. With the cursor in the 3D View window, press F.

41. Move the cursor toward and away from the center of the circle to make the brush the size you want it

42. LClick.

METHOD 3:

43. If you are using a pressure sensitive tablet, you can use pen pressure as you paint to control the brush size by enabling the pressure sensitivity button to the right of the "Radius" button:

END OF METHODS

44. Do you want to change the strength of your weight-painting brush?

       Yes: Go to **45**.

       No: Go to **46**.

45. To change the strength of your brush's effect: if you have chosen brushwork functionality "Mix," "Blur," "Darken", or "Lighten": In the Tool Shelf, go to the "Brush" panel > adjust the "Strength" button. If you chose brushwork functionality "Add" or "Subtract": In the Tool Shelf, go to the "Brush" panel, adjust both the "Weight" and the "Strength" buttons—for maximum strength, both must be all the way to the right; if either is all the way to the left, strength will be zero--it seems best with these two functionalities to put "Weight" at maximum and simply adjust the "Strength" button.

       Note that, instead of adjusting the "Strength" button in the procedures above: (a) with the mouse cursor in the 3D View window, press SHIFT+F > move the cursor toward or away from the center of the circle to give the brush the strength you want it to have: making the circle smaller increases the strength, OR (b) if you are using a pressure sensitive tablet, use pen pressure to control the brush strength as you paint by enabling the pressure sensitivity button to the right of the "Strength" button:

.

46. Do you want **to change how gradually or abruptly your brush's effect falls off**, outward from the center of the brush?

       Yes: Go to **47**.

       No: Go to **51**.

47. In the 3D View window, in "Weight Paint" mode, go to the window's Tool Shelf (if it's not there, press T) > Go to the "Curve" panel. (LClick on the little, black triangle to expand the panel, if necessary.)

48. Look at the curve diagram:

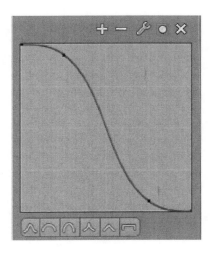

49. You can change how your brush's effect falls off by changing the curve shown in this panel. To do this, you can adjust the curve by LClicking & holding the curve itself, and dragging its nodes.

50. To set the curve in accord with certain basic shapes, LClick one of the "Set brush shape" buttons beneath the curve.

51. When you leave Weight Paint mode, go to the "Properties" window > > LClick the

"Object" button: > Go to "Display" panel > Make sure the little box next to "Wire" is unchecked.

T92. If you want to practice constructing your armature for a human-shaped figure, and skinning the model, here are steps for creating a crude human-shaped figure that you can work with:

1. Start with the default cube.

2. In Object mode, select the cube > Press numpad 1 (you should be looking at it more or less from the front).

3. Press S > Press SHIFT + Z > Type the number *.8* > LClick.

4. Go to Edit mode > Select the bottom face of the cube > Press E > Type *2.5* > LClick > (I will call these two cubes the "big" cubes).

5. Select the right face of the upper big cube (you might want to press numpad 1 again to orient yourself; that is, to make sure you are selecting the right-side face) > Press E (don't move the mouse!) > LClick > Press S > Press Y > Type *.6* > LClick > Press S > Press Z > Type *.45* > LClick > Press G > Press Z > Type *.4* > LClick > Press E > Type *4* > LClick.

6. Select the bottom face of the lower big cube > Press E (don't move the mouse!) > LClick > Press S > Press SHIFT + Z > Type *.7* > LClick > Press E > Type *5* > LClick.

7. Select the upper-left edge of the upper big cube > Press SHIFT + S > LClick "Cursor to Selected" (this puts the 3D cursor onto that edge) > Select the top face of the upper big cube > Press E (don't move the mouse!) > LClick > Press the (regular, non-numberpad) period [.] > Press S > Press SHIFT + Z > Type the number *.25* > LClick > Press CTRL + comma [,] > Press E > Type *1* > LClick.

8. Go into Object mode > Make sure that the 3D cursor is still at the upper-edge of the upper big cube, where you put it at step **7** > Go to the 3D View window header > LClick "Object" > Hover over

"Transform" > LClick "Origin to 3D Cursor" > Go to the "Properties" window: > LClick the

"Modifiers" button: > Go to the "Modifiers" panel > LClick "Add Modifier" > LClick "Mirror" > LClick "Apply".

9. LClick "Add Modifier" again > LClick "Subdivision Surface" > Set both "View" and "Render" to 2 > LClick "Apply".

10. Go to Edit mode > To add vertices to the body and arms: Press A once or twice to select all > Go to the Tool Shelf > LClick "Subdivide".

11. To add the head: Press SHIFT + A > LClick "UV Sphere" > Press G > Press Z > Type *1.6* > LClick.

12. Go to Object mode > Go to the Tool Shelf (if it's not there, press T) > Go to the "Shadings" buttons > LClick "Smooth".

13. Press SHIFT + S > LClick "Cursor to Center" > In the 3D View window header: LClick "Object" > Hover over "Transform" > LClick "Origin to 3D Cursor" > LClick "Object" > Hover over "Transform" > LClick

"Geometry to Origin".

T93. To pose your armature

1. Definition: A "bone chain" is a set of bones such that each bone is the parent of the next, and such that the bone at one end, the chain's "first" bone, is a parent that has no parent and such that, the bone at the other end, the chain's "last" bone, is a child that has no child. A "bone-chain segment" is some part (or all) of the bone chain.

2. *To pose your armature, you have to go into Pose mode.*

3. In general, to change bones' position and rotation (without breaking the chain): select a bone > Use a transformation method as covered in **T25, p. 33** ; for instance, press G or R and move the mouse. You can pose your armature using a very simple, very basic procedure, called "Forward Kinematics" (FK), where you start posing a bone-chain segment starting with its first bone (first parent) and ending with its last bone (last child). But, using this method, it is difficult to end up with the last bone of the chain segment being positioned just where you want it to be. That is why it often makes sense to use the "Inverse Kinematics" method, whereby you can position the last bone of the chain segment and have its parent and the other bones in the segment position themselves accordingly. Do you want to use Forward Kinematics?

Yes: Go to **4**.

No: To use "Inverse Kinematics" (IK), so as to be able to place the last bone of a bone-chain segment where you want it, and have its parent and the parent's parent, etc. automatically move with it, go to **6**.

4.

(a) If you want to rotate a bone whose head sphere is not connected to another bone: Use a rotation method as covered in **T25, p. 33** ; for instance, press R and move the mouse to rotate the bone.

(b) To move, from place to place, a bone whose head sphere is not connected to another bone: Use a method for moving an object from place to place, as covered in **T25, p. 33**; for instance, press G and move the mouse to move the bone.

(c) To rotate a bone whose head sphere is connected to another bone: Use a method for rotating an object or for moving an object from place to place, as covered in **T25, p. 33**; for instance, press G and move the mouse to rotate the bone.

5. To pose a bone-chain segment: position its first bone > move or rotate the next bone, then the next bone, etc. Stop after positioning the last bone of the segment. To continue posing your armature, go to step **3**.

6. Do you want to use a quick, minimally controllable, inverse kinematics method?

Yes: Go to **7**.

No: To use a more controllable inverse kinematics technique, the technique that some call "Classical Inverse Kinematics", go to **8**.

7. Select the last bone of the chain segment > Go to the Tool Shelf (if it's not there: Press T) > Go to the "Pose Options" panel > Put a check mark in the little box next to Auto IK > To place the segment's last bone where you want it, use a method for moving an object from place to place, as covered in **T29**; for instance, press G and move the mouse to move the bone (and the rest of the chain with it). To continue posing your armature, go to **3**.

8. When you apply Classical Inverse Kinematics to a bone, say, to Bone1, you will be able, by moving Bone1, to move Bone1's parent, and the parent's parent, etc., throughout the length of the bone-chain segment (and you will be able to specify the length of the segment). In addition, you will have the opportunity to designate a bone that is not in the chain, or to designate another object, as Bone1's "target;" to say that a certain bone or object is Bone 1's target is to say that, as much as possible, the tail-sphere of Bone1 will follow, or track, the origin of this bone or object as you move it. For instance, if you are rigging a character, and you want to keep the knees bending the right way, apply IK to the upper leg bone, and create a target for the bone, in front of the knee. A second example: So that a leg (foot) will keep pointing toward a place on the ground as the body is moved: Apply IK to the lower leg bone, and create a target for the bone, under the feet. Do you want to apply IK to a bone, say Bone1, in a way that immediately designates—or creates and designates—another bone or object as Bone1's *target*? (If you don't designate a target now, you can do it later.)

Yes: Go to **9**.

No: Go to **10**.

9.

(a) To apply IK to a bone, say, Bone1, while creating a new Empty object and designating it Bone1's target: In Pose mode, select Bone1 > (i) With the mouse in the 3D View window, press SHIFT+I > LClick "To New Empty Object" OR (ii) In the 3D View window header, LClick "Pose" > Hover over "Inverse Kinematics" > LClick "Add IK to Bone" > LClick "To New Empty Object."

(b) To apply IK to a bone, say, Bone1, while designating another bone, say, Bone2, as Bone1's target: In Pose mode, select Bone2 > SHIFT+RClick to select Bone1 > (i) With the mouse in the 3D View window, press SHIFT+I > LClick "To Active Bone" OR OR (ii) In the 3D View window header, LClick "Pose" > Hover over "Inverse Kinematics" > LClick "Add IK to Bone" > LClick "To Active Bone."

(c) To apply IK to a bone, say, Bone1, while designating an object, say, Obj1, as Bone1's target: In Pose mode, select Obj1 > SHIFT+RClick to select Bone1 > (i) With the mouse in the 3D View window, press SHIFT+I > LClick "To Active Object" OR (ii) In the 3D View window header, LClick "Pose" > Hover over "Inverse Kinematics" > LClick "Add IK to Bone" > LClick "To Active Object." Go to **11**.

10.

(a) To apply IK to a bone, say, Bone1: In Pose mode, select Bone1 > (i) With the mouse in the 3D View window, press SHIFT+I > LClick "Without Targets" OR (ii) In the 3D View window header, LClick "Pose" > Hover over "Inverse Kinematics" > LClick "Add IK to Bone" > LClick "Without Targets."

(b) To apply IK to a bone, say, Bone1: In Pose mode, select Bone1 > Go to the "Properties" window:

> Enable the "Bone Constraints" button: > LClick "Add Constraint" > LClick "Inverse Kinematics."

11. The Inverse Kinematic effect extends from the tail-sphere of the bone it's applied to back, from child to parent, to parent's parent, etc. To specify how many bones back the effect extends, go to the

"Properties" window: > Enable the "Bone Constraints" button: > Go to the "Inverse Kinematics" panel > Adjust the "Chain Length" button (0 = entire chain, 1 = one bone, 2 = two bones, etc.).

12. **To add a target after Classic IK has been applied to a bone**: Select the bone > Go to the "Properties"

window: > Enable the "Bone Constraints" button: > Go to the "Inverse Kinematics" panel > LClick in the "Target" field.

13. (a) If the target is to be a bone, LClick the name of the armature that the bone is in > LClick in the "Bone" field > LClick the bone's name; (b) if the target is to be an object, LClick the name of the object.

14. Note how, in the "Inverse Kinematics" panel (see **11**), **by adjusting the "Influence" button you can move the bone** toward and away from its target. So, for instance, if the target of a leg bone is a bone in front of the knee, you can move the leg forward by increasing the value of the "Influence" button.

15. **To delete a target**: Go to the "Properties" window: > Enable the "Bone Constraints"

button: > Go to the "Inverse Kinematics" panel > LClick the "Target" field > Press Delete > Press Enter.

16. To continue posing your armature, go to **3**.

The following Topics, T94 through T103 describe what are called "constraints":

T94. To stretch an object or a bone, which is named, say, Item1, toward object or bone, Item2:

1.

(a) If Item1 is an object: In Object mode, select Item1 > Go to the "Properties" window: >

Enable the "Constraints" button: > LClick "Add Constraint" > LClick "Stretch To."

(b) If Item1 is a bone: In Object or Pose mode, select Item1 > Go to the "Properties" window:

> Enable the "Bone Constraints" button: > LClick "Add Constraint" > LClick "Stretch To."

2. In the "Stretch To" panel that appears, LClick the "Target" field > LClick Item2's name. (If Item2 is a bone, LClick the name of the armature > LClick in the "Bone" field that appears > LClick the name of the bone.)

3. To control the length of the stretch, adjust the "Rest Length" button (You might have to expand the Properties window to be able to read this button); to reset it, LClick "Reset."

4. To adjust the degree to which Item1's volume gets thinner as it is stretched, adjust the "Volume Variation" button.

5. To specify along which of item1's local axis/axes the volume will get thinner as Item1 is stretched, choose one of the "Volume" buttons.

6. To increase or decrease the effect, adjust the "influence" button.

7. To delete the "Stretch To" constraint, LClick the "X" at upper right in the "Stretch To" panel.

T95. To have an object or a bone, which is named, say, Item1, track object or bone, Item2 (for instance, to have a character's eyes follow an object, or to have the camera track an object):

1.

(a) If Item1 is an object: In Object mode, select Item1 > Go to the "Properties" window:  >

Enable the "Constraints" button:  > LClick "Add Constraint" > LClick "Track To."

(b) If Item1 is a bone: In Object or Pose mode, select Item1 > Go to the "Properties" window:

> Enable the "Bone Constraints" button: > LClick "Add Constraint" > LClick "Track To."

2. In the "Track To" panel that appears, LClick the "Target" field > LClick the name of Item2. (If Item2 is a bone, LClick name of the armature > LClick in the "Bone" field that appears > LClick the name of the bone.)

3.

(a) To have Item1's Local positive X (or Y, or Z) axis point to Item2, LClick X (or Y, or Z) (so long as the axis you choose is not the one named on the "Up" button).

(b) To have Item1's Local negative X (or Y, or Z) axis point to Item2, LClick –X (or –Y, or –Z) (so long as the axis you choose is not the one named on the "Up" button).

4. To choose which of Item1's local axes will tend to point "up"; that is, will tend to be aligned with the Global Z axis (if "Target Z" is unchecked) or with Item2's Local Z axis (if "Target Z" is checked): LClick the "Up" button > Choose which of Item1's Local axes you want to point "up".

5. To increase or decrease the effect, adjust the "influence" button.

6. To delete the "Track To" constraint, LClick the "X" at upper right in the "Track To" panel.

T96. To create an invisible plane (which you might make coincident with a visible plane) which your object, which is named, say, Obj1, must stay on one side of:

1. Say that the object whose change in location you want to limit is Obj1. To create the invisible plane, you must choose another object, or a bone—call it, say, Item1—whose center point will define a point on the invisible plane. (Item1 can be a horizontal, vertical, or slanted plane, or any object or bone).

2. Select Obj1 > Go to the "Properties" window: > Enable the "Constraints" button: > LClick "Add Constraint" > LClick "Floor."

3. In the "Floor" panel that appears, LClick the "Target" field > LClick the name of Item1. (If Item1 is a bone, LClick the name of the armature > LClick in the "Bone" field that appears > LClick the name of the bone.)

4. Do you want the plane to be a Global XY, XZ, or YZ plane?

Yes: Still in the "Floor" constraint panel, make sure that the box next to "Use Rotation" is unchecked. Go to **6**.

No: Go to **5**.

5. LClick the box next to "Use Rotation" to put a check in it. Now the plane will be an XY, XZ, or YZ plane of Item1's local coordinate system—this allows the plane to be slanted with respect to the Global coordinate system.

6.

(a) To make the plane an XY plane, and

(i) the *allowed* side in the positive Z direction, LClick "Z".

(ii) the allowed side in the negative Z direction, LClick "-Z".

(b) To make the plane an XZ plane, and

(i) the *allowed* side in the positive Y direction, LClick "Y".

(ii) the allowed side in the negative Y direction, LClick "-Y".

(c) To make the plane an YZ plane, and

(i) the *allowed* side in the positive X direction, LClick "X".

(ii) the allowed side in the negative X direction, LClick "-X".

7. If you want Obj1 to stick to the plane (and not even be able to slide on it), make sure there's a checkmark in the box next to "Sticky".

8. To put some space between the plane and Obj1 when it's closest to the plane, adjust "offset".

9. You can move Obj1 into the "forbidden" area *internally*; that is, Blender puts it into the area but *shows* it as being blocked from entry. You can see where Obj1 is internally: Go to the Properties Shelf (if it's not there, press N) > Go to the "Transform" panel > Look at the "Location" buttons. (If you've moved Obj1 only internally into the forbidden area, you can move it visually there by adjusting the "Influence" button. If Obj1 is inside the forbidden area, you will have to move it out of this area before you can move Obj1 away from the plane—Obj1 will appear to be unmoving as you do this. (If you want to *animate* Obj1's change of location, and If Obj1 is internally inside the forbidden area: if you simply insert a Location keyframe, Obj1 will be keyframed in the forbidden area, but if you insert a Visual Location keyframe, you'll keyframe Obj1 at its visual location.)

T97. To put a limit on how close to or how far from some object or bone, call it Item1 (the "target"), object Obj1 can be:

1. Select Obj1 > Go to the "Properties" window:  > Enable the "Constraints" button: > LClick "Add Constraint" > LClick "Limit Distance."

2. LClick the "Target" button > LClick Item1's name. (If Item1 is a bone, LClick the name of the armature > LClick in the "Bone" field that appears > LClick the name of the bone.)

3. Do you want to make sure that Obj1 gets no closer to Item1 than some distance?

Yes: Go to **4**.

No: Go to **8**.

4. If the "Clamp Region" button does not say "Outside", LClick the "Clamp Region" button > LClick "Outside".

METHOD 1

5. Set the "Influence" button to 0 > Put Obj1 at the desired distance limit > Set the "Influence" button to 1 > LClick the "Reset Distance" button.

METHOD 2

6. Suppose that you want Obj1 to get no closer to Item1 than 3 Blender units: Set the "Distance" button to 3.

END OF METHODS

7. Stop. You are finished.

8. Do you want to make sure that Obj1 stays within some distance of Item1?

> Yes: Go to **9**.
> No: Go to **13**.

9. If the "Clamp Region" button does not say "Inside", LClick the "Clamp Region" button > LClick "Inside".

METHOD 1

10. Set the "Influence" button to 0 > Put Obj1 at the desired distance limit > Set the "Influence" button to 1 > LClick the "Reset Distance" button.

METHOD 2

11. Suppose that you want Obj1 to stay within, say, 3 Blender units of Item1: Set the "Distance" button to 3.

END OF METHODS

12. Stop. You are finished.

13. To make sure that Obj1 is always a certain distance from Item1:

14. If the "Clamp Region" button does not say "On Surface", LClick the "Clamp Region" button > LClick "On Surface".

METHOD 1

15. Set the "Influence" button to 0 > Put Obj1 at the desired distance limit > Set the "Influence" button to 1 > LClick the "Reset Distance" button.

METHOD 2

16. Suppose that you want Obj1 to stay exactly, say, 3 Blender units from Item1: Set the "Distance" button to 3.

END OF METHODS

17. You can move Obj1 into the "forbidden" areas *internally*; that is, Blender puts it into the area but *shows* it as being blocked from entry. You can see where Obj1 is internally: Go to the Properties Shelf (if it's not there, press N) > Go to the "Transform" panel > Look at the "Location" buttons. (If you've moved Obj1 only internally into a forbidden area, you can move it visually there by adjusting the "Influence" button. If Obj1 is, at any time, inside the forbidden area internally, you will have to move it out of this area before you can move Obj1 away from the border of the forbidden area—Obj1 will *appear* to be unmoving as you pull it out of the forbidden area. (If you want to *animate* Obj1's change of location, and If Obj1 is internally inside the forbidden area: if you simply insert a Location keyframe, Obj1 will be keyframed in the forbidden area, but if you insert a Visual Location keyframe, you'll keyframe Obj1 at its visual location.)

T98. To put limits on where, in the Global coordinate-system space, an object, which is named, say, Obj1, can be located:

1. To limit an object's location on, say, the X axis to, say, between X = -2 and X = 5: Go to the "Properties" window: 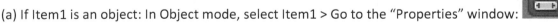 > Enable the "Constraints" button: > LClick "Add Constraint" > LClick "Limit Location."

2. LClick the little box next to "Minimum X" to put a check mark into it (you may have to expand the Properties window to see this label in full) > Set the button under it to -2 > LClick the little box next to "Maximum X" to put a check mark into it > Set the button under it to 5.

3. As you move the object, you can move it "internally" beyond the limit; that is, if you try to move Obj1 beyond the limit, Blender will keep moving it, but *shows and renders* its movement as having been limited. To move Obj1 *visually and in the render* to the internal position, either uncheck the little box next to "Maximum X" or "Minimum X" or set the "influence" button to 0. If Obj1 is, at any time, inside a forbidden area internally, you will have to move it out of this area before you can move Obj1 away from the border of the forbidden area—Obj1 will *appear to be unmoving* while you pull it out of the forbidden area. (If you want to *animate* Obj1's change of location, and If Obj1 is internally inside the forbidden area: if you simply insert a Location keyframe, Obj1 will be keyframed in the forbidden area, but if you insert a Visual Location keyframe, you'll keyframe Obj1 at its visual location.)

T99. To make an object, say, Item1 the child of another object, say, Item2 (or of a vertex group of Item2, say Group1), in a way that gives you more control over the parenting than the CTRL+P method does, and in a way that allows you to make Item1 the child of more than one parent:

1. To make Item1 the child of Item2:

(a) If Item1 is an object: In Object mode, select Item1 > Go to the "Properties" window: 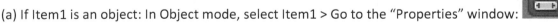 >

Enable the "Constraints" button: 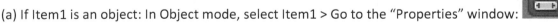 > LClick "Add Constraint" > LClick "ChildOf."

(b) If Item1 and Item2 are two bones in an armature: In Object mode, select the armature > in Pose

mode, select Item1 > Go to the "Properties" window: 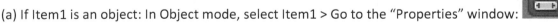 > Enable the "Bone Constraints"

button: 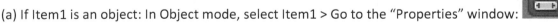 > LClick "Add Constraint" > LClick "ChildOf."

2. Go to the "ChildOf" panel > LClick the "Target" field > LClick the name of Item2 (If Item2 is a bone, first LClick the name of the armature, then LClick the name of the bone)—now Item2 is the parent of Item1. Note that, by default, the child's origin, rotation and scale will be visually (but not actually, as you can see by looking at the Property Shelf, in the "Transform" panel) offset to the origin, rotation and scale of the parent. If you don't want this offset to be there, LClick "Set Inverse"; if you then want it back, LClick "Clear Inverse". (To make Item1 the child of one of Item2's *vertex groups*, say, Group1: First, LClick the name of Item2, then LClick the "Vertex Group" button > LClick Group1.)

3. Check or uncheck the little boxes in accord with which axes you want Item1 to follow.

4. To reduce the parenting effect, adjust the "Influence" button. Notice how Item1 will move gradually back to its unparented location, rotation and scale.

5. To give Item1 one or more additional parents, repeat steps **1** and **2** above for each parent. The relative influence of Item1's parents can be controlled by adjustments of the "Influence" buttons.

T100. To place object, Obj1, visually (but not actually) at the location of object or bone, Item1 (which may be an Empty)—or of a vertex group of Item1, say Group1, in a way such that you can re-position Obj1, placing it at locations intermediate between its original location and Item1's location:

1. In Object mode, select Obj1 > Go to the "Properties" window: > Enable the "Constraints"

button: > LClick "Add Constraint" > LClick "Copy Location."

2. LClick the "Target" field > If Item1 is an object, LClick the name of Item1; If Item1 is a bone, first LClick the name of the armature, then LClick the name of the bone (if you want Obj1 to move to the location of one of Item1's vertex groups: First, LClick the name of Item1, then LClick the "Vertex Group" button > LClick Group1) —Obj1 will jump to the target's location > Go to the "Copy Location" panel > Check or uncheck the little boxes next to "X", "Y" and "Z", in accord with which axes you want Obj1 to move along. Use the "Invert" buttons to move Obj1 in the negative direction along an axis instead of the positive, or in the positive direction instead of the negative direction.

3. To reduce the location copying effect, adjust the "Influence" button. Notice how Obj1 will move gradually back to its original location.

4. If the "Influence" button is set to 1 (full influence of the constraint): To (visually) offset the location of Obj1 from its target by the same X, Y and Z amounts as Obj1, when unconstrained, is (actually) offset from the Global origin, LClick the little box next to "Offset" to put a check mark in it.

T101. To set things up so that object or bone, Item1, visually (but not actually; that is, not internally) will rotate in sync with object or bone, Item2 (or with a vertex group belonging to Item2, say, Group1) when Item2 (which may be an Empty) (or its vertex group) is rotated:

(a) If Item1 is an object: In Object mode, select Item1 > Go to the "Properties" window: >

Enable the "Constraints" button: > LClick "Add Constraint" > LClick "Copy Rotation."

(b) If Item1 is a bone: In Object mode, select the armature > In Pose mode, select Item1 > Go to the

"Properties" window: > Enable the "Bone Constraints" button: > LClick "Add

212

Constraint" > LClick "Copy Rotation."

1. LClick the "Target" field > If Item2 is an object, LClick the name of Item2; If Item2 is a bone, first LClick the name of the armature, then LClick the name of the bone (if you want Item1 to rotate with one of Item2's vertex groups: First, LClick the name of Item2, then LClick the "Vertex Group" button > LClicktGroup1) —Item1 will rotate with the target > Go to the "Copy Rotation" panel > Check or uncheck the little boxes next to "X", "Y" and "Z", in accord with which axes you want Item1 to rotate around. Use the "Invert" buttons to rotate Item1 in the negative direction around an axis instead of the positive, or in the positive direction instead of the negative direction.

2. To reduce the rotation copying effect, adjust the "Influence" button. Notice how Item1 will rotate gradually back to its original location.

3. If the "Influence" button is set to 1 (full influence of the constraint) and if Item1 when *not* constrained is rotated, say, 10 degrees around the X axis: As item1's rotation tracks with that of Item2, to (visually) offset Item1's rotation by 10 degrees, LClick the little box next to "Offset" to put a check mark in it.

T102. To set things up so that object or bone, Item1 visually (but not actually; that is, not internally) will scale in sync with object or bone (or with a vertex group belonging to Item2, say, Group1), Item2 when Item2 (which may be an Empty), is scaled:

(a) If Item1 is an object: In Object mode, select Item1 > Go to the "Properties" window: >

Enable the "Constraints" button: [icon] > LClick "Add Constraint" > LClick "Copy Scale."

(b) If Item1 is a bone: In Object mode, select the armature > In Pose mode, select Item1 > Go to the

"Properties" window: [icon] > Enable the "Bone Constraints" button: [icon] > LClick "Add Constraint" > LClick "Copy Scale."

1. LClick the "Target" field > If Item2 is an object, LClick the name of Item2; If Item2 is a bone, first LClick the name of the armature, then LClick the name of the bone (if you want Item1 to scale with one of Item2's vertex groups: First, LClick the name of Item2, then LClick the "Vertex Group" button > LClick Group1) —Item1 will scale with the target > Go to the "Copy Scale" panel > Check or uncheck the little boxes next to "X", "Y" and "Z", in accord with which axes you want Item1 to scale along. Use the "Invert" buttons to rotate Item1 in the negative direction along an axis instead of the positive, or in the positive direction instead of the negative direction.

2. To reduce the scale-copying effect, adjust the "Influence" button. Notice how Item1 will scale gradually back to its original size.

3. If the "Influence" button is set to 1 (full influence of the constraint) and if Item1 when *not* constrained is scaled, say, 2 units along the X axis: As Item1's scaling tracks with that of item2, to (visually) offset Item1's scaling by 2 units, LClick the little box next to "Offset" to put a check mark in it.

T103. **To make an object follow a curve:**

1. You can set things up so that you can change the apparent location of an object, say, Obj1, in such a way that Obj1 will be restricted to a path defined by a curve object. (These changes will be only apparent, in the 3D View and in the render, because, as you will see by looking at Obj1's unchanging coordinates in the Property Shelf's "Transform" panel, Obj1 will not actually move at all.) To set things up this way:

2. Let's say that Obj1 already exists in your scene. Add the curve object to your scene like this: In Object mode, place the 3D cursor roughly wherever you'll want Obj1's path to be located > (a) Press SHIFT + A OR (b) Go to the Info window & LClick "Add".

3. Hover over "Curve" > LClick "Path" > With the new curve selected, Go to the "Properties" window: > Enable the "Object" button: ![] > LClick the long field at the top to change the name > Type the new name > Press ENTER > remember the curve's name—say, its name is "Curve1" > In Edit mode, and using the methods in **T60, p. 99**, shape the curve into the path that you will want Obj1 to take.

4. In Object mode, select Obj1 > Go to the "Properties" window: ![] > Enable the "Constraints" button: ![] > LClick "Add Constraint" > LClick "Follow Path."

5. LClick the "Target" button > LClick the curve's name (in this case, "Curve1").

6. In the steps below, I will refer to two different controls, **"Evaluation Time,"** and **"Influence"**—here's how to find them:

   (a) To find the "Evaluation Time" button: In Object mode, select the curve > Go to the "Properties" window: ![] > Enable the "Object Data" button: ![] > Go to the "Path Animation" panel (make sure there's a check mark in the little box next to "Path Animation") > Here is where the "Evaluation Time" button is.

   (b) To find the "Influence" button: Select Obj1 > Go to the "Properties" window: > Enable the "Constraints" button: ![] > Go to the "Follow Path" panel > Here is where the "Influence" button is.

7. With the "Evaluation Time" button set to zero, and the "Influence" button set to 1.000: Is Obj1 not appearing to be located at the beginning of the curve (and so, Obj1's path will be offset from the curve), but you *want* it to be at the beginning of the curve?

   Yes: Go to **8**.

   No: Go to **9**.

8. Select Obj1 > With the mouse cursor in the 3D View window, press ALT + G. (This should take Obj1 in *actuality*, to the Global origin, and thus will put its *apparent* location at the beginning of the curve object, wherever that may be in the scene. If you want to see Obj1's actual location before and after you press ALT + G: set the "Influence" button [see step **6** above] to 0.000.)

9. With the "Evaluation Time" button set to zero, and the "Influence" button set to 1.000 (see **6** above). If you want to *offset* Obj1 from the beginning of Curve1 (and thus offset Obj1's path from the curve that defines it); for instance, if you want Obj1 to be visually located (roughly or exactly) two Blender Units in the Y direction away from the beginning of the curve object:

10. select Obj1.

METHOD 1 (precise)

11. In Object mode, go to the Properties Shelf (if it's not there, press N) > Go to the "Transform" panel > Go to the "Location" buttons > Set Y at 2.000.

METHOD 2 (approximate)

12. Set the "Influence" button (see step **5** above) to 0.000 > move Item1 roughly two Blender Units along the positive Y axis > Set the "Influence" button to 1.000.

13. Note that if you, say, double the size of curve1 by scaling it, you will also double the size of any offsets (see **9-12** above).

END OF METHODS

14. To move Obj1 along the curve: Select the curve > adjust the "Evaluation Time" button.

T104. To set things up so that a set of vertices (in a mesh) or a set of control points (of a curve object) will be moved, rotated or scaled by moving, rotating or scaling another object, an Empty, and so that the amount of such control by the Empty over the vertices or control points can by made greater or less —That is, to create a *Hook*:

1. In the 3D View window, in Edit mode > Select the vertex/vertices or control points > Press CTRL + H > LClick "Hook to New Object". This creates a new Empty object at the mid-point of your selection.

2. Go to Object mode > Move, rotate or scale the hook (= the Empty, which should still be selected).

3. To change the influence of the hook: In Object mode, select the object whose vertices or control

points have been modified with the hook > Go to the "Properties" window: 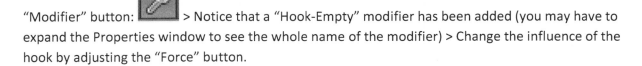 > Enable the

"Modifier" button: 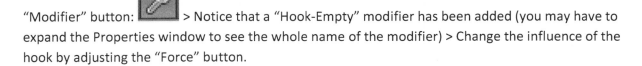 > Notice that a "Hook-Empty" modifier has been added (you may have to expand the Properties window to see the whole name of the modifier) > Change the influence of the hook by adjusting the "Force" button.

T105. To create a bundle of shaping data, and to shape the object in accord with that data: *Shapekeys*:

1. By moving vertices around in Edit mode (without adding or deleting vertices--without extruding for instance), you can *shape* a given mesh in an infinite number of different ways without changing the mesh *structure* (defined by which vertices are connected with which vertices) at all. For instance, you might, for different images, want to give your character a smile, a frown, raise or lower the eyebrows, etc.

2. A "**shapekey**" is a little packet of data that you create that directs Blender to displace, in a certain way, one or more (perhaps many) vertices in a given mesh object. A shapekey might tell Blender to displace, for instance, *Vertex One* from its present location 1 unit in the X direction, 2 units in the Y direction, and 3 units in the –Z direction, and to displace, say, *Vertex Two* 3.3 units in the X direction, etc. etc. So, **a shapekey is a little packet of data that directs Blender to *shape* a mesh object in a certain way**.

3. **You can adjust a shapekey's power to shape the mesh by adjusting the shapekey's *value*.** Setting its value to 0 depletes 100% of a shapekey's power to make its displacements; setting its value to 1 empowers the shapekey 100%.

4. You can create any number of different shapekeys for a given mesh. When more than one of these shapekeys are empowered (their values set above 0), their effect on the mesh will be additive—they will all act together to shape the mesh.

5. When you create your shapekeys, you first pick a mesh shape that you want to consider "undeformed," for instance, you might pick the shape of the mesh of your character's face where he's expressionless—this undeformed shape is called the "basis." Then, changes to that shape will be thought of as deformations of that basis.

6. In the steps below, I will refer to the "'**Shape Keys**" panel—here's how to locate that panel: With the object selected, go to the "Properties" window: > Enable the "Object Data" button: > From here, you can locate the the "Shape Keys" panel.

7. You first have to create a shapekey of data for the *basis* shape (note that a shape*key* is different from a *key*frame, which has to do only with animation): In Object mode, select the undeformed mesh > Go to the "Shape Keys" panel (see **6**) > LClick the "Add Shape Key" button: . This will create the "basis" Shapekey, a bundle of shaping data that defines the *basis* shape.

8. To create another shapekey, in this case a bundle of shaping data that defines a *deformation* of the basis: still in the "Shape Keys" panel (see **6**), LClick the "Add Shape Key" button again: . This creates the new shapekey > To change the name that Blender automatically gave it: LClick in the "Name" field > type the new name; let's say you name it "MyKey1" > Press ENTER > Go to Edit mode > Move the vertices to make the deformation—say, to put a smile on your character's face. So long as"MyKey1" is highlighted in the big box in the "Shape Keys" panel, any change you make in shaping the object in Edit mode will instantly change MyKey1's shaping data to reflect the object's current shape.

9. You may want to create a third shapekey; to do this: Go to Object mode > In the "Shape Keys" panel (see **6**), LClick the "Add Shape Key" button again: . This creates the new shapekey > Let's say you rename it "MyKey2" > Press ENTER > Go to Edit mode > Move the vertices to make the deformation— say, to raise your character's eyebrows. Again, so long as"MyKey2" is highlighted in the big box in the "Shape Keys" panel, any change you make in shaping the object in Edit mode will instantly change MyKey2's shaping data to reflect the object's current shape.

10. **To apply a shapekey, say, MyKey2, to your mesh to see how it shapes the mesh**: In Object mode, select the object > Go to Edit mode > Go to the "Shape Key" panel (see **6**) > In the big field, select the shapekey's name, in this example "MyKey2" > What you see in the 3D View window, in Edit mode, is the object as shaped by the shapekey.

11. **To edit, at any time, a shapekey's—say, MyKey2's—shaping data**: In Object mode, select the object > Go to the "Shape Keys" panel (see **6**) > In the big field, select the shapekey's name, in this example "MyKey2" > Go to Edit mode > In the 3D View window, move vertices around to change the shape (don't extrude; just move things around). So long as"MyKey2" is highlighted, any change you make in shaping the object in Edit mode will instantly change MyKey2's shaping data to reflect the object's current shape.

12. **To shape the object in the 3D View window in Object mode, and in the render, using a shapekey— say, MyKey2, and perhaps using other shapekeys as well, by changing the *values* of the shapekeys** (remember that by changing the "value" of any shapekey, you will be able to change that shapekey's power to deform the shape) : In Object mode, select the object > Go to the "Shape Keys" panel (see **6**) > In the big field, select the name of each shapekey in turn, except for "Basis" and "MyKey2" and for each selection, set the "Value"* button to 0 > Select "MyKey2" > then, still *in Object mode*:

(a) To give the object, as you see it in Object mode and in the render**, the shape that reflects MyKey2's data: set the "Value" button to 1.

(b) To give the object, as you see it in Object mode and in the render**, the shape that reflects the *Basis* Shapekey's data: set the "Value" button to 0.

(c) To give the object, as you see it in Object mode and in the render**, a shape that reflects some intermediate stage between the basis shapekey's shaping data, and MyKey2's shaping data: set the "Value" button to an intermediate position. Note that if you are in object mode, when you slide the "Value" button* from 0 to 1, you are increasing MyKey2's power to deform the basis shape, and so the object's shape will morph from the basis shape to the MyKey2 shape.

(d) To give the object, as you see it in Object mode and in the render**, **a shape that *combines* the shapes generated by MyKey2 and some other shapekey(s)**: Do step (a) or (c) above > select other shapekey name(s) in the big box in the "Shape Keys" panel (see **6**) and adjust the "Value" button using step (a) or (c) above as a guide.

* Notice the numbers to the right of the shapekey names in the big field. These numbers can be changed in the same way that you change the settings of the"Value" button (you can LClick on them and drag, for instance). But whereas the "Value" button shapes the object to reflect the *selected* shapekey's shaping data, a number next to, say, "MyKey2" shapes the object in accord with shapekey MyKey2. Aside from this difference, these numbers behave very much like the "Value" button.

if you have, say, "MyKey2" selected in the big box in the "Shape Keys" panel (see **6), and if the "Value" button in that panel is yellow or green, this means that you have used MyKey2 to create a keyframe (see **T107, steps 22-46, p. 228**), and, although you can change the object's shape in the 3D View window in Object mode by using the "Value" button, you will not be able to change its shape in the *render* using the "Value" button—you can change shape in the render only by changing the keyframe, and you can do that in the Shapekey Editor or in the Properties window, with "Object Data" enabled, in the "Shape Key" panel: RClick the "Value" button > LClick "Insert Keyfram." Yellow and green surrounding the numbers next to the shapekey names in the "Shape Key" panel's shapekey list mean the same thing.

PART SIX: ANIMATION

T106. To animate your scene—an overview:

Blender's animation system is complex. I hope that this short *overview*, though not set out in step-by-step format, will help you to understand how animation works in Blender.

1. The Blender Timeline: Blender, from the first time you open it, presents you with a timeline, which is like an open-ended 3D movie strip, made up of frames. When you go to the Timeline window and put the green animation cursor on a frame, you see in the 3D View window, in Object mode, the 3D content of that frame. You can move the green animation cursor through the frames of the timeline, either simply by dragging it or by pressing ALT+A. When you do this, each frame becomes visible in the 3D View window, in Object or Pose mode, in sequence. (Of course, when you first open Blender and before you animate anything, when you move the cursor through the frames each frame will be the same as every other, and so no change will occur.) I will describe frames of a lower number than a given frame as being "to the left" of that frame, and frames of a higher number as being "to the right" of it.

2. My Definition of "Element": In Blender, an ***Elementary Property***, or ***Element*** (I'll always capitalize the word to show that it has a special meaning), is what I will call any adjustable property that isn't made *up* of adjustable properties. For instance, an object's *location* is not an *Element* of that object because location is made *up* of Elements, namely, the *Elements* of *X-location*, *Y-location* and *Z-location*. Here's another example: A material's *diffuse color* is not an Element of the material because diffuse color is made up of the *Elements* of *diffuse-redness*, *diffuse-greenness* and *diffuse-blueness*.

3. The list of properties in Blender that I am calling "Elements" is large. The following vastly abbreviated enumeration at least shows what I mean by "Element"—Notice that **I am focusing on 4 kinds of Element: Object, Shapekey, Material and World** (see T130, step 30(e) p. 271, for the example of an element, "Blend Opacity," of another kind):

    (Object Elements:)

        X-location (of an object [mesh, curve, armature, camera, etc.] or of a bone)

        Y-location

        Z-location

        X-rotation

        .

        .

        X-scaling

        .

        .

    (Shapekey Elements:)

        value for Shapekey 1 (Shapekey 1's power to change the shape of an object) value for Shapekey 2 (Shapekey 2's power to change the shape of an object)

.

.

(Material Elements:)
    diffuse-redness (of an object's material)
    diffuse-greenness
    diffuse-blueness
    specular-redness

    .

    .

    transparency-alpha
    transparency-IOR [Index Of Refraction]

    .

    .

    mirror-intensity
    mirror-fresnel

    .

    .

(World Elements:)
    stars-separation
    stars-intensity

    .

    .

    mist-intensity

    .

    .

4. **Definition of "Keyframe":** To animate an Element of an object or bone (or world) in Blender, you start by "keyframing" it. You give the Element the value you want it to have at a given timeline frame, then you *record the value it has at that frame* in a little packet of data that you create called a **Keyframe**—a Keyframe will be represented in the DopeSheet window and the NLA Editor window (see below) as a diamond-shaped symbol on the relevant frame. (A Keyframe is not really a frame; actually, you can have many keyframes on a single timeline frame.)

5. **Definition of "Action":** An Action is simply a structure that holds Keyframes. An Action can be applied to, or removed from, an object, a bone, an object's material, or the Blender world. Note that *every Keyframe must reside in an Action*. So, either you create a Keyframe within an existing Action (an Action that you create just before creating the Keyframe, or an Action that was already in existence) or you create an Action simultaneously with creating a Keyframe.

6. **The #1 thing to remember about animation in Blender:** *In Blender, you animate an Element by "keyframing" it using a Keyframe, which is contained within an Action.*

7. Actions and Keyframes are classified on the basis of the kinds of Elements that are keyframed:

    (a) An **Object Action** holds only **Object Keyframes**, which keyframe **Object Elements** (see **3**).

(b) A **Shapekey Action** holds only **Shapekey Keyframes**, which keyframe **Shapekey Elements** (see **3**).

(c) A **Material Action** holds only **Material Keyframes**, which keyframe **Material Elements** (see **3**).

(d) A **World Action** holds only **World Keyframes**, which keyframe **World Elements** (see **3**).

8. Here is a diagram that I will refer to in the steps below:

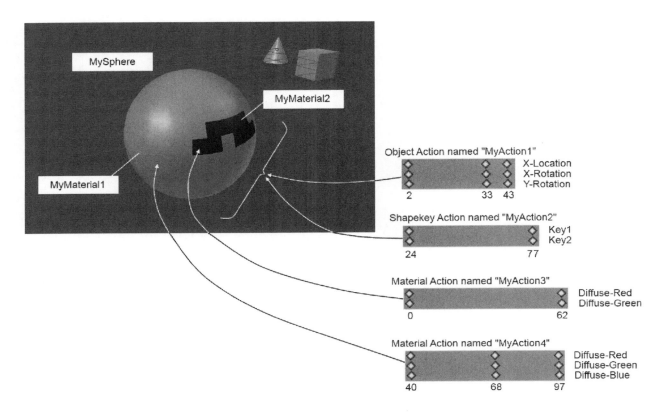

This shows an object, in this example a UV sphere, MySphere, which has four Actions currently applied to it.

(a) MyAction1 applies to the whole object. It holds 9 Object Keyframes that keyframe, at frames 2, 33 and 43, the Object Elements of X-Location, X-Rotation and Y-Rotation.

(b) MyAction2 applies to the whole object. It holds 4 Keyframes that keyframe, at frames 24 and 77, the values of two different shapekeys.

(c) MyAction3 is applied to MyMaterial2 and holds 4 Keyframes that keyframe, at frames 0 and 62, the Material Elements of Diffuse-Red and Diffuse-Green.

(d) MyAction4 is applied to MyMaterial1 and holds 9 Keyframes that keyframe, at frames 40, 68 and 97, the Material Elements of Diffuse-Red, Diffuse-Green and Diffuse-Blue.

9. In general, only one Object Action can be applied to an object or bone at a time. Only one Shapekey Action can be applied to an object at a time. Only one Material Action can be applied to an object's material at a time. Only one World Action can be applied to the Blender world at a time. So, if you have on hand a "walking" Object Action and a "hand waving" Object Action, you cannot use these together in a direct way to make your character wave while walking. (There is a way to blend the contents of two Actions of the same kind in 3D View and in the renders, however. See **17**.)

10. Keyframed or not keyframed: Every Element is either keyframed by a Keyframe which is in an Action which is currently applied or it's not—and note that, by default (that is, before you start to animate your scene, before you actually begin to create keyframes), none of the Elements are keyframed.

• **What happens to an Element which is _not keyframed_ by any Keyframe in a currently-applied Action:**

Looking at the diagrammed example: MySphere's _Y-Location_ (among many other Elements too numerous to mention, which include Z-Location, Z-Rotation, X-Scaling, etc., Diffuse-Blue for MyMaterial2, Specular-Red, etc., Transparency, etc.) is not keyframed. Therefore:

(a) MySphere's Y-Location has the same value in every timeline frame (see 1 above) **in the 3D View in Object and Pose modes and in the renders**. Let's say that MySphere is at Y=3. So, if you drag the animation cursor or press ALT+A, no animation of MySphere's Y-Location at all will occur. If you put the green animation cursor on _any_ frame and _render_ the 2D camera view of the scene, you will see, in the still image, MySphere at Y=3. If you render a 2D _animation_ of the scene, viewing the scene as a movie will be exactly the same as viewing the still image.

(b) If you change MySphere's Y-Location (by pressing G > Y for instance) and moving the sphere in the 3D View window to, say, Y=5, the change will "stick" and will be reflected in every frame in the 3D View in Object and Pose modes and in the renders of the scene.

• **What happens to an Element which _is_ keyframed by a Keyframe in a currently-applied Action:**

Let's suppose that, in MyAction4, MyMaterial1's Diffuse-Redness is keyframed at .308 at frame 40 and at .523 at frame 68, like this:

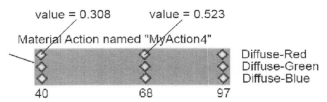

And let's take the first Keyframe, which keyframes MyMaterial1's Diffuse-Redness at .308 at frame 40, as our example:

(a) This single Keyframe (which is represented by a single diamond) does not affect any Element other than MyMaterial1's Diffuse-Redness.

(b) Whenever the current frame is frame 40 (that is, if you manually set the animation cursor to frame 40, or if you press ALT+A and the playback reaches frame 40, or if you create an animation file and the render gets to frame 40), Blender will set MyMaterial1's Diffuse-Redness to .308;

(c) Since there is no other Diffuse-Redness Keyframe in MyAction4 to the left of frame 40, Blender will set MyMaterial1's Diffuse-Redness to .308 for _all_ frames to the left of frame 40; So, if you set the animation cursor on frame 0 and press ALT+A, and play the animation up to frame 40, you will see no change in the material's Diffuse-Redness.

(d) If there _had been_ a Diffuse-Redness Keyframe in MyAction4 to the left of frame 40, then Blender would have **_interpolated_** the frames in between the two Keyframes; that is, in the intervening frames, Blender would have set MyMaterial1's Diffuse-Redness to a different value for each frame such that as the timeline played, there would have been a smooth Diffuse-Redness transition between the two Keyframes.

(e) If there had been no Diffuse-Redness Keyframe in MyAction4 to the right of frame 40, then Blender would have set MyMaterial1's Diffuse-Redness to .308 for all frames to the right of frame 40.

(f) But, in fact, there *is* a Diffuse-Redness Keyframe in MyAction4 to the right of frame 40, at frame 68, so Blender will **interpolate** the frames in between the two Keyframes. In this case, Blender will produce an animation so that if you play frame 40 to frame 68, you will see MyMaterial1's Diffuse-Redness change smoothly from .308 to .523.

(g) Blender will allow you to change the keyframed Element's value, in this case, you can change the diffuse redness of MyMaterial1 by LClicking the color swatch and adjusting the color palette, but it will not "stick;" that is, if you LClick the animation cursor, or if you render the scene, the Element's value will jump back to the keyframed value.

11. In the diagram above, 4 Actions are applied to MySphere. If you wish, you can unlink the Object Action or the Shapekey Action from MySphere. And, you can store the Object and Shapekey Actions so as to be able to re-apply them at any time. In fact, **you can actually apply the very same Object Action to a different object or to a bone**. You control which object Action is the currently-applied one for an object by going to the DopeSheet window in "Action Editor" mode. You control which Shapekey Action is the currently applied one for an object by going to the DopeSheet window in "ShapeKey Editor" mode.

12. An Action can be long, with many Keyframes in it and spanning many timeline frames; or, an Action can be very short—for instance, you can create a "smile" Action, which you can apply to your character when you want her to smile, or you can create a "walk-cycle" Action, etc. Therefore, you do not have to create a new Action each time you want your character to walk or to smile.

13. Note that **every Action has a name**. To see the name of the Object Action that's currently applied to an object: If you go to the DopeSheet window and put it into "Action Editor" mode, you can see the name that either you or Blender gave to the Action. To see the name of a Shapekey Action that's currently applied to an object: If you go to the DopeSheet window and put it into "ShapeKey Editor" mode, you can see the name that either you or Blender gave to the Action. You can see the name of a Material Action or a world Action in the DopeSheet, in the NLA (see **17**) or in the Outliner window.

14. FOLLOW THESE STEPS TO ANIMATE AN ELEMENT—A QUICK GUIDE: So after all this, a succinct procedure for animating an Element can be given: Put the animation cursor at, say, frame 1 > Give the Element, let's say it's MySphere's X-Location, the value you want it to have at frame 1; create an X-Location Keyframe (if an object Action wasn't already applied to mySphere, the mere act of creating this Keyframe will also create an object Action to hold it) > Move the animation cursor to, say, frame 30 > Change the value of MySphere's X-Location > Create another X-Location Keyframe (*both Keyframes must keyframe the same Element in order to animate that Element*).

15. FOLLOW THESE STEPS TO CREATE KEYFRAMES—A QUICK GUIDE (for a fuller account, see T107, p. 224):

(A) To create an Object Keyframe for an object or bone: Select the object or bone, then (where "Item1" is an object or a bone):

(i) To create a **Location Keyframe for Item1**: (a) In Object mode, select Item1 > Go to the

222

Properties Shelf (if it's not there, press N) > Go to the "Transform" panel > RClick any "Location" button > LClick "Insert Keyframes"; OR (b) with the mouse pointer in the 3D View window, press I (the letter i) > LClick "Location"; OR, (c) if there is a Location channel in the DopeSheet window in DopeSheet or Action Editor mode, and in the Graph Editor window in F-Curve Editor mode: move the relevant slider (You can make sliders visible, so long as the channel is there).

(ii) To create a **Rotation Keyframe**: (a) In Object mode, select Item1 > Go to the Properties Shelf (if it's not there, press N) > Go to the "Transform" panel > RClick any "Rotation" button > LClick "Insert Keyframes"; OR (b) with the mouse pointer in the 3D View window, press I (the letter i) > LClick "Rotation"; OR (c) if there is a rotation channel in the DopeSheet window in DopeSheet or Action Editor mode, and in the Graph Editor window in F-Curve Editor mode: move the relevant slider (You can make sliders visible, so long as the channel is there).

(iii) To create a **Scaling Keyframe**: (a) In Object mode, select Item1 > Go to the Properties Shelf (if it's not there, press N) > Go to the "Transform" panel > RClick any "Scale" button > LClick "Insert Keyframes"; OR (b) with the mouse pointer in the 3D View window, press I (the letter i) > LClick "Scaling"; OR (c) if there is a scaling channel in the DopeSheet window in DopeSheet or Action Editor mode, and in the Graph Editor window in F-Curve Editor mode: move the relevant slider (You can make sliders visible, so long as the channel is there).

(iv) To create a set of Object Keyframes, for instance, to create **Location and Rotation Keyframes**: With the mouse pointer in the 3D View window, press I (the letter i) > LClick "LocRot"; etc.

(B) To create a Shapekey Keyframe for an object: Create your shapekeys for that object (see **T105, p. 215**) > In Object mode, select the object > (a) Go to the "Properties" window: > Enable the "Object Data" button: > Go to the "Shape Keys" panel > In the big box there, select the shapekey that you want to animate > Adjust the "Value" button > RClick the "Value" button > LClick "Insert Keyframe" OR (b) Go to the ShapeKey Editor > Move a shapekey slider (see **T107, step 22, p. 228**).

(C) To create a Material Keyframe for an object's material: In Object mode, select the object > Go to the "Properties" window: > Enable the "Material" button: > In the big box at the top with the list of materials in it, select the material that you want to animate > (a) RClick on the button which controls the Element that you want to animate; for instance, to create a **Diffuse-Color Keyframe**: Go to the "Diffuse" panel > RClick the color swatch > LClick "Insert Keyframes"; OR (b) if there are diffuse color channels in the DopeSheet window in DopeSheet mode, and in the Graph Editor window in F-Curve Editor mode: move the relevant slider (You can make sliders visible, so long as the channel is there). Similarly, to create a **Transparency-Alpha Keyframe**: Go to the "Transparency" panel > RClick the "Alpha" button > LClick "Insert Keyframes"; etc.

(D) To create a World Keyframe: RClick on the button whose value you want to animate; for instance, to create a **Stars-Separation Keyframe**: Go to the "Properties" window: > Enable the "World" button: > (a) Go to the "Stars" panel > LClick the little box next to "Stars" to put a check mark into it > RClick the "Separation" button > LClick "Insert Keyframe"; OR, (b) if there is an "Average Separation" channel in the DopeSheet window in DopeSheet mode, and in the Graph Editor window in F-Curve Editor mode: move the relevant slider (You can make sliders visible, so long as the channel is there).

16. In the **F-Curve Editor**, you can **edit the Blender-generated interpolations** between Keyframes of an Action. You do this by manipulating the "Ipo" curves that are showing in this editor's window. Every keyframed Element gets its own "**channel**" in the F-Curve Editor.

17. I said in **9** that only one Object Action can be applied to an object or bone at a time, and only one Shapekey Action can be applied to an object at a time, and only one Material Action can be applied to an object's material at a time, and only one World Action can be applied to the Blender world at a time, and I said that there is, in fact, a way to blend the contents of two Actions of the same kind in the 3D View and in the renders, so that, for instance, you can make your character give a friendly wave while walking. When an Action is applied to an object, an object's material, or the world will you see a representation of that Action in the ***Non-Linear Animation (NLA) Editor window***; The Action will appear there as a bright orange band, dotted by diamond-shaped signs that represent the frames where there are Keyframes. I will call such a band an "**Action band**." The Actions that are represented in the NLA Editor via Action bands are those that are presently applied to the scene's objects and materials, as they are referred to by name in the Action Editor, the ShapeKey Editor, and in the animation windows. In the NLA Editor, you can change any bright orange Action band into a yellow "**Action strip**". **You can merge an Action *band* together with an Action *Strip* of the same kind (or you can merge two Action strips of the same kind)**, so that, for instance, your character can wave while walking.

18. In the NLA Editor, you can also place any given Action strip wherever you want it along the timeline; and you can make copies of Action strips and put them where you want them along the timeline. You can, for instance, take a very short "walk cycle" Action strip, duplicate it many times and put the duplicates together, end to end along the timeline, to make your character keep walking. Essentially, the NLA Editor controls the values of the keyframed Elements (and only the keyframed Elements) in the 3D View and in the renders. For more on the NLA Editor, see **T116, p. 237** and **T117, p. 239** .

19. If you are working with a complex, articulated model, such as a human figure, you will find that, as you create your Keyframes, it will be much easier for you to put your model into different poses if you put an "armature," composed of "bones," inside it. This is known as "**rigging**" (and a rig can be helpful in posing your model for stills as well). As a way of *preparing* your scene for animation, rigging was covered in **T88-T92**.

20. Keep focused on the changeable *Elements*. Remember this: To create an animation in Blender, you ***keyframe Elements inside an Action***; then you can repeat and mix animations in the NLA Editor by turning Action bands into Action strips; then you can modify the animation in various ways using the Compositor (see); then you can import the scene, as influenced by the NLA Editor and the Compositor, into the VSE via "Add" > "Scene", where you can cut and splice, etc. (see **T130, p. 264**).

T107. To animate an Element:

1. For an explanation of Keyframes, read the overview at **T106, step 4, p. 219**.

2. In what follows, I will refer to the **DopeSheet Mode button**. To find this button, go to the DopeSheet window header: The DopeSheet Mode button is the button with one of these expressions on it: "DopeSheet", "Action Editor", "ShapeKey Edi", "Grease Pencil".

3. To animate an **Object Element**: Go to **4**; To animate a **Shapekey Element**: Go to **22**; To animate a **Material Element**: Go to **48**; To animate a **World Element**: Go to **51**.

To animate an Object Element of an object or bone:

4. Select the object (in Object mode) or bone (in Pose mode).

5. You animate an Object Element by creating Keyframes (see the Quick Guide: **T106, step 15(A), p. 222**); but, an Object Keyframe cannot exist unless it is in a Keyframe holder called an Object *Action* (see **T106, p. 218** for more about Actions).

6. Go to the DopeSheet window > Go to the DopeSheet mode button (see **3**) > Make sure it is set to "Action Editor" mode > Is there a button in the Action Editor's header that has the word "New" on it?

 (You might have to scroll in the header to see this button)

    Yes (that is, there is no Object Action presently applied to the object): Go to **7**.

    No (that is, there is an Object Action presently applied to the object): Go to **11**.

7. Do you want to put your new Keyframe into an Action you have already created and saved?

    Yes: Go to **8**.

    No: Go to **9**.

8. LClick this button:

    > LClick the name of the Action that you want to use > Go to **18**.

9. Do you want to first create a new Object Action and then put the Keyframes into it?

    Yes: LClick the "New" button > Go to **10**.

    No: To create an Action automatically when you create the Keyframe, go to **18**.

10. To change the name that Blender has just given to your new Action, LClick the name:

    > Type the new name > Press ENTER > LClick the "F" button:

(The Action must be applied to an object or a so-called "false object" in order for the Action to be saved when you save the .blend file. Since an Action may or may not be applied to an object when you save your .blend file, you need to press the F button so as to permanently link the Action to a false object.) > Go to **18**.

11. Do you want to put your new Keyframes into the Object Action that is currently applied to the object; that is, do you want to put the Keyframes into the Action whose name appears in this field?:

    Yes: Go to **18**.

No: Go to **12**.

12. Do you want to put your new Keyframe into an Action you have already created and saved?

Yes: Go to **13**.

No: To create a new Object Action, go to **14**.

13. LClick this button:

 > LClick the name of the Action that you want to use > Go to step **18**.

14. LClick the "+" button:

 > Go to **15**.

15. In the right-hand panel of the DopeSheet window (still in Action Editor mode), the diamonds represent Keyframes; delete the diamonds that represent Keyframes that you do not want in the new Action. Do you want to delete all of them?

Yes: Go to **16**.

No: Go to **17**.

16. Remember the name that Blender gave to your new Action after you LClicked the "+" button at **14** > You can now use the "B" key to draw a selection box around all the diamonds to select them, or just press "A" once or twice to select them all > Press X > LClick "Delete Keyframes". Once you delete all of them, you will have to LClick this button:

LClick the name that Blender gave to the Action at step **14** > Go to **10**.

17. Select all the diamonds that you do not want in the new Action (you can press B, then drag a border around them) > Press X > LClick "Delete Keyframes" > Go to **10**.

18. Move the green animation cursor to the frame where you want to place the Keyframe > In the 3D View window, adjust the object or bone so that the Element you want to animate has the value that you want it to have at that frame.

19. Do (a), (b), (c) or (d):

(a) With the mouse pointer in the 3D View window, press I (the letter i) > If you want to Keyframe a location Element, LClick "Location," "LocRot," "LocScale," or 'LocRotScale"; If you want to keyframe a rotation Element, LClick "Rotation," "LocRot," "RotScale," or "LocRotScale," etc. (If you want to keyframe, say, X-Location and you LClick "Location," you will also keyframe Y- and Z-Location. If you LClick "LocRot," you will also keyframe the rotation Elements, etc.)

(b) Go to the Tool Shelf (If it's not visible, press T) > Go to the "Keyframes" buttons, LClick "Insert" > If you want to keyframe a location Element, LClick "Location," "LocRot," "LocScale," or 'LocRotScale"; If you want to keyframe a rotation Element, LClick "Rotation," "LocRot," "RotScale," or "LocRotScale," etc.

(c) Go to the Property Shelf (if it's not there, press N) > Go to the "Transform" panel > If you want to keyframe a location Element, RClick any "Location" button > LClick "Insert Keyframes"; If you want to keyframe a rotation Element, RClick any "Rotation" button > LClick "Insert Keyframes"; If you want to keyframe a scaling keyframe, RClick any "Scale" button > LClick "Insert Keyframes".

   (d) if there's already a channel in the DopeSheet window in DopeSheet mode and Action Editor mode, and in the Graph Editor window in F-Curve Editor mode (The Graph Editor Mode button is the button with one of these expressions on it: "F-Curve Editor" or "Drivers"), *for the Element you want to ani*mate, and sliders are present, move the relevant slider (any movement of the slider will create, or change, a Keyframe):

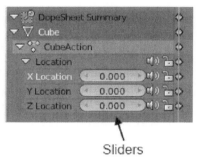

Sliders

If there is a channel for the Element, but there are no sliders there: In the window's header, LClick "View" > "Show Sliders" > Move the relevant slider.

20. **To create another Object Keyframe at a higher-numbered frame, so that you will animate the Element(s) that you chose in step 18:** Move the green animation cursor to a higher-numbered frame > In the 3D View window, adjust the object or bone so that the Element you want to animate has the value that you want it to have at that frame > Repeat step **19**, *making sure that the Element(s) that you want to animate are keyframed in both the earlier and later Keyframes.*

Example 1—a cube: Suppose that your cube is at a certain location at frame 87, and you want it to move to a different location, arriving there at frame 110; and, suppose that, during the same span, you want the cube to rotate, say, around 45 degrees around its Y axis:

In the DopeSheet or in the F-Curve Editor LClick the green animation cursor (the frame number can be found at the bottom of the cursor) and drag it to frame 87 > (a) Go to the Tool Shelf > Go to the "Keyframes" buttons > LClick "Insert" OR (b) with the mouse pointer in the 3D View window, press the letter I (= i) > Because you want to make changes in the cube's location and rotation, LClick "LocRot"— this creates the first Keyframe of this animation sequence > Drag the animation cursor to frame 110 > In the 3D View window, change the location of the cube and rotate the cube > with the mouse pointer in the 3D window, press the letter I (= i) > Now suppose that you suddenly decide not to incorporate the *location* change after all, so: LClick "Rotation," not "LocRot" ("Location and Rotation"). Now the new Keyframe will incorporate the cube's new orientation, but its location will remain as it was in the previous Keyframe—If you had chosen "LocRot" instead of "Rotation," the change in both Elements would have been incorporated in the new frame.

Example 2—an armature: To create an Action for an armature animation that you will want to use more than once, perhaps in more than one context; for instance, you might want to create an Action for a character's walk cycle (one foot forward followed by the other foot forward), a sitting-down motion, etc:

In Pose mode, put the Timeline window's cursor at frame 87 > Press A to deselect all > Create a new

Object Action > Pose the armature > Select the bones that will be moved or rotated > (a) Go to the Tool Shelf > Go to the "Keyframes" buttons > LClick "Insert" OR (b) with the mouse pointer in the 3D View window, press the letter I (= i) > LClick "LocRot" > Move the Timeline window's cursor to 110 > Re-pose the armature > Select the bones that will be moved or rotated > (a) Go to the Tool Shelf > Go to the "Keyframes" buttons > LClick "Insert" OR (b) with the mouse pointer in the 3D View window, press the letter I (= i) > LClick "LocRot".

21. Go to **53**.

22. To animate the Shapekey Element of a shapekey (that is, to animate the shapekey's *value* Element, to animate the shapekey's power to change an object's shape—see the Quick Guide at T106, step 15(B), p. 223):

23. Select the object.

24. You animate a Shapekey Element (a shapekey's value) by creating Keyframes; but, a Shapekey Keyframe cannot exist unless it is in a Keyframe holder called a Shapekey *Action* (see **T106, p. 218** for more about Actions).

25. Go to the DopeSheet window > Go to the DopeSheet mode button (see **2**) > Make sure it is set to "ShapeKey Editor" mode > Is there is a button in the ShapeKey Editor's header that has the word "New"

on it?,  (You might have to scroll in the header to see this button)

   Yes (that is, there is no Shapekey Action presently applied to the object): Go to **26**.

   No (that is, there is a Shapekey Action presently applied to the object): Go to **30**.

26. Do you want to put your new Keyframe into an Action you have already created and saved?

   Yes: Go to **27**.

   No: Go to **28**.

27. LClick this button:

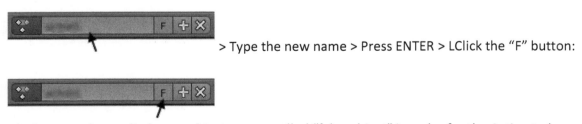

> LClick the name of the Action that you want to use > Go to **37**.

28. Do you want to first create a new Shapekey Action and then put the Keyframes into it?

   Yes: LClick the "New" button > Go to **29**.

   No: To create an Action automatically when you create the Keyframe, go to **37**.

29. To change the name that Blender has just given to your new Action, LClick the name:

> Type the new name > Press ENTER > LClick the "F" button:

(The Action must be applied to an object or a so-called "false object" in order for the Action to be saved when you save the .blend file. Since an Action may or may not be applied to an object when you save your .blend file, you need to press the F button so as to permanently link the Action to a false object.) > Go to **37**.

30. Do you want to put your new Keyframes into the Object Action that is currently applied to the object; that is, do you want to put the Keyframes into the Action whose name appears in this field?:

    Yes: Go to **37**.

    No: Go to **31**.

31. Do you want to put your new Keyframe into an Action you have already created and saved?

    Yes: Go to **32**.

    No: To create a new Object Action, go to **33**.

32. LClick this button:

                                        > LClick the name of the Action that you want to use > Go to

step **37**.

33. LClick the "+" button:

                      > Go to **34**.

34. In the right-hand panel of the DopeSheet window (still in Action Editor mode), the diamonds represent Keyframes; delete the diamonds that represent Keyframes that you do not want in the new Action. Do you want to delete all of them?

    Yes: Go to **35**.

    No: Go to **36**.

35. Remember the name that Blender gave to your new Action after you LClicked the "+" button at **33** > You can now use the "B" key to draw a selection box around all these diamonds to select them, or just press "A" once or twice to select them all > Press X > LClick "Delete Keyframes". Once you delete all of them, you will have to LClick this button:

LClick the name given to the Action in step **33** > Go to **29**.

36. Select all the diamonds that you do not want in the new Action (you can press B, then drag a border around them) > Press X > LClick "Delete Keyframes".

37. To create a Shapekey Keyframe at, say, frame 40, then another at, say, frame 70, during which interval there occurs a change in the *shape* of an object, say, a cube

Here is a picture of the ShapeKey Editor with my own names for the features that will show up once you create the shapekey(s):

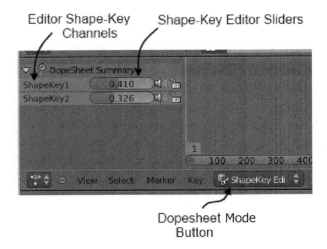

Editor Shape-Key Channels   Shape-Key Editor Sliders

Dopesheet Mode Button

38. Remember (see **T105, p. 215**) that once you have created shapekeys (so that you can later keyframe them, for instance) for an object, you can shape that object in Object mode and in the render by adjusting the *value* Element of a given shapekey, or, in combination, the *value* Elements of several shapekeys at the same time—that is, you can shape the object by adjusting the power of these shapekeys, separately or together, to change the object's shape.

39. The steps here, under this Topic, presume that you have already created the shapekey(s) that you will need in order to give your object the shapes that you want it to have at the animation keyframes that you are about to create. (For each shapekey whose value you adjust in order to animate the shape-change, you will produce a separate keyframe.)

40. In any of the animation windows: Make sure that the green, animation cursor is at frame 40, because, in this example, this is where you want to place your first keyframe in the sequence.

41. Do (a) or (b):

   (a) In Object mode, select the object > (a) Go to the "Properties" window: ![icon] > Enable the "Object Data" button: ![icon] > Go to the "Shape Keys" panel > In the big box there, select, in turn, each of the shapekeys that you want to use to shape the object for frame 40, and adjust the "Value" button for each until the object has the shape you want it to have at frame 40; in this instance, let's suppose that you want the object to have the *basis* shape at frame 40; therefore, you should make sure that for each shapekey, the value is set to 0 so that the object will have the basis shape at frame 40 > For each shapekey whose value will change in the animation: RClick the "Value" button and then LClick "Insert Keyframe" (so, if you intend to adjust more than one shapekey value to produce the frame-70 shape, you will end up producing more than one Shapekey Keyframe at frame 40).

   (b) Go to the ShapeKey Editor Sliders (see picture above). These sliders work just like the "Value" slider in the "Shape Keys" panel (see **T105, p. 215**), except that when you adjust a slider, a keyframe is created (if none already exists for that shapekey) > Go to, in turn, each of the sliders for the shapekeys that you want to use to shape the object for frame 40, and adjust the slider for each until the object has the shape you want it to have; for instance, you might make sure that for each shapekey, the value is set to 0 so that the object will have the basis shape at frame 40. (If you want a slider—one of those that must be adjusted to create the animation—to remain where it is for frame 40, you should still move it, then reset it)—the very act of setting each slider will create a Keyframe for frame 40.

42. In any of the animation windows: Drag the green, animation cursor to frame 70.

43. Do (a) or (b):

(a) In Object mode, select the object > (a) Go to the "Properties" window: > Enable the

"Object Data" button:  > Go to the "Shape Keys" panel > In the big box there, select, in turn, each of the shapekeys that you want to use to shape the object for frame 70, and adjust the "Value" button for each until the object has the shape you want it to have at frame 70 > For each shapekey whose value will change in the animation: RClick the "Value" button and then LClick "Insert Keyframe".

(b) Go to the ShapeKey Editor Sliders (see picture above). These sliders work just like the "Value" slider in the "Shape Keys" panel (see **T105, p. 215**), except that when you adjust a slider, a keyframe is created (if none already exists for that shapekey) > Go to, in turn, each of the sliders for the shapekeys that you want to use to shape the object for frame 70, and adjust the slider for each until the object has the shape you want it to have—the very act of setting each slider will create a Keyframe for frame 70.

44. After you've set the sliders to set the object shape at frame 70, if you want to watch the animation: *Make sure that the 3D View window is in Object mode* > Put the animation cursor to a frame before frame 40 > Press ALT+A . To stop the playback, press ESC.

45. To make sure that the new Shapekey Action is saved when you save your .blend file: Go to the DopeSheet window > Make sure the DopeSheet Mode button (to locate it, see **5** above) is set to "ShapeKey Editor" mode > LClick the button with the "F" on it:

46. Note: Be careful not to confuse the *shapekey* with the *Shapekey Action*. A multiplicity of *shapekeys* (packets of data that shape the object in a way that can be adjusted using sliders) can, together, give a single *Shapekey Action* (a keyframe holder whose keyframes were created using shapekeys) its shapes.

47. Go to **53**.

48. To animate a material Element of an object's material (see T106, step 15(C), p. 223):
Select the object. When you create a first Material Keyframe for the material of an object, a material Action is automatically created.

49. To create a Material Keyframe from, say, frame 201 to frame 224, during which, there occurs a gradual change in a *material quality* of an object's material, a change, say, in the diffuse color of a material on a cube:

Suppose a material on your cube is yellow, and during the span between frames 201 and 224, you want this material gradually to change from yellow to red: In any of the animation windows: Drag the green, animation cursor to frame 201 > Do (a) or (b):

(a) With the cube selected in the 3D View window, go to the "Properties" window: >

Enable the "Material" button: 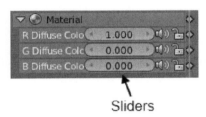 > In the big box at the top with the list of materials in it, select the material that you want to animate > Go to the "Diffuse" panel > RClick the color swatch, which in our example is yellow, but which in other cases could be white, black, or any color. (Here, you are RClicking the color swatch; but, in general, RClick whatever control it is that sets the particular material quality that you want to keyframe) > LClick "Insert Keyframes"—this creates the first Keyframe of this animation sequence > Drag the animation cursor to frame 224 > With the cube selected in the 3D View window, go back to the "Properties" window: > Make sure the "Material" button is still enabled: > Go back to the "Diffuse" panel > LClick the color swatch > Use the palette to change the cube's color to red (see   ) > LClick outside of the palette > RClick the color swatch, which is now red > LClick "Insert Keyframes"—this creates the second Keyframe of the sequence and completes the effect. OR,

(b) Go to the DopeSheet mode button (see **2**) > Make sure it is set to DopeSheet Mode > For you to be able to use this method, there must be a channel there for each and every Material Element that you want to animate. If there *is*, in fact, a channel there for every Material Element that you want to animate, but *sliders* are not present, then LClick "View" > "Show Sliders" > Go to the slider for each of the Elements that you need to change in order to animate the material (In the present example, you will only need to change "G Diffuse Color") > Move each of these sliders and then move it back where it was (any movement of the slider will set a keyframe):

Sliders

> Drag the animation cursor to frame 224 > Move one or more sliders to change the Material Element(s) and to create one or more new Keyframes (In the present example, you will only have to set "G Diffuse Color" to 0 in order to produce red).

50. Go to **54**.

51. To animate a World Element (see T106, step 15(D), p. 223):

When you create a first World Keyframe, a World Action is automatically created.

52. To create a World Keyframe, from, say, frame 40 to frame 70, during which, there occurs a change in the "*world*" settings; say, you want to add stars:

Suppose that at frame 40 there are almost no stars in your scene's sky, and during the span between frames 40 and 70, you want the stars gradually to appear more and more numerous: In any of the animation windows: Drag the green, animation cursor to frame 40 (the frame number can be found at the bottom of the cursor) > Do (a) or (b):

(a) Go to the "Properties" window: 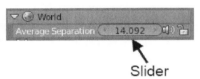 > Enable the "World" button: > Go to the "Stars" panel > LClick the little box next to "Stars" to put a check mark into it > If the "Stars" panel is collapsed, LClick the little black triangle to expand it > Set the "Separation" button to 50.000 (you might have to expand the "Properties" window to see the entire name of this button) > RClick the "Separation" button > LClick "Insert Keyframe"—now your first Keyframe has been created > Drag the animation

cursor to frame 70 > Go back to the "Properties" window: > Make sure that the "World"

button is still enabled: > Go back to the "Stars" panel > Set the "Separation" button to, say, 4.000 > RClick the "Separation" button > LClick "Insert Keyframe"— this creates the second Keyframe of the sequence and completes the effect.

(b) Go to the DopeSheet mode button (see **2**) > Make sure it is set to DopeSheet Mode > if there's already a channel here for the World Element, in this example, "Average Separation," that you want to animate, and a slider is present, move the slider (any movement of the slider will set a Keyframe—you can, for instance, move the slider then move it back):

Slider

If there is a channel for the Element, but there is no slider there: In the window's header, LClick "View" > "Show Sliders" > Move the slider to create the Keyframe > Drag the animation cursor to frame 224 > Move the slider to change the value of the Element and to create a new Keyframe. Go to **54**.

53. If you chose "No" at step **9** or step **28** (that is, if you created the Action automatically when you created your keyframe(s)):

To change the name that Blender has just given to your new Action, LClick the name:

> Type the new name > Press ENTER > LClick the "F" button:

(The Action must be applied to an object or a so-called "false object" in order for the Action to be saved when you save the .blend file. Since an Action may or may not be applied to an object when you save your .blend file, you need to press the F button so as to permanently link the Action to a false object.)
54. When you keyframe an Element for the first time in an Action, the button (in the Properties window, or wherever it is) that controls that Element becomes green, or, if the animation cursor is on the keyframe, yellow. Or, if the control is a color swatch, it gets a green or yellow *border*. So, when a button is green or yellow, you know that the relevant Element is no longer un-keyframed.

T108. To apply (link) a saved Object Action to an object, or to apply (link) a saved Shapekey Action to an object:

(Read **T106, p. 218**.) Recall that only one Object Action can be applied to an object at a time, and only one Shapekey Action can be applied to an object at a time; therefore, if you are applying either a saved Object Action to an object that already has an Object Action applied to it, or are applying a saved Shapekey Action to an object that already has a Shapekey Action applied to it, the new Action will replace the old one. To apply an Object Action: Go to **1**. To apply a Shapekey Action: Go to **2**.

1. **To apply a saved Object Action to an object:** In Object mode, select the object > Go to the DopeSheet

window ( ) > Make sure it is in "Action Editor" mode > In the DopeSheet header, LClick this button, which is at the left end of a connected row of buttons (if an Object Action is currently applied to the object) or which is to the left of the "New" button (if no Object Action is currently applied to the

object): (You might have to scroll in the header to see this button—do not confuse this button with the DopeSheet window icon at the far left of the DopeSheet header) > LClick the name of the Action that you want to apply to the object. If another Object Action had already been applied to the object when you applied the new one, the old Action has now been removed from the object; unless and until it is re-applied to the object, it will no longer be represented in the NLA Editor (see **T106, step 17, p. 224** and **T116, p. 237**), and it will no longer play in the 3D View when you press ALT + A—the new Object Action will replace the old one in the NLA Editor, and will be the Object Action that now plays in the 3D View when you press ALT + A.

2. **To apply a saved Shapekey Action to an object:** In Object mode, select the object > Go to the

DopeSheet window ( ) > Make sure it is in "ShapeKey Editor" mode > In the DopeSheet header, LClick this button, which is at the left end of a connected row of buttons (if a Shapekey Action is currently applied to the object) or which is to the left of the "New" button (if no Shapekey Action is

currently applied to the object): (You might have to scroll in the header to see this button— do not confuse this button with the DopeSheet window icon at the far left of the DopeSheet header) > LClick the name of the Shapekey Action that you want to apply to the object. If another Shapekey Action had already been applied to the object when you applied the new one, the old Action has now been removed from the object; it will no longer be represented in the NLA Editor (see **T106, step 17, p. 224** and **T116, p. 237**), and it will no longer play in the 3D View when you press ALT + A—the new Shapekey Action will replace the old one in the NLA Editor, and will be the Shapekey Action that now plays in the 3D View when you press ALT + A.

T109. To unlink an Object Action from a bone or object, or to unlink a Shapekey Action from an object:

1. (i) To unlink an Object Action, go to **2**. (ii) To unlink a Shapekey Action, go to **3**.

2. With the object or bone selected, go to the DopeSheet window > Make sure it is in "Action Editor" mode > Go to **4**.

3. With the object selected, go to the DopeSheet window > Make sure it is in "ShapeKey Editor" mode > Go to **4**.

4. LClick the button with the "X" on it:

5. Note that *the "X" does not delete the Action*—it merely unlinks the Action from the bone or object. The Action remains available and can be re-applied to the bone or object at any time.

T110. To see what Object Action is currently applied to an object or a bone—or to see what Shapekey Action is currently applied to an object:

1. To see what Object Action is currently applied to an object or bone: With the object or bone selected, go to the DopeSheet window > Make sure it is in "Action Editor" mode > You will find the Action's name in the Action Editor's header here:

2. To see what Shapekey Action is currently applied to an object: With the object selected, go to the DopeSheet window > Make sure it is in "ShapeKey Editor" mode > You will find the Action's name in the ShapeKey Editor's header here:

T111. To copy a rigged model's pose at, say, frame 30, and paste it at say, frame 60:

1. In any one of the animation windows, move the green animation cursor to frame 30.

2. With the 3D View window in Pose mode: (a) Press CTRL + C; OR: (b) Go to the 3D View window's header > LClick "Pose" > LClick "Copy Pose"; OR: Go to the 3D View window's header > LClick the pose

copy button,  .

3. Move the animation cursor to frame 60.

4. Do you want to paste a pose at frame 60 which is a mirror image of the pose at frame 30?

Yes: Go to **6**.

No: To paste the pose at frame 60 which is just like the pose at frame 30: Go to **5**.

5. (a) Press CTRL + V; OR: (b) Go to the 3D View window's header > LClick "Pose" > LClick "Paste Pose";

OR: (c) Go to the 3D View window's header > LClick the pose paste button, . Go to **7**.

6. (a) Go to the 3D View window's header > LClick "Pose" > LClick "Paste X-Flipped Pose"; OR: (b) Go to

the 3D View window's header > LClick the flipped pose paste button, .

7. To make the copy permanent, create a Keyframe.

T112. With any given frame of an armature/character animation showing in the 3D View window: To see a "ghost" image of previous and subsequent frames ("onion skinning"):

1. In Object mode, select the armature > Go to Pose mode > Go to the "Properties" window:

> Enable the "Object Data" button:  > Go to the "Ghost" panel > To choose the "Around Current Frame" method, make sure that the "Around Frame" button is enabled (blue) > Adjust "Range" to specify how many ghost frames to show > Adjust "Step" to specify how many frames will separate each ghost frame.

T113. To manage the DopeSheet Modes (or "Contexts"), namely, the DopeSheet Mode, the Action Editor Mode, and the Shapekey Editor Mode—and to manage the F-Curve Editor:

1. **To find the *Graph Editor Mode button*,** go to the header of the Graph Editor window. The Graph Editor Mode button is the button with one of these expressions on it: "F-Curve Editor" or "Drivers".

2. **"channels":**

(a) In the DopeSheet window, with the DopeSheet Mode button set to "DopeSheet," there are channels which include those for every keyframed Element in every currently-applied Action for every object, bone or material and for the Blender "world."

(b) In the DopeSheet window, with the DopeSheet Mode button set to "Action Editor," there's a channel for every keyframed Element in the selected object or bone's currently-applied Object Action.

(c) In the DopeSheet window, with the DopeSheet Mode button set to "ShapeKey Editor," there's a channel for every keyframed shapekey Element (value) in the selected object's currently-applied Shapekey Action.

(d) In the Graph Editor window, with the Graph Editor Mode button set to "F-Curve Editor," there are channels which include those for every keyframed Element in the Object, Shapekey and Material Actions that are currently applied to the selected object (or in the Object Action that's currently applied to the selected bone) and in the World Action. **In this F-Curve Editor, you can see the interpolated values for each of the channels, these values being represented by curves** ("Ipo" curves).

3. **The little diamond-shaped symbols** in the right-side panel of the DopeSheet window show the positions, along the time line, of the keyframes.

4. **To change the time interval between keyframes:** Go to the DopeSheet > Select the keyframes > Press

S > Scale the interval > LClick.

5. **In the F-Curve Editor: to make a curve disappear:** LClick the eye in the colored square to the left of the channel name; to make the curve reappear, LClick the square again.

6. If you animated an effect in the Visual Sequence Editor (see **T130, step 29 p. 270**), the name(s) of the feature(s) you animated will appear in the Graph Editor window, in F-Curve Editor Mode, but only if the effect strip is selected in the VSE (see below, **T130, p. 264**).

T114. To edit a Keyframe

1. In the Timeline window, use these buttons: and OR use the "Up" and "Down" arrows on your keyboard to go to the frame that you want to edit.

METHOD 1: To change the keyframe by making changes to the object directly:

2. Make changes > Insert keyframe as described in **T107, p. 224**.

METHOD 2: To edit an interpolated curve of an animation:

3. Go to the Graph Editor window, F-Curve Editor Mode: The list on the left includes an entry for each of the object or bone's features that you've animated: a change of an object, bone or material's Element, or of a World Element gets its own channel (the VSE animations might not be listed here—see **T113, step 6, p. 237**). Each channel correlates to one of the curves in the window. The color of the square to the left of the channel name will be the same as the color of the curve.

4. To edit the curves, manipulate the curve handles and control points. Some experts recommend that, when dealing with pose animations, to tweak *rotation*, you should insert intermediate keyframes rather than struggling to understand how the "Quaternion" channels work.

5. To *select* a curve that is visible in the Graph Editor window: Go to the left side panel of the window and LClick the name of the relevant channel.

6. To select a curve's control points: In the Graph Editor window, make sure that the eye symbol to the left of the relevant channel is showing > (a) Go to the right-side panel of the DopeSheet window > RClick the diamond symbol for the curve's channel OR: (b) Go to the right-side panel of the Graph Editor > RClick an end point (little black dot) of the curve.

7. (You can *select all* in steps **5** and **6** above by pressing A once or twice.)

T115. To loop an Action in the 3D View window:

1. Let's say that you've animated your character's legs so that the action segment consists of one walk cycle: In the Timeline window's header, set the "End" button to the length of the segment, 24 frames, for instance. (Now, if you press ALT + A, you will see the looping effect as the legs keep walking.)

T116. To combine the content of two or more Actions:

1. When an Action is applied to an object, to an object's material, or to the world, you will see a representation of that Action in the *Non-Linear Animation (NLA) Editor window*; The Action will appear there as a bright orange band, dotted by diamond-shaped signs that represent the frames where there are keyframes. Such a band, which I will call an "**Action band**", appears to the right of the Action's name and below the name of the object, bone or material to which it is applied. (If only one frame in the Action has keyframes, the bright orange color will not be visible.) You can think of the **gray-orange bands** that flank the bright orange one to left and right as being film clips, every frame of which contains a duplicate of the nearest frame in the bright orange Action band. (For instance, if the last keyframe in the Action band places Obj1 at 0,2,-5, then the gray-orange band that extends to the right of the bright orange band can be thought of as representing a film clip that has Obj1 located at 0,2,-5 in every frame.)

2. The Actions that are represented in the NLA Editor via Action bands are those that are presently applied to the scene's objects and materials. If you remove an Object or Shapekey Action from an object, and apply a new one to that object, a representation of the new Action will automatically replace that of the old Action in the NLA Editor.

3. In the NLA Editor, you can change any bright orange Action band into a yellow "**Action strip**". To do this, LClick the little "snowflake" to the right of the Action's name. So, in the NLA Editor, you will have bright orange Action bands, with their flanking gray-orange bands, and the (initially at least) yellow Action strips and their flanking gray-yellow strips.

4. In the Overview, **T106, step 9, p. 220** above, it was said that you cannot merge two Object Actions together, and (although you can merge two shapekeys within a Shapekey Action) you cannot merge two Shapekey Actions together. **You can, however, merge an Object Action *band* together with an Object Action *Strip*, and you can merge two Object Action *strips*, in the NLA Editor**, so that, for instance, your character can wave while walking; similarly, **you can merge a Shapekey Action *band* together with a Shapekey Action *strip*, and you can merge two Shapekey Action *strips*, in the NLA**. To adjust the degree of influence an Action strip will have over another: Select the Action strip > To display a window of controls at the right side of the NLA Editor window: With the mouse pointer in the NLA Editor window, press N > Go to the "Evaluation" panel > Adjust the Influence button.

5. Example: You can, for instance, combine a walk-cycle Action strip, with a moving-forward Action strip: Suppose you created a 24-frame-long walk cycle Action (left foot forward-right foot forward-left foot forward—while the character stays in place) and you created another Action, an 88-frame-long Action where the whole character moves ahead in the scene (and the legs don't move). You've gone to the Action Editor and made the *walk* Action the current action, that is, you've applied the *walk* action to the character (see **T108, p. 234**). Then you went to the NLA Editor and LClicked the snowflake next to the *walk* Action's name, turning the Action into a yellow NLA Editor Action strip. Then you went to the Action Editor and made the *move-forward* Action the current Action, that is, you've applied the *move-forward* action to the character (see **T108, p. 234**). Then you went to the NLA Editor again and LClicked the snowflake next to the *move-forward* Action's name, turning this Action into a yellow NLA Editor Action strip. Now you have two, plain yellow, Action strips in the NLA Editor, one for walking, and one for moving forward. But remember that the *walk* track is 24 frames long (one cycle), and you want your character to walk across the room; yet, the *moving-forward* track, which moves her across the room, is 88 frames, long. The character will move across the room, but will be moving her legs for only 24 of those 88 frames. To make the legs move for all of the 88 frames, select the *walk* track > To display a window of controls at the right side of the NLA Editor window: With the mouse pointer in the NLA Editor window, press N; or LClick the tiny "+" at the upper right corner of the NLA Editor > In the NLA properties window that appears, go to the "Action Clip" panel > Set "Repeat" to 4.

6. To put a *transition* strip between two Action strips on the same horizontal track: Select the two strips

> In the NLA Editor header, LClick "Add" > LClick "Transition".

7. To join two or more Action strips into a group, a "meta strip" that can be moved around as a unit: Select the strips > In the NLA Editor header, LClick "Add" > LClick "Add Meta-Strips".

8. To change the Keyframes in an Action strip, that is, to edit the Action strip: Select the strip > (a) Press TAB; OR: (b) in the NLA Editor header, LClick "Edit" > LClick "Start Tweaking Strip Actions". When in Tweak mode, an Action strip will be Green, and its Keyframes will be positioned in a green strip above it above it. To leave Tweak mode: Select the strip > (a) Press TAB; OR: (b) in the NLA Editor header, LClick "Edit" > LClick "Stop Tweaking Strip Actions".

9. To create a copy of an Action strip: Select the strip > (a) Press SHIFT+D; OR (b) In the NLA Editor header: LClick "Edit" > LClick "Duplicate Strips". If you tweak (see **8**) a duplicate, the original will be changed also and if you tweak an original that's been duplicated, the duplicate will be changed also.

10. To display other controls, if they are not already displayed: with the mouse pointer in the NLA Editor window, press N.

T117 A note about the NLA Editor:

1. If an Element of an object (or bone, or shapekey or material or world) has been incorporated in any way into the NLA Editor—that is, if it is keyframed there in an *Action band* (see T116, p. 237), or if it is present there in an *Action strip* (see T116, step 3, p. 238), then you can see the NLA Editor as that which governs the appearance and animation *of that Element* in the 3D View window in Object and Pose modes. This 3D View, then (with both its NLA-animated Elements and those elements that have not been incorporated into the NLA Editor at all) is what controls the render (both single-frame still renders and animation renders). This means that once the Element is incorporated this way into the NLA Editor, then you cannot anymore change the Element via manipulations in the 3D View window such that it will "stick" (see **T106, step 10, p. 221**). On the other hand, if an Element is *not* present in any way in the NLA Editor, then the Element is in un-keyframed state (see **T106, step 10, p. 221**), and you *can* change the element via manipulations in the 3D View window—and the change will control how that element appears (as a static component in the animation) in the 3D View window—in Object and Pose modes—and therefore in the render. If there is, for instance, only a Location Action band or Location Action strip for an object in the NLA Editor, this band or strip will govern the 3D View and will override changes you try to make to the object in the 3D View window; *but it will override only changes in **Location** Elements of the object—its Rotation and Scaling Elements will still be governed by the way that you set the object's rotational orientation and scaling in the 3D View.*

T118. To play your animation in the 3D View window:

1. Press ALT + A.

PART SEVEN: CREATION AND ANIMATION OF PARTICLES, HAIR, FLUIDS, CLOTH, SOFT BODIES:

T119. To create and animate hair (grass is similar); an example: long, brown hair blowing in the wind:

1. Go to the Timeline window header > Set "Start" to 1 and "End" to, say, 120.

2. In Object mode, select the mesh object, part or all of which is the head that you have modeled and to which you want to add hair. (Here, it is assumed that you have already added a material to this object) > Go to Edit mode.

3. To create your hair strands: Go to the "Properties" window: > LClick the Particle button: (You may have to scroll in the buttons band to see this button) > Add a particle system to the list in the big box at the top: LClick the "plus" button: > LClick the "Name" button > Type a new name, such as "HairSystem" > Press ENTER > LClick the "Type" button > LClick "Hair" > To view the hair in the 3D View window, go into Object mode—at this point, the hair covers the whole object > Go to the "Emission" panel > Keep the "Number" set to 1000 > Set the "Hair Length" (you might have to expand the window to the left to see the whole name of this button) while watching the hair in the 3D View window, to give the hair the length you want it to have.

4. To put the hair only on the scalp:

5. Go to Edit mode > In the 3D View window: Select the vertices that define the part of the head, the scalp, that you want to add hair to > In the Properties window header (identified by at the left): LClick the "Object Data" button: > Go to the "Vertex Groups" panel > LClick the plus sign (+).

6. Blender will automatically give your new vertex group a name, for instance, "group"; to change this automatically-generated name, LClick the "Name" field > type in the new name, for instance, "Scalp" > Press ENTER.

7. LClick "Assign"—This puts the selected vertices into the "Scalp" group.

8. To verify that the group has been created, LClick "Deselect" to deselect the group. If it deselects it, you know that you have successfully created the group > LClick "Select" to select it again.

9. Go into Object mode > Go to the "Properties" window: > LClick the Particle button: (You may have to scroll in the buttons band to see this button) > Go to the "Vertex Groups" panel > LClick the "Density" button > LClick the name that you gave to the vertex group you created in steps **5-8**; that is, in this example, LClick "Scalp.

10. Go to the "Render" panel > Put a check mark next to "Strand render" > Put a check mark next to "B Spline" > Leave "Steps" set to 3.

11. To add strands of hair in order to produce a full head of hair: Go to the "Children" panel > LClick "Simple" (Notice that the hair has now filled in) > Set "Render" to, say, 230 or so > Experiment with "Clump", which makes the hair look less or more spiky > Experiment with "Shape", which makes the hair take on the shape of wetter or drier hair > Set "Random" to some low number.

12. To comb, cut, lengthen, smooth, or puff the hair, go to the 3D View window header > LClick the mode button > LClick "Particle Mode" > Go to the Tool Shelf (If it's not there, press T) > Go to the "Brush" panel > experiment with the brush functionalities such as "Comb", "Smooth", etc., while adjusting the brush "Radius" and "Strength".

13. To use the comb to comb and to produce different amounts of separation between strands: Go to the "Options" panel > Make sure that "Children" is unchecked > Make sure there's a check mark next to "Deflect emitter" and experiment with changing the "Distance" control while combing.

14. To work on a full head of hair while combing, cutting, etc.: Still in the Tool Shelf, still in the "Options" panel, put a check mark next to "Children".

15. When you are finished combing, etc. the hair, return to Object mode.

To give the hair its final color in the 3D View window and in the Render—in this case, to make the hair brown:

16. The head mesh, it is presumed, already has a material applied to it; create another material which will be applied to the hair as follows: Go to the "Properties" window: ⬜ > LClick the "Material" button: ⬜ > Add a material—Note that adding a new material here will not change the look of the head itself—its original coloring, etc., will continue to be applied to it > Let's say that this new material is second from the top in the material list—let's suppose you name it "HairMaterial"

17. Go to the "Properties" window: ⬜ > LClick the Particle button: ⬜ (You may have to scroll in the buttons band to see this button) > Go to the "Render" panel > Set "Material" to 2—this applies HairMaterial to the particles (to the hair), because HairMaterial is second from the top in the materials list.

18. Go to the "Properties" window: ⬜ > LClick the "Material" button: ⬜ > In the materials list, select HairMaterial > Go to the "Shading" panel > Set "Translucency" to a low number, perhaps .05 > Put a check mark next to "Tangent Shading" > Put a check mark next to "Cubic Interpolation".

19. Go to the "Transparency" panel > Put a check mark next to "Transparency" > Set "Alpha" to 0 > Set "Specular" (specular opacity) to 0.

20. Go to the "Strand" panel > To taper each strand from root to tip: Set "Root" to 1 and "Tip" to, say, .4 or .5 > Put a check mark next to "Tangent Shading".

21. In the "Properties" window: ⬜ > Enable the "Texture" button: ⬜ > Make sure that the "Show Material Textures" button at upper left (in the group of 3 buttons) is enabled (bright):

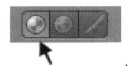

22. Add a new texture (see **T74, p. 120**) (for the hair's diffuse color) > Change the new texture's name; name it, for instance, "HairTexture1" > Set "Type" to "Blend" > In the "Preview" panel, make sure "Texture" is enabled (blue) > Put a check next to "Show Alpha".

23. Go to the "Colors" panel > Put a check mark next to "Ramp" > Add one color, a light brown with 0.5 alpha, to the ramp (see **T79, p. 165** for a guide to working with ramps) and keep it in the middle > Make the color to the left dark brown, with alpha = .9 > Make the color to the right black with alpha = 0.

24. Go to the "Preview" panel > LClick "Material" > LClick the "Strands" button.

25. Go to the "Influence" panel > Go to the "Diffuse" buttons > Put a check mark next to "Color" > Put a check mark next to "Alpha".

26. Go to the "Mapping" panel > LClick the "Coordinates" button > LClick "Strand/Particle" (so that the ramp colorband will determine the color of each strand, root to tip) > Set "Projection" to "Flat".

27. Add another new texture (see **T74, p. 120**) for **the hair's specular color** > Change the new texture's name; name it, for instance, "HairTexture2" > Set "Type" to "Blend" > In the "Preview" panel, make sure "Texture" is enabled (blue) > Put a check next to "Show Alpha".

28. Go to the "Colors" panel > Put a check mark next to "Ramp" > Add one color, a dark brown with alpha = 1, to the ramp (see **T79, p. 165** for a guide to working with ramps) and keep it in the middle > Make the color to the left very dark brown, with alpha = 1 and bring the color's vertical line in toward the center > Make the color to the right black with alpha = 1 and bring the color's vertical line in toward the center.

29. Go to the "Influence" panel > Go to the "Diffuse" buttons > Uncheck "Color" > Go to the "Specular" buttons > Put a check mark next to "Intensity" > Put a check mark next to "Color".

30. Go to the "Mapping" panel > LClick the "Coordinates" button > LClick "Strand/Particle" > Set "Projection" to "Flat".

31. To see the hair as it is now colored, render it.

32. Do you want the hair to move in animation—for instance, do you want it to blow in the wind?

> Yes: Go to **33**.

> No: Stop. You are finished.

33. Set up a force-field object, say, a wind-generating plane, as follows: Add a mesh plane > position it so that its local Z axis points in the direction in which you want the wind to blow > With the plane selected, go to the "Properties" window: > LClick the Physics button: (You may have to scroll in the buttons band to see this button) > LClick "Force Field" > Go to the "Force Fields" panel > Set "Type" to "Wind" > Adjust the wind's "Strength"—You can now see the hair as blown by the wind; but if you press ALT + A to animate, you'll see that the hair is not yet animated.

34. With the mesh with the hair on it selected, go to the "Properties" window: > LClick the Particle button: (You may have to scroll in the buttons band to see this button) > Go to the "Hair dynamics" panel > put a check mark next to "Hair dynamics"—Now you can watch the hair blowing in the wind by pressing ALT + A. If the hair is blowing into the mesh interior, try increasing the "Stiffness" setting. Notice that the first time you play this animation from start to end, the play is slow; that's because the frames are being stored into the "**cache**" memory. After the first play-through, if you don't change any settings, the animation will be fast and smooth because Blender doesn't have to recompute the frames—since they're cached. If you make a change to your settings, though, and play the animation, the animation will be re-cached during playback (unless it's been locked by "baking" it [see step **39**]).

35. To change the way that the hair blows in the wind: In Object mode, select the object with the hair on it > then use one or more of the following methods:

METHOD 1:

36. Still in the "**Hair dynamics**" panel, experiment with the controls for "Stiffness", "Mass", "Bending", "Spring, "Internal Friction" (hairs holding eachother in place or not), etc.

METHOD 2:

37. Go to the "**Field Weights**" panel > Adjust the button that corresponds to the particular force field involved—in this case, adjust the "Wind" button—while watching how the movement of the hair is affected by the change.

METHOD 3:

38. You can use a "**weight painting**" brush to paint resistance-to-the-force-field (in this case, wind resistance) directly onto the hair: In the 3D View window header, LClick the Mode button [see ***Introduction*** for its location] > LClick "Particle Mode" > Go to the Tool Shelf (If it's not there, press T) > Go to the "Options" panel > make sure that "Children" is unchecked > Go to the "Brush" panel > LClick "Weight" > To paint lower resistance-to-wind onto, say, the hair ends (so that they will move more in the wind), set "Strength" to a lower number; To paint higher resistance-to-wind onto, say, the hair roots (so that they'll stay put), set "strength" to a higher number. Lowest resistance (= highest responsiveness) will appear as blue paint; moderate resistance: green to orange; highest resistance: red. (These colors will appear in Particle mode only.)

END OF METHODS

39. To lock the cache memory so that it cannot easily be changed, you have to ***bake*** it: Save the .blend file (for instance, press CTRL + S) > With the object with hair on it selected, go to the "Properties" window: > LClick the Physics button: (You may have to scroll in the buttons band to see this button) > Go to the "Cache" panel > Set "End" to 125 (see **1**) > LClick "Bake" > Wait while it bakes—the baking locks the cache, preventing it from being easily changed; to change it, LClick "Free Bake".

T120. To create a smoke/fire animation:

1. Go to The Timeline window's header > Set "Start" to 1 and "End" at, say, 125.

2. Start with the default cube, which has a material applied to it, and whose edges are each 2 Blender units long > The name of this cube should be "Cube" > Double its size: Press S > Press 2 > LClick > Make Cube higher: Press S > Press Z > Type the number *1.75* > LClick > Go into wireframe: Press Z.

3. Create a particle system: Press SHIFT + A > Hover over "Mesh" > LClick "Plane" > Reduce the size of the plane: Press S > .7 > LClick > Make sure that the plane is centered inside the cube, quite near the bottom of the cube.

4. In Object mode, with the plane selected, go to the "Properties" window: > LClick the

Particle button: (You may have to scroll in the buttons band to see this button) > Add a particle

system to the list in the big box at the top: LClick the "plus" button: > LClick the "Name" button >
Type a new name, such as "Fire" > Press ENTER > If the "Type" button does not have the word "Emitter"
on it, LClick the "Type" button and LClick "Emitter".

5. Go to the "Emission" panel > Set the "Number" button to a large number—for instance, 75000 > Set
the "Lifetime" button to 1 > Press ENTER > Still in the "Emission" panel, make sure that "Start" is set to 1
> Set "End" to 125 (see 1 above) > Put a check mark next to "Random".

6. Go to the "Velocity" panel > Set "Random" to 1.2.

7. Go to the "Render" panel > uncheck "Emitter" > LClick "None".

8. Go to the "Display" panel > LClick "Point".

9. **Turn the cube (named "Cube") into a _domain_ for the smoke and fire:** In Object mode, in the 3D View

window, RClick the cube to select it > go to the "Properties" window: > LClick the Physics

button: (You may have to scroll in the buttons band to see this button) > LClick "Smoke" > Go to
the "Smoke" panel > LClick "Domain". You have now made the cube the smoke "domain".

10. **Turn the plane into a smoke emitter:** In Object mode, in the 3D View window, RClick the plane to

select it > go to the "Properties" window: > LClick the Physics button: (You may have
to scroll in the buttons band to see this button) > LClick "Smoke" > Go to the "Smoke" panel > LClick
"Flow" > Put a check mark into the little box next to "Initial Velocity" > Now if you press ALT + A to play
the animation, you should be able to watch, in the 3D window, the smoke being generated—but the
smoke will not yet render.

11. In Object mode, select the domain (the cube) > Go to the "Properties" window: > LClick

the "Material" button: > Since you started with the default cube, it should already have a
material; if it doesn't have one, add one (see **T62, p. 107**) > Assuming that the domain now has a
material applied to it, LClick "Volume" > Go to the "Density" panel > Set "Density" to 0.000 > Set
"Density Scale" (you may have to expand the window to see the full name for this button) to 4 > Go to
the "Shading" panel > Set "Scattering" to .5 > Set "Emission" to 8 > (Experiment with these settings.)

12. With the cube, the domain, still selected: Go to the "Properties" window: > LClick the

Physics button: (You may have to scroll in the buttons band to see this button) > Go to the
"Smoke" panel > Put a check mark into the little box next to "Dissolve" > Set "Time" to 5 > Keep

"Vorticity" at 2 or 3 > For better resolution, set "Divisions" to 64 (this will slow down the playback) > Go to the "Smoke High Resolution" panel > Put a check mark next to "Smoke High Resolution" > Set "Noise Method" to FFT > Set the "Divisions" to 1.

13. **To give the smoke/fire a texture:** Make sure that the cube (domain) is selected > Go to the

"Properties" window: > Enable the "Texture" button: > Make sure that the "Show Material Textures" button at upper left (in the group of 3 buttons) is enabled (bright):

14. Add a new texture (see **T74, p. 120**) > Change the new texture's name; name it, for instance, "FireTexture1" > Set "Type" to "Voxel Data" > Go to the "Voxel Data" panel > LClick "Domain Object" button > LClick "Cube" (= the name of the cube domain) > "Go to the "Influence" panel > uncheck "Emission Color" (you may have to expand the window to see the whole name) > Put a check mark next to "Density".

15. Add another texture (see **T74, p. 120**), which, since it is lower in the texture stack, will be visually layered on top of the texture you created in step **14**, FireTexture1—name this new texture, for instance, "FireTexture2" > Set "Type" to "Voxel Data" > Go to the "Voxel Data" panel > LClick "Domain Object" button > LClick "Cube" (= the name of the cube domain) > "Go to the "Influence" panel > Put a check mark next to "Emission" > Put a check mark next to "Emission Color" (you might have to horizontally expand the window to see the full name of this control) > LClick the purple color patch > Use the color picker to set it to white.

16. Go to the "Colors" panel > Put a check mark next to "Ramp"—the right side of this ramp represents the color at its base of the fire; the left side represents the smoky part above the flame > LClick "Add" to Add a color in the middle of the colorband (see **T79, p. 165** for how to use the ramp) > LClick the color swatch and change this color to a bright yellow, with an alpha of 1 > move this color somewhat toward the right > Add another color > make it a bright red, with alpha = 1, and move it toward the left > Add another color > make it dark red, with alpha = 1, and move it very close to the left end > With the animation cursor, in the Timeline window, at frame 1, press ALT + A to play the animation > At any point during playback, press F12 to render the image > Adjust the ramp to get the colors you want > Keep rendering and changing the ramp until the fire looks like you want it to look.

17. If you play the animation, by pressing ALT + A: Notice that the first time you play this animation from start to end, the play is slow; that's because the frames are being stored into the "**cache**" memory. After the first play-through, if you don't change any settings, the animation will be fast and smooth because Blender doesn't have to recompute the frames—since they're cached. If you make a change to your settings, though, and play the animation, the animation will be re-cached during the initial play-back.To lock the cache memory so that it cannot easily be changed, you have to *bake* it: Save the .blend file (for instance, press CTRL + S and LClick the file path) > With the cube (domain) selected, go to the

"Properties" window: > LClick the Physics button: (You may have to scroll in the buttons band to see this button) > Go to the "Smoke Cache" panel > Set "End" to 125 (see **1**) > LClick "Bake All Dynamics > Wait while it bakes—the baking locks the cache, preventing it from being easily changed; to change it, first LClick "Free Bake".

T121. To create flowing water:

1. Go to The Timeline window's header > Set "Start" to 1 and "End" at, say, 125 > Put the animation cursor at 0.

Create a "domain":

2. Start with the default cube, which has a material applied to it, and whose edges are each 2 Blender units long > To change the name of this cube, go to the "Properties" window > > LClick the "Object" button: > LClick the long button at the top > Type the new name—for instance, "Cube1" > Press ENTER > To make Cube1 larger, and make it longer in the Y direction, do the following: In Object mode, with Cube1 selected, press S > 2 > LClick > Press S > Y > 2.5 > LClick > Put it into wireframe by pressing Z.

3. With Cube1 still selected, go to the "Properties" window: > LClick the Physics button: (You may have to scroll in the buttons band to see this button) > LClick "Fluid" > Go to the "Fluid" panel > LClick the "Type" button > LClick "Domain".

Create a "fluid cube":

4. Press SHIFT + A > Hover over "Mesh" > LClick "Cube" > go to the "Properties" window > > LClick the "Object" button: > LClick the long button at the top > Type the new name (for instance, "Cube2") > Press S > Y > .15 (so it takes on the shape of a wafer or tile—its shape will define the shape of the water as it pours into the domain) > LClick > Make sure that Cube2 is inside Cube1 and centered; place it near Cube1's left end:

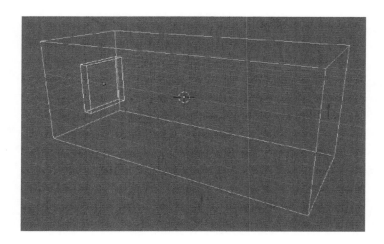

5. With Cube2 selected, go to the "Properties" window: > LClick the Physics button: > LClick "Fluid" > Go to the "Fluid"panel > LClick the "Type" button > LClick "Inflow" > Set "Volume Initialization" to "Both" > Set the Y "Inflow Velocity" button to 0.650.

Bake, as follows:

6. Still in Object mode: RClick Cube1 to select it > go to the "Properties" window: > LClick the

Physics button: > Go to the "Fluid" panel > LClick "Bake" > To monitor the progress of the bake,

go to the "Info" window's header (the window header with to the left) > Watch the changing "Fluid Simulation" line.

To see the animation:

7. When the "Fluid Simulation" (see **6**) line shows that baking is finished, press Z to go out of wireframe > (Note that, if you move the animation cursor in the Timeline window, the domain, Cube1, will be visible at frame 0, but at frame 1 will turn into the water) > You can watch the full animation by putting the animation cursor at 0 and pressing ALT + A.

8. Go to the Outliner window: > LClick the eye symbol next to "Cube2" to make the eye disappear.

9. Select the lamp in your scene > Go to the "Properties" window: > Enable the "Object Data" button (see **T11** for how to find it—if your lamp is the default lamp, a point lamp, it will look like this:

) > Go to the "Lamp" panel > LClick "Sun" > Go to the "Sky and Atmosphere" panel > Check the "Sky" checkbox.

10. RClick Cube1 (the water) to select it > Go to the Tool Shelf (if it's not there, press T) > Go to the "Object Tools" panel > LClick "Smooth" > You can further smooth the water: Go to the "Properties" window: > Enable the "Object Modifiers" button: > LClick "Add Modifier" > LClick "Subdivision Surface" (you'll only need to do this once).

11. Go to the "Properties" window: > LClick the "Material" button: > Go to the "Diffuse" panel > LClick the color swatch > Set the color to blue-green white (move the tiny circle in the color circle straight up, to a point halfway between the center of the color circle and its upper edge, and move the other tiny circle to the very top of the value slider).

12. Go to the "Transparency" panel > Put a check mark into the check box next to "Transparency" > Enable "Raytrace" > Set "Alpha" to .3 > Set IOR to 1.3.

13. At this point, you can render the water as a still image or as a video.

T122. To create a soft, bouncing, jiggling object—an example: dropping a soft cube onto a plane:

1. Go to The Timeline window's header > Set "Start" to 1 and "End" at, say, 125 > Put the animation cursor at 0.

2. Start with the a cube hovering above a plane: In Object mode, select the cube > Go to the

"Properties" window: > LClick the Physics button: > LClick "Soft Body" > Go to the "Soft Body Goal" panel > uncheck the "Soft Body Goal" check box > Go to the "Soft Body Edges" panel > Make sure that the "Soft Body Edges" check box is checked > Go to the "Soft Body Self Collision" panel > Put a check mark in the "Soft Body Self Collision" check box.

3. Select the plane > Go to the "Properties" window: > LClick the Physics button: > LClick "Collision".

4. If you press ALT + A, you will see the cube fall, land on the plain, bounce and scrunch elastically.

5. To make the cube quiver: In Object mode, select the cube > Go to Edit mode > Press W > LClick "Subdivide" > Press W > LClick "Subdivide" > Go to Object mode > Go to the Tool Shelf (if it's not there,

press T) > Go to the "Object Tools" panel > LClick "Smooth" > Go to the "Properties" window:

> Make sure that the Physics button is enabled > Go to the "Soft Body" panel > Set "Friction" to 3 > Go to the "Soft Body Edges" panel > Make sure that there's still a check mark next to "Soft Body Edges" > Put a check mark in the "Stiff Quads" check box > Set "Bending" to .5.

6. If you play the animation by pressing ALT + A: The first time you play this animation from start to end, the play is relatively slow; that's because the frames are being stored into the "**cache**" memory. After the first play-through, if you don't change any settings, the animation will be fast and smooth because Blender doesn't have to recompute the frames—since they're cached. If you make a change to your settings, though, and play the animation, the animation will be re-cached during the initial play-back.To lock the cache memory so that it cannot easily be changed, you have to *bake* it: With the cube selected, go to the "Properties" window:  > LClick the Physics button: (You may have to scroll in the buttons band to see this button) > Go to the "Soft Body Cache" panel > Set "End" to 125 (see **1**) > LClick "Bake" > Wait while it bakes (you can monitor the progress by watching the numbers in the little floating squares that appear)—the baking locks the cache, preventing it from being easily changed. You can test this by, for instance, elongating the cube. Note that when you play the animation, the cube snaps back to its original shape. To make lasting changes, LClick "Free Bake".

T123. To create a piece of cloth; one, for instance, that falls onto another object, draping itself over that object:

1. Go to The Timeline window's header > Set "Start" to 1 and "End" at, say, 125 > Put the animation cursor at 0.

2. Start with the default cube > In Object mode, press SHIFT + A > Hover over "Mesh" > LClick "Plane" > Enlarge the plane: Press S > Press 3 > LClick > Raise the plane up, some distance above the cube.

3. With the plane still selected, go to Edit mode > Go to the Tool Shelf (if it's not there, press T) > Go to the "Mesh Tools" panel > Go to the "Add" buttons > LClick "Subdivide" five times > Go to the "Shading" buttons > LClick "Smooth".

4. Go to Object mode > With the plane still selected, go to the "Properties" window:  > LClick the Physics button: (You may have to scroll in the buttons band to see this button) > LClick "Cloth" > Go to the "Cloth" panel > Set "Steps" to, say, 25 > Set "Structural" to, say, 124 > Go to the "Cloth Cache" panel > Set "End" to, say, 125.

5. RClick the cube to select it > go to the "Properties" window: > LClick the Physics button: (You may have to scroll in the buttons band to see this button) > LClick "Collision".

6. Go to the Timeline window > Set the animation cursor to 1 > Play the animation, by pressing ALT + A. Notice that the first time you play this animation from start to end, the play is slow; that's because the frames are being stored into the "**cache**" memory. After the first play-through, if you don't change any settings, the animation will be fast and smooth because Blender doesn't have to recompute the frames—since they're cached. If you make a change to your settings, though, and play the animation, the animation will be re-cached during the initial play-back.To lock the cache memory so that it cannot easily be changed, you have to **bake** it: Save the .blend file (for instance, press CTRL + S and LClick the file path) > With the plane selected, go to the "Properties" window: > LClick the Physics button: (You may have to scroll in the buttons band to see this button) > Go to the "Cloth Cache" panel > Set "End" to 125 (see **1**) > LClick "Bake" > Wait while it bakes—you can watch the progress of the baking by looking at the numbers in the little floating squares that appear. The baking locks the cache, preventing it from being easily changed—notice how, after baking, if you move the cube away and press ALT + A, the cloth will fall and drape itself as if the cube is still there; to make changes in the way the cloth drapes, you have to LClick "Free Bake", then make the changes.

T124. To have a stream of particles emitted into the scene, to have the particles effected by a force field and to have them bounce off of a surface. For example, to shoot a stream of little yellow cones into the scene, to have them blown by the wind and bounce off of a wall:

1. Go to The Timeline window's header > Set "Start" to 1 and "End" at, say, 125 > Put the animation cursor at 0.

Set up the objects for the example:

2. Start with the default cube > make sure that the 3D cursor is still at the Global origin and at the center of the cube (to put the cursor at the origin: Press SHIFT + S > LClick "Cursor to Center") > Press S > Press 5 > LClick > Press S > Press Y > Press 3 > LClick > Zoom out so that you can see the whole cube > To

change the name of this cube, go to the "Properties" window > > LClick the "Object" button:

> LClick the long button at the top > Type the new name (for instance, "FloorWall") > Press ENTER > With the mouse cursor in the 3D View window, press numpad 3 > Go into Edit mode > Press A to deselect everything > Select the front face > Press X > LClick "Faces" to delete the front face > Delete the left and right sides and the top > Go to Object mode > Press SHIFT + A > Hover over "Mesh" > LClick "Cube" > Press S > Press Y > Type .1 > LClick > Press G > Press Y > Press 12 > LClick > Rename the second cube (for instance, "Emitter"). The two objects, FloorWall and Emitter should now be set up like this:

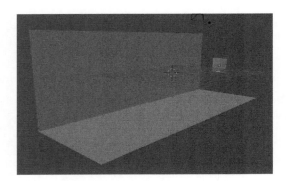

3. Still in Object mode, make sure that Emitter (the smaller object) is still selected > Go to the

"Properties" window: > LClick the Particle button: (You may have to scroll in the buttons band to see this button) > Add a particle system to the list in the big box at the top as follows:

LClick the "plus" button: > LClick the "Name" button > Type a new name, such as "BounceCones" > Press ENTER > Make sure that the "Type" button is set to "Emitter" > Go to the "Physics" panel > Make sure that "Newtonian" is enabled. (If you enabled "Boids" instead, the stream of particles would tend to act like a group living creatures, such as a cloud of gnats or a school of fish; if you enabled "Fluid" the particles would behave like a splashing liquid.) > To watch particles being emitted from Emitter, press ALT + A > (To stop it at any time, press ESC) > While watching the particle-emission animation, go to the

"Properties" window: > Make sure the Particle button ( ) is still enabled > Go to the "Emission" panel > Adjust the "Number" button until there are as many particles in the stream as you want > Set "End" to 125 (see **1**)—You may have to expand this window horizontally to see the names of these buttons > To set the particle lifetime (at the end of which, the particle will disappear), adjust the "Lifetime" button—75 is a good number for this example > Go to the "Velocity" panel > Go to the "Emitter Object" buttons > Adjust the Y button in the negative direction until the particles are going through the "floor" about halfway between Emitter and the floor's left end; -10 is a good velocity.
4. To make the particles bounce off the floor instead of passing through it: In Object mode, select

FloorWall > Go to the "Properties" window: > LClick the Physics button: (You may have to scroll in the buttons band to see this button) > LClick "Collision" > Now, if you press ALT + A you can see the particles bouncing off the floor > Notice that if you render your image at this point [F12], the particles will appear as glowing embers—you can control the way they look by doing the following:

Select Emitter: Go to the "Properties" window: > LClick the Particle button: > Go to the "Render" panel > Enabling "Halo" gives the particles the glowing appearance that they have; to render them as short, linear, marks instead, enable "Line"—but below, you will change them to little yellow cones.
5. Set up a force-field object, in this example, set up a wind-generating *plane* as follows: Add a mesh plane, let's say it's called "Plane" > Position it so that its local Z axis points in the direction in which you want the wind to blow so that the particles will be blown against the wall > With Plane selected, go to

the "Properties" window: > LClick the Physics button: (You may have to scroll in the buttons band to see this button) > LClick "Force Field" > Go to the "Force Fields" panel > Set "Type" to "Wind"—You can now see the particles as blown by the wind > Adjust the wind's "Strength" while watching the animation (you should not think of the wind-generating object as a fan; rather, the circles simply show the direction of the wind, which is blowing evenly in every part of the scene).
To turn each particle into a little yellow cone:
6. In Object mode, press SHIFT + A > Hover over "Mesh" > LClick "Cone" > Go to the "Properties"

window: > LClick the "Material" button: > Go to the "Diffuse" panel > LClick the color swatch > Set the color to yellow > Move the cone—let's say it's named "Cone"—somewhere in the scene where it will not be visible in the render > Select the Emitter > Go to the "Properties" window:

> LClick the Particle button: > Go to the "Render" panel > LClick "Object" > LClick the "Dupli Object" button > LClick "Cone" > While watching the animation, adjust the "Size" button to see

that the particles are now cones > If you want to randomize the sizes, adjust the "Random Size" button.

7. You can render the simulation as an image or as a movie.

PART EIGHT: CREATING AND RETRIEVING SCENES

T125 To create a new scene:

1. To create a new scene, go to the Info window  , then, in this window's header, go to this set of buttons:

LClick the "+" button.

2. (a) If you want a new scene that has no objects in it, where your render settings are the default settings, LClick "New." (b) If you want a new scene that has no objects in it, where your render settings are the same as in the old scene, LClick "Copy Settings." (c) If you want a new scene that has all the objects of the old scene in it, and where any change made to any object in one scene will automatically be made to its counterpart in the other scene, LClick "Link Objects." (d) If you want a new scene that has all the objects of the old scene in it, and where any shape or material change (but not location, rotation or scale change) made to any object in one scene will automatically be made to its counterpart in the other scene, LClick "Link Object Data." (e) If you want a new scene that has all the objects of the old scene in it, and where no change made to any object in one scene will automatically be made to its counterpart in the other scene, LClick "Full Copy."

T126 To retrieve a stored scene:

1. To retrieve a stored scene, go to the set of buttons pictured above (**T125, p. 252**) > LClick the icon at the left end > LClick the name of the scene you want to retrieve.

PART NINE: POST-PROCESSING

T127 About post-processing

1. *In Blender, a **scene** is a representation of a 4D reality—a 3D space and a period of time—containing still or changing objects and world properties. In parts ONE through SEVEN, the topics have shown how to build a single scene and how to render images and movies that correspond to that single scene. In the paragraphs above, the word "render" has been used in this context. Part EIGHT deals with creating new scenes and retrieving old ones. But, beyond this, you can do **post-processing**: you can add effects to your scenes using the Compositor and you can take a finished scene, move it around in the timeline, and splice* *it together with still pictures (each of which has been turned into a sequence of frames that show an unchanging image), with other scenes, with movie-renders of the scene and other scenes, and with sound tracks. Then, a kind of* **final** *render can be made.*

T128. To use the *Compositor* or the *Sequencer* (*Video Sequence Editor*) to do post-processing.

1. As covered in previous sections, you can model your scene, adjust the lighting and the camera, then render your *still* image in accord with **T16**; or, if you have created an *animation*, you can render it in accord with **T17**.

After you have completed your scene, that is, after you have constructed your objects and the scene's "world" features, and (with the help of the NLA Editor) after you have stipulated how the scene's Elements change in time—after you have done all this, following the steps in the sections above, you can do "post-processing" with the **Compositor** and/or with the **Sequencer (the VSE)**, and then create a final render

You can use the *Compositor* to **do color correction, to insert a background image, to combine renders, to insert a motion blur into an animation, to make an object glow, to insert depth of field & out-of-focus blur, or to do any of a variety of other tasks.** To use the Compositor, go to **T129, p. 253**.

On the other hand, **do you want to bring parts of your movie footage together into a single movie? That is, do you want to splice video clips together, or take your animated scene and add on to it, or splice already-created movie files onto it or onto one another, or add a still image such that Blender will instantly convert the image into a multiframe film segment that can be used as, say, an unchanging establishing shot in your movie or as a backdrop for animated characters which can be superimposed onto it, or insert effects, such as transitions between strips—dissolves, fade ins & outs, and wipes—or add an audio track? And, then, do you want to render and save the whole movie as an .avi or .mov file?** If so, you can use the *Video Sequence Editor*: Go to **T130**.

T129. To use the "Compositor" function of the Node Editor window to add post-processing to your still or animated ordinary renders—that is, to use the compositor function of the Node Editor such that, when you render, the render will happen in two stages: the first, ordinary, render will be automatically and immediately followed by a final render, which will add post-processing effects:

1. The layers that are covered in **T41** to **T44** are actually called *scene* layers—these are the layers that you routinely manipulate to show and hide objects as you construct your scene and when you do a simple render. But, in addition to these scene layers, your scene will also have one or more *render* layers applied to it. A *render* layer consists of, or has in it, one or more *scene* layers. Although scene layers are *numbered*, render layers are *named*. (As I see it, a layer is actually just a special kind of group, and in this section, I am going to talk about layers as *groups*. So, I will not say that something is *on* a layer, but *in* it.)

Now, to more fully understand rendering, go to the "Properties" window: > Enable the

"Render" button: > Go to the "Layers" panel > Look at the large box at the top: In this box is a list of your scene's render layers—if you are looking at this panel for the first time, there will only be one render layer, named "RenderLayer" listed there and highlighted (active). Underneath this box are two very important blocks of scene-layer buttons, the "**Scene**" scene-layer buttons and the "**Layer**" scene-layer buttons:

The "**Scene**" block of scene-layer buttons is a duplicate of the block of scene-layer buttons in the 3D View window header in Object mode (see **T41** to **T44**). The "**Layer**" block of scene-layer buttons shows which *scene* layers are contained in the active *render* layer—that is, the render layer whose name is highlighted in the big box that lists the render layers. Again, if you're accessing this panel for the first time, the active render layer will be RenderLayer—notice, by looking at the "Layer" buttons, that RenderLayer contains all the scene layers, which is why you can normally use just the scene-layer buttons in the 3D View header to show or hide layers in the render (see immediately below).

When you *view* your scene in the 3D View window, you see whatever scene layers are enabled (darkened) in the 3D View window header; but, **when you *render* a scene in Blender, you render every single scene layer which is enabled (darkened) in *both* the "Scene" buttons *and* the "Layers" buttons, and no other scene layers will be rendered.** For directions on rendering in a way that incorporates the Compositor effects, see **T131, p. 271** and **T133, p. 274**.

2. The following example (which I will call my "primary" example) illustrates how the Compositor functions. In this example you can use the compositor to make a red sphere and a blue sphere glow in the final render: Suppose you've set up your scene and put your objects where you want them. Let's say, for instance, that you've got a cube in the center of the scene, with two small, shiny, spheres, a red one and a blue one, resting on the cube's top surface; and, you've lit the scene with a point lamp that puts a single highlight on each sphere. Your background is just the default background of the 3D View window.

Suppose, also, that you've put the cube and both spheres into scene layer 1, the red sphere into scene layer 2, and the blue sphere into scene layer 3; your point lamp is in scene layers 1, 2 and 3 (use M to put an object into a layer—see **T41, p. 74**). Make sure that all three scene layers are selected (in the 3D View window header). And suppose that you want to make the spheres to appear to be *glowing* in the render.

Suppose, also, that you've animated the scene: you created a keyframe with the red sphere sitting on the cube (where it is now in the 3D View window) and one, 30 frames later, where it's in the air to the right of the cube. In your animation, it floats up off of the cube and over to the right.

3. You will want to design your own render layers; for instance, suppose you want one render layer, which you will call "MyCube," to contain scene layer 1, and another render layer, which you will call "TwoSpheres", to contain scene layers 2 and 3. Here's how to do this:

4. To create a new render layer and define it as one of your planned render layers (see **3**), in this example, as the planned MyCube or TwoSpheres render layer: Still in the "Properties" window:

, with the "Render" button enabled: , in the "Layers" panel, LClick the plus-sign button to the right of the big box, the render layers list, at the top: > LClick the "Name" field > Type a name for your new render layer (in this example, "MyCube" or "TwoSpheres") > Press ENTER > Go to the "Layer" buttons > LClick the button(s) corresponding to the scene layers that you want your render layer to contain (in the case of MyCube, you should select scene layer 1; in the case of TwoSpheres, you should select scene layers 2 and 3; etc.).

5. Do you want to add another render layer (in the example, you should make sure that both render layers, "MyCube" and "TwoSpheres," are added)?

> Yes: Go to step **5**.

> No: Go to **7**.

6. Go to the Compositor: Open a Node Editor window. You can use the methods described in **T1** and **T2** to do this, but it is easier to go to the Info window: > LClick the "Screen lay out" button: > LClick "Compositing." Even easier: From the default layout, press CTRL + Left Arrow Key. The Node Editor window will be the window at upper left.

7. Have you worked with the Video Sequence Editor (see **T130, p. 264**) yet?

> Yes: Go to **8**.

> No: Go to **10**.

8. Are there one or more strips in the Video Sequence Editor?

> Yes: Go to **9**.

> No: Go to **10**.

9. Go to the "Properties" window: > Enable the "Render" button: > Go to the "Post Processing" panel > If there is a checkmark in the little box next to "Sequencer", LClick the little box to un-check it. (Go to **10**.)

10. In the Node Editor window's header, make sure that the "Compositing Nodes" button is enabled (bright): > Make sure that there is a check mark in the little box next to "Use Nodes"> Go to the "Properties" window: > With the "Render" button enabled: > Go to the "Post Processing" panel > If there is no check mark in the little box next to "Compositing", LClick the little box to put a check mark into it.

11. Go back to the Compositor (see **6**). When you first turn on the Compositor (the steps in **10** will turn it on), Blender will automatically place two "nodes" into the Node Editor—*nodes* are little, floating panels that represent various things, as described below. In this case, the left-hand node is a kind of *input* node called a *Render Layer* node, which represents a render layer. If you look at the dark button at the bottom of this node, you will see that this particular node represents the render layer that is highest in the list of render layers (see **4** above). The node on the right in this initial, default set-up is a kind of *output* node called a *Composite* node. The two nodes are connected by a line, called a "connector," that stretches from an *output* "image" socket on the right side of the Render Layer node to an *input* "image" socket on the left side of the Composite node. (Output sockets are on the right edge, and input sockets are on the left edge, of a node.) Note that, in the Compositor, many operations are done in the same way as, or in a similar way to, those that you perform in the 3D View window: selection (but: LClick *and* RClick will select a node), panning, zooming, deleting, and copying.

12. Once the Compositor is turned on, for you to be able to render anything, you have to have at least one input node and at least one output node in the Node Editor window. It's good to keep your input nodes toward the left side of the window. In order to get any kind of output, you need to have an output node. To be able to render, you should have a Composite node, which is a kind of output node.

13. In general, to add a node to your Node Editor window: Go to the Node Editor window's header > (a) LClick "Add" > Hover over the general type of node that you want > LClick the specific type of node that you want OR (b) With your mouse cursor in the Node Editor window, press SHIFT + A > Hover over the general type of node that you want > LClick the specific type of node that you want > If you add a Render Layer node and set it to represent a certain render layer, you may have to render (F12) in order to finalize the assignment.

14. First, make sure that the Render Layer nodes that represent the render layers that you want to use are in the Node Editor window—for our primary example, LClick the large, dark button at the bottom of the Render Layer node on the left > LClick "MyCube"—now the existing Render Layer node represents your MyCube render layer (and thus represents *scene* layer 1) > Press SHIFT + A > Hover over "Input" > LClick "Render Layers"—this will create a new Render Layer node in the window > LClick the large, dark button at the bottom of the node and LClick the name of the render layer you want the new node to represent; in this case, for our primary example, LClick "TwoSpheres" > Press F12 to render—now the new node represents your TwoSpheres render layer (which represents *scene* layers 2 and 3).

17. You can allow or prevent the output of certain data from a given Render Layer node. What you intend to accomplish, of course, will determine what you want to allow or prevent; in our primary example, when you make the spheres glow, you will have to prevent the *Sky* in the TwoSpheres render layer from being rendered (see (e) below).

18. In general, you can prevent individual kinds of data from being output from a render layer node as follows: by going to the "Properties" window: , with the "Render" button enabled: , in the "Layers" panel, in the large box: Select the relevant render layer.

Method 1:
Go to the "include" buttons > Here are some of the choices you can make:

(a) If you want **to exclude all solid faces** from the output of this render layer's node: Make sure that "Solid" is unchecked. (Only lights, halos and particles will be output from this render layer's node to be rendered.)

(b) If you want **to exclude any halo** from the output of this render layer's node: Make sure that "Halo" is unchecked.

(c) **If you want any object whose material has Z Transparency applied to it (even if its "alpha" is set to alpha = 1) to be excluded** from the output of this render layer's node (so that the object will be invisible in the render): Make sure that "Ztransp" is unchecked.

(d) If you want **to exclude all strands** from the output of this render layer's node: Make sure that "Strand" is unchecked.

(e) If you **want to exclude the sky** from the output of this render layer's node: Make sure that "Sky" is unchecked. Note that in our primary glowing sphere example, you should exclude the sky from the output of the "TwoSpheres" Render Layer node.

Method 2:
Go to the "Passes" buttons, LClick the button with the camera icon on it, to the right of the name of a kind of data, to darken the button. For instance, **to keep specular highlights from being output** from the Render Layer button, enable **the button to the right of "Specular"; to keep ambient occlusion from being output**, enable **the button to the right of "AO"**

End of Methods

19. **In general, to extend a connecting line from any output socket—on any node—and attach it to another node's input socket:** LClick the output socket and drag the line over to the input node and release the mouse button. (You can drag a connector from an input node to an output node in the same way.) By default, a *Render Layer* node has 3 output sockets on it from which you can extend connectors. **You can give your Render Layer node more sockets, each of which will output only certain data from the node into the line that extends from it. To add such an output socket to your Render Layer node:**

Go to the "Properties" window: , with the "Render" button enabled: , in the "Layers" panel, in the large box: Select the render layer that the node represents > Go to the "Passes" buttons > Here are some of the choices you can make (some of the "passes" you can choose):

(a) To add a socket that outputs only data about an object's movement in an animation, for instance, if you want to use a blurring node in order to give a realistic blur to a moving object in an animation: Put a check mark into the little box next to "**Vector**".

(b) To add a socket that outputs only data about the normals (perpendiculars) of your objects' surfaces, put a check mark into the little box next to "**Normal**".

(c) To add a socket that outputs only data about the UV mapping of a material's texturing; for instance, you might make use of this socket if you want to change, in the Node Editor, the material's texturing: Put a check mark into the little box next to "**UV**".

(d) To add a socket that outputs only data concerning the pass indices of the render layer's objects. You will use these index numbers to identify which objects in a render layer that you want to apply an effect to: Put a check mark into the little box next to "**Object Index**". (You give an object, to identify it in the Node Editor, a *pass index* this way: In the 3D View window, select the object > Go to the

"Properties" window: > Enable the "Object" button: > Go to the "Relations" panel > Go to the "Pass Index" button and set a number for the object, a number that no other of the render layer's objects have; you might, for instance, give it a pass index of 1 or 2.)

(e) To add a socket that outputs only data about the (diffuse) color of a material, and no data about the shadows or highlights: Put a check mark into the little box next to "**Color**".

(f) To add a socket that outputs only data about the (diffuse) color of a material and its shadows, and no data about the highlights: Put a check mark into the little box next to "**Diffuse**".

(g) To add a socket that outputs only data about the specular highlight of a material: Put a check mark into the little box next to "**Specular**".

(h) To add a socket that outputs only data about the shadows: Put a check mark into the little box next to "**Shadow**".

(i) To add a socket that outputs only data about the render layer's ambient occlusion (see <u>T83, p. 171</u>): Put a check mark into the little box next to "**AO**".

<u>Now that you've added your Render Layer nodes to your Node Editor, you'll want to finish setting up your Node Editor in order to produce the effect that you want to produce—in our primary example, you want to make the red sphere glow, but there are many other effects you can produce:</u>

20. To keep setting up your Node Editor, you will add more nodes: (a) Go to the Node Editor's header > LClick "Add" OR (b) With the mouse pointer in the Node Editor window, press SHIFT + A.

21. (The following does not cover every kind of node that you can add.)

(a) To add a node that can put an image (or an animation) into the Compositor, hover over "Input" > LClick "**Image.**"

(b) To add a node that can put a texture into the Compositor, hover over "Input" > LClick "**Texture**".

(c) To add a node that can change the combined, red, green, and blue colors of an image: Hover over "Color" > LClick "**RGB Curves.**"

(d) To add a node that can correlate a time interval with a change in some value (for instance, a change in the transparency of a black foreground image, so that the background image will fade to black): Hover over "Input" > LClick "**Time.**" Once you set it all up, you will, of course, render it as an animation.

(e) To add a node that can combine two images in any one of 16 different ways: Hover over "Color" > LClick "**Mix.**" The lower input socket inputs the foreground image; the upper input socket inputs the background image.

(f) To add a node that can layer one image over another, the foreground image having more or less transparent areas: Hover over "Color" > LClick "**AlphaOver**". The lower input socket inputs the foreground image, the upper input socket inputs the background image. Use the "Prem" control to get rid of unwanted black and white borders around the foreground elements. See Example 2 below.

(g) Different parts of an image in Blender can be associated with the same or different closeness-to-camera ("Z-depth") information; for instance, in the camera-view image of a render layer containing a blue cube, each of the various parts of the blue cube will carry information about how far that part is from the camera. Suppose that the same scene also has a red sphere in it, in another render layer, and, in the camera-view image of this render layer, each part of the red sphere carries information about how far that part is from the camera. Suppose further that all parts of the cube are closer to the camera than all parts of the sphere are. You might want to recombine the two images in the compositor so that the cube appears to be in front of the sphere in a composite image. If an image doesn't itself carry closeness-to-camera information, you might want to apply such information from a second image, an image that does carry such information, to the first image; or, you might want to assign closeness-to-camera information directly. **To add a node that can combine two images, so that the closeness-to-camera information of their parts will place them in front of or behind one another in the composite image** in accord with that information: Hover over "Color" > LClick "**Z Combine.**"

(h) To add a node that can apply a blur evenly over an input image—for instance, you might be working with a render layer that has only a car's tail lights in it and you want to blur them—Hover over "Filter" > LClick "**Blur.**" Adjust the X and Y buttons to change the blur size. See Example 1 below.

(i) To add a node that can apply a motion blur to a moving object in an animation: Hover over "Filter"

> LClick "**Vector Blur.**" See Example 5 below.

(j) To add a node that can simulate the depth of field (DOF) effect that can be seen in actual photographs, where only objects that are at a certain distance from the camera are in focus: Hover over "Filter" > LClick "**Defocus**". See Example 6 below.

(k) To add a node that can take any scale of values as input and turn these values into a range of color as output: Hover over "Convertor" > LClick **ColorRamp**. For instance, you can use ColorRamp to convert the closeness-to-camera values [Z values] of the parts of an image into black-to-white coloring, so that the closeness-to-camera properties of image parts can more easily be visualized. See Example 7.

(l) To add a node that can isolate one object in a render layer so that you can work on it in the Compositor without affecting other objects in the render layer: Hover over "Convertor" > LClick "**ID Mask.**" See Example 4.

(m) Suppose you have an image where action is happening against a green or blue screen. **To add a node that can take the green/blue out and replace it with another background image**: Hover over Matte > LClick "**Chroma Key.**"

(n) To add a node that can move your image around: Hover over "Distort" > LClick "**Translate.**"

(o) To **add a node that can rotate your image**: Hover over "Distort" > LClick "**Rotate.**"

(p) To add a node that can scale your image: Hover over "Distort" > LClick "**Scale.**"

(q) To add a node that can flip your image: Hover over "Distort" > LClick "**Flip.**"

(r) To add a node that can crop your image: Hover over "Distort" > LClick "**Crop.**" 0,0 is at bottom left. "Left" refers to the left edge; "Right" refers to the right edge; etc.

(s) To add a node that can distort an image in accord with another image's color patterns: Hover over "Distort" > LClick "**Displace.**"

(t) To add a node that can take UV information from an object in a render layer, combine it with a new image, and thereby replace that object's UV texture with the new image: Hover over "Distort" > LClick "**Map UV.**" See Example 3.

(u) To add a node that can distort an image in a way that mimics various kinds of lens distortion: Hover over "Distort" > LClick "**Lens Distortion.**"

Example 1: Glow; Use of Blur, RGB Curves, and Mix nodes—Use this setup to create the glowing sphere in our primary example

The two Render Layers nodes, one for MyCube and one for TwoSpheres, are at left. TwoSpheres' output goes to two Blur nodes, both of which are set to "Fast Gaussian"; the top one is set to X=10 and Y=10, and the bottom one is set to X=40 and Y=40. The outputs of each Blur node goes to an RGB Curves node. In both of these, the "C" curve is bowed up and to the left. The outputs of the two RGB Curves nodes both go to a single Mix node, set to "Add," with "Fac"=1. The output from the MyCube node goes to a second Mix node, set to "Add," with "Fac"=1, to the right of the first one—the first Mix node's output goes to the input of the second one. The output of the second Mix node goes to the input to the Composite node.

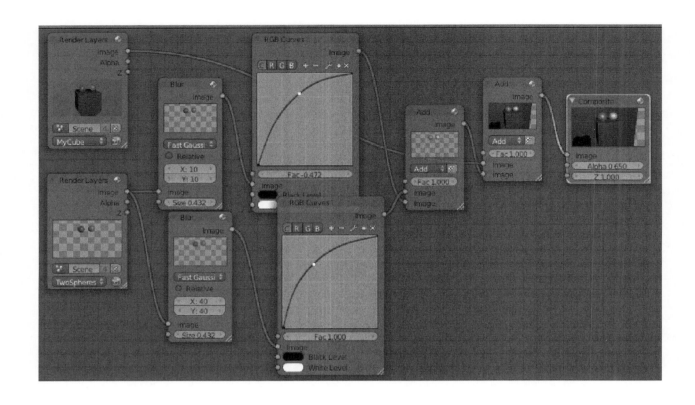

Example 2: Background; Use of AlphaOver node—see 21(f)

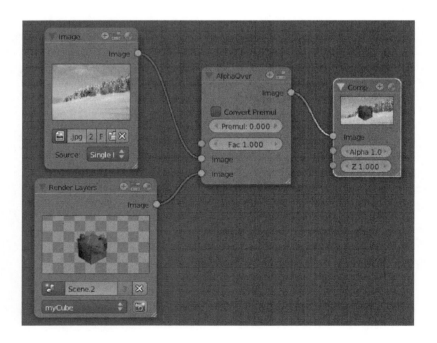

Example 3: Replace UV with different images—see **21(t)**

Suppose you have in your scene a cube with a UV image texture applied to it and you want to change this UV texture: Make sure the Compositor is turned on (see **10**) > In the Compositor window, make sure you have a Render Layers node that has the cube in it and add a UV socket to it > Go to the Compositor's header > LClick "Add" > Hover over "Distort" > Add a Map UV node > Add an Image node > Put the image for the new UV texture into this Image node > Select the Render Layers node with the cube in it >

Go to the "Properties" window: [image], Make sure that the "Render" button is enabled: [image] > Go to the "Layers" panel > LClick the little box next to "UV" to put a check mark into it—this puts a UV socket onto your Render Layers node > To replace the old UV texture with the new one, set up your nodes like this:

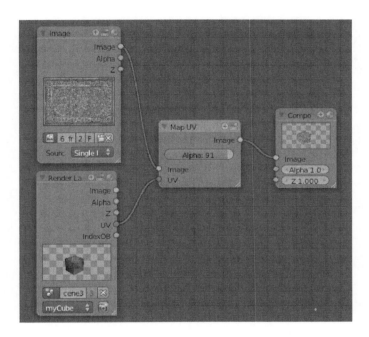

Then render it to see it in the UV/Image Editor.

Example 4: Replace a cube's UV texture (cover it). Use Pass Index (ID Mask node)—See steps **19(d)** and **21(l)**.

The nodes used are, at top left: an Image node; below it: a Render Layers node, which represents a render layer with a cube and a sphere in it, to which a UV socket and an Object Index socket have been added; upper middle left: an ID Mask node, whose ID value socket is connected to the Render Layers node's IndexOB socket; lower middle left: a Map UV node, whose UV socket is connected to the UV socket on the Render Layers node; middle right: a Mix node set to "Mix"; to right: a Composite node. The ID Mask's "Index" is set to 1, because, let's say, you have set the "pass index" of the cube to 1 (see step **19 (d)**).

261

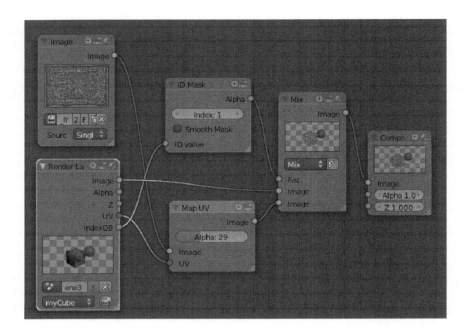

Example 5: Vector Blur

Suppose that, in the 3D View window, you used keyframes (**T107, p. 224**) to create an animation, say, a cube moving from location A to location B > Use the timeline to put the cube at a place where it's in motion in the animation > Go to the Compositor (Press CTRL + Left Arrow) > Make sure the Compositor is turned on (see **10**) > In the Compositor window, make sure that there is a Render Layers node that represents the render layer that the cube is in > add a *Vector Blur* node > Go to the "Properties"

window: 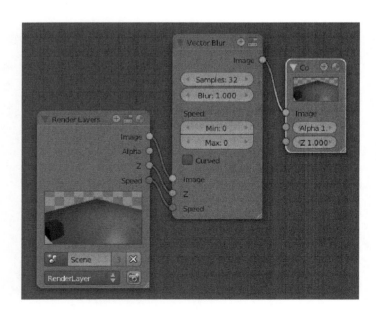 > Make sure that the "Render" button is enabled: > Go to the "Layers" panel > LClick the little box next to "Vector" to put a check mark into it—this puts a "Speed" socket onto your Render Layers node > Set up your nodes like this:

Put a check mark into the little box next to "Curved" > Press F12—you should be able to see the motion blur in the still image that's in the UV/Image Editor window > To render the animation: Go to the

"Properties" window:  > Make sure that the "Render" button is enabled: [icon] > Set up your animation render (see **T133**) > Go to the "Render" panel > LClick the "Animation" button.

Example 6: Defocus

Looking at your scene in the 3D View window, decide at what location in the scene you want your

object(s) to be in sharp focus > Select the camera > Go to the "Properties" window: [icon] > LClick

the Object Data button: [icon] > Go to the "Display" panel > Put a check mark in the little box next to "Limits"—this allows you to look in the 3D View window and see at what distance from the camera the focus will be sharpest: an X will mark this distance > Go to the "Depth of Field" panel > Adjust the "Distance" button while watching the movement of the X until it's where you want it > Make sure the Compositor is turned on (see **10**) > In the Compositor window, add a *Defocus* node > Set up your nodes like this:

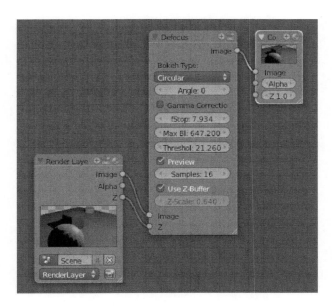

Make sure that the little box next to "Use Z Buffer" has a check mark in it > To increase/decrease the effect, adjust the "fStop" button: 128 means that nothing is out of focus. As you lower the fStop value, the blurring will increase.

Example 7: Use of Map Value and Ramp—see 21(k)

Here, parts of the scene become darker or lighter gray, depending on whether they are closer to or farther from the camera. In this set-up, the Render Layers node's Z socket is connected to the Map Value node's input Value socket; here, the Map Value node's "Offset" control is set to -9.7 and its "Size" control is set to .0559. The Map Value node's output Value socket connects to the ColorRamp node's Fac socket.

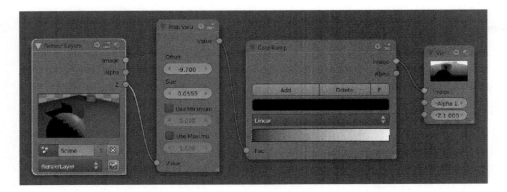

22. **You can create a group of nodes**, which you can apply to more than one place in your node network. To create a group of nodes: Select the nodes that you want to be in the group > Press CTRL + G.

23. To rename a node group: Expand the group if necessary (see **24**) > LClick the name field at the top > type the new name > Press ENTER.

24. To expand a group, to see what's in it: Select the group > Press TAB.

25. To re-collapse an expanded group: Select the group > Press TAB.

26. To put a copy of the group in a different place in your node network: Go to the Node Editor's header > LClick "Add" > Hover over "Group" > LClick the name of the group; OR (b) With the mouse pointer in the Node Editor window, press SHIFT + A > Hover over "Group" > LClick the name of the group.

27. To un-group the nodes of a group: Select the group > Press ALT + G.

28. If you want to expand/collapse a node: LClick the little triangle at top left of the node.

29. To expand/collapse a view window in a node, LClick the little round icon at the top right of the node.

30. For directions on rendering in a way that incorporates the Compositor effects, see **T131, p. 271** and **T133, p. 274**.

T130. To use the SEQUENCER (the Video Sequence Editor):

1. Go to the "Properties" window: > With the "Render" button enabled: ⬛ > Go to the "Post Processing" panel > If there is no check mark in the little box next to "Sequencer", LClick the little box to put a check mark into it.

2. Open the Video Sequence Editor (VSE) window. To do that, (a) you can use the methods described in

T1 and **T2**—go to the "Video Sequence Editor"; But (b) it is easier to go to the Info window: ⓘ >

LClick the "Screen lay out" button: ⬛ > LClick "Video Editing". Even easier: (c) From the default layout, press CTRL + Left Arrow Key three times.

3. The big area with the horizontal stripes is the VSE. Make sure that the VSE is in *Sequence mode* by making sure that the Sequence mode button in the VSE header is enabled (bright): .

4. <u>Overview:</u> The horizontal stripes represent "channels." The green cursor in the Video Sequence Editor is the animation cursor.

To show a number in a little green box at the bottom of this cursor, a number that shows the cursor position along the time line in seconds-plus frames (for instance, "2+20" means "2 seconds plus 20 frames"): Go to the VSE header > LClick "View" > Put checkmarks next to *both* "Show Frame Number Indicator" *and* "Show Seconds."

To show a number in a little green box at the bottom of this cursor, a number that shows the cursor position along the time line in frames (for instance, "68" means "frame 68"): Go to the VSE header > LClick "View" > Make sure that there is a checkmark next to "Show Frame Number Indicator," and that there is *no* checkmark next to "Show Seconds."

(If only "Show Seconds" is checkmarked, or if neither is checkmarked, there will be no little green box at the bottom of the cursor.)

You will add and work with *strips* in the VSE; they can be put into different channels. These strips represent (a) *scenes*: the 3D + time (that is, 4D) camera view of the 3D View window, (b) *single images* that are turned into sequences of frames all showing the same image, (c) *sequences of movie frames*, like lengths of film, (c) *sound tracks*, and (d) *control features* that span a number of frames and affect the movie elements that they span. When you play or render the movie, the strips, in the different channels, all coalesce into one single movie, one strip of film. In your "Video Editing" Screen layout (see step **2 (b) and (c)**), the screen at upper right is a Video Sequence Editor window in *Preview* mode. To play the movie and view it in this window, you can (a) LClick the green vertical cursor and drag; OR (b) press ALT+A; OR (c) go to the Timeline window and LClick the forward arrow.

5. If it is not already open, open the VSE's Properties Shelf by (a) Pressing N; OR In the VSE's header, LClick "View" > LClick the little box next to "Properties" to put a check mark into it. If there are no strips in the VSE, the Properties Shelf will be blank.

 6. Do you want to add a strip derived from your 4D scene, or an image, a movie, a sound track, or a series of individual image files that you created if you saved an animation in an "Image" type animation render (see <u>T17, step 9, p. 17</u>, <u>T133, step 5, p. 274</u>, and <u>T134, step 7, p. 276</u>) (always keep in mind that some files will be very large, so it may take a while to load them)?

Yes: Go to **7**.

No: Go to **9**.

7. To add a strip, (a) Go to the Video Sequence Editor window's header > LClick "Add"; OR (b) With your mouse pointer in the VSE window, press SHIFT + A:

(a) To add a strip that is a sequence of frames that presents **what's in your 3D View window, that is,** the 3D + time (that is, 4D) camera view of the 3D View window (moving the animation cursor over the strip will play the scene's animation): Hover over "**Scene**" > LClick the scene you want to add.

 (b) To add a strip that is a sequence of frames that presents an **image**, that is, an image file (the image will be transformed into a series of frames, a movie clip, all frames showing the same image): LClick "Image" > Navigate to the image file that you want to add > LClick "Add Image Strip".

(c) To add a strip that is a sequence of frames that presents a **movie**, a movie file: LClick "Movie" > Navigate to the movie file that you want to add > LClick "Add Movie Strip"

(d) To add a strip that is an **audio** track: LClick "Sound"> Navigate to the audio file that you want to add > LClick "Add Sound Strip".

(e) To add a strip that is composed of **a set of sequentially-named images that you saved if you used an "Image" type animation render to save your animation**: LClick "Image" > Navigate to the folder that these image files are in > Select these image files (if you saved them as advised in **T17, step 9, p. 17**, **T133, step 5, p. 274**, and **T134, step 7, p. 276**, you will have put them all together and by themselves in a folder, and so you can easily select them all by pressing A) > LClick "Add Image Strip"

8. To **select** one or more strips: (a) RClick in the middle area of the strip—to select another strip also: SHIFT + RClick in the middle area of the strip; OR (b) Press B and drag a rectangular box around the strips you want to select.

9. To move a strip, laterally or horizontally:

METHOD 1:
a. RClick in the middle of the strip & drag > LClick to fix the position.

METHOD 2:
b. RClick in the middle of the strip > Press G > Move the mouse > LClick.

METHOD 3:
c. Select the strip > Go to the VSE's Properties Shelf (if it's not there, press N) > Go to the "Edit Strip" panel > To move the strip horizontally: Adjust the "Start Frame" button; to move the strip vertically: Adjust the "Channel" button.

10. If you want **to join two strips**, just move them next to one another.

11. To **change the length of a strip**:

METHOD 1:
a. RClick on one of the end-arrows on the strip & drag > LClick to fix the length.

METHOD 2:
b. RClick on one of the end-arrows on the strip > Press G > Move the mouse > LClick to fix the length.

METHOD 3:
c. RClick anywhere on the strip to select it > Go to the VSE's Properties Shelf (if it's not there, press N) > Go to the "Edit Strip" panel > Adjust the "Length" button.

12. To turn several strips into one strip (a "metastrip"): Select the several strips > (a) In the VSE header: LClick "Strip" > LClick "Make Meta Strip" > LClick "Make Meta Strip"; OR (b) Press CTRL + G > LClick "Make Meta Strip".

13. To transform a metastrip back into its component strips: Select the metastrip > (a) In the VSE header: LClick "Strip" > LClick "UnMeta Strip" > LClick "UnMeta Strip"; OR (b) Press ALT + G > LClick "UnMeta Strip".

14. To delete a strip or strips: Select the strip(s): In the VSE header: (a) LClick "Strip" > LClick "Erase Strips" > LClick "Erase Strips" OR (b) Press X > "Erase Strips".

15. To duplicate a strip or strip(s): Select the strip(s) > (a) In the VSE header: LClick "Strip" > LClick "Duplicate Strips" > Move the duplicate > LClick to place it; OR (b) Press SHIFT + D > Move the duplicate > LClick to place it.

16. To cut a strip at the position of the green cursor: (a) Select the strip > LClick "Strip" > LClick "Cut (hard) at frame"; OR (b) Select the strip > Press SHIFT + K.

17. You can "cut" a strip at the cursor in a special way, where what happens is that Blender creates a copy of the strip, then divides the original into a left-side segment (every part of it to the left of the cursor) and a right-side segment, and divides the copy the same way; then Blender collapses the right-side of the original to the right edge of the original's left-side segment, and collapses the left-side of the copy to the left-edge of the copy's right-side segment. This, in effect, cuts the strip into two parts, left and right—but you can always pull the collapsed parts out again, by RClicking on the strips' arrows and dragging (Or, by RClicking on an arrow and pressing G). To "cut" a strip at the cursor this way: (a) Select the strip > LClick "Strip" > LClick "Cut (soft) at frame"; OR (b) Select the strip > Press K.

18. To snap the beginning of a strip to the cursor position: (a) Select the strip > In the VSE header, LClick "Strip" > LClick "Snap strips"; OR (b) Select the strip > Press SHIFT + S.

19. If, at some time in the past, you chose to render an animation as an "image" type animation render, Blender will have saved your animation as a set of image files, one for each frame, and will have automatically sequentially named these files. You can bring these into the VSE as a single strip by going to the VSE header, LClicking "Add" and LClicking "Image" > Navigate to the sequentially-named files > Select the files (if these files, and only these files, are in their own folder, you can select them by pressing A) > LClick "Add Image Strip". Now you will have an *image sequence strip* in the VSE. (If, at any point, you wish to turn such an image sequence strip into a set of independent strips, each one representing a frame: (a) Select the strip > In the VSE header, LClick "Strip" > LClick "Separate Images"; OR (b) Select the strip > Press Y.)

20. To change the name of a strip: Select the strip > Go to the VSE's Properties Shelf (if it's not there, press N) > Go to the "Edit Strip" panel > LClick in the "Name" field > Type the new name > Press ENTER.

21. To flip the images in a strip: Select the strip > Go to the VSE's Properties Shelf (if it's not there, press N) > Go to the "Filter" panel > Go to the "Flip" checkboxes > LClick the checkbox next to "X" and/or the checkbox next to "Y".

22. To reverse the direction of the animation of a strip: Select the strip > Go to the VSE's Properties Shelf (if it's not there, press N) > Go to the "Filter" panel > LClick the checkbox next to "Backwards" to put a check mark into it.

23. To put one strip over another so that both appear in the render at the same time (like a double exposure), and where the background colors mix with the overlay colors in an "additive" way (as colored lights mix—red and green make yellow):

(a) In the VSE, put one strip into a higher channel than the other strip is in, the one strip on top of the other strip so that they overlap in time.

METHOD 1:

(b) Select the top strip > Go to the VSE's Property Shelf (if it's not there, press N) > Go to the "Edit Strip" panel > LClick the "Blend" button > LClick "Add".

METHOD 2:

(c) RClick to select one of the two strips > SHIFT + RClick to select the other strip > (i) In the VSE header, LClick "Add" > Hover over "Effect Strip" > LClick "Add"; OR (ii) Press SHIFT + A > Hover over "Effect Strip" > LClick "Add".

END OF METHODS

24. To put one strip over another so that both appear in the render at the same time (like a double exposure), and where the background colors mix with the overlay colors in a "subtractive" way (for

267

instance, since red, green and blue lights make white light, subtracting blue from white leaves red and green—and red and green lights make yellow; so, subtracting blue from white leaves yellow):

(a) In the VSE, put the strip that you want to subtract from the other into a higher channel than the other strip is in, the one strip on top of the other strip so that they overlap in time.

METHOD 1:

(a) Select the top strip > Go to the VSE's Properties Shelf (if it's not there, press N) > Go to the "Edit Strip" panel > LClick the "Blend" button > LClick "Subtract".

METHOD 2:

(b) RClick to select one of the two strips > SHIFT + RClick to select the other strip > (i) In the VSE header, LClick "Add" > Hover over "Effect Strip" > LClick "Subtract"; OR (ii) Press SHIFT + A > Hover over "Effect Strip" > LClick "Subtract".

END OF METHODS

25. Where a movie, image, or scene strip, let's say it's called "WinterScene," is positioned to the left of a movie, image, or scene strip, let's say it's called "SummerStorm," and where WinterScene and SummerStorm overlap for some number of frames (which they might do if they are in different channels), or where the two are separated by some number of frames: **To fade WinterScene *out* while fading SummerStorm *in*:** RClick to select WinterScene (Always select the strip that you are fading *from* first) > SHIFT+RClick to select SummerStorm > (i) In the VSE header, LClick "Add" > Hover over "Effect Strip" > LClick "Cross"; OR (ii) Press SHIFT + A > Hover over "Effect Strip" > LClick "Cross".

The **Cross** effect strip will be inserted in the middle, as shown here:

26.

(a) Where a movie, image, or scene strip, let's say it's called "WinterScene," is positioned to the left of a movie, image, or scene strip, let's say it's called "SummerStorm," and where the two are separated by some number of frames: **To fade WinterScene *out to black* and then fade SummerStorm *in from black*:** (i) In the VSE header, LClick "Add" > Hover over "Effect Strip" > LClick "Color"; OR (ii) Press SHIFT + A > Hover over "Effect Strip" > LClick "Color".

(b) Move and adjust the length of the *Color* strip so that it is in a higher channel than, up above, both the WinterScene and SummerStorm strips, between the two and overlapping the right end of WinterScene and the left end of SummerStorm > Making sure that the Color strip is still selected, go to the VSE's Properties Shelf (see **5**) > Go to the "Effect Strip" panel > LClick the "Color" swatch to make sure it's set to black.

(c) RClick the WinterScene strip to select it (Always select the strip that you are fading *from* first) > SHIFT+RClick the Color strip > (i) In the VSE header, LClick "Add" > Hover over "Effect Strip" > LClick "Cross"; OR (ii) Press SHIFT + A > Hover over "Effect Strip" > LClick "Cross". This sets things up for the fade-to-black effect.

(d) To set things up for the fade-from-black effect: RClick the Color strip to select it (Always select the strip that you are fading *from* first) > SHIFT+RClick the SummerStorm strip > (i) In the VSE header, LClick "Add" > Hover over "Effect Strip" > LClick "Cross"; OR (ii) Press SHIFT + A > Hover over "Effect Strip" > LClick "Cross".

The **Color** strip and the two **Cross** effect strips will have been added as pictured below:

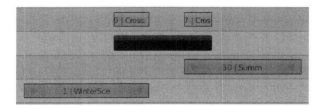

27.

(a) Where a movie, image, or scene strip, let's say it's called "WinterScene," is positioned to the left of a movie, image, or scene strip, let's say it's called "SummerStorm," and where WinterScene and SummerStorm overlap for some number of frames (which they might do if they are in different channels), or where the two are separated by some number of frames: **To transition from WinterScene, in the playback or movie render, to SummerStorm using a method where part of the new image (SummerStorm) appears in one small part of the old image (WinterScene) and spreds until the old image has been replaced by the new; that is, to transition from one to the other using a "wipe":** RClick WinterScene to select it (Always select the strip that you are transitioning *from* first) > SHIFT+RClick to select the SummerStorm strip > (i) In the VSE header, LClick "Add" > Hover over "Effect Strip" > LClick "Wipe"; OR (ii) Press SHIFT + A > Hover over "Effect Strip" > LClick "Wipe".

The **Wipe** effect strip will be inserted in the middle, as shown here:

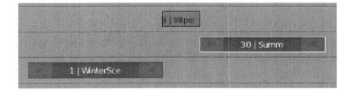

(b) By default, the edge separating the two images in the wipe, moves straight across the image field. Whatever wipe mode is in effect, **to change the wipe mode**, go to the VSE's Properties Shelf (if it's not there, press N) > Make sure that the Wipe strip is selected > Go to the "Effect Strip" panel > LClick the "Transition" button:

(c) To make the edge *rotate* in the wipe like the hand of a clock: LClick "**Clock**".

(d) To make the new image appear in a tiny central circle that grows until the old image is replaced: LClick "Iris"> Make sure that the "Out" button is enabled (blue).

(e) To make the new image appear around the outside of a large central circle that gets smaller until the old image is replaced: LClick "**Iris**"> Make sure that the "In" button is enabled (blue).

(f) To have the new image appear as a central sliver that gets wider until the old image is replaced:

LClick "**Double**" > Make sure that the "Out" button is enabled (blue).

(g) **To have the new image move in from opposite directions until the old image is replaced:** LClick "Double" > Make sure that the "In" button is enabled (blue).

(h) **To go back to the default wipe, where the edge separating the two images moves straight across the image field:** LClick "**Single**". To change the direction of this wipe mode, LClick "Out" or "In".

(i) **To blur the edge(s) of the wipe:** Adjust the "Blur Width" button.

(j) **To change the angle of the wipe edge(s) when the transition is of type "Single" or "Double":** Adjust the "Angle" button.

28.

(a) **To place a semi-transparent color overlay over a movie, image, or scene strip's images:** For instance, suppose you want to put a red overlay over an image strip called "CityStreet.jpg": (i) In the VSE header, LClick "Add" > Hover over "Effect Strip" > LClick "Color"; OR (ii) Press SHIFT + A > Hover over "Effect Strip" > LClick "Color".

(b) Move the new Color strip into a channel above the CityStreet.jpg strip, directly above the frames of CityStreet that you want to overlay, and adjust its length > With the Color strip selected, go to the VSE's Properties Shelf (if it's not there, press N) > Go to the "Effect Strip" panel > LClick the "Color" swatch and, in the color-picker, set the color to red > Go to the "Edit Strip" panel > Adjust the "Opacity" slider to set the degree of transparency of the red overlay.

29.

(a) **To animate one or more properties of an effect strip**; for instance, to animate the degree of opacity and color of the red overlay created in step **28**—let's say you want the overlay to change from red to yellow as it becomes completely transparent: Put the green cursor where you want the animation to start > with the Color strip selected, go to the VSE's Properties Shelf (if it's not there, press N) > Go to the "Edit Strip" panel > The "Opacity" slider should be set to the degree of transparency that you set in step **28(b)** > RClick the "Opacity" slider > LClick "Insert Keyframe" > Move the green animation cursor to where you want the animation to end > Set the "Opacity" slider to full transparency > RClick the "Opacity" slider again . LClick "Insert Keyframe" again—now the change-to-transparency animation is finished > Put the green cursor back to the beginning of the animation > Go back to the VSE's Properties Shelf > Go to the "Effect Strip" panel > RClick the "Color" swatch > LClick "Insert Keyframe" > Move the green cursor to where you want the color animation to end > LClick the "Color" swatch > In the color-picker, set the color to yellow > LClick outside the color-picker > RClick the "Color" swatch > LClick "Insert Keyframe".

(b) You can adjust these settings in precise ways by adjusting the curves in the Graph Editor window, F-Curve Editor mode: adjust the curve in much the same way as you would adjust any Bezier curve: see topic **T60, steps 20-24**—RClick and drag a control point or end point > LClick to fix the position, OR Select the control or end point(s) > Press G > Move the handle(s) > LClick to fix the position.

(c) For instance you can make the opacity fluctuate over the length of the image strip; or you can make the color change from red to green to yellow to blue, etc.

30.

(a) Let's suppose that, in the 3D View window, you have created an object, say, a character (a soldier, say, which you may or may not have animated) and that its background in the 3D View window is the default Blender background, or, suppose that you have created the image of, say, the soldier character, and have used a graphics program to make the background of the image transparent.

Suppose also that you have created an image, or animation (where, for instance, a fan blade is turning), of a room interior (with no transparent areas in it).

In addition, suppose that, in the VSE, you have created a strip—called, say, "Character"—from the character image (which, again, might be animated) and a strip—called, say, "Room"—from the room image (which might be animated).

Further suppose that you want to superimpose the "Character" strip over the "Room" strip such that, when the sequence is played back or rendered as a movie, the character will appear to be in the room.

To superimpose one strip, whose images have transparent components (a default 3D View background will act as a transparent component) over another strip (as in the example above):

(b) To illustrate the process using our example: In the VSE, move the "Character" strip into a channel above the "Room" strip, directly above the frames of the "Room" strip that you want to superimpose over.

(c) Make sure that the "Character" strip is selected > Go to the VSE's Properties Shelf (if it's not there, press N) > Go to the "Edit Strip" panel > LClick the "Blend" button > LClick "Alpha Over."

(d) To make the character more transparent or more opaque against the room background: RClick the "Character" strip to select it > Go to the VSE's Properties Shelf (if it's not there, press N) > Go to the "Edit Strip" panel > Adjust the "Opacity" slider.

(e) To animate the opacity of the character: With the "Character" strip selected, put the green animation cursor where you want the animation to start > go to the VSE's Properties Shelf (if it's not there, press N) > Go to the "Edit Strip" panel > Make sure "Blend" is set to "Alpha Over" > Adjust the "Opacity" slider to the value you want it to have at the start of the animation > RClick the "Opacity" slider > LClick "Insert Keyframe" > Move the animation cursor to where you want the animation to end > Open a DopeSheet window > In the DopeSheet window's header, LClick "View" > Put a check mark next to "Show Sliders" > In the left-hand side of the DopeSheet window, adjust the slider next to "Blend Opacity" to the value you want the opacity to have at the end of the animation.

31.

(a) To reposition a strip's images in the image field, or to scale the images, or to change their rotational angle (orientation): RClick the strip to select it > (i) In the VSE header, LClick "Add" > Hover over "Effect Strip" > LClick "Transform"; OR (ii) Press SHIFT + A > Hover over "Effect Strip" > LClick "Transform" > With the Transform strip still selected, go to the VSE's Properties Shelf (if it's not there, press N) > Go to the "Effect Strip" panel.

(b) To reposition the strip's images: Adjust the "**Position**" buttons.

(c) To scale the strip's images: Adjust the "**Scale**" buttons.

(d) To rotate the strip's images: Adjust the "**Rotation**" button.

32. For directions on how to render stills from the movie in the sequencer or to render the movie in the sequencer, go to **T132, p. 273** and **T134, p. 275**.

T131. To *render* a Compositor-modified still image of the 3D View (that is, if you have set up the Compositor to add effects to your scene, follow these steps so

that Blender will create a simple render of the 3D View window's scene as a preliminary and transitory render, and so that it will then immediately and automatically create a final render that incorporates your Compositor effects):

1. Have you worked with the Video Sequence Editor (see **T130, p. 264**) yet?

> Yes: Go to **2**.
> No: Go to **4**.

2. Are there one or more strips in the Video Sequence Editor?

> Yes: Go to **3**.
> No: Go to **4**.

3. Go to the "Properties" window: 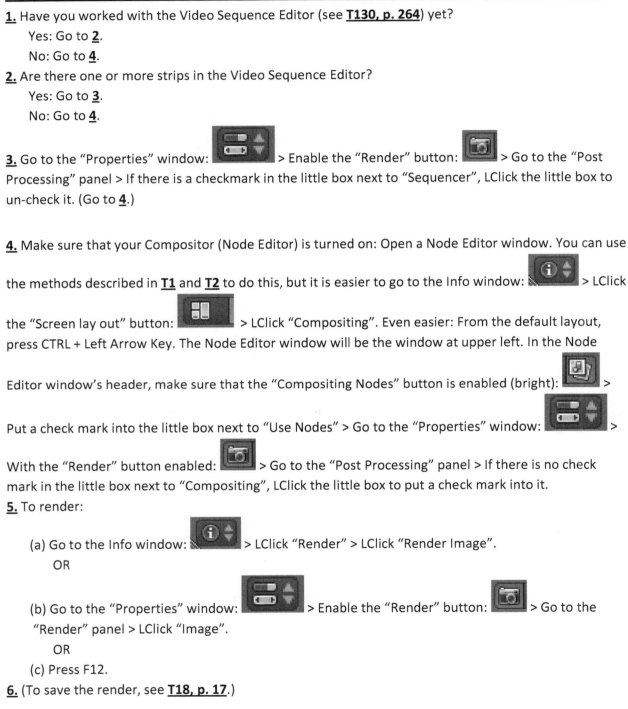 > Enable the "Render" button: > Go to the "Post Processing" panel > If there is a checkmark in the little box next to "Sequencer", LClick the little box to un-check it. (Go to **4**.)

4. Make sure that your Compositor (Node Editor) is turned on: Open a Node Editor window. You can use the methods described in **T1** and **T2** to do this, but it is easier to go to the Info window: > LClick the "Screen lay out" button: > LClick "Compositing". Even easier: From the default layout, press CTRL + Left Arrow Key. The Node Editor window will be the window at upper left. In the Node Editor window's header, make sure that the "Compositing Nodes" button is enabled (bright): > Put a check mark into the little box next to "Use Nodes" > Go to the "Properties" window: > With the "Render" button enabled: > Go to the "Post Processing" panel > If there is no check mark in the little box next to "Compositing", LClick the little box to put a check mark into it.

5. To render:

> (a) Go to the Info window: > LClick "Render" > LClick "Render Image".
>
> OR
>
> (b) Go to the "Properties" window: > Enable the "Render" button: > Go to the "Render" panel > LClick "Image".
>
> OR
>
> (c) Press F12.

6. (To save the render, see **T18, p. 17**.)

T132. To render a still image of a frame from a strip in the Video Sequence Editor:

1. Make sure that your Video Sequence Editor is turned on: Go to the "Properties" window: 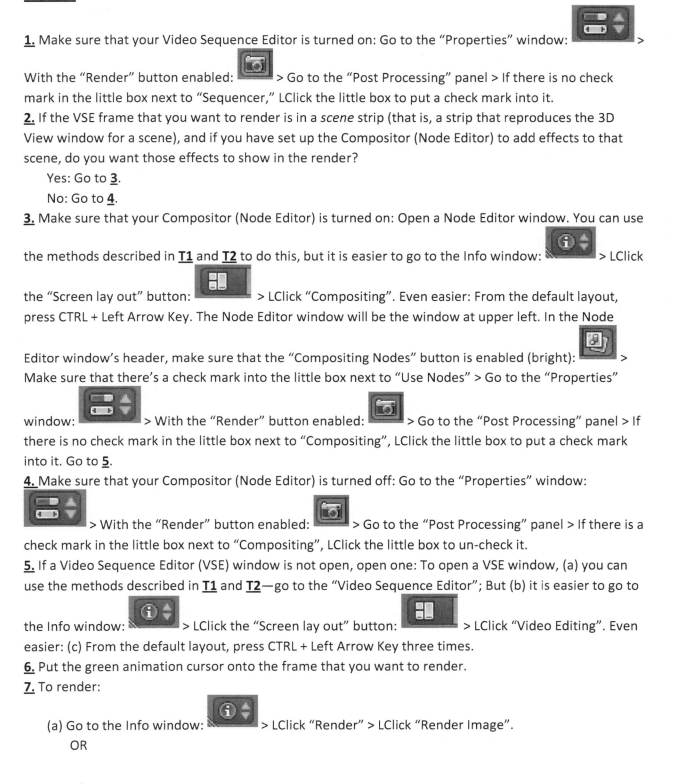 >

With the "Render" button enabled: 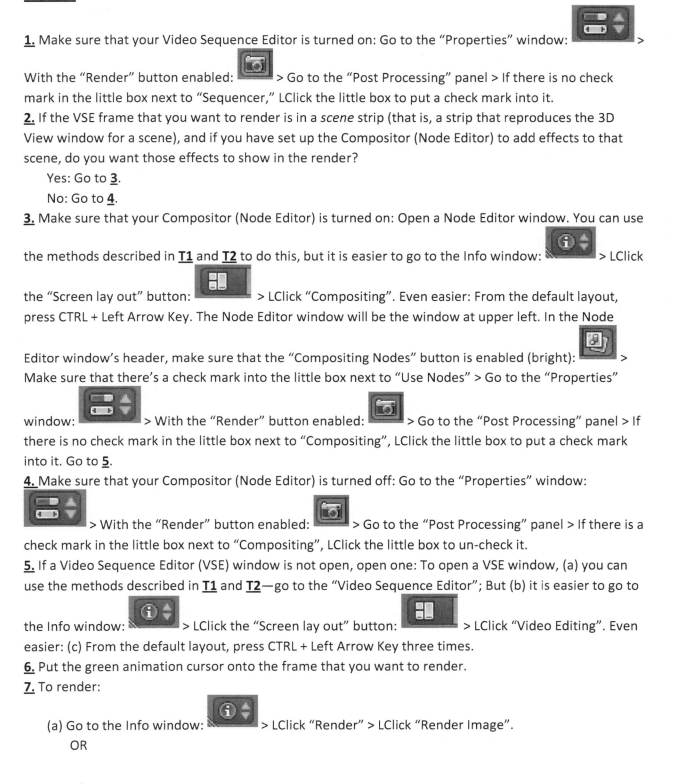 > Go to the "Post Processing" panel > If there is no check mark in the little box next to "Sequencer," LClick the little box to put a check mark into it.

2. If the VSE frame that you want to render is in a *scene* strip (that is, a strip that reproduces the 3D View window for a scene), and if you have set up the Compositor (Node Editor) to add effects to that scene, do you want those effects to show in the render?

Yes: Go to **3**.

No: Go to **4**.

3. Make sure that your Compositor (Node Editor) is turned on: Open a Node Editor window. You can use the methods described in **T1** and **T2** to do this, but it is easier to go to the Info window: 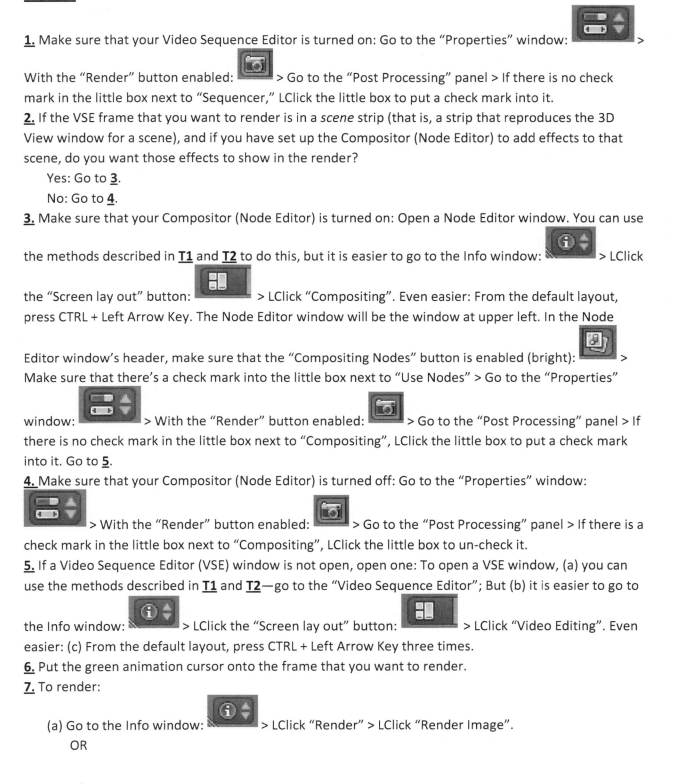 > LClick the "Screen lay out" button: 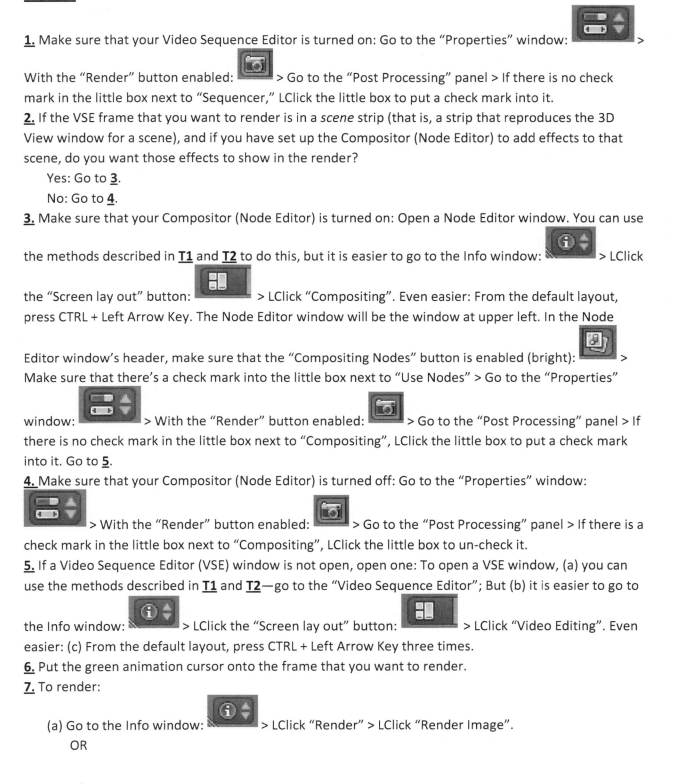 > LClick "Compositing". Even easier: From the default layout, press CTRL + Left Arrow Key. The Node Editor window will be the window at upper left. In the Node Editor window's header, make sure that the "Compositing Nodes" button is enabled (bright): 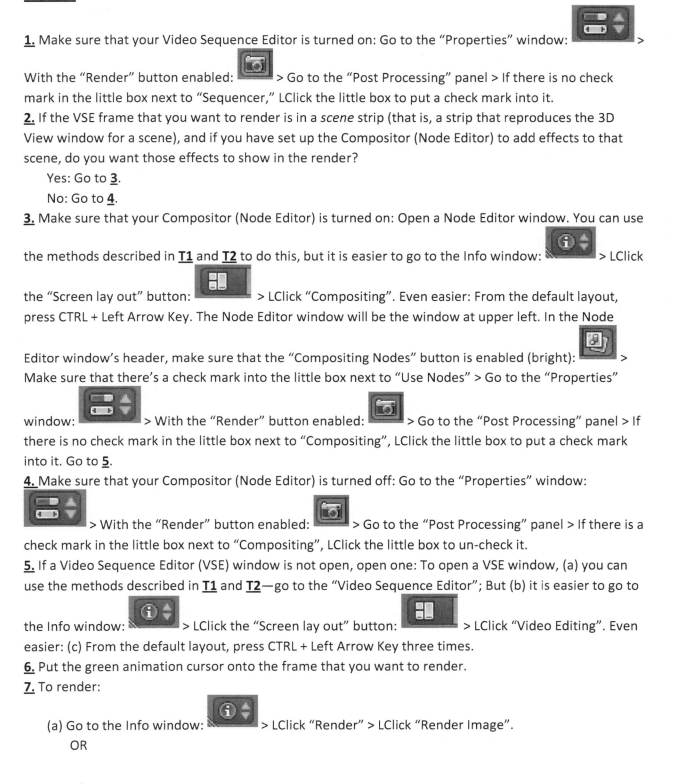 > Make sure that there's a check mark into the little box next to "Use Nodes" > Go to the "Properties" window: 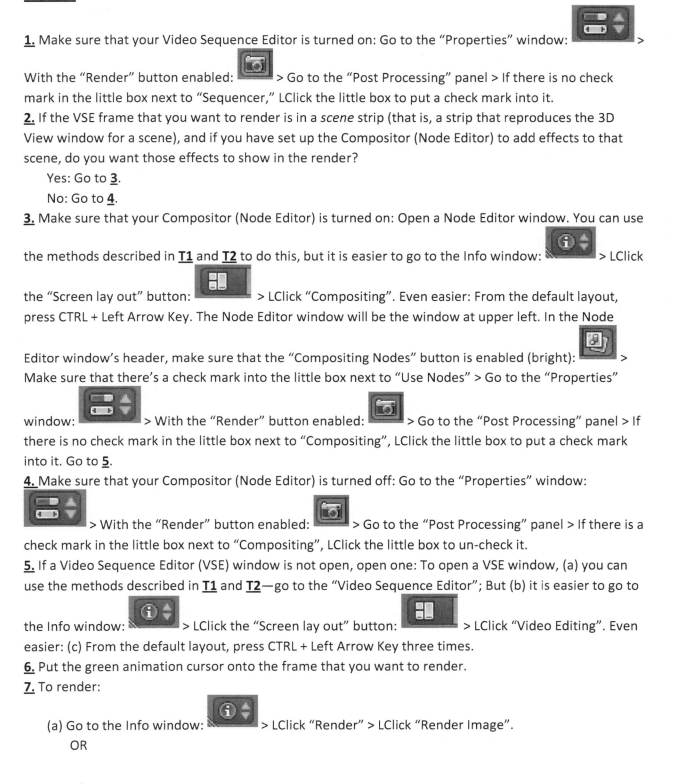 > With the "Render" button enabled: 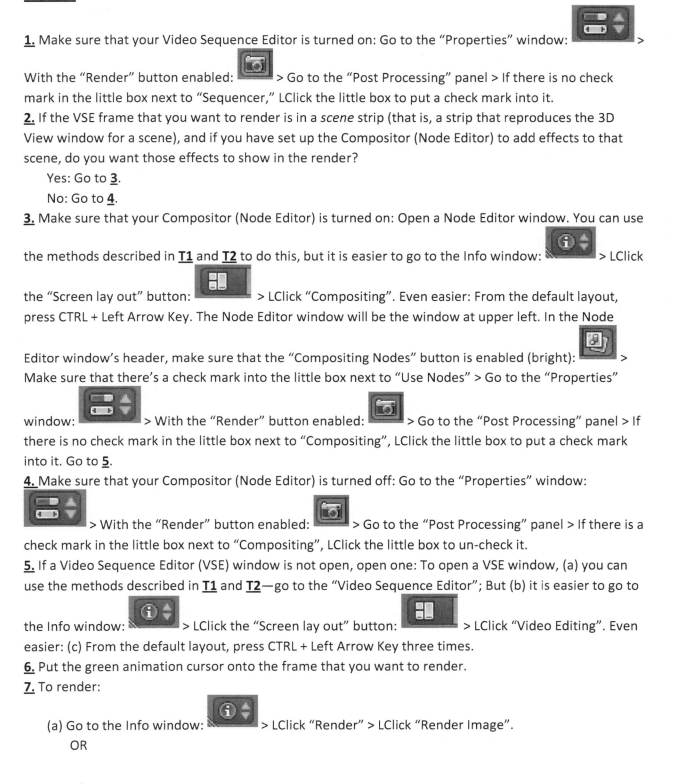 > Go to the "Post Processing" panel > If there is no check mark in the little box next to "Compositing", LClick the little box to put a check mark into it. Go to **5**.

4. Make sure that your Compositor (Node Editor) is turned off: Go to the "Properties" window: 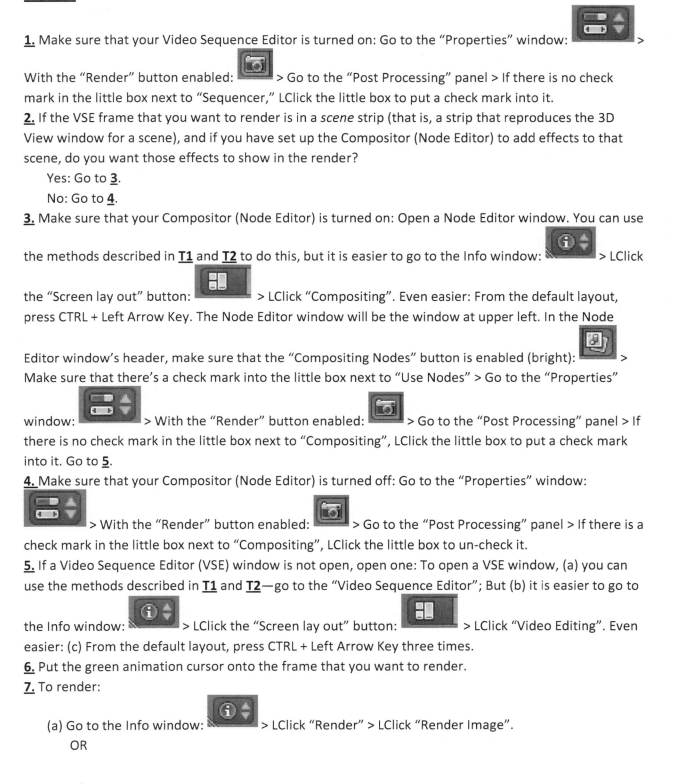 > With the "Render" button enabled: 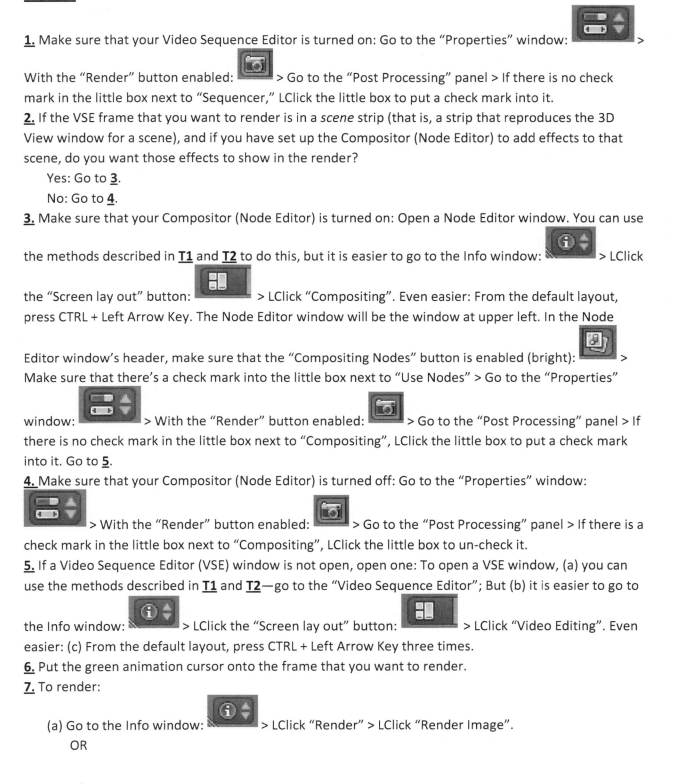 > Go to the "Post Processing" panel > If there is a check mark in the little box next to "Compositing", LClick the little box to un-check it.

5. If a Video Sequence Editor (VSE) window is not open, open one: To open a VSE window, (a) you can use the methods described in **T1** and **T2**—go to the "Video Sequence Editor"; But (b) it is easier to go to the Info window: 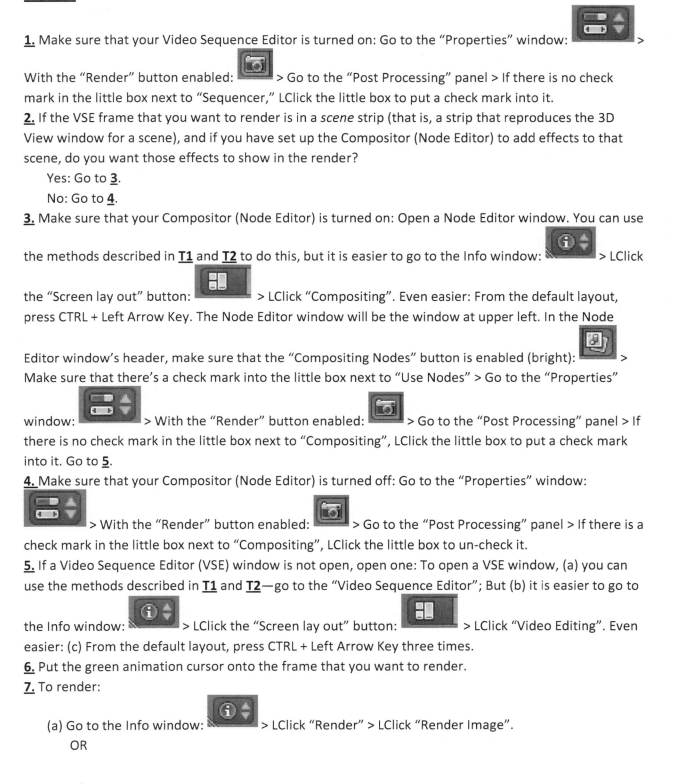 > LClick the "Screen lay out" button: 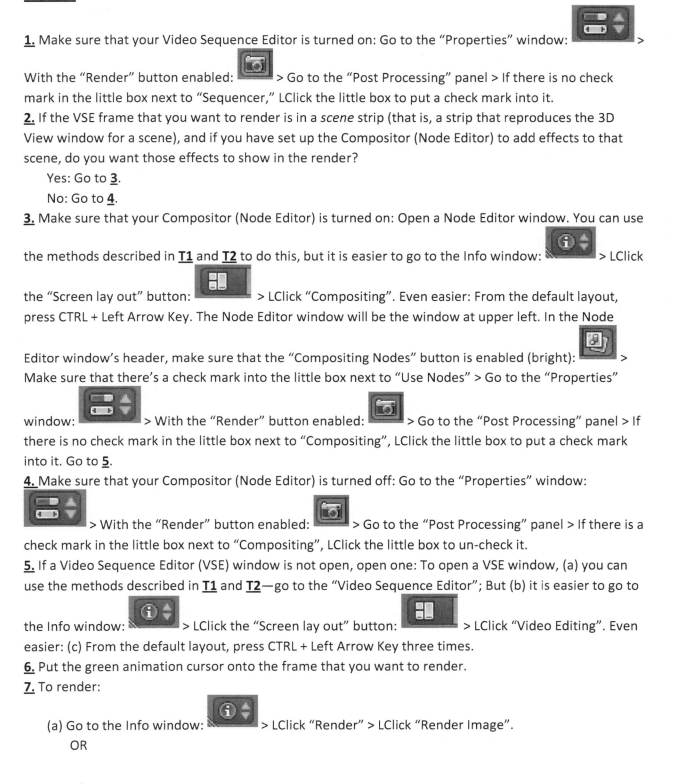 > LClick "Video Editing". Even easier: (c) From the default layout, press CTRL + Left Arrow Key three times.

6. Put the green animation cursor onto the frame that you want to render.

7. To render:

(a) Go to the Info window: 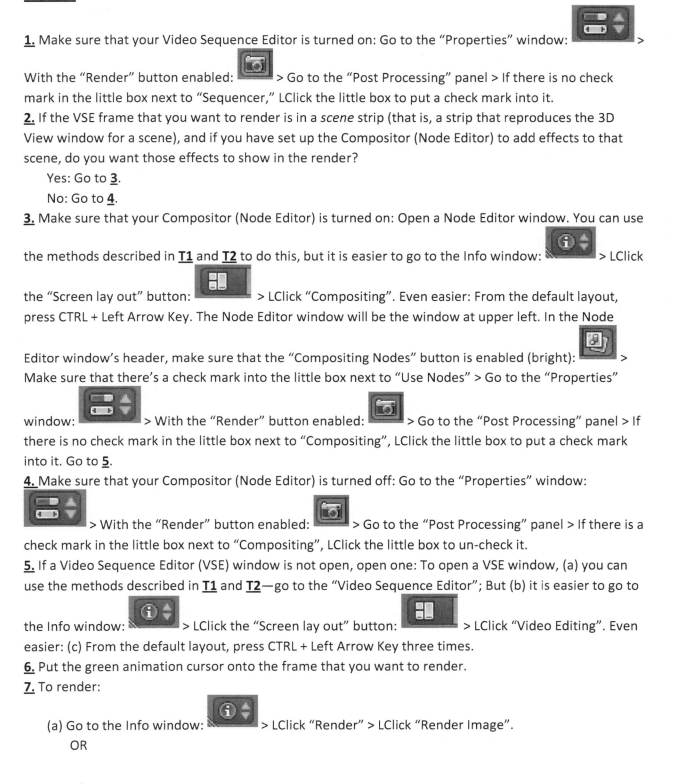 > LClick "Render" > LClick "Render Image".

OR

(b) Go to the "Properties" window: > Enable the "Render" button: > Go to the "Render" panel > LClick "Image".

 OR

(c) Press F12.

8. (To save the render, see **T18, p. 17**.)

T133. To render *and save* a Compositor-modified animation of the 3D View (that is, if you have set up the Compositor to add effects to your scene, follow these steps so that Blender will create an animation in a way such that, for each frame: a simple render of the 3D View window's scene will be created as a preliminary and transitory render, and then, immediately and automatically a final render of the frame will be created, a render that will incorporate your Compositor effects):

1. Have you worked with the Video Sequence Editor (see **T130, p. 264**) yet?

 Yes: Go to **2**.

 No: Go to **4**.

2. Are there one or more strips in the Video Sequence Editor?

 Yes: Go to **3**.

 No: Go to **4**.

3. Go to the "Properties" window: > Enable the "Render" button: > Go to the "Post Processing" panel > If there is a checkmark in the little box next to "Sequencer", LClick the little box to un-check it. (Go to **4**.)

4. Make sure that your Compositor (Node Editor) is turned on: Open a Node Editor window. You can use the methods described in **T1** and **T2** to do this, but it is easier to go to the Info window: > LClick the "Screen lay out" button: > LClick "Compositing". Even easier: From the default layout, press CTRL + Left Arrow Key. The Node Editor window will be the window at upper left. In the Node Editor window's header, make sure that the "Compositing Nodes" button is enabled (bright): > Put a check mark into the little box next to "Use Nodes" > Go to the "Properties" window: > With the "Render" button enabled: > Go to the "Post Processing" panel > If there is no check mark in the little box next to "Compositing", LClick the little box to put a check mark into it.

5. Go to the "Properties" window: > Enable the "Render" button: > Go to the

"Dimensions" panel and make changes if you wish > Go to the "Output" panel > In the long field at the top, LClick and type in a destination for your movie file (if you want to change what's in the field) OR LClick the little button on the right end of this field to browse for a destination > Go down to the next button and LClick it > LClick the name of the file format you want—(a) if you choose an "image" type animation render, Blender will save your animation as a set of image files, one for each frame, and will automatically sequentially name these files; Later, you will want to bring these together into a movie clip in the Video Sequence Editor; to be able to select them all easily, you should put them all by themselves into one folder. To bring these together into a movie clip: bring them into any *empty* VSE as a strip (see **T130, step 7(e), p. 266**), then animation-render the strip using a movie type animation render as described in this step; for shorter animations, you probably don't want to use the image type animation render (but for longer animations, you do want to.); (b) If, on the other hand, you use a "movie" type animation render (you might use H.264 for instance) Blender will create a movie file (.avi or .mov) .

6. To render:

    (a) Go to the Info window: > LClick "Render" > LClick "Render Animation".
       OR

    (b) Go to the "Properties" window: > Enable the "Render" button: 📷 > Go to the "Render" panel > LClick "Animation".
       OR

    (c) Press CTRL + F12.

T134. To render *and save* an animation of the material in your Video Sequence Editor:

1. Make sure that your *Video Sequence Editor* is turned on: Go to the "Properties" window: 📊 >

With the "Render" button enabled: 📷 > Go to the "Post Processing" panel > If there is no check mark in the little box next to "Sequencer," LClick the little box to put a check mark into it.

2. If any VSE strip is a *scene* strip (that is, a strip that reproduces the 3D View window—together with its changing Elements as reflected along the timeline in the NLA—for a scene), and if you have set up the *Compositor* (Node Editor) to add effects to that scene, do you want those Compositor-generated effects to show in the animation render?

    Yes: Go to **3**.
    No: Go to **4**.

3. Make sure that your Compositor (Node Editor) is turned on: Open a Node Editor window. You can use

the methods described in **T1** and **T2** to do this, but it is easier to go to the Info window: ⓘ > LClick

the "Screen lay out" button: 🔲 > LClick "Compositing". Even easier: From the default layout, press CTRL + Left Arrow Key. The Node Editor window will be the window at upper left. In the Node Editor window's header, make sure that the "Compositing Nodes" button is enabled (bright): 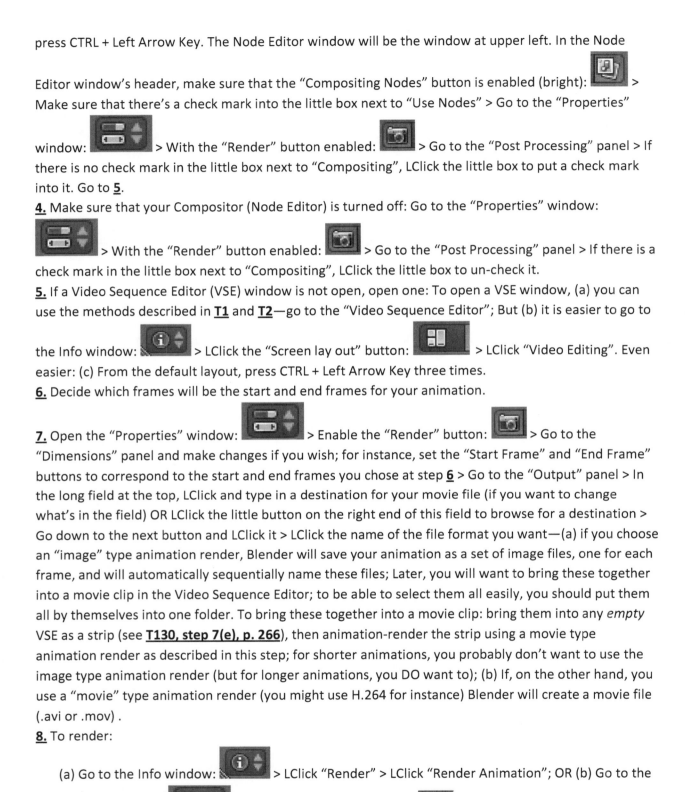 > Make sure that there's a check mark into the little box next to "Use Nodes" > Go to the "Properties" window: > With the "Render" button enabled: > Go to the "Post Processing" panel > If there is no check mark in the little box next to "Compositing", LClick the little box to put a check mark into it. Go to **5**.

4. Make sure that your Compositor (Node Editor) is turned off: Go to the "Properties" window: > With the "Render" button enabled: > Go to the "Post Processing" panel > If there is a check mark in the little box next to "Compositing", LClick the little box to un-check it.

5. If a Video Sequence Editor (VSE) window is not open, open one: To open a VSE window, (a) you can use the methods described in **T1** and **T2**—go to the "Video Sequence Editor"; But (b) it is easier to go to the Info window: > LClick the "Screen lay out" button: > LClick "Video Editing". Even easier: (c) From the default layout, press CTRL + Left Arrow Key three times.

6. Decide which frames will be the start and end frames for your animation.

7. Open the "Properties" window: > Enable the "Render" button: > Go to the "Dimensions" panel and make changes if you wish; for instance, set the "Start Frame" and "End Frame" buttons to correspond to the start and end frames you chose at step **6** > Go to the "Output" panel > In the long field at the top, LClick and type in a destination for your movie file (if you want to change what's in the field) OR LClick the little button on the right end of this field to browse for a destination > Go down to the next button and LClick it > LClick the name of the file format you want—(a) if you choose an "image" type animation render, Blender will save your animation as a set of image files, one for each frame, and will automatically sequentially name these files; Later, you will want to bring these together into a movie clip in the Video Sequence Editor; to be able to select them all easily, you should put them all by themselves into one folder. To bring these together into a movie clip: bring them into any *empty* VSE as a strip (see **T130, step 7(e), p. 266**), then animation-render the strip using a movie type animation render as described in this step; for shorter animations, you probably don't want to use the image type animation render (but for longer animations, you DO want to); (b) If, on the other hand, you use a "movie" type animation render (you might use H.264 for instance) Blender will create a movie file (.avi or .mov) .

8. To render:

(a) Go to the Info window: > LClick "Render" > LClick "Render Animation"; OR (b) Go to the "Properties" window: > Enable the "Render" button: > Go to the "Render" panel > LClick "Animation"; OR (c) Press CTRL + F12.

INDEX

CAMERA P12

I have made every effort to ensure that this book is free from errors; but a step-by-step guide to Blender requires a complex treatment, and no doubt some mistakes remain. Because I conceive of *Blender Steps* as a *Truth Engine* book, I view it as being perfectible by means of reader suggestions. If you encounter an error, I encourage you to contact me—you can reach me at www.truthenginebook.com. Click on "company/contact." Put "Blender Steps" in the subject line. Future editions of this book may well reflect your input.

—Richard Crist

Printed in Great Britain
by Amazon.co.uk, Ltd.,
Marston Gate.